WHAT
NEXT?!

THE AUTOBIOGRAPHY OF
DAVID VINCENT AINSWORTH

FOREWORD

"One damn thing after another" is a well-known paraphrase of Arnold Toynbee's definition of history. He was arguing (with opposing viewpoints held by some historians in the 1950s) that that there is no discernable drift or pattern or cycle to unfolding history. History, he thought, was just a sequence of random kinetics among the planet's population and features.

In the case of my personal history, although of course influenced by my genetic nature and cultural nurture, the forks in my path that have largely determined my life trajectory have been arrived at by random happenstance as much as choice. I chose which fork to take sometimes. In others, I was no more in control than a pinball in an arcade game. As I write this at age eighty one, battered but not diminished, I incline more toward the Toynbee view. The title of this book is a sly reference to the duality of life. Do our lives unfold according to our plan, step by step, or do life events blindside us with random and often exasperating kinetics?

Nevertheless, the reactions, sensations, thoughts and emotions I have experienced and decisions I made as I encountered life were my own, and those were enabled by my genes or cultural conditioning. I am satisfied with my genes. (See Genealogical Appendix) I am also satisfied with the various cultural environments in which my yeast was allowed to rise. Lastly, I am satisfied with the choices I made, the endeavors I undertook, and the hand I was dealt generally. I am delighted with my progeny. I am content. Not everyone can say that.

The average life expectancy of an American male when I was born in 1940 was 63 years. Today it is 76 years. Among those who attain the age of 81 as I am now, it is 88 years. For me, every day is found money now.

I have undertaken this volume at the suggestion of my son and daughter-in-law, Gray and Laura Ainsworth. Maybe there is an interesting story here, at least for family and friends. The truth of that will be in the telling and for others to judge. At least I have lived through one third of the life of the Republic. I see my audience for this book as being generations of descendants to come who might find it interesting to compare their histories to that of an ancestor. Motivations and stimuli aside, it is unlikely that this chronicle would have actually been written but for the prolonged period of enforced idleness by the Covid 19 pandemic of 2020-2021. Every cloud has a silver lining.

My formative years are covered in chronological order for ease of telling and reading. My adult years are treated sometimes as autobiography, rarely as memoir, sometimes as travel journaling, and, at the end of the book, as a few topical essays on matters that I feel certain will affect my descendants in important ways. That, as the saying goes, is the story of my life.

David Ainsworth

Napa, CA

For Joka

"There is no cure for birth or death.
The best therapy is to enjoy the interval."

George Santayana

CONTENTS

CHAPTER 1

HOLLAND

It all started in Holland, Michigan on a day when the tulip bulbs planted by descendants of the city's Dutch founders lay inert under a thick layer of snow. I was born, the second son of my parents, on February 10th in the year 1940. I am informed and believe, unlike David Copperfield, my first cries did not coincide with the stroke of midnight.

The nation was then in the eleventh year of the Great Depression and times were hard, although my father provided us with a middle class standard of living from his oil well acidizing business which he operated with a silent partner. We lived in what my mother described as, and I could see in early photos to be, a white traditional two story house on a tree-lined residential street. My maternal grandmother lived with us at the time, perhaps to help with my older brother Bill and me and not entirely to my father's liking. During unwelcome, and not infrequent, episodes of his intoxication, he reportedly referred to his mother-in-law as "Buttercup." I don't know why he thought that term was apt, but it shows wit and belligerence.

My father, William Earl Ainsworth was born in a one room home, circa 1903, in Star, Mississippi. Star is a village in the hill country of Rankin County, not far from the state capitol, Jackson. His mother, my grandmother Inez, later had two other sons (Thomas Grey and Edgar Carl) and a daughter (Ina Mae). Inez died at the tragically early age of 29, reportedly from pellagra, a disease caused by a dietary deficiency in Vitamin B-3 (niacin) commonly found in meat, poultry and fish. Their diet at the time reportedly consisted of cornbread, some pork, black-eyed peas, and a few vegetables like okra and collard greens.

My paternal grandfather, William Augustus Ainsworth, was the last cotton farmer in my line of Ainsworths, thus extinguishing the connection

1

between his family and the textile industry in Lancashire, England. (See Genealogical Appendix.) Lacking the economic leverage of near slave labor and plantation scale farming operations enjoyed by major cotton growers, cotton farming on a small scale finally played out for the Ainsworths of Rankin Country. After that, "Daddy Will" moved to Jackson and became a policeman.

As a family, they were poor, and my father left home at the age of sixteen to find work in the oil fields of Oklahoma. He worked as a roustabout on oil rigs first in Oklahoma and then also in Kansas and made the transition in his early thirties from oil rig laborer to white collar office work with the Kansas State Proration Commission. That agency monitored and regulated the amount of crude oil and natural gas extracted by each of the states that spanned the vast and productive Hugoton Gas Field beneath Kansas and the panhandles of Texas and Oklahoma. It is the second largest natural gas field in the world.

My father met my mother, Carmen Sylvia Vincent, at the beginning of the Depression in Wichita, Kansas where my mother was a librarian in the public library. One of five surviving children of Harry and Grace Vincent of Winfield, Kansas, she earned a bachelor's degree in library science from Southwestern College in Winfield—the only member of her family to graduate from college. She had been born in a village named Bustinari near Ploesti, Romania in 1908 when her father, an oil well driller from the oil-storied town of Titusville, Pennsylvania, had been sent by the Standard Oil Company to Romania to work in the large, shallow oil field there. My mother was named Carmen Sylvia after the then queen Elizabeth of Romania, who was a prolific writer of poetry, novels and music under the literary name of Carmen Sylva meaning "red woods" of the sort found in the Carpathian Mountains.

My mother's birth certificate, though issued in the Romanian language, legally established her American citizenship as being born to two American parents, even though abroad. However, nearly a century later when I used her birth certificate to satisfy a California government requirement of citizenship as a prerequisite for receiving MediCal benefits, a humorous adventure in bureaucracy followed that ended only when the bureaucrats accepted her untranslated Romanian birth certificate as evidence of her American citizenship.

After several years in Romania, Harry Vincent and his family returned to the United States before the outbreak of World War I. Whether this was at their request or Standard Oil's direction is not known to me, but Harry left first to commence his new job in Vincennes, Indiana, again working as a driller for Standard Oil. My grandmother Grace and her five children followed, taking *five months* to make the trip from Ploesti, Romania by train to an unknown European port, thence by steamship across the North Atlantic to New York, and finally, by rail to Vincennes. Within a decade or so, the family subsequently moved from Vincennes, Indiana to Winfield, Kansas, another oil town, where my mother went to high school and college. My grandfather Harry died there of Hodgkin's disease in his late 50s, no doubt caused by all the first class carcinogens in his oil field work environment. My grandmother Grace returned to Pennsylvania, her childhood home, settling in the town of Warren where she lived until her death at age ninety seven in a home for "gentlewomen" operated at no charge to the residents by the Freemasons, of which Harry had been a member in good standing.

During the early years of the Depression, my mother was the only one of her siblings to have a job. Her income as public librarian meant that her sister Corelia's two boys could have shoes for school and winter. It was during that time that she met and married my father in Wichita. My older brother William Earl Ainsworth, Jr. was born there in 1937.

Thereafter, my parents migrated from Kansas to Holland, Michigan when my father joined forces with another man to start an oil well acidizing business in Holland. Apparently, his partner had the resources and contacts in Holland and was looking for someone who knew oil rigs and production methods. My father had that background. The company was named the Ainsworth Acidizing Company as his partner apparently wanted to remain a silent partner.

Acidizing oil wells was a method of extracting residual oil and gas from wells that had been substantially depleted. Pouring hydrochloric or sulfuric acid into the *permeable* sandstone and limestone rocks in depleted oil wells would partially dissolve those rocks and release residual oil and gas which would then flow to the drill hole. A good living could be made from selling that extra margin of recovered oil and gas after acidizing. [That is not to be confused with hydraulic fracking today which involves injecting water and chemicals at high pressure into wells drilled into *impermeable* oil shale to break up the rock. Oil from millions of years of accumulated marine deposits locked into the fine crystalline structure of the shale will then flow to the drill hole through the fracked fissures. These oil shales are the source rocks from which all oil and gas comes.]

I go into this level of detail because oil and gas consumption is a matter of substantial concern as I write this and represents a threat to those who come after me. That is because oil shale reserves deplete faster than conventional wells, and after the oil shales are depleted, there isn't any more oil. (See my novel *In Extremis* for a meditation on how that might bring about collapse.) Absent a timely discovery of one or more new sources of energy to replace oil and methane gas, and the hard work of building an infrastructure to accommodate the new energy sources, sapiens may be in for a rough patch. I wish, gentle reader, that there could be a way for you to let me know how it comes out. For more on this subject, see also the essay on energy at the end of the book.

My only knowledge of what happened to my father's acidizing business is hearsay from my mother. My father died of a heart attack in 1961 just before my twenty first birthday while I was a junior at Kansas University, so I never had a chance to interrogate him on that and many other adult matters. However, my mother told me that the silent partner in the Ainsworth Acidizing Company absconded with the funds of the business when my father was unable to work due to a severe back injury on the job.

With my father's inability to work due to his injury, my parents packed up and drove from Michigan at the beginning of 1941 to my father's home and family support unit in Mississippi. My mother drove the car with my brother and I in the front seat, and my father stretched out in the back seat for what was for him an agonizing journey. We settled in Biloxi, Mississippi.

[Notes: Google Maps can locate the dwelling presently situated at the Holland, MI address of my parents listed on my birth certificate as 195 West 11th Street, Holland, MI. The existing house as I write this probably post-dates the house we lived in.

A Genealogical Appendix at the end of this volume contains a sort of bouquet of genealogical tidbits about the bloodlines of my paternal and maternal grandparents. Readers of this chronicle may wish to read that appendix before continuing because I make reference to those genealogical matters from time to time herein.]

Chapter 2

Biloxi/Yazoo City, Mississippi

Since everyone with knowledge of why my parents settled in Biloxi and what they did there are long dead, I am left with only my dim recollections of that time. It must have been either just before or just after Pearl Harbor. I had an older cousin named Dorothy (early teens), daughter of my Uncle Grey and his wife Eula, all of whom must have been there in Biloxi as well. My earliest memories are of playing with my cousin Charles (my Uncle Carl's son) in Biloxi when we were perhaps three or four (1942-43). We were allowed to walk to the neighborhood market (a small store) and buy a half stalk of sugar cane for a nickel. Then we would break it into its cane segments and chew on them for days. Another memory involved Charles and I discovering that a rubber bulb with an attached pointed tube could vacuum up water which we could then shoot by squeezing the bulb. We were severely reprimanded for squirting water on Charles' baby sister Carla in her crib. All of that tends to confirm that a sort of gathering of the clan for mutual support during the Great Depression took place.

We also at some point relocated to Yazoo City, Mississippi during that period, perhaps because of a work opportunity there for my father as he recovered from his back injury. My mother used to reminisce about a Portuguese fisherman and his wife who lived next door to us in Yazoo City. "Mr. Da Silva" used to bring her homemade fisherman's soups which she loved.

Given the fact that my father went back to Mississippi for support while recuperating from his back injury, and confirmed by my own early childhood memories of other relatives on my father's side being in proximity, I know that Mississippi is ground zero for my family genealogy on my father's side. I have no contacts there anymore and haven't personally been back there since my father's death sixty years ago. My uncle Carl moved to Southern California, and he died there in his fifties of a heart attack. My uncle Grey lived in Iowa, Louisiana and died there into his seventies, also of heart disease.

Late in my life (2016), I disembarked from a Holland America Line cruise ship named the *MV Veendam* in Edinburgh, Scotland with my bestie, Johanna Van Egmond. It was at the end of a cruise around the Baltic and North Seas. (See Chapter 24) We made our way to the Manchester area of England and to the village of Ainsworth. I wanted to have a better understanding of who the Ainsworth's were, where they came from and what made them emigrate, seemingly in waves, to the new world over four centuries. The result of that inquiry produced some answers to those questions that may be found in the Genealogical Appendix. Since it does not bear on this history, I omit discussion of it here except to note that a large number of Ainsworths may be found in the cotton belt states of the South, notably Mississippi. They are descendants of Ainsworths who migrated from Lancashire in England in the late 1700s and early 1800s. Residents of the Bolton-Manchester area of Lancashire, the center of the textile industry in England, would have known that the source of the cotton that drove their economy was the American Piedmont, specifically Charleston and Savannah, which were the ports naturally tributary to the plantations that grew the cotton. So, during hard times in England, they gravitated to the American South in search of new opportunities. For my family line, that migration, in turn, led to the Mississippi cotton fields, as well as those of South Carolina, Texas and Louisiana. It was from those Ainsworths—the Williams and Jameses and Levins and their descendants—that my father came.

My mother used to talk about being a fish out of water as a Yankee in the Deep South. Huey Long was the governor of neighboring Louisiana and a very notorious character. He was a populist and would work up a rural crowd by railing against the banks and oil companies in Shreveport and Baton Rouge. I have dim memories of visiting someplace in Louisiana, perhaps the home of my uncle Grey and Aunt Eula in Iowa, Louisiana. My mother, who was accustomed to speaking her mind, told me she was instructed by the family to stop saying critical things about Governor Long, even inside the home, because he had spies everywhere.

The family could get into trouble, they said. My mother understood her in-laws to be referring to the state police which were controlled by Governor Long.

Governor Huey Long lived in a suite in the Roosevelt Hotel in New Orleans. That Roosevelt would be Teddy Roosevelt, not Franklin Delano Roosevelt who came later and was the populist Long's rival for the Democratic nomination for President in 1936. (I am remotely related to both Roosevelts. See Genealogical Appendix.) Long had an always-open jail cell built in the basement which initially contained "the deduct box." This was a locked metal box with a slot at the top into which state government employees, all of whom owed their jobs to Long, together with any bag men for the oil and other companies that did business with Long's government, dropped periodic cash payments. The deduct box was later moved to the lobby of the hotel for the convenience of everyone, a dressy brass version of which may be found there still. No record was ever kept of the receipts thereof, and its contents were for the personal use of Huey.

Long, aka "The Kingfish," boasted that he "bought legislators like sacks of potatoes and shuffled them like a deck of cards." He built a network of one lane roads between rural towns in the state and provided the poor with free textbooks. He dispensed patronage jobs and built hospitals and universities. He taxed the wealthy and corporate businesses to finance his "Share the Wealth" populism and was as popular with the rural poor as he was despised by the elite. In his later years as governor, he invalidated laws passed by the legislature by edict, fired his elected lieutenant governor, packed the judiciary, and put the state police under his personal command. He famously said that "if tyranny ever comes to America, it will be in the name of one hundred percent pure Americanism."

The Roosevelt Hotel had, and still has, the famous Sazerac Bar, an ornate, art deco lounge that served up the eponymous Sazerac rye whisky cocktail. In 1935, an unsuccessful assassination attempt was made on Huey Long in the bar resulting in a bullet hole in the wall that may or may not still be visible. The next day, Long was shot on the steps of the state capital in Baton Rouge in a successful attack. While Long lay mortally wounded in his hospital room, Seymour Weiss, Long's chief of staff, urgently asked him for the key to the deduct box so the contents would not be discovered. Long reportedly whispered "Later, Seymour, later" and then died. The deduct box was never found by the authorities. His family members were elected to numerous positions in the Louisiana government and the U.S. Senate for decades afterward.

My college educated, Yankee mother arrived from Kansas, via Michigan, and lived in a Jim Crow, Huey Long-influenced, South more alien than anything she had ever experienced. I was, of course, oblivious to all of that as a three or four year old, and was happy in the company of my cousins and with my Uncle Grey, a charming and superb teller of stories. For some reason, I have no memories at all of my brother during that time. He would have been playing with older kids, but he would have been a lot more aware of any underlying tensions and racism then than I. My brother and I never had a chance to talk about that period while he was alive as we were estranged for a good forty years until his death from lymphoma in April, 2002.

The war was raging in Europe and the Pacific from early 1942 through the late summer of 1945, and my father was extremely frustrated by being too old (late thirties) to wear the uniform. With his back injury healed, he cast his eye around for industrial work in support of the war effort. Shipyards were heavily recruiting both Southern whites and blacks for shipbuilding work in Northern cities. So, he moved our family to Vancouver, Washington to build aircraft carriers.

CHAPTER 3

VANCOUVER AND BREMERTON, WASHINGTON

Again, owing to my tender age in the 4-6 years old range at the time, the absence of any survivors at the time of this writing, and there being no documentation of any kind left behind during those tumultuous war years, information about this period is sketchy. The snippets of recollection that I do have are anecdotal. My father, I now realize, would have been in Vancouver, Washington during the 1943-45 years in order to work in the Kaiser shipyard there which was engaged in building escort aircraft carriers for use in convoys. My mother told me he was a pipefitter. His work environment would have been a cloud of asbestos fibers because ship pipes were covered with asbestos lagging. Fortunately, he never developed the mesothelioma that fell like an avalanche onto industrial workers of that era much later.

Henry J. Kaiser, a larger-than-life, "big iron" industrialist, built dams and bridges and ships, among other things, before, during and after the war. Across the Columbia River from Vancouver, his Portland, Oregon shipyard built Liberty ships during the war. I know now that Liberty ships were an emergency hull design modified by the U.S. Maritime Commission based on naval architecture borrowed from British "ocean" class merchant ships. Their mission was to carry military supplies for all of the armed forces in both the European and Pacific theaters—a staggeringly vital role. That role was made more daunting because the infrastructure for building those ships in Depression-mired America did not exist. So, the Big Iron guys and their Merchant Navy policy-maker sponsors in the Federal Government started from scratch in 1941.

The war in Europe had broken out in October, 1939 when Hitler's army invaded Poland. Britain, Poland's ally, declared war on Germany because Hitler broke his pledge to British Prime Minister Chamberlain, after annexing first Austria and then the German-speaking parts of Czechoslovakia, that Germany sought no more territory. Germany then occupied not only Poland but virtually all of continental Europe not already under fascist regimes. For the first two years and two months of that European war, the United States remained neutral, the prevailing sentiment in the U.S. Congress being intolerant of "old Europe" and the tendencies of its monarchies to make war with one another over obscure grievances. This animosity toward old Europe was especially strong in America at the time, coming so soon after the ghastly carnage of World War I, the so-called "war to end all wars."

When Japan attacked Pearl Harbor in December, 1941, however, America declared war on Japan, Germany's ally. Germany had welcomed America's "neutrality" in 1939-1941 war in Europe even though America was violating the rules of neutrality by shipping supplies and providing merchant ships to Britain. This aid stood in breach of the German Navy's embargo on Great Britain to starve it into surrender. Hitler tolerated America's actions at first because he wanted to keep the American army and navy out of the Atlantic war. However, following the Japanese attack on the American fleet at Pearl Harbor on December 7, 1941, Hitler reasoned that America, in its 12th year of the Great Depression, would not have the industrial capacity to effectively fight two wars simultaneously. It would, of necessity, focus on Japan. So Germany declared war on America and began to attack American shipping in the Atlantic.

In the space of a week in December, 1941, America found itself a combatant in two wars, across two oceans, with essentially no merchant navy to carry military supplies for all its armed services and a major part of its warship fleet having been sunk at Pearl Harbor. So, building Liberty ships to carry supplies and building warships became a top national priority to support any trans-oceanic military response by America. America's old WW I era ships were hopelessly few, small, and obsolete. Shipyards like Kaiser's Portland yard recruited heavily from the under-employed ranks of older men, African Americans, housewives and immigrants to build ships. So, Rosie the Riveter and men like my dad volunteered in droves to work in the shipyards. They "built ships by the mile and cut off by the yard" as one wag characterized the enormous production line.

By the time our family got to Vancouver in 1943, the war effort was two years old and the shipyards were in full production building new ships and repairing war-damaged ones. I remember my mother talking about my father working on repairs to the carrier *USS Ticonderoga* after it had been hit by a *kamikaze* attack in the Pacific.

At some point my dad's employment shifted to the naval shipyard in Bremerton, Washington and we moved to Bremerton. My dad worked there on newbuildings and repairing more war-damaged ships until the end of the war in the Pacific. I don't have a sense of the relative duration of our stays in either Vancouver or Bremerton, but it would have been approximately a year in each place.

My recollections from those days—again, I'm not sure which events transpired in which town—are limited to just a few childish experiences. Items:

I remember being put in a pre-K "nursery" school, I think in Vancouver. On the first day, there came a time where we children were to rest. I and the other boys were told to remove our pants (were some of the children bed-wetters?) and lie down on a mat on the floor with the other children. That struck me as a profoundly intimate thing to be doing with my fellow students, especially the girls, and it embarrassed me greatly. So, when the teacher wasn't looking, I got up, put on my pants, left the building, ran across a lawn and climbed over a fence to walk home. As I climbed over the fence, I could hear the teacher calling, "David, David, come back," but I made my escape. My mother didn't make me go back after that.

One time I went out to play, I think also in Vancouver, and left the yard at our house. I have an image in my head of that house as part of a wartime housing development for shipyard workers consisting of a long series of identical duplexes that ran for several square blocks. At some point, two policemen in a police car took notice of my wandering the streets, stopped, and put me in the back seat of their car. We then proceeded to drive around as they asked me if any of the houses we passed was my house (no), and did I perhaps live down that street (no)? They stopped at a store and bought me an ice cream cone, and we continued to drive around. When I overheard them wondering how they were going to find out where I lived, I helpfully gave them the street address of our house, to which they delivered me with ice cream cone in hand to the shock and surprise of my mother.

In Bremerton, I was old enough to go to public school kindergarten at the same school my brother Bill attended. So, we walked to school every day along a route my brother knew and my mother did not think to check. She just saw us off every morning with our lunch boxes and relied on my brother to get me there and back. Unbeknown to her, my brother and his friends, and we younger siblings, took a "short cut" through the woods to get to school. This being the Pacific Northwest, woods were omnipresent and so were watercourses. So, our path to school took us over a substantial, deep, rocky and fast running creek spanned by "King" Log and "Queen" Log, two massive, mossy, sometimes wet and slippery logs that had fallen across the chasm of the creek. The older kids were proud to take the smaller "Queen" Log while the younger kids took "King" Log, which offered a bigger pathway. I remember slipping one rainy day and falling to my knees on King Log and looking down into the creek cascading over the rocks beneath me. It frightened me, but I recovered and went on. We continued to take that route to school until my mother became intrigued by our childish chatter about King Log and Queen Log. She made us show her what we were talking about, and, as soon as she saw the logs and the chasm under them, she gave us both the biggest scolding I can ever remember her giving us. We were never allowed to go there again.

I do remember the end of the war in Bremerton. That would be the Pacific War. The end of the war in Europe had come in May of 1945, but the War in the Pacific raged on until VJ Day. Our war in the Pacific shipyards was the war against Japan. Still, I was just a kid playing in the neighborhood during the summer months we were out of school while the adults engaged in the war effort. However, one day—I now know it was August 15, 1945—a woman stuck her head out of a second story window of one of the identical duplexes and started shouting "The war is over! The war is over!" The men and many of the women were at work in the shipyard at the time, so the there weren't many people to hear the woman's shouts. I just remember thinking that this must be very good news that would affect our family. I don't recall any other public marking of the end of the war in my household or my neighborhood.

I was not aware of it at the time, but relations between my mother and father were strained to the breaking point due to his periodic lapses into heavy drinking. My mother did not drink alcohol of any kind and considered drinking a sin under her Methodist credo. They quarreled over it, and my mother took the opportunity of the end of the war and the provocation of increased drinking by my father as he now had time on his hands, to leave my father. Taking my brother Bill and I, my mother drove with her sister Corelia ("Coe") and her husband Dick Stanhope, who must have been working in the shipyard also, back to Kansas to start over.

The drive back was a long one on two lane roads that took perhaps three or four days. However, I remember being mesmerized by the vastness and beauty of the American West as we "rode with the tumbling tumbleweeds" across expanses of basin and range with a continuing panorama of purple sage, herds of antelope, red rocks, towering forests and cascading rivers.

CHAPTER 4

WICHITA, KANSAS

I have a pretty clear recollection of the house that we moved into in Wichita. It was just my mother, brother and I living in the upstairs apartment of a two story frame house in a neighborhood of modest homes. The street in front of the house was made of brick and had a deep slope from each curb down to the center of the street which served as a drainage channel during heavy rains.

I received my first tricycle shortly after we arrived. None were to be had during the war, and my mother gave me one soon after manufacturers began to make then again. It was shiny and red but of very poor quality. In just a matter of months my brand new trike simply broke in half as I was pedaling it on the sidewalk. I was crushed after being so thrilled when I received it new. Those were the days of *caveat emptor*, and my mother had no remedy with the seller, so I just did without again.

It was in that neighborhood that I developed my first important relationship with a girl. Annie Macomb lived a half block down the street and we became fast friends, first, riding our tricycles up and down the sidewalk, and then hanging around her great uncle George, a carpenter who lived with the family and helped her mother Elsie out while Annie's father was away a good deal of the time as a long haul trucker. Uncle George was a patient, quiet man who did endlessly fascinating things with his tools, and we would watch him for hours at a time. In retrospect, I think he was just making what-not shelves and the like rather than paid carpentry jobs, but he and Annie and Elsie, and later Annie's father Floyd became extended family. More later on the Macombs.

We lived in that apartment only a matter of months before my father arrived back in Wichita to live with us. Apparently, he and my mother worked out some terms by which he was allowed back in the family. Those matters were never discussed with my brother and I, but I'm guessing the terms involved no drinking and going to church. My mother was raised as a Methodist, and Methodists were pretty straight-laced types.

My brother and I were obliged to attend Sunday school during the hour the minister preached his sermon on Sunday. The Sunday school lessons were a collection of Old Testament stories about Daniel in the lion's den, Jonah and the whale, Lot's wife being turned into a pillar of salt for her perfidy in turning to gaze at God descending to destroy Sodom and Gomorrah, and the like. At the tender age of six or seven, I *knew* those stories were baloney. The fact that an adult was reciting these biblical stories that I knew to be untrue made me extremely uncomfortable, and I found it personally embarrassing to have to sit and listen to them. But, I kept my opinions to myself and just went along out of an intuitive awareness that, however, factually absurd those stories seemed, any public challenging of them by me would have been very unwelcome. No third party ever whispered any words of denial in my ear or otherwise planted the seeds of doubt in my mind at that tender age. I just *knew.*

The point of the Old Testament stories was to demonstrate how miraculous the God of Abraham was, thereby engendering a fledgling faith in young minds. As I said, they had the opposite effect on me. I have always thought that experience was a curious one to have at my then age, since it necessarily followed that adults were not to be trusted to tell the truth, about religion anyway. I don't remember ever having any conversations even with my brother Bill about it, but then he was three and a half years older than I, and we did not share our thoughts with each other.

Not long after my father rejoined the household, we rented a slightly larger, single family house at 411 South Rutan Street. I recall a good deal about the years we spent at that house. It was a special treat to get a bag full of hamburgers from the neighborhood White Castle for 15 cents each. It should be noted that the White Castle hamburger spots in Wichita, Kansas, developed what eventually became known as "fast food."

My nursery school experience at Vancouver had been brief and unsatisfactory. However, I started kindergarten and first grade at the neighborhood elementary school in Wichita and fit in just fine. I remember it as a fun and formative time. I had a crush on a popular girl named

Becky, and my recollection is that it was reciprocated. More interestingly, I made friends with some fraternal twins named David and Billy Koch—boys that were destined for extreme prominence.

David was a popular boy but Billy was awkward and the last to be chosen for teams on the playground. Other boys would tease and even bully him, but David seemed strangely indifferent to those situations. I don't recall him ever defending his brother. It usually fell to me to tell the boys that were picking on Billy to stop it. In any event, the three of us would play together on the school playground. At one point, the twins' mother Mary Koch extended an invitation to my mother for what we would now call a play date. The Koch's chauffer would come to my house and take me to the Koch household to spend the day, after which I would be returned by chauffeured limousine. That did indeed happen. It was handled that way because the Koch household was a large property well out of town. There were no neighborhood kids for the twins to play with. There was no neighborhood.

The estate house was large (I remember getting lost upstairs when I went to the bathroom and wandered from room to room to room looking for a way out) and the grounds were to me huge. There were three polo fields. There was a skeet shooting range. The twins fired off multiple clay pigeons just to show me how they worked.

There was a stables. The stable hands must have selected and saddled the horses, but one day the twins and I were each given a horse and we went out for a ride. I had never been on a horse before and yet there I was, on a polo horse on my own. I tried to follow the twins as they rode ahead, totally at ease with their horses, but as we got some distance away from the stables, my horse must have sensed that it was free to do what it wanted to do, which was return to the stables. So, it turned and began to gallop back from whence we had come. The twins were galloping after me calling "Pull back on the reins!" What I heard was "Let go of the reins!" And I did. I managed to hang on to the saddle horn and we, the horse and I, made it back to the stables in relatively short order. There were no further horseback riding excursions.

To reciprocate, my mother invited the twins to come and play at my house one day. They were delivered to our front door by the same chauffeur who had picked me up the time before. We did what kids in our neighborhood did, which was wander the neighborhood seeking opportunities to amuse ourselves and play with other kids. At the end of the day, Fred Koch, the twins' father himself, stopped by to pick up his sons. He knocked on our screen door, my mother answered, and they made their introductions. My mother later described the situation that followed many times over the years. Fred asked where the boys were and my mother answered, "Oh, there are around somewhere." Koch's face suddenly turned white and he started to panic. My mother realized at that point that people in the Koch's stratum of wealth were in constant fear of kidnapping, and that his distress was real. She quickly stepped to the porch railing and called out "David, boys, come home!"

We three came running out of a house diagonally across the street where a kindly music teacher was entertaining us with cookies and riffs on the piano. Fred Koch made his exit with the boys, and they never again visited our house to play. I made one or two more trips out to their estate, but the school year ended and the twins were sent to private schools from then on.

The twins had two older brothers. Fred, Jr. was the oldest and grew up to be a somewhat reclusive art collector and mansion renovator. Reportedly, he took no interest in the family business, which was buying oil leases and developing oil fields, among other investments. That is how Fred, Sr. made his fortune. The second son, Charles, was smart and business oriented and took over the family business after being groomed for it by his father.

Fred, Sr. had an interesting and uneven career, an examination of which is beyond the scope of this account. It included, among other things, some years doing oil development business with Joseph Stalin in Russia, where Fred, Sr. acquired a life-long hatred of not only Soviet-style communism, but of any form of political collectivism in general, including public welfare programs like Social Security. I suppose he considered public welfare programs as the camel's nose under the tent. His four sons followed his lead and became life-long opponents of any political measures to foster public welfare such as FDR's New Deal. Fred co-founded the John Birch Society and was a reliable funder of conservative candidates and ballot measures opposing liberal/progressive measures to expand government welfare programs and the taxes to pay for them.

After Fred Sr. died in 1967, Charles expanded Koch Enterprises into a vast diversified corporate holding company. Of the twins, David worked with Charles in the business for many years and together they perfected the conservative political activism started by their libertarian father as major donors to conservative Republican candidates and organizations. They funded the Cato Institute, a conservative think tank, among other right wing groups. David died of cancer a year ago as I write this. Charles is in his late-eighties and still runs Koch Enterprises. He also continues to fund Republican causes and candidacies, but he withheld any funding of the candidacy of Donald Trump on the purist of libertarian grounds, namely, that Trump's trade tariffs against China constituted unreasonable interference with free trade.

Billy, the other twin, was always the odd man out. Like his father and brothers, he was an MIT engineer by training, but, like Fred Jr., distained the family business controlled by Charles. He saw himself as forced to engage in bitter litigation for many years against his mother and brothers to get control of his share of the estate in liquid funds so that he could pursue his passions for yacht racing and art collecting. He built an America's Cup boat called America 3, or America to the Third, and won the Cup in 1996, taking America's premier yachting event out of the hands of traditional single-hulled sailors like Dennis Connor and introducing the computer technology-driven boats we see today. Bill lives in West Palm Beach, Florida and is founder and Chief Executive of Oxbow Carbon LLC, a specialized energy company that markets petroleum coke. He made headlines several years ago, first, by being defrauded by people selling him expensive bottles of wine purportedly from Thomas Jefferson's cellar, and then hounding the perpetrators into penury with lawsuits.

My early grammar school years were spent, pleasantly enough, playing sandlot baseball with my friends and going to school. For some reason, I was directed to "skip" the second grade and went straight to third, which put me behind everyone else in learning the multiplication tables. Grammar school was generally hard for me from then on whereas it had been easy before, and I was always younger than my peers.

CHAPTER 5

OMAHA, NEBRASKA

After fourth grade, my parents moved to Omaha, Nebraska. My father was able to parlay his experience with the Kansas Proration Commission into managerial skills with Omaha-based Northern Natural Gas Company in their Proration Department. As mentioned earlier, the energy companies drawing oil and gas from the Hugoton Field had to conform to the regulatory requirements of the States of Kansas, Oklahoma and Texas. My impression is that he had a successful career in middle management with NNG in Omaha. He seemed to enjoy the work and his colleagues and over the years gained authority and responsibility. I remember seeing his photo in the *Omaha World Herald* in an article about his opening a company office in Calgary, Alberta.

We lived in a two-story frame house at 4004 Paxton Boulevard in North Omaha where I followed my brother in the progression from Central Park Elementary School into North High School. Though I was unaware of it, one Marlon Brando was following a similar path in Omaha's South High School at the same time. Also, while I was in Central Park Elementary School, I was classmates with Don Orris, who would later become my client at American President Lines as he almost singlehandedly transformed the freight side of the American railroad industry from boxcar carriers of cargo to unit trains of flatcars carrying cargo in ocean shipping containers. Neither one of us could remember knowing the other in grammar school though.

I have lots of boyhood memories from those Omaha years—just vignettes from the life of a boy in the mid-West in the 1950s, a period many now regard as probably the zenith of American prosperity and happiness. I had neighborhood chums with whom I played sports and tried scouting. I wore a flat top crewcut which cost twenty five cents at the barbershop. We had snow, snow, and more snow during our long winters that fostered sledding on the local hills and streets, ice hockey at the neighborhood park golf course pond, and endless shoveling from sidewalks and driveways.

In grammar school, I was a 'traffic guard" on the street in front of school. It involved holding a stop sign out to allow kids to cross the street. In the winter on very cold days, we would have to be relieved every 10 minutes or so to avoid frostbite.

I had a girlfriend in 5th grade named Ann. She was a tall, pretty brunette and, like most girls at that age, was light years more mature and emotionally intelligent that I was. I don't remember how we got to be close, but she want to "go steady" and so she gave me a ring to wear not on my finger but on a chain around my neck. After some months, for some reason—or probably no reason—I decided that was a nuisance, so one day I gave her ring to the PE teacher to give back to her later in the day during her recess. That afternoon, as I walked away from school to go home, I looked back up to the school door and there she was, watching me with a dark, hurt expression on her face that I still remember. The following day, the PE teacher told me in an icy voice "next time, do your dirty work yourself." I remember feeling not only like a complete jerk, but bewildered, like I didn't know how to handle affairs of the heart at all, which was of course true.

I received a bow and arrow for my birthday one year, and there was a green space across the street from our house of about two square blocks. So, one spring day, I was arcing arrows into the ground about 50 yards away when I spotted a robin. Robins were welcomed in the spring as harbingers of summer. Without thinking much about it, I took aim at my avian target at that impossible distance away to see how close I could come to it. The arrow went right through the robin's neck, fixing it to the ground where it stood. I was appalled. It was the first time I killed anything bigger than an insect, and it felt awful.

A few years later, when "squirrel hunting" with friends—really just an excuse to shoot a .22 rifle in the woods—I spotted a squirrel on a fencepost, drew a bead on it and fired. The squirrel exploded in a puff of fur and disappeared. When I walked over and observed the mangled body of the squirrel in the blood-stained snow, I confirmed a judgement, first made after shooting the robin with my bow and arrow, that hunting animals for sport was, for me, never going to be fun. I have never hunted animals with anything other than a camera since that day.

I had a buddy named Billy Atkinson whose father was in the freight salvage business. Billy's dad used to hire us for fifty cents an hour to do menial work around his store. One day he had a big sack of "red hots," a spicy candy popular at the time. We were to take red hots out of the big bag and put them into small, individual sized bags for retail sale. It took all day, and I became sick as a dog from eating red hots all day. My mother wouldn't let me work there anymore.

I had another buddy named Lee Haver. His dad managed a gas station and arranged for Lee to gradually start learning auto mechanics. Lee was a hard worker and like to have spending money. He was the first kid in high school to get a car, which we tooted around in endlessly. When he graduated from high school, he went directly to work in a gas station and over the years ended up the affluent owner of several gas station franchises.

My dad would put my brother and I to work at three specific jobs in summer—two of which I came to loathe. The one I didn't mind was mowing the lawn with an old push-style mower. It was hard work and Omaha summers were hot and humid, but I didn't mind the work. I even free-lanced around the neighborhood mowing lawns for elderly ladies at fifty cents a lawn.

The jobs I hated involved painting. One recurring job was to paint the picket fence that surrounded our large back yard. I felt like Tom Sawyer before I'd ever heard of Tom Sawyer. Slapping white paint on the face of the pickets was manageable because it was easy, but getting the edges of each picket right took an eternity. Fortunately, I only had to do it once every second or third year. My least favorite painting job though was a major, annual task: painting the screens and storm windows. In a northern climate, in summer, the outer windows were screens. In the absence of air conditioning, it was critically important to have all windows open with fans nearby, but no mosquitoes in the house. In the bitterly cold winters, the outer windows were "storm windows"—a separate glass window that provided an air space in between the inner and outer windows for insulation. So, every spring, the heavy storm windows had to be removed from all the windows of the two story house, wrangled into the garage, and then replaced with the screens. But first, the screens had to be painted because the extreme heat and sunshine would reliably cause some of the paint to peel off the wooden frame of the screen. In the fall, the three of us would again remove the screens and store them, wrangle the storm windows back from the garage and reinstall them. After, that is, painting them—always with the same forest green paint on the storm windows and screens to contrast with the white salt box house.

As miserable as I was doing that work as a ten or twelve year old, and as much as I hated it, I'm sure I did a very poor job of it. But, my father was patient and never scolded me. I just had to complete it more or less satisfactorily. It was one of the early lessons in Midwestern male stoicism I received as a boy.

My father and mother had a continuing conflict in their marriage about his drinking. He enjoyed alcoholic drinks, but my mother regarded liquor as immoral and would not allow him to drink in the house. So, he fell into a pattern whereby he would finish his chores on Saturday by mid-afternoon, shower, change clothes and then walk up to the neighborhood commercial area "to get some razor blades." There was a bar there and he would invariably return hours later noticeably under the influence. That would trigger bitter quarreling with my mother for the rest of the night. I came to dread those episodes. It only happened on Saturdays. Dad never drank on workdays. Or Sundays, but then the bars were closed then in Nebraska.

When he was drunk, he reserved his sarcastic, argumentative side for my mother. He never spoke harshly or in any way mistreated my brother or me. But he was nasty to my mother. Not physically abusive, but verbally so. I was rarely witness to the beginnings of their arguments at the time as I tended to isolate myself in my room on Saturday evenings to avoid being present during their fights. So, I can't say whether my mother initiated the quarrels by complaining about his being under the influence, or whether he initiated it out of some latent resentment loosed by the lowering of inhibitions from bourbon. Later, though, after they were divorced and my dad remarried Marge Gibson, the widow half of a couple who had been old acquaintances, Marge and Dad enjoyed what we would now call happy hour in their home in the early evening. My dad's disposition during those cocktail hours was sunny, more in keeping with his normal disposition and that of his friendly, story-telling, funny brothers. My uncle Grey, as mentioned earlier, was a renowned story teller and jokester.

So, while I was a preteen lad, my sympathies were with my mother as the victim of my dad's snarky verbal abuse. With the benefit of hindsight, however, I would have to say that my mother's religious single-mindedness about alcohol consumption was the root cause of their incompatibility. Dad was good company with a daily cocktail after he divorced my mother. With my mother, however, he would binge drink only on Saturday and then, when drunk, became sarcastic and argumentative with my mother. Neither of them was culpable; they were just incompatible.

I don't want to portray my mother as a dour, strict, colorless person. She wasn't. She had a great sense of humor and was whip-smart, educated and a good conversationalist. She took excellent care of my brother and me and, like most mothers, sacrificed greatly over the years so that we would have what we needed, or thought we needed. She just had a thing about alcohol and disliked being around people under the influence. Ironically enough, in her eighties and nineties living in Sonoma wine country, she became quite fond of a glass of "white zinfandel" at the end of her day, as she learned to experience the sense of well-being that washes over one after a glass of wine.

The recurring rows of my parents over drinking had a sustained adverse influence on me as a youngster. I was in constant fear that my family would break up or that some violence would result. That anxiety was prescient. When I was thirteen my father simply announced that he was not happy in the marriage and wanted a divorce. He was seeing a widow named Marge at that time, though my mother did not know it.

I was fourteen when they divorced, and my mother moved back to Wichita. She could work there as a librarian and had friends there. I moved with her. My brother Bill started college at Cornell as a freshman just before the move.

My father married Marge, and they bought a home, almost certainly with Marge's money inherited from her late oilman husband. The home was in West Omaha, an expanding part of the City populated with upper middle class custom homes. Dad continued to work at Northern Natural Gas Company, and I would visit him and Marge for a month or so during my summer vacations from high school and college. I always felt welcome there.

During one of those visits, I think when I was a freshman in college, he invited me to attend his Toastmasters Club. I did so, and learned that whenever an invitee visits a Toastmasters meeting, he is obliged to stand up, introduce himself and tell the assembly something about himself. As a kid addressing adults, I was nervous, but did a workmanlike job of introducing myself, or so I was told. I took note that he had surprised me with that and sort of appreciated his gamesmanship in testing me in that small way.

I attended a few more of his meetings and learned that his speeches to Toastmasters were serious, deep-thinking efforts for which a better education than a rural Mississippi high school might have prepared him. One of his talks was a defense of then Governor Orval Faubus of Arkansas, who was engaged in resisting racial integration in Arkansas public schools. In 1957, Faubus ordered the Arkansas National Guard to enforce segregation in a Little Rock High School, which President Dwight Eisenhower countered by deploying the 101st Airborne Division to Little Rock. The good citizens of Little Rock then voted by a large majority to close the public schools rather than accept the horror of integrated schools. My father, apparently ignoring the new 1955 Supreme Court decision holding in *Plessy v. Ferguson*, that the "separate but equal" doctrine was unconstitutional, argued that Governor Faubus was in the right. But it was a reasoned argument based upon the 10th Amendment of the U.S. Constitution reserving rights not expressly delegated to the Federal government to the States.

He also made a point of not expressing the racist views he held as a Mississippian at home or to my brother or me privately. Ever. I took that to mean that he was unsure in his own mind whether his racist past (he had belonged at one point to the Ku Klux Klan) was defensible. In any event, he left it to us to make up our own minds, something I realized at the time and gave him credit for.

CHAPTER 6

LAWRENCE, KANSAS

I can't remember my graduation from Wichita East High School. I don't even recall seeing a high school diploma. It's possible I didn't even attend it. I never made a circle of friends at East High, never played a sport there, didn't have any steady girlfriends, and never joined any clubs or participated in extracurricular activities. I don't know why. I just considered that the full social life I'd had at Omaha North High School before the divorce was enough. It wasn't possible to replicate that in much bigger Wichita East High starting as a junior and knowing no one. I don't remember it as being a stressful period, certainly not traumatic. I was just disinterested in high school, and spent all my spare time reading novels.

A girl with whom I was slightly acquainted *asked me* to the senior prom, but I made excuses and didn't go. She was the daughter of a friend of my mother's, so that was awkward for my mother. I was a knee-jerk loner by then.

I read a ton of novels my last two years of high school and took hard courses in physics, chemistry and foreign languages. I was preparing for college. I was shy and was a year younger than my peers at East High. This indifference stood in stark contrast to my brother who at North High School in Omaha had been President of the Senior Class, made National Honor Society, played varsity tennis, and won a scholarship to Cornell in Chemical Engineering. I felt guilty about my blank record at East High, but I did look forward to college.

Our finances were not such as to lead me to consider any schools other than the University of Kansas in Lawrence. I must have done passably well on my entrance exams because I don't remember feeling any stress about being admitted. In those days, getting into State U was not hard.

My brother was an SAE (Sigma Alpha Epsilon fraternity) at Cornell, and so I was a legacy at the SAE chapter at KU. I was invited to join the fraternity after rush and did. I lived comfortably in the fraternity house for the first two years and did a normal amount of dating around the sorority houses. Mostly, I studied geology and chemistry and English literature.

In the spring of my sophomore year, my roommate was my pledge father, John Garrett, who was a year ahead of me. We took to grousing about how stultifying school was and how much we wanted to go to Europe. I was majoring in geology and didn't enjoy my minerology and paleontology classes all that much. A year wandering in Europe sounded just about right. John had worked the previous summer as a fireman for the Rock Island Railroad and knew that the Rock Island hired college boys to work as firemen on the extra trains hauling the summer grain harvest. So, following his instructions, I applied for and got a job as locomotive fireman with the Rock Island that summer.

A fireman's job was not difficult. I rode in the engine with the engineer and did what the engineer told me to do. Fill the sand box so that sand could be sprinkled on the rails when more traction was needed. Inspect the journal boxes on the car wheels to make sure they were oiled and not overheating. Relaying the signals from the switchmen on my side of the track. Mostly, though, it was just riding along. The collective bargaining agreement mandated the job. It was the career development route for future engineers and served as a safety back up in case the engineer became incapacitated. Management thought the position was unnecessary "featherbedding" and sought to eliminate the position, but, I had no skin in that game. In the summer of 1959, my only interest was that the job allowed me to earn union wages and save practically all of them for my trip to Europe.

I had two Rock Island runs that summer. One was a night freight train between Kansas City and Herrington, Kansas. The second was a night freight train between Herrington and Caldwell, Oklahoma. If I needed a place to stay in either town for the turnaround trip, I just rented a room.

In between fixed runs, I worked on switch engines in the Kansas City yard. There is a good deal of work that goes into the making up of a freight train. We would get orders to find certain railcars, unblock them by switching other cars out of the way, and putting the string of desig-nated railcars together on a siding and ready to be pulled off by an engine for transportation out on the main line.

On Friday nights, the engineer that I worked with would game the system by timing a trip to a remote part of the yard to get certain cars just before a scheduled passenger train or freight train was coming through. That would mean that we had to stay off the main line back to the terminal for a couple of hours. My engineer would then park the engine and we would walk to his favorite bar to watch the prize fights on TV for two hours until we were cleared to come back. I came to the conclusion that management was probably right about "featherbedding," at least on switch engines.

I saved a thousand dollars in three months, which was a lot of money then. Through American Express, I bought my passage on a Holland America Line ship named the *SS Groote Beer* sailing from Montreal, Canada to Rotterdam in early October, 1959. I had several hundred dol-lars left over. Then I told my parents that I was going to Europe for a year. Neither one objected. I arranged with my father to suspend my monthly child support payments ($125 per month) with which I was paying for my college expenses. He agreed to hold them for my final two years of college when I got back.

At the end of the summer, my roommate John informed me that he was not going to be able to go. He was getting pressure from his parents, it was his senior year, and he was slotted to start Medical School. He also had a girlfriend named Celia Welch in the DG house with whom he was going steady. So he bailed. I never considered cancelling. I saw no reason why I couldn't go anyway. My pledge son, Sam Davis, had secretly cov-eted my trip and, without telling me, booked the same passage on the *Groote Beer*. When it was a *fait accompli*, he told me he was coming with me. It was a lucky break.

When the time came, my dad arranged for Sam and me to fly on a Northern Natural Gas company plane from Omaha to New York City. In New York, we spent a day riding the Staten Island Ferry (for a nickel) and dodging security in Grand Central Station where we spent the night waiting for our bus to Montréal. I recall a lovely, resplendently leafy

October bus ride through New England to Montreal and a brief stay at the YMCA there. Groups of girls were riding around in horse-drawn cabs singing *When the Saints Go Marching In* in French. I was charmed by the vibe and vowed to return to Montreal as I boarded the ship. I never did.

CHAPTER 7

EUROPE (1959-60)

This chapter relies heavily on a journal I kept during my nine months in Europe in 1959-60. I wrote it in pencil and now it has faded into near illegibility. So, its substance is hereby preserved. The trip, predictably enough, turned into one of the major formative experiences of my life—my coming of age story. It appears in considerable detail because the journal carefully recorded these events.

The late September trip across the North Atlantic at the tail end of hurricane season was predictably rough, and the *Groote Beer,* a Holland America Line C-3 hull design dating to WW II was small and "tender," that is, rolled a lot. The name of the ship in Dutch means "Great Bear" which is the common European name for the constellation Ursula Major, or as we call it, the Big Dipper. The ship rolled constantly in the big swells, and there were no stabilizer fins on ships in those days. It was queasy-time for six days, during which, at age 19, I wrote a poem that I read aloud at the urging of my table mates in the dining room, to wit:

Ah, the Sea, fantastic! As it rolls and pitches like a giant in agony.

Ah, the Sea, historic! As old as Man's intelligibility and Man,

Who knows not, occupies his Firth of Forth, his berth of barf.

People actually got mad at me for that doggerel.

Sam and I disembarked in Rotterdam, and we each bought a small, used motorcycle by which we planned to get around. Mine was a black 175cc German Maico I dubbed "Snowball." Sam had a pretty, burgundy, 150cc Jawa, a Czech brand. Each had a "banana" seat (for 2 persons) and a luggage rack. We strapped our suitcases and duffle bags on the luggage carrier of our bikes with bungee cords and set out for London where Deana Grimm, a friend and daughter of one of my dad's co-workers was an exchange student. Sam and I had seen her off on the *SS United States* in New York. We took a car ferry from the Hook of Holland to Harwich and rode on to London.

Somehow we found low rent digs in working class Earl's Court in the East End near where Deana was staying. (We ran into a rule that youth hostels in the UK were not available to persons on motorcycles, so our plan to stay in hostels in the UK was scratched.) I contacted Deana, and we called on her host family at their home. The family she stayed with were lovely working class folks and were very welcoming. We spent over a week chumming around with Deana and her friend Nancy from Montana and their English friends. We did low budget things like riding the subways and busses to see the sights of Westminster Abbey, Buck-ingham Palace, Tower of London, the British Museum and the Tate, Trafalgar Square, changing of the Guard at Whitehall, a concert by the Academy of St. Martin in the Fields, Harrods and Windsor Castle. It was well into October by then, and Sam and I decided that we should get on with our planned excursion to northern England and Scotland before the weather closed in.

We were, of course, way too late. Our first day on the road north was cold and raining, and we didn't have fairings (windscreens) on our bikes or proper rainwear, so the heavy truck traffic insured that we were covered in rainwater infused with road grit. Sam and I got separated on the motorway, and I proceeded on to Litchfield, our planned destination for the day. I couldn't find him at the hostel or American Express, so, cold, wet and miserable, I holed up for the night and called Deana in London the next day to see if she had heard from him. I learned that Sam had returned to London when we got separated.

After realizing that the weather commentary I had read in the guide-books that English weather was "mild" in October was disputable, I hopped on a train with "Snowball" in the baggage car, and rode back to London in comfort. Sam was right. A motorcycle trip into the north of England and Scotland in October was a bad idea. After another few days of touring with Deana and Nancy in London, we again said our good-byes and sensibly headed south. Destination: Paris.

The *modus operandi* we used to enter Paris was one that we adopted for each city we visited thereafter, namely, we followed the signs to the *Centre Citi* and then sort of circumnavigated the neighborhoods ("arrondissements") outward until we found one that seemed suitable. We settled in Clignancourt, a northern suburb. There wasn't much going on there in 1959, although there is a huge and famous flea market domiciled there now. The only thing I remember about Clignancourt is that Sam and I immediately acquired a taste for a bottle of wine with lunch. I'm sure it was plonk that we drank, but it was cheap and served with our meal in an unmarked liter carafe. The house charged us by the amount we drank. We took our time at lunch and dinner and got buzzed pretty much every meal, thinking, hey, these French know a thing or two about the good life! We then either motorcycled in to the First Arrondissment to visit the famous sites or took the Metro.

After a few days, in an inspired move, we took a room at the Hotel Saint-Louis on the Ile Saint-Louis. The Ile Saint Louis is a small, unreasonably charming island in the Seine just over a short bridge from the Ile de la Cite where Notre Dame sits. The left bank and Saint-Germaine is to the south across a bridge and the right bank and the upscale commercial part of town and museums over another bridge across the opposite half of the Seine to the north. We stayed there a month. Versailles, Eiffel Tower, Le Marais, Les Halles, the Louvre, the Opera, the Pantheon, Conciergerie, Notre Dame and Saint Chappelle, the Left Bank (Café Dieux Maggots), Montmartre and the Sacre Coeur, all the art museums, the Tuileries, Champs Elysees and Arc de Triomphe, Parcs Luxembourg and Monseau, and on and on. It was magical and made more so by fine fall weather and Berthillion, the landmark ice cream store on l'Isle.

I grew a beard in Paris. (Of course I did.) My motivation was actually to reduce the pain of being struck in the face by insects at high speeds on my motorcycle. I had neither a windscreen nor a helmet. The beard, when trimmed and accessorized with tear-drop motorcycle sunglasses, created a Brando-esque Joe Cool look. We didn't know anyone in Paris, couldn't speak the language, and couldn't afford any gastronomical landmarks, so after seeing the sights for a month, we were ready to move on.

It was mid-November, and Sam and I headed south to Avignon to see the Palace of the Popes built during The Schism. The palace was modest, but the Schism had been a big deal at the time. The Bridge at

Avignon has to be one of the great icons in France. It is an 800 year old stone bridge that broke in half centuries ago in the Rhone floods, and the part still standing has been allowed to continue spanning half the river, a minor hazard to navigation, and beckoning to nowhere.

From Avignon, we motored across Southern France toward our winter destination, the Costa Brava and Balearic Islands in Spain. Our first stop was a pension in a small town on the coast northeast of Barcelona called Cadaquez. Run by a gracious couple, the pension offered a room with two meals per day included for 100 pesetas per night each ($1.60). We spent a week there just soaking up the atmosphere, eating seafood, motoring around on our cycles, and hiking the coastline. As you have likely come to understand, gentle reader, we had no plan. No schedule. We arrived at a place at the end of a day, and if we liked it, we stayed until we felt like moving on.

The Cadaquez highlight was our discovery that Salvador Dali lived there in a little cottage on a rocky beach near town. Our beachcombing took us right past his house. He wasn't home during that time, and we peeked through a beachside door in a wall that led to a courtyard of the sort known as the "Spanish surprise." It is typical in Spain to have a high stone or stucco wall on the street with a double door. The wall conceals the house itself, and you have to breach the wall by entering the door to the courtyard and the house beyond. The surprise part is that the wall is universally plain, undecorated and offers no clue what lies inside, but upon entering through the door, the visitor is usually stunned by a landscaped, floral, ornate courtyard and whitewashed villa beyond. In Salvador Dali's case, however, the courtyard was stark, gothic and filled with the sort of ornamentation one finds in his paintings. Mobiles of driftwood, an altar with a cracked ostrich egg suspended above it, melted pieces of metal and plastic flowing over the edge of an unpainted table. On one stone platform, an elephant's skull was placed with its jawbone sitting on top of the skull. On top of that, the lower jaw of a horse sat crosswise, forming an X of jawbones on top of the elephant's cranium. Hmm, different, I thought. At the time that I was trespassing on his property, I had never seen a Dali painting. When I did several months later in the Prado Museum in Madrid, it was an aha! moment. Many of the objects on his patio appeared in his paintings.

I must have bought my Spanish classical guitar there in Cadaquez because I didn't have it in Paris, but I had it by the time I got to Mallorca. The inside label showed that it was made in Spain. I played the ukulele in college and wanted to graduate to guitar when I could take some lessons.

About the time the pension proprietors started feeding us roasted seagull for lunch and dinner (the fishing boats were not going out as often during the approach to winter), Sam and I determined it was time to shift our base of operations to Palma de Mallorca. So, we packed up and drove down the coast to Barcelona, the port for ferries to the Balearic Islands. On the way, we were periodically stopped on the mountain roads and my guitar case searched by the *Guardia Civil* carrying machine guns. Francisco Franco was Spain's fascist ruler then, and the government had a sinister vibe to it. Also, in Cadaquez, we had heard the Americans had a military installation high in the Pyrenees nearby and that a number of suspected foreign spies could be found in the area. Perhaps the American Government had found a way to work with the Franco regime since both were paranoid about communists.

I don't recall how we found a place to stay in Barcelona or what it looked like, so, it must have been an unremarkable pension or hostel. We spent several days in Barcelona seeing the sights. The *Sagrada Familia* was just a big construction site at the time so we were unaware of it but did visit the old cathedral.

Barcelona claims "Cristobal Colon" like Hannibal, Missouri claims Mark Twain. Columbus sailed from Barcelona before he stopped at Lisbon, and it was here that Ferdinand and Isabella received him after his return with six Amerindians who were promptly baptized in the cathedral. One theory I heard in Tenerife, Canary Islands just a few years ago was that Columbus wasn't Italian at all, that he was from Catalan Province (Barcelona is the chief city in Catalan.) Since Castile Province (Madrid) and Catalan were historic enemies, Columbus thought it politic, so the story goes, to represent himself to potential financiers Ferdinand and Isabella as being from Genoa. Columbus's surviving son, however, always claimed that his father was an Italian from Genoa.

Sam's and my grandest excursion out of Barcelona was to drive up to the mountain monastery at Monserrat and see its famous statue of the black virgin. There, in the company of several sailors from the U.S. Navy, we were treated to a concert by the Monserrat Boys Choir, a group second only to the Vienna Boys Choir in prestige we were told. The fact that the cloister of the monastery was a perfect acoustical venue for the choir may have enhanced their reputation.

On Thanksgiving Day, 1959, Sam and I embarked on the car ferry to Palma. It was an overnight passage, and we opted to sit up all night to save money. We arrived bleary-eyed early the next morning and drove our motorcycles ashore onto bone-jarring cobblestone streets. On an empty stomach, it was painful. I stopped at a street vendor's cart and bought a sandwich of sautéed octopus and onions just to get something in my stomach.

Later, at a waterfront café in Palma, we ran into an English nightclub singer/comic named Dickey Bennet and his Danish girlfriend Anna. They were well connected among the foreign expatriate crowd in Mallorca and graciously took us under their wing and helped us look for an apartment. We found a brand new, well-situated, furnished two bedroom apartment in a suburb called Terreno on the flank of a hill topped by the resident castle. We signed a one month lease for the place, including daily maid services, for the princely sum of US$ 20 per month. We shopped and cooked for ourselves, and paid for our Spanish brandy (Fundador, 60 pesetas or .85 cents per liter) and wine (2 liters, .25 cents), bars and nightclubs, petrol for the bikes, and miscellaneous expenses for another $35 per month. Fresh citrus was there for the picking.

There were two alternative Mallorca's then, and possibly now as well. The dominant Spanish one was quiet and not terribly different than I imaged it was in 1500 after the moors left. The church was omnipresent, as was the Franco regime through the Guardia Civil, but life there for the locals amounted to a pleasant, Mediterranean existence somewhat above subsistence level, with a few aristocrats, bourgeois merchants and political elites who were wealthy.

The other Mallorca consisted of foreigners. They were from all over Europe with a few Americans tossed in. Australian actor Errol Flynn's black-hulled schooner *Zaca* was berthed in Palma while we were there. (He died that year.) The foreign expats were there because the sun shined a lot, it didn't snow, and the rent, food and liquor were cheap. There were writer alcoholics, painter alcoholics, actor alcoholics, family black sheep, homosexuals (at a time when society would grant them no quarter), idle wealthy, and a scattering of tourists. Sam and I, at the tender age of nineteen, got a lot of exposure to that fast-living crowd for what turned out to be two full months.

Some of these folks were enormously entertaining and generous—great company. We were lucky in that we met two American girls from Baltimore just out of college and touring on their own in the off season. Bernice and I paired off, and Sam and Nancy did likewise. We shared the Mallorca experience like wholesome young couples, motoring around to various beaches and observing the Christmas season with a young pine tree liberated from the castle grounds and decorated with orange peels cut in continuous strips around the orange at which we had become dexterous.

The nights were spent clubbing on a civilized basis, with one exception. A party at our apartment turned ugly one night when Dickey's girlfriend Anna cut her wrists with one of our kitchen knives, showed her bloody wrists to everyone, and then ran out into the night. Dickey's response was indifference, and, in my view, shocking. I felt obliged to go after her. The problem was that it was a moonless night and there were no streetlights, so as I was chasing down the street after her footsteps, I ran at full speed into the grill of an unseen black car. The sound of that crash and my subsequent howling and cursing motivated Anna, who was nearby as it happened, to return with me to the apartment. Her cuts were not deep and were judged later to be only a "suicidal gesture" for which Dickey berated her publicly. I was gobsmacked by the whole experience.

At the end of our two months of play in Mallorca, Bernice's time ran out, and she had to go home. We said our goodbyes to each other, and I packed up to head for the South Coast of Spain via Ibiza, a neighboring island. Sam and Nancy planned to go to Austria together to ski, but rode along over to Ibiza to have a look-see. The ferry ran on Monday and Friday, so we took the Monday ferry and got off at Ibiza. I intended to take the Friday ferry on to Alicante and Sam and Nancy planned to return to Mallorca until time to depart for Austria.

While in Ibiza, Sam and Nancy were strolling around town and came upon a flamenco bar called Casa Pepe. They alerted me to the place, and we went back the following night for the flamenco guitar show. I was quite taken with the music and asked the guitarist, Pepe Madrid, if he would give me lessons, to which he agreed. So, I scratched the plan to depart on Friday and instead rented a room for a month to study guitar. I stayed in Ibiza for the two months of January and February having the time of my life.

I said farewell to my faithful travelling companion Sam who, along with Nancy, was off to Kitzbuhel to ski. [Fast forward: they got married later that year, settled in Baltimore and had a family. Sam completed college there and went on to enjoy a successful career in senior management with a multinational company. For some of that time, he lived in Germany. Our trip was a major junction in the trajectory of his life.]

In early February, I learned by phone call that Sam and Nancy were still in Mallorca because Nancy lost her passport and it took nearly a month to get a new one. So, to visit them and get some supplies, I took the ferry back to Mallorca for a weekend. I was gratified to be welcomed expansively by the expat community as one of their own, making me feel very sophisticated indeed. While there, I met Dutch, an American graduate student from Minnesota, who was headed for Ibiza to explore the old Phoenician tombs under the town. He took the same ferry I did returning to Ibiza, and we spent two or three days together crawling around in caves under the hilltop town of Ibiza. We found a few shards of broken pottery and glass in the long-since-plundered tombs, but we had no way of knowing whether they were Phoenician, Greek, Roman, or World War II for that matter. Dutch took them back to Minnesota when he left.

My routine in Ibiza for two months was unbroken. I would wake up in the spare, unheated, whitewashed second story room in my cot, take a sometimes cold shower, walk across the street to the bakery and get a fresh, sugar-dusted, bun-like pastry and an orange from the market next door. Next, I would climb up to the third story open roof of my building, stopping at my room to pick up my guitar and music. I would eat my breakfast on the roof in the sunshine and practice my guitar for two hours before my daily lesson at Casa Pepe. At about two o clock, I would walk to a restaurant called Los Caracoles (the snails) for lunch. I never ordered from a menu; rather I would sit at the same table every day that the proprietor had set for me and eat whatever hot meal he prepared along with a glass of *vino blanco*. It was always delicious and the *prix fixe* was about 50 pesetas (less than a dollar). In the afternoon, I would have my guitar lesson and read or write or hop on Snowball and go exploring the various beaches and towns on the island. At that time, there were no other foreigners to be found on the island. [At this writing, of course, Ibiza has become one of the most notorious playgrounds in Europe, filled with resorts and populated with beautiful people. I have trouble getting my head around that.]

Each evening, I would go to another restaurant called Los Pasajeros (the passengers) near the ferry dock. Conveniently, it was owned by the brother of the owner of Los Caracoles. The brothers would have spoken about what I was served for lunch, and around eight o'clock, I would arrive and sit at the table that had been set for me. Then the proprietor would serve me whatever meal he chose to cook, with a glass of *vino tinto*. The lunches and dinners were Mediterranean-style seafood dishes, including various paellas, and seemed uniformly delicious to my untutored palate. After dinner, I would always adjourn to Casa Pepe for a glass or two of Fundador brandy and listen to Pepe's guitar performance along with the evening crowd. I *loved* that routine, and I was living it for about three dollars a day.

One day during my last week on Ibiza, I met an Australian named Mike from Tasmania who was himself touring on his motorcycle. He also had stopped off at Ibiza for the interval between the Monday and Friday ferries from Mallorca to Alicante. We were sitting in a bar after the show at Casa Pepe late one night, and a group of English thespians came in and sat next to our table. Their group was noticeably deferential to one older man in their midst who excused himself at one point and asked me if he could borrow my fedora-style hat as a prop for whatever scene he was about to act out for his mates. I said sure and he did. It was Peter Finch, the star of the movie *Network*, among many other major stage and screen successes. I wasn't star struck at all; we were just bohemians having a good time yukking it up one brandy-fueled evening.

I caught the Friday ferry to Alicante, as did Mike, so we agreed to join forces since we were both headed for Granada. The evening of our departure, Pepe Madrid limped down to the dock to say goodbye and tell me to *practica*. The two brothers at whose restaurants I had eaten every day also came down to wish me bon voyage. I was surprised and touched by the discovery that they considered me a friend and not just a tourist kid. I found the departure from Ibiza wrenching. I had just turned twenty.

We spent the night on the ferry *SS Jaime II* in the first class bar and third class dormitory. There were no real cabins that I could see. I remember getting up once during the night to go to the head which was located in the foc'sle. To get there meant crossing the pitching foredeck on a moonless light. Both coming and going, I tripped over a large, slippery object that covered the entire deck. I fell down both times. I didn't think much about it, but the next morning I saw what I had fallen over the night before. It was a huge skate (like a manta ray) on deck being taken to market in Alicante. Eeeww.

When the ferry docked at Alicante, Mike and I 'rassled our motorcycles down the gangway and started off on what turned out to be a long, hard slog to Granada 400 km away. It took us through picturesque arid lands populated with gypsies and over the Sierra Nevada mountain range that rings Granada. We found a pension for our base of operations and explored the absolutely gorgeous Alhambra, a showpiece built by the moors before they were expelled in 1492. We also quaffed a few glasses of Fundador and ate our share of paellas. Nearby Valencia is ground zero for paella, and, since saffron infused rice is basically a host for lots of things, there are a great many paella recipes. We were happy to sort through as many as we could.

From Grenada, Mike and I drove back to the coast and the seaside town of Malaga. After checking into our pension, I was sitting in our room with a door open to the courtyard playing my guitar. Immediately I heard a voice from a room on the other side of the courtyard.

"Dave? DAVE?"

It was Dutch, the Minnesotan we hung with in Mallorca. He had migrated south from Mallorca about the time Mike and I set out from Ibiza and just happened to end up at the same place and at the same time we did. My guitar repertoire consisted of only a few pieces, and Dutch had heard all of them in Mallorca, so when he heard those same sounds over the courtyard, he knew it was me. Wild! The three of us went out for dinner and thence to a flamenco bar. Somehow, three Australian girls also got involved and the six of us struck up a conversation with two Spaniards, one of whom was a lawyer. In any event, on the subject of flamenco and my pursuit of it, it turned out that both of the Spaniards knew who Pepe Madrid was and were impressed that I had managed lessons from him. I, of course, knew he was talented, but it turned out that he had a national following. I was more fortunate that I realized to have his instruction all those idyllic weeks Ibiza.

From Malaga, Dutch left for Morocco and Mike and I departed for Marbella, a coastal town popular with the Spanish aristocracy and English expats. In our search for a pension, we were referred to a "hostel" which turned out to be a grand, baronial estate owned by the regional government and used by the officials of the Falange, the political party of Franco. When not in use by the party bigwigs, it was used as a youth hostel! The rooms were spare, but the common areas were large with glass cases filled with antique armor and weapons. High on the walls were the mounted heads of game animals. The dining room was vast with a long banquet table and upholstered brocade armchairs. A broad, curving stairway led from the great hall to the rooms upstairs. The charge was 12 pesetas per night, including breakfast, or about US$ .20 cents. I can't guess how they arrived at that charge.

In town, there was more flamenco at more flamenco bars. This was Andalucía, after all, the province from whence the music came. Always there are dancers stamping their heels rhythmically, and always there are castanets clacking in dexterous fingers twisting over the heads of the women in red ruffled dresses. And always there were guitars beating out a haunting, violent rhythm.

The music is associated with gypsies by outsiders, but the flamenco artists are rarely gypsies; they represent a culture to themselves. And Flamenco, which means "flamingo" after the vast flocks of flamingoes that migrate through Andalusian marshlands twice a year, has Moorish origins, whereas the gypsies migrated from Eastern Europe. Flamenco is its own music, sprung from its own culture centered in Andalucía, and its practitioners may be found throughout the province. In Barcelona, it is a sound as alien as Dixieland jazz.

From Marbella, we pointed our bikes toward Gibraltar and its neighbor, Algeciras. We finished March by touring Gibraltar, where I was almost knocked off a high trailside rock wall by a gamboling Barbary Macaque (good sized ape.) I was sitting on the wall admiring the view all the way to Africa when the ape flew by and hit me hard on the shoulder with his. It was like an NFL collision. I knew it was deliberate; he was probably just letting me know I was on his turf. A colony of about three hundred of them were residents of The Rock and very much protected by the British.

Mike and I contemplated the risks and rewards of taking our motorcycles into Morocco, a French protectorate until 1956 just four years earlier. We decided that we would ferry to Ceuta, a Spanish Morocco enclave on the North African Coast, stash our bikes somewhere in Ceuta, and then take a bus to Tangiers. We did exactly that and spent just under a week in Tangiers and intermediate points exploring the souks and having tea. Just performing subsistence functions seemed to take all day in these places.

We stayed at a clean, well-located *residencia* for 85 Moroccan francs per night (about US$ .17 cents.) It wasn't much of an irritant (because we had very little money with which to shop) but purchasing anything meant an elaborate negotiation. Nothing was marked with prices, which was okay if you were indifferent whether you want to buy something. You just say no, "too much" and keep walking, and they will chase you dropping the price until you buy it. If it is something you want to buy, though, like cigarettes, they've got you. They start at a sky high price and then you negotiate against yourself until you tire and then just pay something close to their price. Mike was a journalist and had travelled in Turkey, the Middle East, India and Malaysia, so he was better at it that I was. We went to the American Express office in Tangier (the place all travelers go to exchange mail and money) to see if we had a message from Dutch, whom we left at Granada as he departed for Morocco. But no message. We lost his trail there.

Things were unsettled in Tangier at that time as a large earthquake just days before had killed some 19,000 people in Agadir 700 kilometers down the coast. We wished that we could have seen the more colorful destinations of Marrakesh and Casablanca, but they were much farther south and, in addition to the infrastructural upset caused by the earthquake at Agadir, we didn't have the time or budget for that trip. So, we rode another bus back to Ceuta with a lot of curious Arabs and collected our bikes. Then, a thrilling and scary ferry ride carried us back across the mouth of the Mediterranean Sea to Gibraltar in twenty five foot waves churned up from a cyclone near Casablanca.

Back on the European mainland, we explored the nearby cities of Cadiz and Jerez. The latter town is famous for its iconic Spanish sherry and the white Andalusian horses that perform all over the world. The horses are a special type that are bred and trained to perform intricate precision movements at the crack of a whip. The colts are born black or dark brown and, oddly as they mature, turn snow white.

From Cadiz, Mike and I set out for Madrid several hundred kilometers inland to the north. On the way, as we passed through a shuttered village interestingly named Orgaz at sunset, a small boy jumped from a doorway into the cobblestone road just as I was passing. I struck the boy with the front of my bike. He went down face first into the cobblestones and came up bleeding profusely from his nose. As I skidded to a halt, dismounted and hurried back to check on him, a woman dressed in mourning black (most married peasant women wore black dresses routinely) rushed out of the same doorway, snatched the boy up and disappeared back inside and closed the door. The houses were set back about 18 inches from the road. I found myself standing in an empty street again, not knowing anything about the boy's condition. Mike had stopped up the road and just looked at me and shrugged. No one else materialized, so we continued on to Seville.

[Note: Orgaz is not sly shorthand for a hotly pursued sexual state. The village is named after The Count of Orgaz (whose surname was actually Toledo) made famous for posterity by one of El Greco's most splendid paintings, "Burial of the Count of Orgaz." It was painted and delivered to El Greco's patron, the Toledo cathedral's bishop in 1588. Under the terms of his contract with the church, El Greco was to be paid according to the painting's appraisal upon completion, which was of course a number disputed by the parties. El Greco, lacking any bargaining power, ultimately accepted his patron's price.]

Seville struck me as a gorgeous city filled with the palaces of aristocrats and bourgeois merchants with a spectacular cathedral. Most Spanish cities of any size have a big cathedral, but the prominent cities have spectacular ones. At the American Express office in Seville, we ran into the three Australian girls we had met previously in the bodega in Malaga. Mike talked the talk with his countrywomen, but we and they had diverging itineraries again and went our separate ways.

From Seville, we headed north to Toledo. Toledo had a crashing torrent of a river than ran through it, and, as I looked up from the river to the hill above it topped with an old Moorish castle and the obligatory cathedral bell tower as a thunderheads gathered darkly over the city, well, let me just say that both I and El Greco have seen a "Storm Over Toledo."

On to Madrid next. We bought tickets to a bullfight, but it was subsequently rained out. I'm sure I would have been appalled at the whole process of picadors sticking *bandilleros* into the bulls' hump to tire it so that the matador could dispatch it with his sword. I would have been rooting for the bull.

The Prado Museum in Madrid is one of the world's great museums. Filled with masterpieces by Goya, El Greco, and the German and Italian Renaissance painters and sculptors, it occupies acres of inside galleries. Interestingly, Goya had two categories of his works. One consisted of the portraits of aristocrats and biblical scenes favored by his church and aristocratic patrons. The other was a collection of his "dark" paintings, which were militantly insurrectionist in their tone. One anti-war painting haunts me to this day. It is called "A Fight With Clubs." It is a protest of the Napoleonic Wars in which peasants were involuntarily conscripted by both sides to fight in barbarous wars as proxies over monarchical ambitions. In the painting, two peasants with truncheons are depicted trapped up to their knees in quicksand facing each other with no option but to fight to the death of one of them.

Mike and I decided to go upscale in Madrid so we checked into a first class pension with two meals included for US$ 1.70 per day while both of our motorcycles were having some 5,000 kilometer M and R.

43

After Madrid, Mike was heading to London to start working as a journalist for a paper or magazine. I planned to head east to the coast,
through Barcelona again, up to Cadaquez again, and across the Mediterranean coast of France to Italy. It was April then, and I was increasingly
aware that my trip was seven-ninths over.

The motorcycle ride from Madrid to Barcelona took me though
Guadalajara and Zaragoza, and along the way it turned bitterly cold.
Two days of that will test your endurance. But, back in Barcelona, I
stayed at the same pension where Sam and I had stayed, and they remembered me. This time, I just wandered the city and its zoo, practiced
my Spanish with the concierge at the pension and saw a great French
movie with a gorgeous and later to become world famous musical soundtrack—*Orfeo Negro,* or "Black Orpheus." It is a love-found-and-lost
story set in Rio during Carnival.

Snowball and I rolled back up the Mediterranean coast to Cadaquez,
where I happily renewed old acquaintances in my former pension for a
few days rest while waiting for warmer weather. Then, when the weather
broke, I made a rush to the border over the flank of the Pyrenees to rest
stops in Narbonne and Montpellier before settling in Marseilles. [I have
often kicked myself for not having had the presence of mind to swing
through St. Tropez, home of the then world famous Brigitte Bardot who
electrified the world as the "sex kitten" in Roger Vadim's *And God Created Woman* and who commonly hung out in the town's waterfront bars
and marina. I eventually did caress Brigitte's stunning bosom many years
later, but she was bronze then and on the waterfront in Buzios, Brazil
where she had been welcomed as the girlfriend of a Brazilian playboy a
decade after I passed through the Riviera as a twenty year old.]

I stayed in a ratty pension in a very ethnic part of Marseilles, co-
habiting with a scattering of merchant seamen and lots of Vietnamese
who were a new demographic for me and my Kansas ways. Vietnam, a
French colony, had been overthrown in a communist revolution ending
in 1954 just six years earlier. So, many Vietnamese who sided with
France were given French citizenship just as those who later supported
the South Vietnamese Government and American troops in our Vietnam
War immigrated to America with the fall of Saigon. I remember liking
Marseilles. It was a colorful port city (I found that I usually liked port

cities—a harbinger of things to come?) with lots of good cheap food (can you spell bouillabaisse?) and a big cathedral a long climb up the prominent hill in town.

In a slightly bizarre vignette, I was sitting in a bar one night when a woman just a few years older than me at the bar kept glancing at me and finally asked whether I was German or American. I should mention that, by this time, I had been knocking around so long and was wearing such an amalgam of locally purchased clothes that, combined with my beard, it was hard to identify my nationality just by look, which is what you usually could do in those days. Feeling playful, I decided to make a game of it and said I was Spanish. I said this in Spanish, which I hoped was good enough to fool this woman who was Scandinavian as I recall. She looked doubtful and asked a bunch of questions about where I lived in Spain and what was I doing in Marseilles and the like, and I fabricated answers to all of them. I never did get busted, but I certainly did get a feeling that she was less interested in a grubby-looking Spaniard than she would have been in a bohemian-looking American. In any event, I didn't have enough money to buy her drinks, so she chatted up someone on her other side.

Other Marseilles vignettes: I was thinking about selling Snowball in Marseilles and hitching/taking the trains from then on because I was feeling pretty road-worn by then, and warm weather had still not returned. However, I found that no French citizen wanted to buy a Dutch registered motorcycle because of customs difficulties, duties due, inspections needed, etc. This was, of course, long before the European Union was even being discussed. Every little country in Europe had its own laws and bureaucracies then. So, I resigned myself to two more months of motorcycle travel.

I went to an American cowboy movie starring Gary Cooper in Marseilles. It had a Spanish soundtrack, and in one scene, Gary Cooper came through the swinging doors of a saloon, bellied up to the bar, and said in a high, ludicrously nasal, dubbed-in voice, "*Cognac solo, por favor.*" At halftime (there was no intermission in the movie, they just stopped the film midway for the intermission show) a tough-looking woman came out and, accompanied by some scratchy audio, did a gratuitous strip tease. After her unerotic performance was finished, she abled offstage and the movie resumed. I would have preferred a cartoon.

On April 13th, 1960, I departed Marseilles for Genoa via the French and Italian Rivieras. I just have images in my head of the towns I rolled though; Cannes, Nice, Antibes, Cap Ferrat, and, of course, Monaco. I had no money for the restaurants, bars, and casinos of those places. They were what we then called "jet set" havens, and the rich and famous were on full display for the media and each other. So, I never saw their venues except from the street as I confined myself to the beaches at such places, and then only for the time it took to have a cup of coffee or a beer while gazing at them.

I did take some time to look Monaco over, however. I scored a pension room in the shadow of the palace (Monaco is tiny, so the palace casts a shadow on much of Monaco) and put on my best clothes (think Ivy League sport coat and rep tie with khakis) and set out to explore *Le Casino* at Monte Carlo, a blindingly white wedding cake of a building in full midday sunshine. At twenty, I could not tell a roulette table from a poker table. So, no gambling, just looked from the lobby. The casino certainly was splendid though and, with its crystal and silk everywhere, had light years more class than anything I'd ever seen.

The Yacht Club marina had *beaucoup* serious yachts in it. The Hungarian Ballet was booked in the Theater that night. A floral cascade rolled down beside the descending roadway from the Palace to the sea. The scent of money, real money, old money, saturated the atmosphere like orange blossoms. I finally decided that our newly married Princess Grace was being well cared for, and I could save my worrying for something else.

I have been to Monaco and Monte Carlo twice since that first visit on occasions when I could afford to dress formally, enter the Casino and place my bets with the other high-roller wannabes, but I was never so entranced by the glamor of Monte Carlo as I was as a twenty year old kid on a beat-up motorcycle. Glamor beyond reach surely is the pinnacle of glamor.

I made it from Monaco to Genoa in one hard day of riding, motivated by the need to outrun a storm that was gathering behind me in the Alps and being blown down to the sea by *le Mistral*. Genoa is broadly spread out along the Mediterranean with its back to the mountains, giving it a good port exposure, but its charms, if any, escaped me during my overnight there. The next day took me to Pisa for an overnight stay—just long enough to see the leaning tower the next morning.

[It would take me twenty five years to return to Pisa with Carol in 1985 and at that time the tower was closed to visitors as engineers worked to cure the gradually increasing inclination of the lovely Medici tower. Another twenty two years after that in 2007, I returned yet again with niece-in-law Jennifer Ingellis to see the reopened tower after extensive anchoring renovations. Carol and her nephew Mike Ingellis were taking wood-fired-oven cooking lessons in Florence while Jennifer and I did the hard work of sightseeing in Tuscany. It was then that I learned the extent of the Medici family's dominance of Pisa and in the building of Pisa's monuments. My people! (See Genealogical Appendix.)]

In 1960, however, I was in a hurry to get to Rome and gave Pisa short shrift, leaving after visiting the Leaning Tower/Cathedral/Baptistery complex. I was, however, impressed that Galileo developed his notions about gravity by dropping objects of various sizes and shapes from the top of that very tower and timing their drop to the ground.

I arrived in Rome and found that the U.S. Navy was there, that the 1960 Summer Olympics were taking place there, and that I arrived on Good Friday before Easter Sunday. It seemed throngs of people wanted, then as now, to go to the Vatican on Easter. So, the City was packed and pension prices were punishingly high. I found a low-end *albergo* with an available garret room out past the Spanish Steps and commenced to see the sights, of which there are a great number. I visited the Forum, Pantheon, Circus, Colosseum, and the various museums, but I don't think much of Rome's history stuck to me. I was more interested in attending the spectacle of Sunday mass at Saint Peters' Square along with a hundred thousand other souls.

It was raining during the ceremony, but no one seemed to care. Pope John XXIII came out on his balcony and blessed our gathered selves, together with our medals, rosaries and Bibles in a fifteen minute oration in which he felt obliged to also bless "the poor communists and the Jews." Even then, I was savvy enough to recognize the slight to those outliers. When he blessed the communists and Jews, it was like a

Southern matron saying "bless their hearts" when referring to Yankees and Catholics. Nonetheless, it was a spectacle writ large and the good will among a hundred thousand pilgrims praying for peace while kneeling in the rain was infectious and calming. And, as my personal takeaway, the St. Christopher's medal that had been hanging around my neck since purchasing it on an impulse in Montreal was now blessed by the Pope! I was bulletproof!

I visited the Sistine Chapel the next day and was disappointed to find the frescoes faded and dimly lit and the room very crowded with visitors who had to be constantly shushed by the security staff shouting "SILENCIO!" every ten minutes. [When I returned with Carol in 1985, the frescoes had been restored and were a delight to see, although the crowds had increased and the period between admonitions for "SILENCIO" had shortened to every five minutes. I learned then that it took Michelangelo only *nine days* to conceive, design and paint the central overhead panel depicting God creating Man. I have never seen a more artful and satisfying visual rendering of that biblical event before or since.]

On the Tuesday after Easter Sunday, I struck out straight across the boot of Italy for the Adriatic and then north to San Marino and Venice as I made my way back to Northern Europe and my transport home. It was fine weather when I left Rome, but there is a substantial mountain range that runs down the spine of Italy. I had to go over it. The higher I climbed, the colder it got until I was literally in the clouds. When a sleet storm hit, I ducked inside a tunnel until it turned to rain, then pressed on. When the rain got heavy, I had to duck under the eve of a closed Red Cross station beside the road. When the rain slacked, I continued up and over Caruso Pass, until, in a white-out fog, I came across an Italian guy on a motorcycle down on the pavement. This was not long after he had roared passed me on the climb up to the pass. I checked to see that he was okay and that his cycle started again. He was wearing full leathers and that kept him from getting a severe case of road burn. I kept going, slowly, in the fog until I noticed the buildings of a town at the edge of the road. I parked and look around until I found a *tobac* shop where I was directed to a house that let rooms. There I found a cheery, stout Italian woman who offered me a room for the night.

I moved Snowball under the eve of her alpine house and pulled all my gear into the front hall out of the rain. My room was in the unheated attic of a narrow, three story house and a bed with the thickest comforter I've ever seen and a big yellow cat asleep on it. After a hot shower took the chill out of my bones, I went down to the kitchen as my landlady had invited me to do when I got hungry. I sat at a small table in the kitchen, and she served me a gigantic bowl of spaghetti dressed with nothing but garlic and olive oil. It was heavenly. I ate a mountain of it as she glanced sideways at me, smiling and shaking her head. After dinner, I climbed the stairs back to my room, got under the comforter with my clothes on and spooned around the cat for a merciful night's sleep.

The next morning, the clouds had disappeared along with the rain cell, and I found myself on the upper edge of a high Alpine meadow with a spectacular view down the glacial valley all the way to the Adriatic below. Snow clouds boiled off the peaks above me, but the road was dry and the sun was warm. So after a cup of coffee and some bread and jam, and after settling up with the proprietress, I saddled up and pointed Snowball downhill for an easy ride to the coast. By the time I reached the pea-green Adriatic, it was toasty warm. I turned left onto the coast road and headed north.

By nightfall, I was checked into a small, pleasant hotel in Pesaro within striking distance of Venice. I drove right past the turnoff to San Marino because I could see weather up there that looked just like the weather at Caruso Pass the afternoon before, and I wanted no more of that. So, I followed the shoreline of the invariably pea-green Adriatic to Pesaro. My small hotel was a favorite of Anna Maria Alberghetti, or so an affectionately signed photo of her on the wall said. Alberghetti, a world class opera soprano and Hollywood and European film actress in the 1950s and 60s, was born in Pesaro. If I were ever to run into her, I thought, we could talk about her home town.

This was the first time I fell in love with Venice. The other times are each subsequent visit I have made over the years to this lovely, decaying, soulful and absolutely unique old city. Twice Carol and I came here on vacation, and after she died I was here once on my own to catch a Norwegian Line cruise ship. Just riding the *vaporetti* (water taxis) up and down the main canals lowers my blood pressure by twenty points. The array of palazzos along the canals with their unique architecture, each with its mysterious opening at water level through which watercraft can enter and leave with any sort of cargo or people, masked or unmasked, costumed or not, is irresistibly captivating. I digress.

When I arrived at the outskirts of Venice, I ran into a problem I should have but hadn't foreseen. My usual *modus operandi*, as I mentioned earlier, was to drive to the city center and then fan out into the neighborhoods to get a feel for the place. Here, the road ended at a vast garage where all vehicles must be parked There are no streets at all in Venice. Just islands with pedestrian bridges between them and footpaths within them. So, I parked my dirty black bike in the garage and made my way to the nearby *vaporetti* pier where I prevailed on the good nature of a German student to tell me how to get to the hostel. This I was able to do without incident, and the hostel had room for me. It was a new, surprisingly large and commodious place with hot water, a cafeteria and a convenient location. *Grazie Venezia!*

The glassblowers of Murano were fascinating to watch at their craft, and the art objects they created were gorgeous, though purchasing something was completely out of the question, given my lack of funds and the necessity of transporting things on the back of my motorcycle.

What can I say about San Marco Square? Starting at the gondola moorings the path led past the bronze figures of Romulus and Remus atop tall pillars at the entry to the vast square itself. All the cafes and shops and *palazzi* around it on three sides circled back to the entry with St. Mark's Cathedral and the Ducal Palace facing the square and adjacent to the campanile on the walkway to the gondolas at water's edge.

St. Mark's was ornamented above the entrance with four great copper/bronze chariot horses, and ornate mosaics carpeted the ground floor of the cathedral. All of the Plaza, including the Cathedral mosaics, flooded routinely, a painful thing to see.

I saw a copy of Rodin's "The Thinker" in the Museum of Modern Art and walked the beach in front of the elegant hotels on Lido Island. I toured the grand Basilicas, inspected the fish and produce markets on the Grand Canal, climbed the Rialto Bridge and strolled a bewildering array of footpaths along and between the small canals that link the countless neighborhoods to each other. Behind the Ducal palace, an ornate bridge over a small canal passes from the second floor of the palace to the adjacent prison. It is over this "Bridge of Sighs" that unfortunate criminals and political prisoners passed after hearing their sentences announced in the palace and were led, one assumes sighing at their last glimpse of Venice, before descending to their none-too-comfortable accommodations in the dungeon.

The Jewish neighborhood was called the Ghetto, and that is where the term comes from. In the Ghetto, the buildings were miniaturized with lower than normal ceilings and smaller than normal rooms, reflecting the relatively lower status to which resident Jews were relegated.

After three days, my time limit was up at the hostel, and I had no money for a proper hotel in Venice, so I reluctantly checked out, schlepped my gear back to the *vaporetti* to collect Snowball at the garage, and continued on the unexpired part of my European adventure. Destination: Trieste and Communist Yugoslavia.

Trieste is an Italian town at the gateway to the Balkans with a turbulent past and a negligible future. I overnighted it there and, in a severe lapse of judgement, decided to buy more Jugoslav dinars than was allowed. Someone told me that I could get many more dinars in Italy than in Yugoslavia for my dollar. So, I bought 7,000 dinars versus the 1,500 allowed, parked my cycle in Trieste, and took an overnight bus into Ri-jeka on the northern Dalmatian Coast of Yugoslavia. I explored Rijeka for three days, just to experience life under communist rule, or at least as much as I could see as a pedestrian. Architecturally, the city had a core of baroque buildings lining the streets, but there was a more recent over-lay of drab Soviet-style concrete block high-rise apartments, office buildings and statuary.

There were statues everywhere of Marshall Tito, either alone or with Vladimir Lenin in some heroic pose. Every public building, hotel and restaurant had a large picture of Tito on the wall. In fact, I sat down in my hotel restaurant for breakfast and looked up to see a large portrait of Tito on the wall as my view. I stood up, walked around to the other side of the table and sat down with my back to Tito to the gasps of more than a few people.

I met a twenty-something Brit at the hotel who told me he had just spent the previous night in jail after having been arrested for drunkenness. He claimed he had been pushed around by his jailors and that he had responded by yelling "Tito blows dead rats!" at them. That didn't strike me as very clever under the circumstances, but they nevertheless let him out that morning.

The hotel manager was quick to point out that the hotel's name "Neboder" meant skyscraper, "just like in America." It was maybe seven stories.

I stood in line at the bakery to get bread and watched a couple of weather-beaten women in rough clothes gazing incredulously at filmy nightgowns in a department store window. I wandered the busy port full of small, coastal ships with trucks coming and going as they delivered and received the cargo to and from those ships. A bookstore window had a display of books on engineering and industrial techniques along with a single novel, *Peyton Place*. No doubt it reinforced the communist party's characterization of American decadence.

I was unable to buy Austrian shillings with my smuggled dinars (I didn't know what I was doing); however, I was able to pretty much pay for my stay in Rijeka with the exchange I'd made in Trieste. So I ended up smuggling my excess dinars right back out again.

On the bus ride back to Trieste, overnight again, the bus halted at the frontier and border guards came aboard to check passports as normal procedure. Then, after leaving, they came back aboard and signaled me, and me alone, to exit the bus and go into the guard building. With knees knocking, I did, and there, to my surprise, was my suitcase which had been in the bus's luggage compartment. I was made to stand there while the guards went through everything in my suitcase and carefully felt the walls of the suitcase for secret compartments. I was in a state of high anxiety because of the excess dinars I was carrying and cursed my stupidity for trying such a lame stunt. Finally, the guard pointed to my passport picture, in which I appeared unshaven, and pointed to my beard and said, "Next time, look the same as your passport picture" and let me go. When the bus cleared the frontier into Italy, I breathed a big sigh of relief.

The following afternoon, Snowball and I crossed the Italian border into Austria, and I visited the currency exchange office at the Customs house in a town called Klagenfurt. A pretty girl who waited on me even exchanged the handful of those lousy, aluminum lire coins I had cramming my pockets. She then proceeded to shower me with maps of Austria and a currency conversion chart which I stuffed with difficulty in my toggle coat pocket along with my other maps of Austria and currency conversion charts. She had no reason to be nice to me as I looked wind-blown and rough, so I knew it was because she was just a nice person. Anyway, it gave my spirits a boost, and I finally unburdened myself of those accursed Yugoslavian dinars.

The Austrian Alps are very beautiful, and I marveled at the vastness of the Alps across northern Italy, eastern France, Austria and Switzerland. The Pyrenees and the mountains in the spine of Italy were big, but lacked the sheer mass of the Alps. Scenic as they were, I spied the huge, craggy, snowy peaks in the distance as far as I could see from high ground and wished that I didn't have to drive through them on a motorcycle. I had a night to spend in Klagenfurt before tackling the Alps, and I had my first, but certainly not my last, Weiner Schnitzel. It tasted like more. Vi-enna, here I come!

It turned out that the Austrian engineers knew how to build their highways in valleys and tunnel through their mountains, so my ride to Vienna was not a hard one. Vienna ranked up there with London and Paris as the most appealing cities I experienced in Europe. First of all, the Danube ran through the place and lots of picturesque old bridges spanned the river. The city had a tired aspect to it that, like Venice, was appealing. It was a very cultured city as I soon found out, with multiple concerts, operas, theater shows and the like *every night*. I could just book what wanted to see and hear on short notice. It was all available at low prices as they always accommodated students in the nosebleed sections.

My reference to a "tired" appearance of the city is an oversimplification of the hangover effects of World War II on the city. Austria had been annexed by Nazi Germany early in 1938, and it was liberated in the spring of 1945. It was occupied after the war under an Allied joint force arrangement much like Germany itself and Berlin. In the vicinity of Vi-enna, the Soviet army had the territory north of the Danube and the

Americans had the area to the south. For ten years after the war, Soviet troops in their section behaved with the same level of criminality toward the Austrian population seen in East Germany. Rape by Russian soldiers was common and went unpunished by Russian officers, I was told. Finally in 1955, concurrently with the nearby and destabilizing Hungarian Revolution, the Allies and the USSR (led by Nikita Khrushchev) agreed to withdraw, and Austria became an independent nation outside the Iron Curtain. When I arrived in Vienna only four years later in 1960, the scars of the war were still visible on the face of the city, and the citizens of Vienna bore invisible scars of war and occupation in their psyches for many years to come.

In Rome, I had met an American girl from the Deep South who was doing her junior year abroad in Vienna. She'd been in Rome on an excursion, and we struck up a conversation in the Forum but then went our separate ways. In a small-world moment on the sidewalk outside the American Express office in Vienna, we ran into each other again, and she offered to show me the sights. We visited Schonbrunn Palace, a Versailles-like Hapsburg palace and attended afternoon performances of "Fidelio" and "Tales of Haufman" at the Staatsoper. By night, we haunted the streets and alleys of a suburb called Grinsing where it was traditional to drink "this year's wine" (raw, cheap) in a wine garden party atmosphere while listening to "The Third Man Theme" played on the zither. There was also the world's largest (at the time) Ferris wheel in the amusement park. We had a fine time over three or four days and then said our farewells again ("If you ever get to Atlanta/Kansas City, give me a call ….") as I was obliged to continue on to Munich. Now, whenever I get a chance to watch "The Third Man" starring Orson Wells on TV, I am immediately transported back to Vienna. It was for me very much a city seen through a black and white lens like in the movie.

I arrived in Munich with my Holland America return trip booking money in one pocket, and sixty pfennig (cents) in the other. Thank God, as the saying goes, the route from Vienna to Munich via Salzburg took me around the Bavarian Alps, which were way up there. I checked into the International Students Home in Munich because, unlike a hostel, it didn't require payment in advance. I went for a walk to consider my conundrum. If I spent my ship passage fare, I had no way to get home. Selling Snowball wouldn't yield much money and then I would have to pay for transport. How could I avoid spending some of my passage money?

As I walked, I passed a wurstel stand on the street. I gazed pathetically at the bratwurst, sauerkraut and buns on display, all of which cost more than the 60 pfennig I had. I finally held out my hand with the pfennig and looked questioningly at the girl dispensing the food. She smiled and pulled out a bread roll, put mustard on it, and handed it to me as she took my pfennig. That was dinner, and it did make the hunger pains in my stomach go away for the time being. I still had no idea how to solve my cash flow dilemma.

The next morning, I went straight to the American Express office to get my mail. It would be hard to overstate how important American Express was as a traveler's aid. The company would accept mail at its offices addressed to anyone at all "care of American Express" in whatever city was specified. The company would hold the mail for seemingly any length of time in its general delivery box until claimed by the addressee. If the good will generated by that service meant more sales of traveler's checks or other AmEx products, so much the better. As I look back at that corporate behavior through my eighty-year-old lenses today, I am stunned by the contrast with the automated, fee-obsessed, callousness of today's corporations.

I had been writing letters and cards to family and friends ever since I leaving Rome asking that they write to me next c/o American Express in Munich. When I stopped in that fateful day and collected my assorted mail, there was a letter from my dear, sweet, mother who had sensed from my letters written as I migrated from Spain through Provence to Italy, Yugoslavia and Austria that I was living hand-to-mouth. So, she sent me US$100! I cannot tell you, dear diary, what an emotional boost that provided to my morale! I now had enough money to not only buy breakfast and pay for my lodgings in Munich, but to fund my (frugal) journey back to England without dipping into my ship passage money. Euphoric after drawing my money in German marks from the AmEx cashier, I went for a walk in a park facing the bombed out ruins of an old government building. In the park, there was a fruit vendor from whom I bought an entire bunch of seven bananas. I sat on a bench and methodically ate all seven bananas, savoring each one as the precious nourishment that it was. I doubt that I have experienced a greater sense of well-being since then.

As my banana-induced starch and potassium high peaked, I became curious about the large building in ruins that I was facing. So, I walked over to it and read the information board in front of it. It was the old Ministry of War building. The Allies bombed it to smithereens and the City fathers decided to leave it as-is. So, with a tree growing out of the debris from the collapsed dome, it served as a reminder to the citizens of Munich of the regrettable political journey the country had undertaken at the hands of the Third Reich just twenty years earlier.

My urge for creature comforts unabated, I adjourned to the one, the only, the three-story stack of beer halls known as the Hofbrau House. It was May, not October, but they were serving up platters of *sauerbraten mit rotkhol* (bratwurst with red cabbage) and beer in any size of stein you chose. I was in there for maybe three hours and came out into the midday heat three sheets to the wind and trying not to stagger. I do remember steadying myself by placing a hand on the wall of the building across the narrow street facing the Hofbrau House door through which I exited and regarding all the bullet holes riddling the wall.

At the International Student's home, I had two other male students in my dorm—an Iranian and a Canadian. The Canadian was good company, and he was the only other person I ran into who wore 501 Levis jeans. Levis were considered uniquely American and thoroughly disreputable by Europeans. [Fast-forward sixty years: every European man, woman and child on the street wears denim jeans.]

The route from Munich to Amsterdam where I could sell my Dutch-registered motorcycle took me through Heidelberg. I had the fantasy of acquiring a saber cut scar across my cheek in Heidelberg that I could sport for the rest of my life. Talk about Joe Cool! So, I stopped for a couple of days in Heidelberg just to experience the place.

It was a small, lovely University town. The University counts as one of Germany's best and was its oldest. A small river ran through the town, and on one side, a popular "philosopher's walk" passed through a fine forest. I walked the walk, even though marginally able to talk the talk. My two years of high school German helped a lot however.

There was a castle with a 55,000 gallon wine barrel—one big enough to have a dance floor at its top. According to the guide, there were legends associating the barrel with a super wine-drinking dwarf called Perkeo, but my German wasn't good enough to sort the stories out into a coherent tale.

I discovered a sure-fire, if surprising way to meet people there. I happened to buy and carry around a can of cigarette lighter fluid one day, and multiple people stopped and asked me if I would be so kind as to let them fill their lighters. I remember obliging an Englishman from Newcastle-on-Tyne and a Hungarian waitress from Budapest, among others.

Past Heidelberg there was an overnight in Dusseldorf, where my strongest impression was of a foggy, industrial city on the Rhine with more beautiful girls than they could ever use. Next, a pastoral ride into Holland and the town of Arnhem of "A Bridge Too Far" fame. Thence, across the flat, manicured spaces of the Utrecht area and the polder fields and canals into Amsterdam. For the first time since Spain, I was stopped on the road by a highway policeman on a motorcycle who was intrigued by the fact that I was obviously a foreigner and the bike was registered the Netherlands. Stolen? He checked my papers, and then we shot the breeze for a half hour enabled by his excellent English, before pressing on into Amsterdam where I managed to locate the clean, well run hostel that had space for me.

A couple of days in Amsterdam was all it took to sell Snowball. I pinned up a for-sale note on the community bulletin board at American Express. The next day I received four offers and sold Snowball after 12,000 kilometers of faithful service. The 200 guilders I earned from that transaction, about US$ 60, when added to the balance of the $100 my mother sent me, inflated my discretionary funds into the comfortable range. After taking my first ever tour (a boat ride around the canals of Amsterdam) and making the obligatory visit to the Rijksmuseum and its amazing collection of art, I checked out of the hostel and taxied to the boat-train to London.

At the Hook of Holland ferry terminal, I met a Scottish merchant seaman whose tanker had just exploded in the English Channel, killing three of his shipmates. I thought he showed a lot of equanimity for such a recent experience since he was good company and we drank good Dutch beer for the six hour trip to Harwich. An early morning arrival, a train to London and a bus ride to Earl's Court had me back in the same lodgings that Sam and I used eight months earlier.

The following week proved a kaleidoscope of social goings on. You would have thought I lived in London. I checked in with the Masters family (Deana's host family) and connected with two of their clan my age, Ronnie and Pauline. Together with their friend Tony who had a car, we toured the City and surrounding countryside. Nancy, Deana's friend, was still in London as well, so our rolling group of five got tickets to "The World of Susie Wong," and "West Side Story" in west end theaters, as well as a performance of the London Symphony. Nancy and I took a daytrip by train to a picturesque village called Richmond and she told me of her life growing up on a thousand acre ranch in Montana.

I also reached out to Mike, my Tasmanian journalist travelling friend from Spain now working in London. He wanted me to experience Hyde Park Corner on Sunday morning, so we went there to listen to the cacophony of speakers on various issues *du jour*. It was nice to know that the crazies had some place to go on Sunday morning to vent their spleens. I attended one of Nancy's school lectures on the American Revolution, as taught from a British point of view. (Whaaaa…?) And my last night saw us all at the Masters' house for a farewell dinner, for which I was very touched and honored. I had always made it a habit to bring Mrs. Masters flowers, and we had this sort of shtick going where she would say "I wish I was thirty years younger, David…," leaving the rest unsaid, while Mr. Masters rolled his eyes. And I would always answer, "I wish you were too, Mrs. M" as their children, my friends, whooped.

I embarked on the *SS Niew Amsterdam* at Southampton the following day, June 7, 1960 and thought it a very good ship and light years more commodious than the *Groote Beer*. I can't remember anything about the voyage back, and my journal doesn't record anything for those eight days. I suspect I just stared at the horizon the whole time trying to put the last nine months, which seemed like years, into meaningful perspective. I never did. I just remember it as a terrific adventure with a steep learning curve about the world outside of the United States.

We docked in Manhattan on June 15, 1960 where I was met by my father who by happy coincidence was on the East Coast on business at the same time my brother was on leave from the Navy. Bill was flying to London to do a bit of touring before joining the fleet and his ship, the carrier Enterprise, on which he was an air intelligence officer. Dad was flying back to Omaha, and we had arranged for me to drive Bill's convertible Triumph TR-3 back to Omaha for storage. The one remark from our conversation at that moment of rendezvous that I can remember was my dad saying to me, "Well, I expect you will want to get to your hotel to shower *or shave* or something." Okaaaay. We went our separate ways that same day.

During the drive back to Omaha, the TR-3 broke down in, would you believe, Ainsworth, Iowa. I had to wait there a couple of days while a part was obtained from wherever. Substitute the name TR-3 for the name Snowball, and it was déjà vu all over again. I had the same conversation many times at the motel and lunch counters about my name and the coincidence of breaking down there.

CHAPTER 8

LAWRENCE, KANSAS (CONTINUED), QUANTICO (1959)

Back at KU for my junior year, I had to make some adjustments starting with my major. The bust part of the bust and boom nature of the oil patch was in full downswing, and jobs for petroleum geologists were nonexistent, according to my father. That intelligence, together with my newly acquired worldview, resulted in changing my major from Geology to Political Science with a specialty in International Relations.

I also felt that I had outgrown (sniff) the SAE fraternity house, so I moved out into an apartment in the basement of an older couple who ran the Dairy Queen franchise in Lawrence. (Free ice cream cones!) I hearkened back to my Heidelberg fantasy and joined the fencing team at KU. I had some ability as it turned out, and I ended up being captain of the foil squad and getting a letter jacket my senior year. A fencing letter, of course, did not carry anywhere near the prestige of a football or basketball letter, but it was fodder for my curriculum vitae. The fencing team made trips around the Big Eight campuses for tournaments, and I enjoyed that. I was fully engaged in my political science courses, applied myself and got As and Bs. I dated a number of girls my junior year, one of whom was Sam's sister, Sandy. She was in the Chi Omega sorority just down the street from the SAE house.

On Thanksgiving and Christmas holidays, I would visit both my mother in Wichita and my father in Omaha. One clear Omaha memory I have was stopping off at a local bar and having a beer with my father on the way home from Toastmasters. I was almost twenty one at the time and already drinking beer at KU. For perhaps the first time, I related to my father as an adult with that simple shared moment. I don't remember what we talked about. Probably school and Toastmasters and Europe. Unfortunately, there were no opportunities to develop an adult relationship with him after that. He died of a heart attack that winter while shoveling snow off his sidewalk in Omaha.

I was in my apartment in Lawrence when Marge called me with the news. I drove to Omaha to attend what turned out to be the first of two memorial services. One service was in Omaha at the church he and Marge attended occasionally. After that service and neighborhood wake (dad was well-liked in his neighborhood,) Marge arranged to have his casket put on a train to Jackson, Mississippi. I rode the train with his body down to Jackson for a second service among his family there.

The last time that I had been in the company of the Rankin County Ainsworths, I'd been a toddler. My grandfather, William Augustus ("Daddy Will") and my uncle Grey were there along with various in-laws and cousins. (Dad's younger brother Carl had predeceased him.) A memorial service was held in Jackson, and then my father was buried in the cemetery of nearby Star, his birthplace. I remember seeing a man walk up a gravel road to the cemetery in Star dressed in bib-style denim overalls and farm boots and being introduced to him as a cousin, once removed. I saw the one room cabin in which my father had been born and in which his mother had died of pellagra. I had never seen such primitive conditions and rural poverty, even in Europe.

Incongruously, the wake turned out to be a very jolly affair, thanks in large part to my Uncle Grey's stories and jokes. I remember riding with him when he went to the bootlegger's store to buy some whisky for the wake. It was across the road from a Mississippi Highway Patrol station. I asked how that could be possible, since Mississippi was a dry state. He explained that law enforcement not only tolerated the sale and consumption of illegal alcohol, but the bootleggers were taxed on their sales. The experience taught me that, in the Deep South, they do things differently. The train ride back to Lawrence was a welcome opportunity to reflect.

Back at KU and behind in my classes from being absent for more than a week, I resumed my studies. And, sometime during the grey, cold days of the winter of '60, I joined the Marine Corps. In those days, America had the draft. Every male in good physical condition had a six year obligation to serve in the U.S. Armed Forces. When we became eighteen, we were eligible to be drafted by the local draft board which had a file on all of us. If we were members in good standing of a college at the time, our draft was deferred until graduation. Then, if you had not voluntarily joined one of the other services or been accepted in an officer candidate program beforehand, you would be drafted into the Army as a private. Though correspondence with my naval officer brother Bill on the carrier Enterprise (he had been in Naval ROTC in college,) we had discussed what I should do for my military service. He wrote: "Well, Dave, since you have to serve in the military, you might as well fly with the finest. Join the Marine Corps." He admired the Marine pilots on the Enterprise.

To this day, I am not sure whether he was giving me good advice or setting me up for some long forgotten offense. In any event, I naively thought, why sure, I'll just joint the Marine Corps and "fly with the finest." In talking to the local Marine recruiter at KU, I learned of an officer candidate program that was unique to the Marine Corps call Platoon Leader's Class. Under that program, I could spend the summer between my junior and senior college years at the Quantico, Virginia officer training center going through boot camp. Upon graduation from college the following academic year, I would then receive my commission and commence active duty. So, I signed up.

During spring break, when I went back to Wichita to visit my mother, I mentioned that I had joined the Marine Corps. She hit the ceiling. "Oh, no you're not!" She said emphatically. I said, "No, mom, you don't understand. I've already joined the Marines. I have to go into the military in some capacity, so I joined the Marines. It's done." Still fuming, she asked rhetorically, "Well, why didn't you just join the French Foreign Legion!" She obviously had a better sense of what was in store for me than I did. From then on, she later told me, she tried not to think about it and just assumed that I would have a wonderful time.

Early that June, after my finals and receiving orders from HQ Marine Corps, I got myself to the airport in Wichita and flew back to a Washington area military base on military transport. I gathered there with other Marine officer candidate recruits from all over the country. When we were all accounted for, it was off to Quantico on a bus. We were all apprehensive and there wasn't much chatter on the bus. When the bus rolled to a stop, things happened quickly. A sergeant with a drill instructor's "Smokey" hat got on the bus, told us there would be no further talking, and directed us to get off the bus and put our feet on any pair of yellow painted footprints on the asphalt outside. The footprints were arranged in the form of three lines, like a platoon with three squads. From there, we were marched to a barber shop where our heads were shaved, then to a warehouse where we were given a couple of sets of fatigues, boots, underwear and some toiletries. Finally, with our GI ("government issue") gear in our arms, we were marched to the Quonset hut that would be our barracks and assigned a bunk. We were given ten minutes to change out of our "civvies" into fatigues, pack our stuff into a trunk at the foot of our bunk, and "fall in" on the company street in the same formation as that in which we arrived. Welcome to the Marine Corps!

The next thirteen weeks were and still are a blur of constant physical training on the obstacle course, rifle care and cleaning, close order drill, classroom lectures on small arms weaponry and military organization, forced marches of twenty miles with full packs and combat gear, and doing endless pushups as punishment for some inadvertent infraction of discipline or wrong answer to a question or no reason at all, at the discretion of the drill instructor. In the mess we could eat as much as we wanted, but we had to eat everything we put on our trays in the cafeteria line. We bussed our own trays after each meal, and the trays had to be empty. We had to shower and be shaved, dressed and on the company street for the morning run by 5:30 am. Fortunately, the oversleeping that would be expected for overtired young men was mooted by the fact that the Richmond, Fredericksburg and Potomac Railroad main line passed less than ten feet from one corner of our Quonset hut, and a freight train came by at high speed at 5:15 am every day. There was no sleeping through that. After a month, we were in terrific shape and most people had lost weight. For some reason, I gained ten pounds, but it was all muscle.

After the first month, we were given "liberty" each Saturday afternoon and Sunday. Mostly, we would catch a bus to Washington, DC and see the sights. During those weekends, I looked up Sam, who was living in Baltimore with his wife Nancy, and my girlfriend from Mallorca, Bernice, also from Baltimore. I got to meet Bernice's family at their home on one occasion and liked them very much. However, I was pretty much unavailable for the rest of the summer, was returning to KU for my senior year, and was committed to the Corps for years after that. She was a year ahead, had graduated from college, and had started a job in Baltimore. She wanted to settle down. We lost track of each other after that.

A goodly number of Marine officer candidates washed out of PLC. Each man who left was declared unfit, usually involving some breach of military rules or a mental breakdown. But, a majority of us finished the summer program satisfactorily and would be commissioned as second lieutenants upon graduation from our universities the following academic year. We left Quantico at the end of that summer pretty much full of ourselves. We considered ourselves Marines at that point.

My senior year at KU was different than the earlier years. Europe had changed me. The death of my father had shocked me. The Marine Corps had already matured me somewhat and set me on a new course. I felt I had to buckle down and finish my studies on a positive note my senior year. In contrast, many of my fellow seniors were coasting and partying. I studied, made good grades, continued to fence on the varsity fencing team, and had less and less contact with the SAE house. Noteworthy, however, was an introduction engineered by my fraternity brother, John Garrett and his then fiancé, Celia Welch, a member of the Delta Gamma sorority. Celia mentioned one of her sorority sisters, one Judy Gail Harman, in the context of one of those casual "Say, you ought to meet my sorority sister friend Judy. She's been to Spain too," remarks. I was pretty sure Judy was in one of my classes, and it didn't take much effort to confirm that. So, I knew who she was. She did not know who I was.

I called her, and we connected on several levels just chatting by phone. She had transferred in to KU from a private girls' college in Baltimore called Goucher, and she was a bit of a bohemian with an interest in theater. We had a love of Spain in common, so I joked that I might just walk up to her on campus one day and say "Ole!" by way of an introduction. A couple of days later, after my last class of the day, I was walking to the fraternity house where I parked my car, and saw her coming down the sidewalk on the other side of the street. So I stepped off the curb and set a course that would intersect with her own. What she saw was a stranger headed toward her and staring. I fell in beside her and said "Ole!" That broke the ice, and we walked back to the Greek neighborhood together.

Over the next weeks, we settled in to an exclusive dating relationship. She was planning to enter the Peace Corps after graduation, and I was entering the Marine Corps after graduation. That meant both of us were headed for Washington after graduation. That was about as far as our thinking got as we finished our senior year at KU.

Evidently, a military uniform salesman came to campus during the spring semester and measured those of us who were going to be commissioned as officers upon graduation. I say that because when the graduation ceremonies were over, I put on my officer's dress whites and someone, probably an ROTC Naval officer, pinned my lieutenant's bars on me. There I stood, the Marine Corps' most newly minted "brown bar" (a second lieutenant's bar is brass; a first lieutenant's bar is silver) with a degree in International Relations and orders to proceed with dispatch to Quantico. I would see Judy just fifty miles up U.S. Highway 1 in Washington when she got settled and I got liberty.

CHAPTER 9

USMC (1962)

The government owned me now so the eight months of basic training required of all Marine officers ("The Basic School") started immediately. I lived in the Bachelor Officer's Quarters in Quantico and attended training classes in a special area of the base reserved for The Basic School. Whether a Marine officer is on a career track to be an infantry officer, a pilot, a special staff officer, a lawyer, or something else, he (now he or she) must become (1) a rifleman in boot camp (I had done that the previous summer) and (2) an infantry officer with the requisite training that qualified him to lead troops (The Basic School.)

In that respect, the Marine Corps differs from the other services where an officer candidate is given three months' training (a "90 day wonder") and given an assigned post. In The Basic School, there is a good deal of classroom work learning military history, small unit tactics (companies, platoons and squads), ground navigation, and military law (there is a one volume bible called the Uniform Code of Military Justice that governs courts martial.) In the field, work is devoted to amphibious tactics, physical conditioning, artillery and air support spotting, and use and deployment of the weapons in the Marine arsenal from pistols to rockets and artillery. That is what I did for eight months from early in the morning to late at night.

However, most Saturday afternoons and Sundays, we got liberty. Up U.S. Hwy 1 I went to keep company with Judy in Washington. It wasn't long before Judy and I realized that we would have to come to terms with the fact that she was scheduled to disappear into the maw of the Peace Corps in rural Costa Rica, while I was destined to places unknown upon completion of The Basic School, thus putting an end to our relationship indefinitely, at best, and permanently, at worst. So, since I had no options,

Judy acquiesced in letting the Marine Corps control our lives, and we decided to get married. The Peace Corps' loss was my gain.

Judy arranged, through the considerable good offices of her mother Thelma, for us to get married in Kansas City one weekend in October. With just a day or two of liberty tacked on, I flew back to Kansas City, and, costumed in my dress white uniform alongside her brilliant white wedding dress, we were married in the family church in a visual whiteout. At the reception, all the family friends and relatives from far and wide gathered to see us off. We flew back to a rental cottage we had picked out on the edge of the leafy campus of Mary Washington College in nearby Fredericksburg, Virginia.

Judy was a fish out of water for a while, since she knew no one there, and the Peace Corps assignment she had been planning on went poof when she couldn't accept her deployment to Costa Rico. But, it wasn't long before I graduated from the Basic School and got orders to report, not to some far-flung outpost of the Corps, but to Schools Demonstration Troops right there in Quantico! Schools Demonstration Troops were a detachment of Marine infantry to provide honor guards for visiting dignitaries to Quantico and to act as "aggressor" troops in the field for the new officer candidates undergoing training in boot camp and The Basic School. I was a weapons platoon leader in a rifle company of Schools Demonstration Troops for a year. An infantry company consists of three infantry platoons of three squads each and a weapons platoon. My platoon had three squads, each with three machine gun teams, plus designated non-commissioned officers to lead the teams and squads, a platoon sergeant and myself as platoon commander. When deployed in combat, two of the three infantry platoons in the company (one would usually be held in reserve) would be assigned up to six machine gun fire teams to give each of three infantry squads a machine gun, grenade launching and mortar-spotting capability. The weapons platoon leader is usually the most senior platoon leader (although rank among lieutenants is said to be "like virtue among whores") and is available to replace any of the platoon leaders, or the company executive officer in the event any of them become casualties.]

Judy and I moved to officer's quarters on base at Quantico. There, Judy was able to make friends with some of the other junior officer's wives on base. She also had a close friend in Washington, with whom, together with her husband (whose cover story was that he worked in the "Department of Defense"—enough said,) we socialized. We enjoyed our new friends and the social benefits of the Officer's Club and settled down for a more or less pleasant time during our tour in Quantico in 1963.

During that year, three noteworthy things happened. The first was the Cuban Missile Crisis. Most historians agree that America came closer to nuclear war with the Soviet Union at that time than at any other time. The Second Marine Division out of Camp Lejeune, North Carolina was loaded onto amphibious naval vessels which sailed to the Caribbean during the period in which President Kennedy faced down the Russians by "quarantining" Cuba. That is, Cuba was surrounded by naval vessels, including a division of Marines, and no ships, Soviet or otherwise, were permitted to enter or leave Cuban waters. This was in response to the intelligence community's discovery via air surveillance that the Soviets were engaged in the installation of ICBM rocket bases in Cuba aimed at the U.S. (This was after the Bay of Pigs fiasco, so Cuba had reason to fear U.S. aggression against it.) Ultimately, Nikita Khrushchev and the Soviet forces blinked, and they dismantled and removed the missile facilities, thus avoiding a nuclear confrontation. At Quantico, other than being placed on high alert for several days, the only manner in which we participated in the confrontation was to give up our bayonets so that they could be sent to Camp Lejeune where they were apparently in short supply.

The second noteworthy event consisted of the March on Washington. In the summer of 1963, my infantry company was put on alert prior to the now famous March on Washington organized by black civil rights leaders. They sought jobs and improved civil rights for minorities. On a hot day in August, more than 250,000 people, preponderantly African Americans, converged on the Mall in Washington to express their demands for reform. President Kennedy was concerned about the potential for uncontrolled rioting with such a huge gathering of angry protesters and took non-public precautionary measures to safeguard against that eventuality. Among them was the activation of my company of Marines. Our orders were to, if so directed, cordon off the U.S. Capitol Building to prevent it from being attacked and damaged by rioters. [Note: Contrast this precaution with the January 6, 2021 insurrection by white supremacists at the Capitol Building incited by Donald Trump after his failed Presidential campaign that was allowed to proceed unmolested.] So, we trained for that unusual mission by such things as conditioning runs with gas masks on and by deploying via open military trucks wrapped in chicken wire to keep objects thrown at our column from striking our troops. We were not issued bayonets or live ammunition initially. They were to be issued only if necessary. Our active involvement in policing civil disturbances, if any, by the protesters was said to be justified by the Insurrection Act of 1807.

On the morning of August 28th, our company deployed in a column of personnel carrier trucks and proceeded to an area near the Navy Yard not far from the Capitol Building in Washington. There, we parked at the ready, out of sight. No one knew what would happen during the March on Washington that day, but City and White House authorities were anxious that the important monuments in Washington would be protected.

Their fears were misplaced, as it happened. Passionate speeches were given by civil rights leaders. Freedom songs were sung by Joan Baez and Bob Dylan. And the final speaker on that long afternoon was Dr. Martin Luther King who, reportedly at the spontaneous urging of Mahalia Jackson, delivered his famous "I have a Dream" oration. Filled with civil resolve after that ceremony and moved by Dr. King's oratory, the quarter million protesters peacefully dispersed and went back from whence they came. So too, our company of Marines drove back to Quantico unnoticed.

As a result of the March on Washington, the speeches that were made, and the political support that materialized out of that event, President Kennedy promoted the landmark Civil Rights Act of 1964 and the Voting Rights Act of 1965. He was assassinated before he was able to see those measures enacted into law, but his Vice President, Lyndon B. Johnson of Texas, succeeded Kennedy and implemented his own vision for America called the Great Society. He courageously signed into law the two pieces of civil rights legislation in question as soon as Congress enacted them, thus bringing an end to many of the grievances of black Americans at the time. He courageously signed those bills into law despite anticipating that his Democratic Party would lose its majority in the South as a result. It did. All eleven former Confederate states subsequently flipped Republican.

My up-close-and-personal experience with the law and order con-cerns arising out of the March on Washington, together with the achievements that flowed directly from it, taught me an indelible lesson about the First Amendment. The careful enumeration of the right of freedom of assembly and of speech created by the States following the Constitutional Convention is expressly unqualified and the courts have imposed only a few, reasonable, public safety-based limits on those rights (e.g., falsely shouting "fire" in a crowded theater, obscenity, inciting to violence, etc. are not protected speech, and violence and blocking public rights of way unsafely are not protected public assemblies.) Neither the letter of the First Amendment nor the spirit of jurisprudence expressed in it are in any way made subject to anticipatory restraints based on claims of public safety. When Americans assemble to non-violently articulate their grievances, the political power structure and its police must stand aside, on alert to the extent needed, and let democracy work.

Prior to and during the training for this potential "insurrection" de-ployment, I developed an exercise-induced "asthmatic bronchitis" for which I was hospitalized at the Bethesda Naval Hospital while they de-layed and delayed diagnosing the problem for what it is. Reading between the lines, I'm sure they were concerned that I might use this development to seek a discharge from the Corps on medical grounds. After three weeks or so of this diagnostic ballet, I caught on. One day I answered the daily question of the doctor, namely, "How do you feel?" with the statement "Fine, I feel just fine." I was immediately returned to my unit. [For the next forty eight years, I suffered from exercise induced wheezing which would subside with rest. At age 79, however, I applied to the Veterans Administration for disability benefits for the Chronic Obstructive Pulmonary Disease or COPD as it is now called, because it seemed to me to be progressing. The VA checked my records, including the hospitalization at Bethesda, put me through some respiration tests, and immediately granted me 30 percent disability based upon test results showing that my ability to exhale was now only 70 per-cent of my capacity to inhale. As a result, I now receive a $450 per month disability payment, but more importantly, I am entitled to VA medical benefits if my COPD worsens and becomes a financial burden.]

The third and easily the most important newsworthy event that took place during my posting at Quantico was the birth of my son, Gray Harman Ainsworth. Gray after my uncle and Harman was Judy's maiden name. So, we had a bouncing baby boy with colic, and we enjoyed wheeling Gray around the neighborhood at night in a magnificent perambulator given to us by one of the other Marine couples we knew whose baby had outgrown it. We, in turn, passed it along to others when we left Quantico.

As my tour with Schools Demonstration Troops grew short, we knew that new orders would be forthcoming. My fitness reports were excellent, and the conventional wisdom was that the better your fitness reports, the more likely you would be to get your requested new post assignment. I had requested Marine barracks in Hawaii as my first choice or in Rota, Spain as my second, confident that Judy would enjoy either as a reward for giving up her Peace Corps opportunity. When the orders came, did I get my chosen assignment? Of course not! I was stunned to receive orders to proceed to Camp Pendleton in California for three months training in preparation to shipping out with my battalion to Okinawa for thirteen months *without dependents*! Judy would spend those thirteen months with a new baby stateside and on her own. So much for staying together.

Surely, I thought, there had been some careless, bureaucratic mistake at the Pentagon. Another platoon commander in my company, a bachelor planning on a career in the Corps, had sought a "line" (command) post like mine but was instead assigned to the Marine barracks in Hawaii, a "with dependents" post. We got each other's orders! So, off to the Pentagon we went, making the fifty mile trip from Quantico to Washington together to try and get the assignments switched.

The visit to the Pentagon proved to be remarkable. First, as we walked up to one of the doors (it is a five-sided building, remember) from the vast parking lot, who should come out of the doors just as we reached for the door handle? David M. Shoop, five star general and Commandant of the Marine Corps, that's who, with a brigadier general as his aide following behind him. What we should have done is snap to attention and salute smartly. Instead, each of us simply froze in astonishment. He evidently had seen the deer-in-the-headlights reaction from junior officers before, so he simply saluted the two of us and kept right on going, as we continued to stand there agape until having the presence of mind to return his salute in the direction of his receding back.

The second memorable aspect of the visit then unfolded. Shaken from our encounter with the Commandant, we proceeded to navigate the labyrinthine halls of the Pentagon seeking the Marine Corps Office of the G-4 (Personnel). We were finally directed to the correct office and asked to see someone having authority over company grade officer assignments. A major came out, greeted us, and listened to our pitch that surely a reversal of assignments would be mutually beneficial. "No. You have your orders," he said. Then he left.

Well, at least we had clarity as we drove back to Quantico. I was headed for Okinawa. Judy was crushed at the news. There was some talk about an offer from her dad to talk to his Congressman to get things turned around, but I quashed that. I joined up, I had orders, and whining about an overseas assignment that many Marines experience seemed dishonorable. So, we prepared for the new reality. We packed up the few personal effects we had (all of the furniture was government-issue that we had picked out of the furniture warehouse when we arrived) and drove to California. I had a used, maroon-red, 1962 Jaguar Mark II that I had acquired during our posting at Quantico, and in that small sedan, filled to the gunwales with baby equipment, we made a leisurely, late summer trip west to Kansas City to visit Judy's family. From there, we drove the storied Route 66 to Southern California. Gray was pushing six months old and would miss splashing around the in the Officer's Club pool at Quantico.

We rented a small, second-story, furnished apartment on the beach in Oceanside just outside one of the gates to the vast Camp Pendleton. From there, I commuted in uniform to the remote camp where the barracks were for the Second Battalion, 5th Marines. For the initial weeks, we conducted amphibious training using landing craft and armored personnel carriers over the beaches of Camp Pendleton.

After a month or so, I received surprise orders to Embarkation School there at Pendleton. Why I was picked for that job and by whom was never revealed to me, however, I learned that career officers avoided "staff" jobs and preferred "command" jobs that would further their careers in the Corps. As a Reserve Officer, I had no plans to stay in the Corps past my six year obligation. I also learned that Embarkation Officers were a vital part of the organization because the Corps is an amphibious force and ships must be loaded with troops and equipment in the reverse order in which they must come off during a combat landing. That, in turn, requires familiarity with the various contingency plans for operations planned by higher commands and a high security clearance. Thus, while Embarkation Officer billets were disfavored by the "regular" career types, incumbents nevertheless had to have some moxie and talent. So, it was a kind of left-handed compliment for me to get the assignment. Embarkation School was a month long classroom affair over long, warm, autumn days during which all I wanted to do was be outside. But I committed the subject matter to memory, got good grades, and did my duty.

The one vivid memory I have of Embarkation School is that of a Marine officer walking into the classroom while in session and whispering something in the ear of the instructing officer and handing him a piece of paper. The instructor then announced that President Kennedy had been assassinated in Dallas that morning. He wondered aloud how something like that could happen in this country. Then he resumed his lecture! Our Commander-In-Chief was President Lyndon Johnson from then on.

At home in our apartment, Judy and I witnessed what may have been the first instance of television saturation news. The screen had non-stop coverage of the Kennedy assassination. We have a poignant photo of Gray at seven months old, just beginning to walk, toddling up to the TV screen showing a full-face image of Kennedy and placing both hands on the screen to look into JFK's face.

Southeast Asia was a hotspot in those days. Genocide was occurring in Cambodia at the hands of Khmer Rouge. There was a communist insurgency in Laos by the Pathet Lao against the Hmong regime. And in Viet Nam, the Viet Mihn, a communist/nationalist insurgent force that had withdrawn to communist North Viet Nam following the partitioning of the former French colony during the French Indochina War, had reactivated their cadres in the South and, under the name Viet Cong, begun an insurgency against the democratic government of South Viet

Nam. This was concerning to the member states of the Southeast Asia Treaty Organization ("SEATO"), a mutual defense treaty organization among the United States, Australia and the democratic governments of Southeast Asia—the Asian counterpart to NATO and all a part of America's foreign policy of "containment" of international communism. The United States under JFK had taken the lead in this fight and had sent U.S. military "advisors" into South Viet Nam to train and work with South Viet Nam Army units. The Viet Cong, under the leadership of Ho Chi Mihn was slowly escalating its insurgency into civil war. It was in this environment that our battalion was deployed to Camp Schwab, Okinawa for 13 months, where we were redesignated as part of the Third Marine Regiment. On her own after I shipped out, Judy made her way back to Kansas City with eight-month-old Gray to stay near her family for the duration.

Our transport to Okinawa from Pendleton involved two highlights worth mentioning. We embarked on Navy APAs (attack personnel ships) designed to carry Marines in four or five high bunks arranged in rows quite close together. With our individual seabags, the quarters were extremely crowded. The entire voyage consisted of conflict between our wanting to be on deck for fresh air and exercise and the Navy captain of the ship who wanted us below decks. The captain didn't welcome Marines aboard because they would smoke cigarettes and either throw the butts overboard, an unsafe, prohibited practice at sea because the swirling winds would blow them back onto the ship, or throw them down on deck and grind them out with their boots, thus, marring the ship's paint and generating debris.

However, the ship stopped in Hawaii for a couple of days, and we officers were able to quarter at Fort DeRussy located on prime Waikiki Beach land. In the officer's quarters there I met two Marine pilots on their way to the Kaneohe Bay Air Station to check out a plane and get some flying hours. They asked if I wanted to ride along. Is a bluebird blue? They were able to commandeer a photography plane, and we flew over all of the Hawaiian Islands that day—Molokai with its old leper colony, the Big Island and its volcanoes, Maui and Mt. Haleakala, and the rainforest coast of Kauai. It was spectacular, although I got a start when a plate in the fuselage between my legs popped off suddenly in flight and I found myself looking straight down at the ocean. It was the housing for cameras taking pictures of surface features directly underneath the plane.

After a long, slow voyage to Korea, we disembarked at Inchon for a day's liberty. We were in our winter green uniform, not fatigues, so we looked good. I just remember the port itself with its extremely high seawalls because of the high tidal range and over which the Marines first landed during the Korean War. We were the first Marines to be in Inchon since the war ten years earlier so our group of eight or ten officers attracted a crowd as we walked around the town of Inchon. Before it was over, we had a group of about fifty kids just following us around jabbering, asking for cigarettes and money and having a good time.

We finally got to Okinawa and were trucked up to the most isolated base in northern Okinawa, Camp Schwab. The Air Force had a large base at Kadena and the officers there had their dependents with them. The Army had a big base and port operation at Naha city, and their officers were posted with dependents. Our officers were the only military types in Okinawa without dependents, and we were stuck in the jungle on the north end of the island. This resulted in innumerable raucous weekend liberty excursions to the Army and Air Force Officer's Clubs in Naha and Kadena, causing our base commander to apologize more than once to those base commanders for the rowdy behavior of the Marine officers for "surrounding the place" as we put it. I, of course, was shocked, shocked, on such occasions and was never involved in any of that.

We had our athletic field, our landing beach, our grinder (asphalt lot) for close order drill, our classrooms and barracks and NCO and Officer's Clubs at Camp Schwab so we could do most of our training and subsisting on base. There was no social life whatever, apart from our sojourns to the south end of the island on weekend liberty. This resulted in a few people going "rock happy" on occasion, and usually alcohol was involved. One night during the monsoon, a captain and a major got into a fist fight and slid, flailing at each other down a rain soaked hillside into the darkness. Another time, a fellow lieutenant from my company found a broom outside our barracks coming home from the club one night and used it to smash the window next to my bed, screaming "Wake up, Ains-worth, you supercilious son of a bitch!" as the window shattered into little pieces all over me and my bed. Whatever disciplinary proceedings flowed from those incidents were kept quiet. (Such incidents were to be expected, after all.) I've often wondered what aspect of my personality or demeanor might have provoked an attack for—superciliousness.

I had collateral duties in addition to my Weapons Platoon Commander duty. Predictably enough, because of my schooling, I was designated Company Embarkation Officer. That did not involve a lot of work—mostly inspecting, inventorying and storing a specified amount of gear that we would have to take with the company headquarters when and if ordered to combat.

Also, as was the case in Quantico and Camp Pendleton, I was appointed to special courts martial as either prosecuting or defense counsel or as a member of the judging tribunal. This is something unique to the Marine Corps, namely, having non-lawyers responsible for conducting criminal trials for lesser offenses in "Summary" and "Special" courts martial. At The Basic School, we read and were taught about the Uniform Code of Military Justice. When I became a lawyer some years later, I marveled at how that could work properly. It was rough justice all right, but the UCMJ was a single volume and it was knowable. In cases involving relatively minor offenses such as being AWOL, insubordination, intoxication, etc., punishment would be decided by "Summary" court martial before the unit commander alone, or "Special" court martial before a tribunal of three or five judges. Both prosecuting and defense "counsel" would argue for the defendant or the command, as applicable, based on the applicable provisions of the UCMJ and the evidence. Guilty verdicts produced reductions in rank, revocation of liberty rights, and brig time for short periods. In such cases, neither the command nor the defendant were represented by counsel who were lawyers. Serious crimes like murder, desertion, armed robbery and the like which could result in confinement in the brig or prison for long periods, dishonorable discharge, etc. were handled by "General" courts martial, in which case both counsel were lawyers and often the panel of judges were as well.

I drew a lot of assignments as counsel or a judge in Special courts martial, which I always enjoyed and took seriously. The most serious case was one at Quantico, where two Marines stole some pistols from the armory and went AWOL into New England, telling their mates they were going on a crime spree. The Base Commander called the FBI (which also has its training facilities headquartered on the Marine Base at Quantico) and the fugitives were picked up in Massachusetts by the FBI two days after they went AWOL. I was defending one of them against the charge of being AWOL for 40 days which included the time they spent in a Massachusetts jail. I maintained that my client was AWOL only two days, the balance of the time in jail in Massachusetts, I argued, they were in "constructive" Marine Corps custody because the base commander asked the FBI to arrest them. I had trouble proving that the base commander made the request, something I had heard from someone, because the base commander was supposed to follow a different procedure and didn't want that to come out. The base legal officer stonewalled me as long as he could, but finally stipulated that my client was in Marine Corps custody two days after leaving the base, so we won. I got some grudging recognition from the Base Commander for "doing a good job."

I probably participated in twenty five or thirty courts martial during my period of active duty, and that experience was a major component of my later decision to go to law school.

I hadn't been in Okinawa three weeks before I was ordered one day to report to the Battalion Commander. Well, *that* was unusual and big medicine because I reported to the Company Commander, and *he* reported to the Battalion Commander. So I proceeded chop-chop to Battalion HQ and was ushered into the Lt. Col's office, where my Company Commander, a captain, was also present. I was very concerned at that point. The colonel started asking me whether I had been involved in any fights or automobile accidents back in California. I was extremely concerned now and assured the colonel I had not. He then broke into a smile and said that must be why I had been promoted to First Lieutenant. He was messing with me! He then pinned my new silver bars on.

It was only a matter of days later that I was appointed Battalion Embarkation Officer. The former Battalion "EmbO" had reached the end of his assignment in Okinawa, and, of the company embarkation officers, I was picked to replace him. That too, did not involve substantial time away from my primary duties as infantry platoon leader, but it did involve three times as much inspection, inventorying and planning for the embarkation of three rifle companies, instead of one, plus the gear and personnel for Battalion Headquarters. Also, the other company EmbOs reported to me.

I held that collateral duty for less than a month before I was promoted again to Regimental Embarkation Officer for the Third Marine Regiment. That was a game changer. It was a full time job at Regimental HQ under the command of a full "bird colonel."

[There were only nine infantry regiments in the Marine Corps. They made up three divisions, each with three regiments. That's it for the Corps infantry. Then there are the three air wings. We were the "Third Marines" as regiments were called. Regiments were commanded by full colonels who wore a silver eagle as rank insignia. A lieutenant colonel was one step below in rank and had a silver oak leaf cluster as a rank insignia. A major was one rank below that wearing a gold oak leave cluster insignia. Below major was captain with two silver bars and below captain were First and Second Lieutenants with silver and gold bars, respectively. The ranks above full colonel were generals, which include one star (brigadier general), two star (major general), three star (lieutenant general), four star (general), and five star (Commandant) ranks.]

I was a twenty-four-year-old first lieutenant and the lowest ranking officer on the regimental staff. The regimental HQ had four sections reporting to the commander. S-1 was personnel, S-2 was intelligence, S-3 was operations, and S-4 was logistics. Administratively, I reported to the S-4, a major named Bell, and we sat in the same large office at separate desks. (I omit the names of most of the officials I dealt with out of an excess of caution.) Operationally, I reported to the S-3 Operations Officer and directly to the colonel. I was solely responsible for loading the regiment and its attachments (a reinforced regiment with motor pool, artillery, engineers, forward air control, medical and other attached units) and all their gear aboard a task force of Navy ships. Whenever the colonel got orders from the Commanding General of the 3rd Marine Division and/or CINCPAC (Commander In Chief, Pacific in Hawaii) to "mount out," my job was to get the reinforced regiment and its vehicles and equipment all loaded to ships in the reverse order they had to come off the ships when we hit the beach wherever we were going. Can you spell intimidating?

As I mentioned, Southeast Asia was a hot spot of communist insurgency at the time. The Third Marines received orders to "mount out" (go to war) twelve times in the ten plus months I was at Regimental HQ. I can't remember a single time that the order to mount out came during daylight. It always came in the middle of the night, and started with the phone ringing on the wall of the barracks room I shared with another lieutenant in my former battalion. I always answered because it was always for me. It would be the colonel himself on the line.

"This is Colonel So-and-so. Report to HQ immediately," he would say.

"Yes sir. On the way," I would reply.

He would hang up as soon as he heard the words. Heart pounding, I would jump into uniform and run to the HQ building maybe three blocks away within ten minutes of the call. There I would meet with the S-3, the Operations Officer, a lieutenant colonel with whom I had worked on a routine basis learning what the top secret contingency plans were for amphibious landings in various places under various circumstances. In a couple of cases, we also had plans for airlift operations to inland trouble spots with manned or unmanned airfields. Each contingency plan had a corresponding Embarkation Plan—mine. Incredibly, none of the other regimental officers ever inspected or reviewed or questioned my work, although my plans and their execution were tested (successfully, he notes modestly) each of the twelve times we mounted out.

In preparation for mount-out events, I spent my days gathering scale drawings of the various holds and decks of Navy AKA (cargo) and APA (personnel) vessels, and making scale templates for *each* type of vehicle, artillery piece, or other form of gear to be loaded on task force ships. On paper and for each contingency plan, I would constructively stow the entire RLT-3 organization and its equipment into cargo spaces on these ships in the reverse order in which they would be called for during an amphibious landing, making certain that each item of gear would fit the weight, height, length and width limitations of the spaces available. All day long I did this, stowing and restowing and checking my work as conditions and developments changed. It was detailed, tedious work, and easy to overlook some space variance that would spell operational disaster when some critically needed artillery piece or ammo or medical truck wouldn't fit on the ship. As mentioned, no one ever checked my work. I always marveled at the fact that such a heavy responsibility fell on such a young and junior person. But no career-minded line officer wanted such a specialized job, both for fear of being pigeonholed in that specialty or for making a mistake that might jeopardize the operation during a landing. Better leave that job to reserve officers like me who were expendable.

For my part, I knew it was heady, important work, and so I did my very best to make my plans perfect, checking and rechecking them. So, when the colonel made one of his middle of the night calls, I could contact the commanding officers of the various battalions and their Embarkation officers and tell them when to deliver their units at which piers alongside which ships at what times. I would then stand on the pier, with my radio and direct the units and equipment to their assigned positions alongside their assigned ships and at the same time direct the deck departments on the Navy ships what equipment and vehicles to load in which spaces in which order, giving them copies of my stowage plans. The troops themselves were much easier to handle. They were directed to certain spaces in APA ships (attack personnel carriers) and their commanders would shoe-horn them into those spaces and await orders.

Once the ships were all loaded, the task force would sail to the destination coast and, when ordered, the landing operation would begin. That would commence with me standing on the bridge of the command ship with my radio (I might be ferried to the command ship) and directing the Navy deck crews to start unloading equipment into landing craft in groupings that made up waves of landing craft. Troop units would go over the side of their APA at their assigned color stations (red, white, blue, yellow, green, black), down the rope nets and into the landing craft. This was hazardous for the troops because this all happens at sea and the swells are constantly tossing the landing craft up and down at the bottom of the nets. So, a Marine in full combat gear could climb down the net, turn and see the landing craft at his feet, and step off seconds later only to fall ten feet onto a boat now at the bottom trough of a swell.

Now the Navy and Marine Operations officers took over. The landing craft containing the various units and their equipment desired by the colonel and his operations officer would form circles in the ocean nearby and continue to circle until all of the desired units were unloaded and in the circle, then they would fan out into a line or "wave" parallel to the beach. When the line was in place, the colonel would give the command to assault the beach, and the wave would race for the beach with naval gunfire and close air support providing cover. We received orders to mount-out for circumstances and specific destinations about which we, or as least I, were rarely told. Some were obvious. The *Plaine Des Jarres* flap in Laos was one. The Gulf of Tonkin flap was another. These were events which were being reported in the media, so we knew what was involved. But most of the time, we didn't. I was just following a plan for a generic landing at a generic beach area with certain units being assigned certain roles. Of the twelve times we were ordered to mount out during my watch, in all twelve occasions we received orders to "stand down" at various stages of the mobilization and embarkation. RLT-3, my regiment, went into Viet Nam thirty days after I returned to the States. Fortunately, all of the embarkation exercises I was involved in went like clockwork. No drama, no recriminations, no embarrassments. All that hard work paid off.

We did have a joint exercise with a division of Chinese Marines for a landing at Taiwan. On that occasion, we went through the entire operation of embarkation aboard the task force, sailed to Taiwan, and made a night landing on the beaches of northern Taiwan. I learned then why it is useful—make that essential—for military units to stage war games. Things go wrong and everyone learns from them. On one occasion, I was standing on the bridge of the command ship listening to radio traffic about the unknown location of five landing craft needed for a wave that was scheduled to hit the beach. A report finally came in saying that they were last seen headed "out to sea." Out to sea meant out into the Taiwan Strait and toward the People's Republic of China! A Navy craft finally chased them down. If five landing craft containing a company of Marines had made a night landing in the PRC, the result could have been a diplomatic embarrassment or it could have been a shooting disaster, depending on the level of self-restraint of the Red Army.

A few hours later, one of the company commanders from one of the battalions, a captain, accosted me on the wing of the bridge and ordered me to disembark his company and equipment on the next available landing craft. I explained patiently that the order in which the cargo was stowed determines when it is available to be unloaded and his company's equipment was still buried, all in accordance with the operation plan. Also, the troops that the operation plan calls for next have debarkation priority. It was like I had said nothing. He repeated his demand, at a slightly higher volume, and a little closer to my face. I'd been up for about forty eight hours straight, and I lost it. I yelled "I am NOT going to unload your company or equipment out of the order prescribed by the Regimental Commander's Operation Plan, and you WILL return to your troops and await instructions." As I shouted my statement, the regimental commander overheard it and walked over and stood beside me, leveling a stare at the captain, but saying nothing. The captain was purple with rage at having been publicly dressed down by a junior officer, and, eyes bulging, looked from my face to the colonel's back and forth a few times until he got it. I spoke with the authority of the Regimental Commander. Then he turned around and disappeared. We resumed the operation until all elements of RLT-3 were ashore. I decided to follow the advancing troops to observe the operation.

Once off the beach, I and the troops ahead of me were dismayed to find that we were simulating an attack through a vast field of hemp. Hemp is a large, yucca-like plant with very sharp pointed needles at the end of their fronds. The plants were planted so closely together that the fronds interlocked with the fronds of the neighboring plant, thus insuring that every step forward we took, we got stabbed in the legs multiple times. By holding a rifle out in front vertically, we could bend the fronds away from us and avoid many of the sharp points. But I was an officer and carried no rifle, only my .45 pistol sidearm. Nevertheless, Marines being Marines, the troops pushed on through a thousand yards of hemp to reach the nearest high ground. It took more than a week for the punc-ture wounds to heal.

The capper of that day for me was resting in the shade of some jungle vegetation and looking up to see a green snake coiled on a branch about eighteen inches above me. It was called a "hundred pacer" snake, so named because that's about how many steps you can take after being bitten. I quickly grabbed a nearby Marine's rifle, loaded only with blank ammo. However, blank ammo has an impact for short distances, so I blew the snake's head off.

One other operation turned out to be noteworthy. Because of communist insurgencies in the interior parts of Laos and South Viet Nam, a contingency plan was formulated for a battalion of Marines to be airlifted into an unmanned airfield for a quick assault exercise. I was picked to be part of the advance team from HQ that went to an abandoned Philippine Air Force base on Mactan Island just off the larger island of Cebu. We flew down on a C-130 and touched down at the airbase and did our recon. Then we were offered a tour of the local town of Lapulapu by our Philippine Air Force sponsors. In the town, we observed a towering statue of a local hero named Lapulapu. When we asked who the esteemed Mr. Lapulapu was to merit the monument as well as having the town named after him, they explained that Ferdinand Magellan, the Portuguese explorer sailing on a Spanish ship in his famous Age of Discovery circumnavigation of the world in 1521, stopped at Cebu across the channel. There Magellan allied himself with a tribe in Cebu that had pledged loyalty to Spain, and they quarreled with the natives on Mactan. Magellan arrived in Mactan with his troops and threatened their chieftain, Lapulapu, with attack unless they converted to Christianity and yielded to the Spanish crown. Magellan was refused and in the ensuing skirmish, Magellan was killed by a poison arrow shot by the Mactan chief. Appropriately, it was the local chieftain who was honored by subsequent generations, and not Magellan. Magellan's expedition completed its circumnavigation of the world without him.

The goodwill of the locals toward Marines was strong throughout the Philippines. Marines and Philippino irregulars had jointly fought the Japanese in WW II, and the locals suffered greatly during that war. The city fathers of Lapulapu made a special point of wanting to introduce us to some "fellow countrymen" present on the island. So, we were led through the town on foot to an unglamorous local house, and one of the villagers knocked on the door. Its occupants turned out to be three young American Peace Corps women posted there. They were visibly appalled to be associated with U.S. Marines in the eyes of the locals and couldn't wait for us to leave. It was sort of funny, but it showed an awkward disconnect among America's various foreign policy influences.

Our subsequent war game involving a surprise airborne landing at Mactan's abandoned airfield two weeks later was a success, but then of course it was unopposed. I did get some experience in the logistics of airborne operations, however.

My thirteen month tour in Okinawa ended just short of my 25th birthday. I was relieved of my duties and ordered to proceed to Treasure Island in San Francisco to be mustered out of active duty. Judy would meet me there, and we would have a few days in the City to get reacquainted. I felt like I had to court her all over again. Our only communication in those days was by letter and the rare phone call, and I was sure she felt as estranged after all that time as I did. I had purchased a new 1965 Plymouth Barracuda through a special deal Chrysler had with the armed forces, and I was to pick it up in Kansas City. Kansas City was to be our headquarters while I interviewed for jobs in New York and Washington, DC after San Francisco.

I felt a powerful attachment to the Third Marines that I wasn't fully aware of until I left it. The experiences I'd had there were the most profound of my young life, and I felt confident and successful. I know of no other organization or activity which would afford someone to have the responsibility and authority I had at such a young age. It is with great trepidation now that I include my fitness report in this record because it seems uncomfortably self-aggrandizing. However, I do so nonetheless because it is the best evidence of the impact my experience there had on me—a measure of myself that would shape me, quite literally, for the rest of my days. I happen to be in possession of it now only by a fluke. I had given a copy of it to my mother when I returned from Okinawa, bragging I suppose to my mother and to show her that my decision to join the Marines had been a good one. She kept it the rest of her life, and I found it only after she died and I was going through her things. The following is an excerpt from the final fitness report prepared by my superior shortly before I left Okinawa:

"Colonel Wheeler: [Regimental Commander] I have never recommended or written such a fitness report and do not expect to ever again, nor have I seen or had the pleasure to have under my command an officer as this. [sic] Lt. Col. George summed it up by saying 'Most lieutenants think it is a pleasure to serve with us; I consider it my pleasure to have served with him.' [Col. George was the S-3, Operations Officer for the 3rd Marines.] Lt. Ainsworth is an absolutely superior officer. He is a mature, poised, sober, quiet and proficient officer capable of handling assignments of far greater responsibility involving those of command due to his present capacities and high growth potential. His duties have involved the closest possible liaison with officers of higher and lower Marine echelons plus those of the Navy and Air Force. He possesses the particular knack of cooperative and personnel [sic] relations to the benefit of all. He has personally supervised the embarkation of officers in the Regiment, helped maintain their highest possible state of readiness and assisted them in their ship and airlift loading plans. Time after time, he has prepared loading plans required to lift an RLT Headquarters, with attachments ranging in size to 8 inch howitzer artillery. His efforts materially affected the success of Reflex I, a Marine Expeditionary Unit airlift exercise from Okinawa to the Philippines."

Evidently, Colonel Wheeler and Lt. Col George felt that I had made them look good, and so were repaying the favor. Still, the report goes beyond a glowing fitness report. It is tangible evidence of the intensity of the experience we shared and the successes we enjoyed. For me, the experience was a sustaining and validating lesson on how to behave, how to lead, and how to cooperate with others engaged in a common and difficult endeavor. It has stayed with me always.

Of course, even though my service had been in the Marine Corps Reserve, namely, what I signed up for to satisfy my military obligation, I had the option of staying in the Corps and making a career of it. My record at that point was a good one, and I was well positioned to have a successful path into field grade ranks and beyond. However, Judy had never been happy in the Marines. It was hard on spouses; no way around that. But I wasn't keen on it either. I saw myself in international work, perhaps the government, perhaps shipping. International politics was my passion after my trip around Europe. Judy's interests also ran to international relations and travel. So, I made no move to stay in the Corps and make a career of it. I think it would have been a great experience and a rewarding career, but I passed. It was one of those big forks in the road, and I took the one more commercially travelled by.

Even though a member of the Regimental Headquarters staff all this time, I was technically detached from the Third Battalion's roster of infantry officers, and the Third Battalion was rotating back to CONUS

(Continental United States) by ship. The battalion commander wanted me to go back with them by ship; I know not why. I don't recall them being short any officers, but maybe they were. In any event, my superior, the Regimental Logistics Officer, was trying to get me back by air, and, if he was successful, it would constitute an "attaboy" from the Regimental Commander, the colonel himself, for a job well done. When I ultimately received my orders, I was to return by aircraft, thus being spared another lovely transpacific cruise in an APA with bunks four or five high and a ship's captain who didn't want to see Marines on the deck of his ship.

I said farewell to Camp Schwab, Okinawa, on a tropical January day in 1965, dressed in my summer khaki uniform, the base uniform for that time of year. My personal effects and other uniforms had been crammed into my seabag, my only luggage. The stereo electronics swag I had acquired in Hong Kong at wonderful prices had been shipped to Kansas City earlier in a thick, padlocked, plywood chest I had hired a local carpenter to build so that no loss or damage would come to the contents. The chest would be transported on the next available military or merchant vessel bound for San Francisco. I embarked, this time as a passenger, on a prop-driven military aircraft bound for Travis Air Force Base in the San Francisco Bay Area, via Anchorage, Alaska for refueling.

The plane flew for nineteen hours before landing at the Anchorage Airport. Seating was not airline seating; it was webbed frame seating that ran along the longitudinal sides of the aircraft with a view of military cargo strapped onto pallets in the middle of the plane. When we landed at 3:00 pm in late January, the sun was a dim, orange ball one finger up from the horizon, and the temperature was below zero. It was only a month after the great earthquake that had leveled the area. The control tower lay horizontally on the tarmac where it had fallen during the temblor, broken into sections on impact when it fell over.

Our plane was parked out on the tarmac some fifty yards from the small terminal building, and it grew cold inside the cabin the instant the doors were all opened. The layover was two hours, so staying in the plane in my short sleeve shirt was out of the question. I sprinted for the terminal building through the thermal shock of Alaskan winter air and found a warm place inside to wait. After dining on candy bars and corn chips and dozing, we ran back to the plane in the now twilight, taxied and took off, this time headed south. After another nineteen hours, during which I dug a field jacket out of my seabag, we landed at Travis AFB, and I and a handful of other Navy types were bussed to Treasure Island in San Francisco. TI had a functioning Navy presence then, with a BOQ, an Officer's Club and a Headquarters. At the former, I changed into clean civilian clothes, checked in by phone with Judy who was flying in from Kansas City to join me the next day, and got some sleep. The next day, I was administratively mustered out of active duty and given my DD-214, a form showing my honorable active duty service particulars. I was a free man—sort of. I was still in the Marine Corps Reserve and by law, the President could call for me to return to active duty at any time at his sole discretion. Those had been the terms of my commission as an officer.

CHAPTER 10

GETTING A JOB (1965)

I had made reservations for several nights at the Sheraton Palace Hotel for a sort of second honeymoon. It turned out that Judy and I fell in love with San Francisco, and we had a splendid time exploring the City and its many attractions while getting reacquainted.

My job-seeking plan was to interview with shipping companies (leveraging my embarkation experience) in San Francisco and New York and then with the CIA in Washington (leveraging my college degree and Marine experience.) Also, I had a contact in the CIA. The only shipping company interviews I could get on short notice were with a general agency representing European carriers on the West Coast, and with Matson Navigation Company, a domestic ocean carrier in the Hawaii trade just down Market Street from the Sheraton Palace. The Personnel Department at Matson (it wasn't called Human Resources then) set up an interview with a manager in the Freight Operations Department which was starting a management training program to feed its satellite offices in other ports. It was a good interview, and I left expecting to receive a call from a more senior manager at the latter's convenience when I was back in Kansas City. The other interview was a waste of time because the European general agent had a sleepy operation and no openings.

Those interviews were the only business interruption Judy and I had during our holiday in the City by the Bay. The food was invariably great, and we got a kick out of the formality of the City. One did not call it "Frisco." Ever. When one went to Union Square shopping, men wore a coat and tie and women ("ladies") wore white gloves. When one rode the cable car, ladies were required to be seated. Only men were permitted to stand on the outside running boards of cable cars, hanging from the poles as each conductor competed with each other conductor in how elaborately and musically they could ring the cable car's bell. The view from the Top of the Mark was gorgeous. Fisherman's Wharf was tacky, even then.

Reentry into civilian life came agreeably in San Francisco, and two interviews down, it was time to get busy. We flew back to Kansas, anxious to see Gray, nearly two, and whom I hadn't seen since he was eight months old. Judy hadn't previously been separated from him at all. When we got back to Judy's parents' house, and I was reintroduced to Gray, he clearly didn't have the concept of Daddy down. The first day back, I walked from the kitchen into the hall carrying him in my arms, and, as we passed the phone on the wall, he pointed at it and said "Daddy." I had made a few phone calls home from Okinawa, something technologically difficult in those days, and on those occasions, Judy would put Gray's ear to the phone and say "daddy" as he listened to my scratchy audio. This was going to take some time.

I set off to New York after a few days and interviewed with Grace Lines, a U.S. Atlantic Coast to South America shipping company, and with another prominent shipping agency representing Scandinavian lines. Both interviews were pleasant, but no more than mildly interesting and neither indicated that they were looking for a new hire. I then proceeded on to Washington DC, where I had an appointment scheduled with the CIA.

The interview was at the big CIA headquarters building surrounded by pastoral woods outside Langley, Virginia near Washington. I had written them from Kansas City requesting an interview, and I had mentioned that fact to a friend who (it was rumored) worked there. Although we never spoke of it, his cover was that he worked for "The Department of Defense" but never talked about what he did there. I put two and two together. My request was confirmed by return mail and the interview scheduled. It was with a senior agent with responsibilities for recruitment and training agents on the covert ops side. On the day of the interview, I drove through a guard post, gave my name, stated my business, and was admitted into the ample parking lot. From there, I was free to just walk through the front doors into the famed building.

After checking in at reception in the large, but spare, lobby and reception area, I was escorted through a grey door and down a long grey corridor with identical grey metallic doors, save an identifying name or number plate at each door. Through one of them, my inquisitor waited. I was introduced to Mr. X and we had a long and agreeable talk about the department's orientation and an agent's career path in covert ops. It involved initial jungle training in Panama and other operational matters. He said a top secret security clearance would be required. I reminded him that I had a top secret clearance from the Department of Defense (required because of my contingency planning work with the Third Marines.) He said yes, he realized that, but "the company" required another, its own, background security check. It would take *six months* to complete, he said. I was crestfallen at that news. I couldn't sit around waiting for six months; I had a family to support. At the end of the interview, likely following some signal that I missed, the door opened and in walked my friend. They had decided to let me in on their secret. My friend gave me some encouragement, and said he thought it would be a good fit for me. Then, I was escorted back to the reception area, leaving the two of them to compare notes.

[As I write this, I am in possession of the obituary of the "friend" referenced above, Monty Rodgers. Monty died of brain cancer in 2012 after a long career in the CIA, including 25 years as chief of clandestine operations in Africa.]

My job-seeking business on the East Coast now completed, I returned to Kansas City to wait for responses from Matson and the CIA. Over the month of so of waiting in Kansas City playing with my young son, I came to discount the likelihood of ending up at the CIA for two reasons. First, five more months was an impractically long time to wait for a job offer under my circumstances. Second, I had gnawing doubts about what a lifetime of work in covert operations would do to my brain. I had met some defense intelligence operatives in the Marines; they would just appear, going by the name of "Sam" or "Joe" and be around for a while, never mixing in, and then disappearing again. It was not normal work.

I assumed that spooks worked constantly to counter the threats presented by some really bad people and the governments that employed them. But, after years of doing that all day, how could that not color your outlook? Would it be possible to lead a normal family life and keep the world in proper focus? Increasingly, I doubted it. Meanwhile, time passed.

Sometime during our stay in Kansas City, my trunk containing the stereo equipment I bought in Hong Kong arrived. The thick, plywood chest arrived with the upper left quarter of the chest completely crushed. It took a lot of force to pulverize that chest and I never learned what had happened. But when I opened the chest, all the gear was intact and functioned perfectly. The chest had given its all but done its job.

During that time same waiting period in Kansas City, I took delivery of the new Plymouth Barracuda I had ordered in Okinawa. It was a blue, racy-looking hatchback, and we were happy to have it to tool around in. I don't remember Judy playing any role in buying that car. I didn't consult her before buying it that I recall. Nor had I involved her in buying the Jaguar that we had in Quantico and Pendleton. It was just one of those sexist norms that prevailed at the time. I don't think Judy ever wanted to be involved with car purchases then, but I don't know that. As I write this, I think most young wives with small children would insist on having a say, likely even the biggest vote, about the car she would be driving around with her kids.

One day about three weeks after returning from Washington, I received a call from the Assistant Director of Freight Operations at Matson, one John Dodge. Would it be convenient to talk about my recent interview with the company in San Francisco and further those discussions, he asked? It would indeed, I said. He introduced himself by saying that, after graduating from Harvard, he took a position in the Peace Corps managing a cohort of many Peace Corps volunteers in several African countries. I told him about Judy's near miss with the Peace Corps. There followed a long, thorough-going interview which I realized was preparatory to making an offer if he liked my responses. Toward the end of the conversation, he asked me the stock interview question, "Where would you like to be in five years?" I answered, "In a position of responsibility and authority in an organization with a prestige product or service." That's what he wanted to hear, and he offered me the job. How soon could I start? I said I would get back to him promptly after talking it over with Judy.

Judy and I took inventory. It was a good job offer. It was in delightful San Francisco. It avoided five more months of waiting for the CIA to decide whether it would make an offer. It would involve a normal family life for us. It would provide us with an income *now*. It would allow us to get our own home and not have to live with her parents. It was a no-brainer. I called John Dodge back and accepted the offer, saying we could be in San Francisco in two weeks.

It was springtime, and we took the southern route via the fabled Route 66 again, except this time, we turned north at Bakersfield toward San Francisco, instead of southwest to Camp Pendleton.

CHAPTER 11

MATSON (1965-1979)

My starting salary at Matson as a management trainee in the Freight Operations Department in 1965 was $6,000 per year, or $500 per month. That contrasted favorably with the $220 per month I earned as First Lieutenant, although in the military, housing was subsidized, medical and dental care was free, and commissary (groceries) and PX (merchandise) privileges were heavily subsidized.

As we searched for an apartment, we realized that San Francisco was much more expensive than any place we had lived. After coming to terms with the fact that we were not going to be living in a stylish apartment with a bay view in Sausalito, we took a furnished third floor apartment on Sacramento Street in the Fillmore neighborhood. That location was in the dodgy transition zone between toney Pacific Heights and the public housing of the Western Addition. I rode the bus to Matson by day, and by night and weekends, we shopped for furniture and cheaper unfurnished apartments. Some months later we moved to a comfortable unfurnished apartment on California Street near the top of Nob Hill. It was right on the cable car line that ended in front of the Matson Building. It was perfect for me, and Judy and Gray spent their days in the park surrounded by the Fairmont Hotel, the Mark Hopkins Hotel, the Pacific Union Club and Grace Cathedral getting to know the nannies and the kids of affluent people living on Nob Hill. On weekends, we piled into the Barracuda and headed for the beaches of Marin and hikes on Mount Tamalpais.

About that time, I got a letter from the CIA congratulating me on having obtained the full top secret security clearance, and inviting me to contact them about my return. I wrote back to say that I was gainfully employed now and would not be following up. Another fork in the road.

We reconnected with John and Celia Garrett who were living in Mill Valley. It will be recalled that John was my pledge father in the SAE house at KU, and the one with whom I was originally going to Europe and who got me the job on the Rock Island Railroad. Celia was Judy's sorority sister and the one who had brokered our introduction. They had since married, and John had been through medical school and was a resident preparing to do his military service as a doctor in the Navy. Judy and Celia got pregnant at about the same time and delivered their babies at the same time. Judy had Erin and Celia had her son Shannon.

Erin was born in St. Francis hospital in the City when we lived on Nob Hill. Gray had cost us $15 in medical expenses to be born at Quantico. Erin cost many hundreds of dollars out of pocket, even with the group health insurance benefits from Matson. I wondered whether I made the right decision when I decided not to re-up in the Marine Corps.

Now, we were a bit cramped in our two bedroom apartment on Nob Hill. We had no savings, but Judy's father Hilton generously offered to give us $5,000 for a down payment on a house. That and my salary would not permit us to buy anything in any of the San Francisco neighborhoods we liked, so we began to shop in Marin. Sausalito and Mill Valley in trendy Southern Marin were also beyond our reach, so we shifted our search further north. We liked the town of San Anselmo in the Ross Valley and concentrated our search there, finally selecting a hillside contemporary A-frame two bedroom house at the end of a cul-de-sac of custom homes.

We bought it and lived there quite happily for two years trying to landscape the wild, hard loam downslope property on the edge of town. The most noteworthy event that occurred in that house involved thirteen beagle puppies. Judy's father was a prominent trusts and estates attorney in Kansas City and a Brethren pastor on the side. He was also a softy who visited a client on his farm one time and found out that the farmer was going to drown a litter of puppies he didn't want. Hilton decided to take them and ship them to us! We received a notification from United Airlines that "the shipment" was arriving at night at SFO that day or the next. We drove down to the airport at the appointed hour and picked up thirteen wormy puppies.

We found deworming medicine for them and kept them in an old playpen of Erin's in the sub-basement. Then we advertised in the Marin newspaper and sold them all. For years after that, we had people coming up to us on the street, remembering themselves to us, and saying that they had bought one of the puppies. I can't remember why we didn't keep one.

Sometime later, our neighbors across the street in a three bedroom house with a pool were suddenly transferred elsewhere for the husband's job as an engineer for Bechtel. They asked if we wanted to rent their house for the two or three years they would be gone. We jumped at the chance, sold our A-frame and moved across the street.

The pool was a hazard, and we had the inevitable scare that involved me lounging beside the pool one day and out of the corner of my eye seeing Shannon crawl up to the edge of the pool and, without hesitation, fall in. He came up from the depths on my extended arm and hand sputtering but unfazed.

Erin was an early riser as a toddler, and she would get up and walk around while Judy and I were still in bed. Early one morning, the doorbell rang. I was surprised to find our neighbor from down the road holding Erin's hand. Erin had managed to unlatch the front door and, dirty diapers and all, head off down the road until being intercepted by our alert neighbor.

Those years were quite pleasant, and we had a growing society of friends. Gray went to the neighborhood grammar school, Erin to preschool and Judy made friends in the League of Women Voters. We also exchanged baby-sitting duties with my superior at Matson who had hired me, John Dodge and his wife, also denizens of San Anselmo.

It was the late sixties and the rock music scene was getting started. If LA had Laurel Canyon, Marin Country was the Bay Area's ground zero for rock. We had the Jefferson Airplane, the Grateful Dead, Country Joe and the Fish, and Carlos Santana, among others, all managed by rock impresario Bill Graham who lived in Larkspur. There were always rock concerts going on at the amphitheater on Mt. Tam. That era capped off its early anti-war idealism and innocence with Woodstock in 1969.

When the owners of our house with the pool came back after their work absence, we had to find another place to live. Using my GI bill benefits, we bought an older four bedroom, two story brown shingle on San Anselmo Avenue in the middle of town. The house was a non-stop do-it-yourself project, but we slowly improved the place to our taste. It was roomy and pleasant and the neighborhood had kids Gray and Erin could play with.

Meantime, I had grown nostalgic about the courts martial experience I'd had in the Marine Corps. My experience as a junior captain of industry at Matson was positive and I was progressing nicely through the ranks, but something was lacking. I just wasn't as passionate about what I was doing as I had been in the Marines. I wanted to go to law school. My notions of the highest and best use to which I could put my talents, whatever they were, seemed to point to the practice of law. And I had my eye on maritime law by virtue of my theater of operations in the shipping industry.

I took the LSAT exam, did passably well, and applied for admission to the Golden Gate University School of Law, located just four blocks down Mission Street from the Matson Building. I was accepted and, again using my GI bill educational assistance benefits, I began attending the night classes offered by GGU's four year night school program—a major fork in the road. I loved it. I found I was able to do my studying ("briefing cases" for my various classes) while commuting between San Anselmo and the City on the Greyhound bus. After work three nights a week, I attended classes up Mission Street until 10 pm, drove home to San Anselmo after class, and ate whatever Judy had left out for me for dinner.

After the first year, I was one of the top three in my class and received an invitation to join Law Review, a very good thing to have on one's resume when looking for work later. At that point, I had a larger opportunity that caused a bit of a flap at home. As one of the top three in my class, I qualified to transfer to Boalt Hall, the Berkeley campus law school of the University of California. A Juris Doctor credential from Boalt, like one from Stanford, Harvard, Yale, Michigan, and a handful of top tier law schools would have opened a lot of employment doors for me later. It would, however, have meant taking day classes because Boalt had no night program.

On the one hand, that would have shortened my law school exercise from three more years to two. On the other, I would have had to quit my job (and salary), do unknown part time work. It would also have forced Judy to take a job and farm the kids out for day care, the parameters and the cost of which were uncertain and would be hard for all of us. So, I swallowed hard and passed on the opportunity. But, I resolved to myself that I would not let the absence of a degree from the UC Berkeley Law School on my *curriculum vitae* keep me from achieving my ambitions. Yet another fork in the road.

I completed law school at Golden Gate, was Editor of the Law Review, and graduated in the same top three standing as at the end of my first year. Thereafter I was offered a position in the Matson Law Department by its then General Counsel, David Anderson, a fine and able lawyer. However, there was a bit of *sturm und drang* along the way inside Matson.

Back in my third year of Law School, I had completed my management training program in the Freight Operations Department and, over the course of two years, had rotated through several jobs that were prerequisites to a position as Freight Operations Manager at one of the ports where Matson did business (LA/Long Beach, San Francisco/Oakland, Seattle, various places in Asia.) My bosses knew that I was going to Law School at night, but it was a matter of time before I got offered one of those jobs. I guess all of us were just ignoring the potential for future conflict.

About that time, a subsidiary company, Matson Terminals, was starting up a training program for stevedore superintendents because Matson Terminals was expanding its scope to include loading and unloading of ships for companies other than its parent Matson Lines, including one of its competitors, Sea-Land. The Regional Manager for Matson Terminals had surreptitiously asked me whether I would be interested in a superintendent's job, technically a promotion. I say surreptitiously because he didn't want to start an unnecessary fight with my boss, the Freight Operations Director of the parent company, his most important client. I said that I would think about it, but emphasized that I intended to finish law school and probably change careers after that. He said if I wanted to take the superintendent's job as a bridging job, it would be okay with him. He needed a superintendent to handle his important clients in the near term, notably Matson and Sea-Land.

As luck would have it, right then I was called in to my boss's office, congratulated and told I was being promoted to Freight Operations Manager in Matson's biggest port, Los Angeles. I was crestfallen. Secretly, I held the view that there were certain things that I just would not do, and work in LA was one of them. I felt like a jerk, and explained that I realized all the training I had received was more than just a day's work for day's pay, that I knew it would lead to one of these regional positions. However, I was in my third year of Law School, I was determined to graduate, and I couldn't go to Los Angeles. He did not see that coming, was shocked, and was not pleased. He gave me some time to think it over.

A few days later, he called me in again to continue this conversation, only he apparently had instructions from above to firmly *tell* me I was going to LA, and that I would have to pick up the rest of my law school in LA, as and when I was able. The job came first. The speech was not unexpected.

I called his hand and raised him one. I apologized again for disappointing the company by declining the position I had been trained for, but explained that my interest in the law had increased steadily and that I would have to pursue it. I said Matson deserved better than someone with divided loyalties and gave him two weeks' notice. He was stunned. I did not tell him that I had spoken again to Matson Terminals and agreed to take the stevedore superintendent's job. Still another fork in the road.

The scat hit the fan. The company's terminals subsidiary had hired me away from the parent shipping company. The President of Matson Terminals, a gregarious executive with an engineering background, was called on the carpet, and he just played dumb. Dave was leaving anyway, he argued, and all he did was keep him (me) in the company. Moreover, he added slyly, I would have responsibilities for the loading and unloading of Matson's own ships—a job I was well suited for. It was win-win. The Director of Freight Operations had no answer to that.

Things died down, and I did take over the stevedoring of Matson's non-containerized ships at Pier 30-32 and sometimes their container ships over at the Oakland container terminal. In the end, Freight Operations Management was happy with the service they got since it was an improvement over what they had received before. I continued to work for Matson Terminals through graduation from law school, at which time I was offered the counsel job in the Matson Law Department. Matson's General Counsel gave me two months off with full pay to study for the bar exam, a very decent thing to do. The expectation was, however, that I should jolly well pass the bar exam. I did and settled into an interesting and rewarding seven years in the Matson Law Department. By that time, I was a peer with the other executives involved in the earlier squabbling and all was forgiven.

At home, however, things had been unraveling for some time. Judy had grown unhappy with her lot as a homemaker and had political aspirations. Feminism was on the march at the time, and I'm sure she took some encouragement from the movement to stretch her interests and her legs. She pursued her citizen's committee work with the city of San Anselmo and the County of Marin while I was attending law school classes at night and working by day. On weekends I was ticking off my do-it-yourself home improvement projects, leaving very little quality time for us. So, shortly before I graduated from law school, we decided to amicably separate. After graduation, I would move out while Judy took the kids to Kansas for a visit, and she would break the news to them while they were away. I would take an apartment in San Anselmo and would see them regularly.

It happened quickly. Gray and Erin came home to a *fait accompli,* and I lived five minutes away. I had them on Wednesday nights and one weekend day, and we managed to have good bonding time together, probably more so than when I had been preoccupied with law school. We took fun camping trips in the Sierra Nevada Mountains in summer, haunted the beaches at Point Reyes National Seashore, and fished in the Water District lakes. I don't think the experience was traumatic for them, and I was comfortable as well.

When I started dating, it was natural that my date would occasionally be around during the times Gray and Erin visited me, but I immediately saw a problem with that. I noticed that the quality of the time I had with Gray and Erin was diluted a lot when a stranger was around. I couldn't have that, so I thereafter made it a habit to see the kids alone, so that we could continue to bond and enjoy ourselves naturally. That became a bone of contention with some of the women I dated as they naturally felt left out. But, arbitrary or not, that's how it was, and I never regretted it. As the kids grew older and their peer groups became the major influence in their lives, they needed me less and grew more independent.

When Erin was thirteen, she asked me brightly one day, "How's your love life? Are you happy?" She was concerned about my solitary status and thought I should be with someone. I wasn't really looking for it, but I now had permission to take another fork in the road.

When Judy and I finally got around to divorcing, I gave her my community property interest in our house and furnishings. Her dad had made our home acquisitions possible with his gift of a down payment, and she had custody of the kids. I thought she should have the household free and clear going forward. I was an attorney and making good money, so I was better positioned to fare for myself. So, I rented an apartment in San Anselmo, first off the Miracle Mile and then later in the newer Parkside Apartments. In a speculative play, I bought some Taco Bell stock on margin and got lucky. Pepsi acquired the company causing the stock to rise sharply. I sold my shares and used the capital gain to buy an older cottage on Belle Avenue near the Seminary, and began the now familiar routine of home renovation again.

At Matson, I enjoyed my work. As a domestic ocean carrier operating between the West Coast and Hawaii, Matson was a Federal public utility and had to get approval from the Federal Maritime Commission every time the company raised its freight rates. So, I spent a lot of time doing administrative litigation along with my colleague in the Department Peter Wilson and under the able tutoring of my boss and our litigation team leader, David Anderson. We won all our cases, primarily because the Pricing Department would consult with the Law Department before raising its rates to make sure that the resulting rate of return for the company was within legal limits.

Beyond that, I was a generalist. I did a broad range of legal work, including transactional work such as ship construction contracts, terminal construction contracts, ship and terminal financings, and gantry crane purchases. I drafted ship charters and bills of lading making up our contracts of carriage, managed litigation placed with outside counsel in places all over the trading area in which the company did business, primarily the U.S mainland, Hawaii, and Guam. I opined on government regulation and compliance matters from antitrust law to Coast Guard regulations on vessel registration. It was a calm, academic, and closely managed legal and business environment, and I got along well with my fellow lawyers and the executives and employees of the company. Mine was a well-paid, not overworked, intellectually challenging professional life, with little excitement. There was one notable exception.

One day I was at my desk preparing for a settlement meeting with counsel for the California Air Resources Control Board. One of our ships had been cited for exhausting black smoke from its stack, a violation of environmental regulations, and the amount of the fine had to be negotiated. It was the noon hour and almost all of the executive suite on the top floor of the Matson Building was out to lunch.

Suddenly, I heard the receptionist screaming my name. I jumped up and ran to the double French doors that separated the Legal Department from the elevator lobby and reception. I pushed open the right door and saw a man with a rifle pointed at the receptionist who was under her desk screaming. As soon as I opened the door, the gunman swung the barrel of the rifle toward me. I jumped back from the doorway, and the right door automatically closed. This put me behind the left door of the two French doors wondering frantically how to get the receptionist out of danger.

Immediately, the door pulled open from the reception area and the gunman stepped through passing not twelve inches from my shoulder. Fortunately, the door opened into the reception area requiring the gunman to elevate his rifle to a vertical position so that he could open the door toward himself. It was in that stance I encountered him as we surprised each other just inside the doorway. My hands closed simultaneously on the barrel and the stock of the rifle and it fired, shooting a small, neat hole in the ceiling above us. There followed a fierce fight for control of the weapon by two adrenaline-charged people as we tussled around the law department area, crashing into furniture and walls. In another piece of luck, the gunman was a Philippino and smaller in stature than I was. With my grip on the weapon the same as that I'd used in "pugil stick" training in the Marines for hand to hand combat, I was able to strike and overpower my assailant, wrest the gun out of his hands, and put him on the carpet.

One of the legal secretaries had locked herself in Pete Wilson's office when the rifle fired, and I hollered for her and the receptionist to call the police as I stood over the man holding the rifle by the barrel like a club. I honestly don't know what kept me from beating the man with it. That was the highest level of fight-or-flight adrenaline I've ever experienced, and I can certify that, when in that state, presence of mind goes out the window. I came within a whisker of clubbing him senseless right there. I think my rage must have been mirrored on my face because when I told him not to move, he didn't.

I was joined by our Controller who heard my hollering from his office and, perhaps ten minutes later, the police cautiously entered the department through the same doors used by the gunman, weapons drawn. They relieved me of the rifle, placed the gunman into custody and took our statements. Then they left.

The legal secretary and I stood there looking at the wrecked furniture and each other in our normally sedate law department. It was surreal. Since I had the aforesaid settlement conference an hour later at the Civic Center, I decided to keep the appointment. I didn't know what else to do. At my meeting with the California Air Resources Board counsel an hour later, I related my experience to him. He remarked that my timely appearance under the circumstances was surprising. That may have put me in good stead with him, because with very little advocacy on my part, I came out of the meeting with a very light penalty for the air pollution offense by the *Matsonia*.

It turned out that the gunman was an ordinary seaman aboard one of the Matson ships. The ship had been placed in routinely scheduled dry dock and the crew laid off. When the crewman applied for unemployment compensation, the California state government office told him that, given the timing of the dry docking midway through their reporting period, his compensation would be prorated, resulting in an amount less than he expected. When he protested to them that he could not live on that money, they apparently just told him there was nothing they could do, because Matson reported the layoff period. When he visited the Matson Personnel Department, he was told that his problem was with the unemployment office. Catch 22.

The enraged man's next move was to come to the Matson Building with a rifle wrapped in his raincoat, get on the elevator unchallenged, and step out into the reception area of the executive offices intending to shoot the CEO of the company. When he pulled out the rifle and demanded to see the CEO, the receptionist started screaming my name as the only man on the floor. That was when I entered the proceedings.

Our CEO, Bob Pfeiffer, happened to be in Honolulu addressing a local business club that day. Since Honolulu was three hours behind San Francisco time, he was briefed on the developments at his headquarters before his speech. When he was introduced to his audience, he opened his remarks as follows:

"Whenever someone is asked to give a talk to you, he or she always says how happy they are to be with you. Well, I'm here to tell you that I am *really* glad to be here talking to you!"

Pfeiffer believed that criminals should not be rewarded with publicity for their crimes, so Matson issued no statement about the incident. Nor did any of the media pick up the story from the police blotter because that night, someone fired gunshots into the front door of Mayor Dianne Feinstein's home, and that incident monopolized the news cycle. The entire compliment of executives in the executive suite, however, took me to lunch at the University Club.

In an executive shake-up at Alexander and Baldwin, the General Counsel of A & B, Willis Deming, was transferred to its subsidiary Matson as Senior Vice President and General Counsel. That meant that David Anderson was demoted to Assistant General Counsel—an undeserved insult to him. Further, it meant that I was then the junior man in a four man law department. Not a lot of growth potential, I thought. However, after working with Willis for two or three years, and getting along well with him, he surprised me with a major career opportunity. He was prepared to engineer a transfer for me to Honolulu as Assistant General Counsel in parent company Alexander & Baldwin's law department. A & B's law department did less work in house than Matson, which, by virtue of its far flung maritime operations, generated many more legal problems. The work at A & B was primarily mergers and acquisitions, financings and corporate governance matters. I had a strong preference for maritime work. However, as Willis pointed out, I would be the second man and in line to succeed the VP General Counsel at a bigger company. It was an offer he was not making to the other, more senior lawyers in our department and would be a good career move for me. But, it would have involved a move to Honolulu.

I thought it over and decided against it. This road now had a lot of forks in it. The divorce was still fresh, and I didn't want to remove myself from the routine lives of Gray and Erin for their sakes, and I would miss them as well. And, as noted, I preferred maritime work. I told Willis of my feelings and he countered that, in the long run, I would be able to offer more financial support to my children if I took the Honolulu job. I thanked him for the opportunity and declined. He was right, as it turned out, because within a few years, the A & B Vice President and General Counsel left and his then number two succeeded him and had a very comfortable twenty year tenure there.

However, opportunities of my own were developing. One of my duties at Matson under Willis, was to attend the meetings of the Bay Area branch of Pacific Merchant Shipping Association Legislative Committee, a California and Pacific Northwest area trade lobby. We formulated joint industry positions with respect to California, Oregon and Washington state legislation affecting our industry, environmental regulations, terminals and pilot issues and the like.

One of my counterparts on the committee was Richard Tavrow, Senior Vice President and General Counsel of American President Lines, Ltd. APL was a much larger, world-wide liner company that had recently gone through a purging of its executive ranks for unlawful "rebating" in the trans-Pacific trades. The CEO had been ousted and so had the General Counsel. APL was owned by Natomas, an oil company with reserves primarily in Indonesia. As a consequence of the trauma at APL, Natomas sent its Chief Financial Officer, Bruce Seaton down to run APL, and the company did a nationwide search for General Counsel resulting in the selection of Tavrow, then a VP General Counsel for the East Coast Shipping Company, Prudential Lines. So, Tavrow was newly in charge of legal affairs at APL, and had hired one newly minted lawyer without any maritime experience. The two of them couldn't keep up with all the work, and he was looking for a lawyer to be his assistant and hit the ground running and work unsupervised. We had worked cooperatively on a number of matters in our committee dealings, and he generally deferred to my superior expertise in the nitty gritty of West Coast shipping. So he called me one day and asked if I would be interested in being his Assistant General Counsel. I said I would indeed be interested and proceeded to have extensive interviews with him and with CEO Bruce Seaton himself, Seaton having a policy of interviewing anyone being hired by anyone reporting directly to him. So, I interviewed with Seaton in the penthouse of the 601 California Building in San Francisco, Natomas' headquarters. We hit it off because he knew Matson's CEO, Bob Pfeiffer well, and we had plenty to talk about. So, I got the job.

When I informed Willis Deming of my decision, he was surprised. He offered me more money to stay, but I declined, pointing to a more promising career path as number two with a global, fortune 500 carrier. I was practically repeating the selling points he had made about the A & B job in Honolulu. He understood that and wished me well. He had even done some of APL's legal work early in his career in a Washington DC law firm called Treadwell and Laughlin. So, my leaving would be amicable with him. Not so, however, with Bob Pfeiffer.

Matson was, and still is, an insular, paternalistic company. Bob called all management employees on their birthday to wish them a happy birthday. He took a dim view of having his executives poached by other companies, and immediately got on the phone with Bruce Seaton and made or implied whatever threats he could manage. But Seaton was a hard case and told Pfeiffer that in his trans-Pacific, intensely competitive trades, such practices are not just common, but essential, citing the number of Sea-Land employees he had recruited as well as APL executives recruited by others. In essence, he just told Pfeiffer to get over it. I was surprised and a bit embarrassed at having been the cause of such a kerfuffle, but after that, my departure went well. I gave Matson a full thirty days' notice and finished up or turned over to Peter Wilson all the files I had open and left on good terms. Bob Pfeiffer even continued to call me on my birthday for two years after I left Matson. But then we had that shooting incident in common.

Efren Sanchez, one of my clients in Matson's Freight operations advised me to be careful at APL. He was mindful of the pressure on operators in the trans-Pacific trade to do things that were not legal in order to be competitive. The ethics of that marketplace were a lot more hazardous, he warned, than in Matson's Hawaii trade. Witness what had happened to the former executives and lawyers at APL, he cautioned. I thanked him and said that I'd withstood pressure before and was confident that I could chart a proper course.

CHAPTER 12

APL (PART I)

Still single, still living in San Anselmo in my renovation project cottage, I began my daily commute, not via bus to the financial district in San Francisco where Matson's offices were any more, but by car over the Richmond Bridge to downtown Oakland where APL's offices were. I needed a good, roadworthy car to commute with, and recalling the pleasurable ride I'd had in my Jaguar in Quantico, I bought a Jaguar Van den Plus sedan the same dark red color I'd had before. I now looked upwardly mobile and the low, heavy car would be able to slip through the winter winds that buffeted the Richmond Bridge like a ghost.

One of the principal functions that Dick Tavrow expected me to cover was regulatory compliance. We were less regulated in pricing our services in the foreign trade than we had been with Matson in the domestic trade. However, because a major share of the carriers in the foreign trade were foreign, state-owned shipping companies with varying levels of subsidy by their governments, pricing was allowed to be set by cartels of carriers operating in shipping "conferences." The conferences were formed by agreements among ocean carriers themselves serving a common trade. These agreements were filed with and approved by the Federal Maritime Commission having jurisdiction over shipping by an act of Congress. To the extent that the carriers' concerted action confined themselves to the authorized activities supervised by the FMC, including price fixing, the cartels, which is what they were, had antitrust immunity. If they departed from the approved regimen, however, they could be prosecuted under both civil and criminal laws and the penalties were draconian.

The general idea behind that regulatory regime was that a nation's merchant marine was vital to the interests of that nation, and it should be conducted without discriminatory treatment of importers and exporters.

The shipping public should all have equal opportunity to access space aboard ships at public rates with the same levels of service. Any secret, discriminatory arrangement with a shipper to capture its volume of cargo in exchange for preferential service was illegal. The prior management team had run afoul of those legal strictures and paid the price for it.

My job was to stay close to what the company did in the conference setting, to conduct educational compliance seminars for the managers involved and to attend the conference "owners" meetings held every six months or so in port cities all over the world where major decisions on price, terms of service, and self-policing were made. So, I travelled extensively with the pricing department executives to owners meetings in Manilla, Hong Kong, Tokyo, Honolulu (convenient mid-Pacific location,) Singapore, Seoul, and occasionally London and other North Europe ports. The other big American carriers were Sea-Land Service and United States Lines who each sent counsel as well, as they too had been caught up in illegal operations at the time APL did, their executives too had been punished, and they too were militant about compliance.

The American carriers operated under a handicap in that foreign flag carriers could enter into illegal arrangements with foreign shippers with lesser risk of prosecution since U.S. law enforcement could not reach foreign parties or their documents, whereas, they could subpoena the witnesses and documents of American carriers readily. All the more reason American carriers were so militant about compliance as to send counsel with their sales and pricing executives who met jointly with their competitor counterparts. I enjoyed that work. We were functioning in a trans-national legal self-policing program entirely unknown to other business entities.

Judy had meanwhile sold the house in San Anselmo, and she and the kids had moved to Point Reyes Station, a small town in West Marin. I wasn't privy to her decision-making, but West Marin was cheaper and she had friends there. It added forty five minutes to my drive when I had the kids with me on weekends, and it had, of necessity, eliminated our Wednesday night get togethers. But, Gray was in high School at Tomales Bay, and Erin was finishing her grammar school at Point Reyes. My presence was not material to their well-being at this point, and that freed me up for a long term relationship with a companionable woman again if I could find one. It was about that time that Erin surprised me with her "How's your love life? Are you happy" question. It was time to seek a personal fork in the road and move on.

The Gods must have heard me ruminating because about this time, I met Carol Ingellis one Friday evening in a Union Street watering hole in 1983. After a very enjoyable set of drinks, I asked her if she would join me for dinner, and she agreed. We walked down to Fillmore Street to a restaurant she liked that has since been bought by Gavin Newsom and one of Gordon Getty's sons and named after the only opera Gordon Getty ever wrote, Plump Jack. The dinner was delightful, and afterward I dropped her at her apartment in Pacific Heights where her widowed father was visiting from Connecticut. I said I would be in touch and drove back to Marin. The following week, I came down with a roaring cold, missed a couple of days work, and generally hunkered down at home. By the next weekend, I was feeling human enough again to call Carol, but she beat me to it. She called me to say hello. She didn't say it, but she was really checking in to see why I hadn't called since our first date had gone so well. "Aha," she said when I told her I'd been sick. She sounded perversely delighted to hear that I'd been sick, because it confirmed her intuition that I surely would not have forgotten her. I asked her out again. That was the beginning of, as they say, a beautiful friendship.

We became an exclusive couple immediately, and I met her friends and colleagues in her communications seminar business. She met Gray and Erin as well and her relationship with them morphed into a sort of worldly older sister role. Erin had theretofore viewed San Francisco with suspicion as a big, dirty city from her point of view in rural Point Reyes. But Erin's conversion to city girl began when Carol took Erin to lunch at the Neiman Marcus rotunda, basically introducing her to San Francisco style.

Carol joined me in San Anselmo for hikes in the Water District at the foot of Mt. Tamalpais and at the Point Reyes National Seashore. Similarly, I joined her on weekends in her Pacific Heights digs for dinners and concerts and prowling the City's neighborhoods. Together we travelled to Lake Tahoe, Mendocino and to Carmel for getaways. It was a charmed courtship.

Carol's father, Victor, and the rest of the Connecticut family were startled when they were told that Carol had a serious boyfriend named David Ainsworth. It is not a common name, and Victor had sold his package liquor store when he retired to a red-headed local guy who everyone knew named—wait for it—David Ainsworth. Not the same guy, she told them.

So, six months after we met, during a weekend in Marin, I proposed and Carol accepted. My little cottage wasn't all that appealing, so we started shopping for real estate. Carol had a preference for the City, but I was partial to Marin. I could not afford to buy a house in any of the San Francisco neighborhoods I would have liked to live in, and my fondness for the quiet and space and loveliness and, most importantly, the weather of the Ross Valley in Marin was powerful. So, Carol gave in. I owed her one. Someday, I told her, we would live in the City.

In a whirlwind-esque series of events, I sold my cottage, we bought a three bedroom, two bath contemporary house on top of a hill in San Anselmo with a good view facing Mt. Baldy and Mt. Tam. An intimate, informal wedding was planned for the manicured garden of Carol's bestie, Michele Monson. Carol's father Victor and brother Bill and sister-in-law Sandy came out for it, and my mother also attended, coming up from her home near Riverside where she was living in retirement after her career as a public and school librarian. Gray and Erin, both teens, dressed up in their finest. Tom and Mary Malone, old friends of Carol's from Palos Verdes came up for it. Carol was raised a Catholic and I was raised as a Methodist, but neither of us practiced a faith. We married in a civil ceremony officiated by a judge.

We honeymooned in Cabo San Lucas in a casita literally in the sand on the beach facing the iconic sea arch off the Cabo headland. Keith Richardson (of the Rolling Stones) and his entourage in the resort next door created a stir of excitement, but otherwise it was an idyllic honeymoon—easy, beautiful, and relaxed—until it was marred by "the Mexican problem." I rented a car one day so that we could tour the area, and, in the town of Cabo San Lucas, I pulled into the central "square," an intersection of dirt roads lined with one story adobe buildings, and turned right. Immediately, a ragged-looking policemen appeared on foot in the street blocking my way. He indicated a nearby tree, high up on which a board painted with an arrow pointing the other direction hung by wires from a nail. Gotcha! I was going the wrong way on a one-way "street." The policeman took my driver's license and told me I could pick it up at the police station when I paid the fine. I knew what was happening. This was Mexico after all. I had walked, well, driven, into their money trap.

We finished our drive around Cabo, seeing the most abject poverty either of us had ever seen with naked children sitting in the dirt outside one room adobe shacks with no doors. These places were within a few hundred yards of the luxurious resorts catering to foreigners. The contrast was jarring and because of it, we could never thereafter get comfortable with the idea of a vacation in a Cabo resort.

When I turned the car in, I walked to the police station, another one-story, adobe building with bars on some of the windows that revealed jail cells. Inside, I showed my ticket to a man in plain clothes at a counter and waited to see how much they were going to gouge me. He presented me with a bill for around two hundred dollars, in pesos, but in two increments. I saw that I was being fined twice. One violation was for going the wrong way on a one-way street. The second was for making an illegal U-turn when I turned around! I exploded before I had a chance to think it over. The second fine was bulls**t, and I said so to the man. He didn't speak English, so there followed a brief search for someone who did. I angrily pointed to the first citation, and yelled, "*esto si*," and at the second "*esto no!*" My translator and the policemen made hand gestures for me to calm down, indicating that this was a negotiation. I got it, and went stoic again. We settled on a discount for the second offense, and I paid the fine in pesos. They gave me back my driver's license. I vowed never to rent a car in Mexico again, if, that is, I ever returned to Mexico. Carol was relieved when I got back, saying she wondered if she would have to visit me in jail.

After the honeymoon, we settled into our two jobs routine. A number of years followed characterized by my working hard at APL and Carol reinventing herself as a head hunter in the field of health care professionals—quite an achievement given her lack of any prior nexus to health care. Nevertheless, she succeeded at it. We began to take long annual vacations to excellent destinations such as Santa Fe, New Orleans, the

Florida Keys, Italy, France, England, Hawaii, Tahiti, Australia, and sub-Saharan Africa. One vacation I took with Gray for his graduation from UCLA—a 12 day oar boat trip on the Colorado River through the Grand Canyon. It was the experience of a lifetime for both of us. Because of the splendor of the country we traversed and the amazing geology of the site, Gray acquired a life-long passion for outdoor adventures.

One year I received an invitation from my daughter Erin to attend "Dads' Weekend" at the University of Colorado where she was a Delta Gamma. I had, in my work preoccupations, missed the opportunity during her freshman and sophomore years, but her junior year I went. What a hoot! A tailgate party in a parking lot before the Big Eight football game in which we stood in a lovely, heavy, snow fall and drank beers and ate snacks with our daughters and the other dads; standing on the stadium seats throughout the football game watching oranges being tossed from the stands onto the field whenever a notable play happened (the ranking team in the Big Eight Conference went to the Orange Bowl in Florida and CU was a contender;) multiple visits to bars in town to meet and greet acquaintances and fraternize with the other dads; and the final, most important event of the weekend, namely, taking our daughters shopping on the last day to make sure they were properly provisioned for the balance of the academic year. I couldn't wait for the next, equally fun Dad's Weekend Erin's senior year.

Among my early legal adventures at APL, three colorful incidents stand out as noteworthy and illustrate why maritime ("admiralty") law is a fascinating field in which to practice. Six months after joining APL, Mount Saint Helens, a volcano in the Cascades Range in southern Washington erupted, creating a huge cloud of ash that carpeted the whole Columbia River basin. We had two "break-bulk" ships in Portland load-ing bulk grain cargoes at the time. It rains in the Pacific Northwest, and a small river called the Toutle River ran down the flank of Mt. St. Helens and discharged into the Columbia River. The ash from the eruption de-posited a vast amount of sediment into the Toutle, which, in turn, deposited it into the Columbia River seventeen miles downstream, com-pletely silting up the ship channel from there to the mouth of the Columbia at Astoria. Mother Nature trumped our ship schedules, and the ships sat in Portland for two months while the Corps of Engineers dredged the Columbia River channel twenty four seven to make it navi-gable again. Meanwhile the cargo interests lodged big claims with us for delay and deterioration of the grain while sitting in a clammy ship's hold in humid weather all that time. However, the cargo owners had declined the option we gave them to unload the grain at their expense and put it back in the grain silos at the port for safe storage. That was the first of two cases in quick succession in which I was able to use the Act of God defense successfully.

The second one involved another bulker in Alaska. One of our ships was moored to an industrial pier near Homer on the Cook Inlet side of the Kenai Peninsula discharging a load of bulk chemicals. The company whose pier it was utilized a conveyor belt with buckets on it housed in a steel truss viaduct and a nose end that mechanically lowered into the ship's hold to scoop out the chemical compound it had purchased. It was springtime and the Cook Inlet contained countless ice floes as the shore ice melted in the warmer weather. On this particular day, a strong westerly wind arose pushing the ice floes in the inlet toward the shore of the peninsula at which our ship was berthed. At the same time, the notorious Cook Inlet tide (ranged up to twenty feet) began to flood.

The consequence of all this was that a miles-long raft of solid ice formed along the eastern shore of the peninsula and began to surge north with the incoming tide. Our ship was at the end of the industrial dock which protruded a more than hundred meters out into the Cook Inlet and in the path of the raft of ice that no one noticed coming. The mass of ice struck the south-facing stern of the ship and shoved the ship forward along its berth, snapping the two steel spring lines and six thick hemp mooring lines like they were string. The nose of the shore side conveyor assembly inserted down into one of the cargo holds was mangled as the ship heaved against it and moved away, scraping the conveyor snout against the ship's gear as the ship went with the ice. Hundreds of thousands of dollars in damages were incurred by the ship and the dock equipment as a result. We claimed ship repair damages against the pier owner for failing to provide a safe berth as required by the charter. The pier owner claimed against the ship and APL for its losses to the conveyor equipment for failure to safely deliver the cargo and negligent navigation. Our defense was *force majeure*, or irresistible force of nature, a defense under the charter party. The case settled with each party accepting its own losses, but the pier owner suffered the greatest damage and it paid a per diem charge for the delay to the ship while it waited at anchor until the pier was sufficiently repaired to unload the rest of the cargo.

Yet another Alaska project occupied a good deal of my early days at APL. It involved building a new dock and terminal at Dutch Harbor, Alaska on the island of Unalaska midway out into the Aleutian Islands chain. The Aleut Indian tribe that owned the land needed a terminal over which to ship its annual seafood catch. This cargo moved in refrigerated containers to Japan, the biggest market for the high end seafood caught in the Behring Sea. Salmon, king crab, black cod and other highly desirable fish products were caught by the local fishing fleet and delivered to the floating and land-based processors in Dutch Harbor. APL was eager to receive and transport that high priced cargo and had the refrigerated containers and ships available to do it. Unalaska sat just on the Great Circle route from Seattle to Japan, and our ships were sailing past it every week. A joint venture terminal was a win-win for both APL and the local fishing industry.

So, the project fell to one Orville (Larry) Creech, an APL terminal operations executive, to make it happen. Creech was crucial to the effort because he was a half-blood Indian from one of the Pacific Northwest tribes, and the Aleut Indians of Unalaska were wary of doing any business with the white man that involved getting control over any of their land. No outside company had ever done a land deal with the locals. So, Creech began to romance the locals about a new terminal with a container gantry crane, and they said they could get tax exempt municipal bonds to finance the native Alaskan development. I hired a Seattle law firm to draft a thirty year terminal lease for a terminal to be built with the proceeds of bonds guaranteed by the state. There followed a long and tortured negotiation of the terms of the lease with drafts mailed back and forth and conference calls to iron out our differences, and finally, we had an agreement. We were ready to commence construction and APL would manage the project as lessee of the land.

One of the requirements of the state before it would issue tax exempt bonds was that the City of Unalaska pass a resolution affirming that the project would benefit the city and its inhabitants. So, off I go with Larry

Creech to Dutch Harbor, flying from Oakland to Seattle, then to Anchorage, then to Kodiak, then to Cold Bay, then to Dutch Harbor on progressively smaller airplanes. At Kodiak, the crew told us that we would have to get off the plane. It seemed that the company's other plane had just burned up in Adak, an Aleutian island at the end of the chain and within sight of Russia. They needed to bring passengers back from Adak, we were told. A handful of passengers did get off, but Creech jollied the crew into letting us stay on as far as Dutch Harbor. By then, Creech was well known to all of the crews. So then we flew the leg from Kodiak to Cold Bay, an airport consisting of a landing strip and two Quonset huts, one of which was the public terminal.

We got off the plane and walked around piles of snow to the "terminal" for a bathroom break, and noticed that there were big holes in the sheet rock of the walls at the entry and a door was swinging on one of its hinges with the wooden door jamb shattered. I asked a young woman at the coffee counter what happened, and she shrugged and said "Oh, a griz got in here last night." I noticed that there was some writing on the corner of one lens of her eyeglasses. I squinted to look at it and it said "Boots." "It's my name," she said.

We took off again for Dutch Harbor a few hours later and made a hair-raising landing alongside the face of a big sheer cliff out of which the airstrip at Dutch Harbor had been bulldozed. Another Quonset hut airport terminal greeted us. This one had a big sheet of plywood over the entry with the exoskeleton of a king crab mounted on it. Below the crab, the sign read: "The reason why we are here." Walking the grounds later, I found that the air strip was a surviving part of a U.S. Army Air Force Base from WW II. There were buildings around it in various states of ruin, windowless, and weathered grey. But the fifty year old wood was not rotted at all. Even the square-headed nails were only slightly rusted. I was told that the extreme weather acts as a preservative for the building materials. Storms knocked the buildings down, but the materials were preserved.

I learned that the Army Air Force had an air station there during the war, and that Dutch Harbor was the only other American territory that Japan attacked when they attacked Pearl Harbor. It was a bombing raid, but the bombs were dropped in poor visibility, and they missed the base altogether.

Creech and I met with the Unalaska tribal elders and their legal counsel go over the process to make sure everyone was agreed on the closing. We prepared the city council resolution affirming the project and, to expedite things, Creech and I set about getting the signatures of the five city council members. The first one was working in a fish processing plant, and we interrupted his work long enough for him to take off his fish processing gloves to sign the resolution. The next three were found in tribal offices doing desk work. The fifth and final councilman we had to chase down over the gravel roads outside town. He was the school bus driver, and we got his signature parked along a country road where we pulled him over.

The closing came off without a hitch, and APL thereafter took possession of the lease parcel while I returned to Oakland. The company then brought in soils engineers, architects, dredges and builders to build the wharf, container yard and office and shop buildings that would accommodate APL's line haul containerships on their eastbound voyages along the Great Circle route. Despite the severe climate and occasional high seas, the construction project went well, with a single exception.

Early on, we chartered a large oceangoing barge in Seattle to carry all the construction materials needed, lashing it on the deck of the barge and stowing the perishable equipment and materials in a tall stack of containers that covered most of the deck. The barge was then towed to Alaska by a powerful ocean-going tugboat with twin screws. As the tug and tow approached the Aleutians in severe weather, the tug lost one of its engines. The cyclonic winds of the storm were pushing the south side of the barge which, given the large stack of containers piled three and four high, created a sail effect that pushed the barge to the north faster than the tug could travel on one engine. The barge eventually overtook the tug and threatened to drag the tug under. At the last minute and to avoid a complete disaster, the tug severed the tow line to the barge, just as the vessels reach the gap between Unalaska Island and its neighbor, thus allowing the barge and all the construction materials to drift into the Behring Sea out of control. The tug and crew were saved, but the barge was adrift. What to do?

Larry Creech, who wore cowboy boots and a ten gallon hat on the jobsite in Alaska, chartered the largest fishing trawler he could find and set out after the barge. When they caught up to the barge, Creech was famously observed standing on the prow of the trawler with a lasso until he got it over one of the deck cleats of the barge. With multiple lines, they were able to control the barge that way for a couple of days until a salvage tug arrived from Kodiak and brought the barge safely in to Dutch Harbor. Larry Creech was thereafter known in APL circles as "Lawrence of Alaska."

The terminal was completed and, when I retired from APL twenty years later, had been generating extremely lucrative cargo for APL all that time. The Native American fishery had prospered greatly and the lease had been renewed and extended well into the future.

Meantime, something novel was happening in shipping. "Multi-modalism" was developing at warp speed, and APL was writing the book on it. In the early 1960s, containerization had been pioneered by Malcom MacLean, a trucker in the Southeastern United States. The U.S. Army had invented the "CONEX box", an 8.5 foot by 6 foot by 7 foot steel box with reinforced corners that would permit stacking the boxes and locking them together for transporting military cargo and household goods on trucks, trains and ships. What MacLean did was engineer the ideal size of container to fit the Puerto Rico trade, that is, to maximize its carrying capacity for the particular cargoes that moved between the Continental U.S. and Puerto Rico. It was designed to fit on a skeletal chassis to make up a roadworthy trailer to be driven over the highway. MacLean came up with a steel container 8 feet wide, 8.5 feet high and 35 feet long. Then he bought some ships and converted them with under-deck cell guides 35 feet apart, allowing his containers to be dropped below deck into the cells and stowed on deck in stacks lashed together at the corner castings. By doing so, he created a lot of extra carrying capacity aboard ship by using the air space above deck, while eliminating the handling of cargo at both ends and with it, the risk of damage to or theft of the cargo. His company, Sea-Land Service was born.

Matson followed closely on the heels of Sea-Land by engineering the optimal container for cargo moving in the Hawaii trade. Matson's containers were the same height and width to meet highway standards but only 24 feet long and the sides and top were made of lighter aluminum to carry more cargo by weight. I loaded Matson containers to and from Matson ships configured for 24 foot containers when I was a stevedore superintendent at Matson Terminals. They were specialized to accommodate bulk materials in tanks, refrigerated cargo in insulated and refrigerated containers and flatracks to carry long, heavy or over-height objects. We even had a "cowtainer" in which twelve head of cattle could stand inside and the sides of the container could be opened on deck into a manger by which a stock tender aboard ship could feed the cattle during their voyage. The big island of Hawaii had a few large herds of livestock for both fresh beef and dairy purposes and shipped live cattle regularly.

Shoreside, the marine terminals became vast parking lots for empty and loaded containers, and the wharf area was equipped with giant gantry cranes which would lift a container loaded with twenty three tons of cargo with one lift. Containerization was light years more efficient than the old "break bulk" operation where individual crates and boxes and drums and vehicles, etc., were manually loaded directly into and out of the ship's holds and had to be stored in a covered building on the dock.

Using the technology Sea-land pioneered, containerized cargo could be placed onto a chassis and trucked over the road. But to move cargo long distances overland, rail transport was more efficient than trucking. Containerized cargo arriving from overseas had for years been manually unloaded from the container and then transloaded into railroad boxcars. That largely defeated the efficiencies of the container and allowed pilferage and damage. To meet the demands of shipping companies carrying an ever-increasing amount of cargo from Asia, railroads quickly began providing flatcars that they had been using for their "piggyback" service (truck trailers were placed on flatcars and transported by rail long distances) in order to transport ocean containers sitting flat on and lashed to the flatcar cross country.

When I had just arrived at APL, containers moved on individual rail flatcars in onesies and twosies and just made up a few cars on a train consisting mostly of boxcars carrying domestic freight. In the course of passing through railroad switching yards as the trains moved cross country, flatcars carrying APL containers would sometimes get "lost." Railroads kept track of railcars, not containers on railcars. In winter, the flatcars would sometimes sit for days in switching yards freezing the cargo inside. And the transcontinental trip took many days, even weeks to reach the main population centers in the country, namely the corridor from Boston to Washington DC ("Boswash").

Bruce Seaton hired a railroad executive named Don Orris to head up our "intermodal" (ship to truck and rail) operations, a misnomer because the operations were not concerned with movements between carriers ("inter" modal) but rather with carriage on several modes of transport ("multi" modal.) Don became my client.

By 1980, every liner shipping company had converted to containerized operations and had standardized the size of container equipment to two lengths, 20 footers and 40 footers. The odd-sized containers of Sea-Land (35') and Matson (24') and Sea-Train (27') had served their purpose initially, but became obsolete as standardized containers were transloaded from ship to ship and carrier to carrier as they moved around the world. Containers and terminal handling equipment and container ships had to all conform to standard sizes.

Don Orris commenced negotiations with the major western railroads in the southern (Southern Pacific and Santa Fe RRs), central (Union Pacific, Denver & Rio Grande RRs) and northern (Burlington Northern RR) corridors to haul unit trains consisting of only APL's containerized import cargo. In the northeastern Boswash corridor, the destination railroads were Conrail and CSX and in the southeast it was CSX and the Norfolk Southern. Orris wanted uniquely designed flatcars that locked into the bottom corner castings of containers to secure them instead of labor intensive lashing containers to a piggyback flatcar. Lastly, he wanted APL to be the master carrier that dealt with both the shipper (seller) and the consignee (buyer) of the cargo, thus making the railroads a subcontractor. The railroads had to swallow hard before accepting that subservient role, as they considered the shippers and consignees to be their customers in the rail move.

The Santa Fe was as bureaucratic as the government and outright refused to play this new role. The Southern Pacific was reluctant. The Burlington was slow to return phone calls. Conrail was testing the wind. However, the Union Pacific was the first to face the fact that the biggest volume of transcontinental rail traffic consisted of imports arriving on the U.S. Pacific Coast destined to Boswash, and the routing of all that cargo among railroads was controlled by the shipping companies. APL was the biggest transpacific carrier and controlled the biggest block of cargo. The Union Pacific wanted to partner with APL and grow with the trade.

Just how much it would grow would surprise all the railroads, but the UP saw the potential first and wanted to be well positioned for it.

So, Don Orris and his staff, working with their counterparts at the UP, put together a concept for a through route from LA to Boswash consisting of the Union Pacific, the Denver, Rio Grande and Western, Chicago & North Western and finally Conrail into the northeast. I was Orris' lawyer. It was up to me to come up with novel contracts by which each railroad in the chain would agree to be bound by the liability and performance terms of APL's contract of carriage and receive a negotiated division of the through freight charges. These operations were largely exempt from the century-old regulations of the Interstate Commerce Commission which had jurisdiction over railroads because, during those Reagan/Gingrich years, the ICC was eliminated and its functions either deregulated or transferred to the newly constituted Surface Transport Board with a smaller regulatory role. Public common carriage had evolved into private contract carriage. It was the Wild West.

My expertise ran toward contracts of carriage, among other things, and so I modified APL's traditional bill of lading to contemplate a unified through rate for freight charges, and for APL to contractually assume liability for the through transport, even for loss or damage to cargo occurring in the custody of connecting railroads and truckers. In turn, APL would enter into connecting carrier agreements (drafted by me) which required the connecting carriers to indemnify (reimburse) APL for any claims APL paid for damage done by connecting carriers. If it could not be determined which carrier had custody of cargo when it was damaged, the liability was apportioned. This was a big change in the way things were done and the way transportation companies were structured with their own legal, insurance and claims departments. Even the insurance industry had to accommodate their policies to these new contractually assumed liabilities and cross-indemnities.

Armed with drafts of these new agreements, we went on the road as the APL team to sell all the railroads on this new way of doing things. We knew that if we could put together one major transpacific/transcontinental, one-stop shipping arrangement, the Asian cargo sellers and their American buyer customers would flock to APL's first class, simplified service. If APL could establish credibility, shippers and consignees could dispense with bank letters of credit, a source of delay and expense. At that point, all other railroads in all other routes to BosWash would have to yield or be left behind. And that is exactly what happened. APL's route to the East Coast using the Union Pacific, Denver & Rio Grande, Chicago and Northwestern and Contrail railroads was an instant success. It became the gold standard. Beginning in the early 80s, the volume of imports arriving at West Coast ports escalated rapidly. By the 90s, the volume of cargo was huge, and it was controlled by the shipping companies, the largest of which by far was APL. And the legal structure worked.

The Southern Pacific and Santa Fe railroads were slow to size up the situation and were left without any through transport arrangements with large shipping companies. As a result, they lost so much import business that they were undergoing orderly liquidation. The SP tried to merge with the Santa Fe, but the merger was denied by the ICC as anticompetitive. (I, as counsel for APL, opposed the merger in the ICC proceedings.) The SP finally was allowed to con-ditionally merge with the Union Pacific. (I also argued APL's position in that proceeding contending that the approval should be granted only on the condition that the southern route across the U.S. be continued.) That condition was imposed on the merger that was granted. The Santa Fe was the last to find a home as a failing company. It was acquired by the Burlington Northern, thus becoming the BNSF that "proudly sponsors" Public Television as I write and sits in the portfolio of Warren Buffet's financial empire, Berkshire Hathaway. When the dust settled, APL had access to transcontinental routes across the northern, central and southern rail corridors over which it could route its major market share of imports throughout the United States in the most efficient manner and under contractual arrangements with all participating railroads that gave APL complete control over the entire multimodal supply chain. That did not give APL complete market power, however, as its competitors simply copied APL's service using the same railroads. And the railroads were happy to give all of our implementing contracts to our competitors to gain additional freight. However, APL was the big dog.

Another unforeseen impact of these events was transpiring along with the multimodal handling of America's imports. The conventional hardware of the railroads disappeared. They stopped buying boxcars.

They bought or leased specialized container-carrying flatcars in greater and greater numbers as imports from China exploded. They trip-leased the empty containers from us on the Atlantic Coast and used them to carry domestic rail cargo back to the Pacific Coast instead of boxcars that required cargo handling in and out. The empty containers would then be returned to us at our Pacific Coast ports (at no cost to us) for movement back to Asia with agricultural products grown in the rich and productive citrus groves and farms of the San Joachim and Sacramento Valleys.

The final evolution of multimodalism was the use of more specialized rail flatcars that could carry ocean containers stacked two high, thus almost doubling the efficiency of the unit trains. To accomplish such "stack train" operations, the railroads would have to raise the clearance of thousands of railroad tunnels throughout the country—a herculean undertaking. But they did it and amortized the cost over the millions upon millions of container units they carried. APL absorbed those costs and passed them along to their shippers. Cargo owners were happy to go along to avoid the much longer all-water route to the U.S. Atlantic Coast through the Panama Canal. The less frequent schedules offered by the few all-water, smaller, slower shipping companies that got left behind in the multimodal sweepstakes were simply non-competitive.

So, as we travel the country by car today and stop at a railroad crossing to wait for a freight train to pass, we look at long unit trains of articulated double stack flatcars groaning with ocean containers rolling by marked "Maersk," "MSC," "CMA-CGM," "Mitsui O-S-K Line," "China Ocean Shipping," etc. These liner shipping companies are heirs of APL's innovations. Gone are the colorfully marked boxcars with old familiar railroad brands like "Erie-Lackawanna—the Route of Phoebe Snow," "Rock Island Lines," "Kansas City Southern," and the rearing figure of a black horse on the Norfolk Southern cars—all gone. The only way to know what railroad is hauling the train is to look at the engines. They will be marked "Union Pacific," "BNSF," "Conrail," "CSX," etc.

Ironically, APL containers are rarely seen nowadays on stack trains. As is more fully described in Chapter 13, APL was sold in 1997 to Neptune Orient Lines, a Singapore government-owned company, and after several more years, resold by NOL to CMA-CGM, a Swiss-owned combination of former French lines. However, lots of CMA-CGM containers are visible on the stack trains, and CMA-CGM are the owners of the old APL container fleet still in use but being phased out as they reach their economic life.

CHAPTER 13

APL (PART II)

In 1983, I received a wad of cash from the sale of vested stock options triggered by a change of control of Natomas (APL's parent) bought by Diamond Shamrock, another oil company. APL was spun off as a new public company. Carol and I invested it in a pair of flats on Telegraph Hill in the City at 364-366 Lombard Street. We updated the apartments slightly, and rented the two units out to two groups of singles. The upper unit had some views and commanded more rent, and the lower was taken by none other than daughter Erin and her friend Mary Waters. Since graduating from the University of Colorado at Boulder, Erin had been leading a nomadic existence as a political and public relations consultant in Denver and Fresno and had settled in the City working for a phone conference calling firm as a sales rep. It was an ideal location for the girls, and they became friends with the group in the upper unit. It was a fun and carefree time as young singles in the City. Each of the girls met their future husbands during that time.

With another infusion of stock option cash two or three years later (my title was Assistant General Counsel and about to become Vice President and General Counsel with the departure of Richard Tavrow in a corporate reorganization) Carol and I decided to renovate our San Anselmo house. A realtor friend in the city who sold us the Telegraph Hill flats recommended an architect she knew, and we invited him over for a consultation about the project. We had a great first meeting with him and asked him to be our architect on the project. We adjourned and convened a follow-up meeting a week or so later to look at some concept drawings he'd prepared. In that conversation, either Carol or I mentioned that we owned a couple of flats on Telegraph Hill in the City that were being rented. He dropped his pen, sat back in his chair and looked at us. "You own a couple of flats WHERE?" he asked.

His meaning was made plain by that one question. We should be talking to him about renovating that property and moving there. I looked at Carol, whose countenance resembled a bank of stadium lights at the notion of living on Telegraph Hill. Since North Beach and Telegraph Hill was one of the City neighborhoods that I *would* live in, I figured it was time for me to make good on my promise that "someday" we would live in the City, a prospect that had never ceased to be Carol's dream.

We thereafter met Paul at the Lombard Street flats and began the process of designing the reconstruction of the two flats into a four story single family house, a project he loved. It was the first of many meetings over the course of the next year and a half, usually held at one of the tables of a bar on upper Grant Street. We agreed on a design, bid the job among a number of contractors and selected one, listed our San Anselmo house for sale and sold it, and moved into a small house (owned by the managing partner of the San Francisco 49er football team) in Cow Hollow for the duration of the construction.

Just before we moved from San Anselmo, Carol spotted a dark growth on my back which I couldn't see. I had suffered blistering sunburns a number of times as a youth working shirtless on summer jobs at the dairy farm, on pipelines, and on seismograph crews, and I had a variety of skin tags, moles, keretoses and other evidence of sun damage to show for it. Carol badgered me into seeing a dermatologist until I did. She likely saved my life. The growth was biopsied, and it was melanoma.

The biopsy showed that it had eaten through the underside of my skin and technically could have spread, although it didn't show up anywhere else in a PET scan. If any melanoma cells had gotten into my lymph system, they would have migrated to lymph nodes and been temporarily captured there. The doctors set up a surgical procedure with the UCSF Medical Center's melanoma team. They incised my back, cutting a small, football shaped biscuit of skin surrounding the melanoma from my back. Then they injected the site with both dye and a radioactive substance and watched with their instruments to see where both went. Both the dye and the radioactive solution migrated over the next hour to the lymph nodes in my right armpit. I was then anesthetized and they surgically removed the lymph nodes in question. I was then good to go.

The melanoma never reappeared in any form, but I continued to receive annual phone calls from the team for five years. I represented a good outcome for their procedure, so they wanted to keep me in their statistical base as such.

During that time, my first grandchild, Brayden Rose was born on September 16, 1996 to my son Gray and daughter-in-law Laura in Los Angeles. While I'd been having my career, my son Gray had launched his own and been wildly successful. He had moved up in a more or less straight line from disc jockey for the campus radio station at UCLA, to technical services jobs at Cannon films, then Pathe Films, and finally MGM studios with custody of MGM's vast film li-brary. Along the way, he married his sweetheart Laura and before too long, we had arrived at the blessed event.

Three weeks after Brayden was born, on November 4th and three days after my melanoma excision, my daughter Erin and her fiancée Eric Fish got married. Carol held baby Brayden while I performed my role as giver-away-of-the-bride at the wedding. I didn't want to color any of those festivities with the melanoma story, so Carol and I just kept quiet. Besides, it was over.

That New Years Eve of 1996, Carol and I bought a bottle of Dom Perignon champagne and a box of See's chocolates and let ourselves into the new house just before midnight. "Villa Lombard's" rough construc-tion had been completed, and the roof, windows and doors were in. We made our way up the stairs in the ample ambient light of the City coming through the skylights over the dining room and French doors in the kitchen. I pulled two folding chairs up to the lone sawhorse in the kitchen area and opened the bottle of champers while Carol unpacked two flutes and the chocolates onto the sawhorse. At the stroke of mid-night, with the Coit Tower bells heralding in the year 1997, we toasted each other, our good fortune, the new house, the new grandbaby, our new son-in-law, and the coming year.

We moved our household goods from the rental house and the fur-niture in storage into Villa Lombard (it had an Italianesque design) in June of 1997. Carol's nephew Michael and his wife Jennifer were our neighbors down the street. They had stayed with us in the San Anselmo house when they first emigrated from New Hampshire to find work in Foodie City. We four subsequently had a great time haunting the North Beach coffee shops and restaurants and sharing bottles of Chianti at the Villa Lombard kitchen table on Friday nights.

For the next three years, we lived the sweet City life. A short commute to work, theater and symphony performances, San Francisco Giants baseball games (Carol cared nothing for baseball until she witnessed the amazing performances of Barry Bonds at the new ballpark, thereafter becoming a superfan,) dining at every trendy new restaurant that got good press and at our old sentimental favorites, working hard at our respective jobs, enjoying our globe-trotting vacation travels, and getting to know our grandchild Brayden and new Fish grandchildren Lauren Elizabeth and Julia Gail.

One night in 2001, flush from another payout of APL bonus money after a good year, we decided to host a get-together in Tuscany for both of our families. My kids and grandkids and Carol's siblings and their kids were all invited to join us at a large villa we rented in the village of Panzano in the Chianti region of Tuscany for two weeks in September. We received no regrets; everyone was coming.

When September came, we all found our individual flights to Florence and made our way to the Villa Santa Lucia di Sopra on a hill outside Panzano with a valley view marked by the estate of Giovanni da Verrazano in the distance. Verrazano was an explorer whose expedition in 1524 to the Atlantic Coast of America, included New York Harbor. The Verrazano Narrows Bridge today spans the narrows between Brooklyn and Staten Island.

We all piled into our rooms in the villa and, over the course of the first week, separately and in groups, explored the town of Panzano (the famous Florentine Steak was the creation of a butcher in Panzano), nearby Greve, the wine capitol of Chianti, the nearby villages of Castellina and Rada, and of course, the twin cultural magnets of Tuscany, the Medici towns of Florence (Firenze) and Sienna. Farther afield, there were day trips to Pisa, Vinci and Lucca. We had a long series of wonderful touring days, capped by large, boisterous dinners back at the villa. Carol's family was, after all, Italian. To ice the cake, the estate made a Chianti that carried the house label of Maxim's in Paris. It was available to us in the cellar of the villa for US $5 per bottle. Our cups ranneth over, so to speak.

When the disaster struck, a line of Kahlil Gibran later came to mind: "Such prophesies of joy awaken the toad who sleeps away the past under the hearthstone, light forsaken." One perfect early autumn day as a group of us were sauntering around Florence, eating gelato, strangers began to come up to us with deeply anxious faces. Gesturing, they invited us to go into a nearby bar and see the TV news. On the Italian station Rai News, we could see a dark, grainy image of a plane crashing into one of the World Trade Center buildings. It was September 11, 2001.

It wasn't long before everyone staying at the villa, wherever they were in Florence, heard about the twin towers attack and made their way back to the villa where we watched the poor coverage of the dreadful New York scene on Rai News, in Italian, not really knowing what had happened. It took a couple of days of scouring the Paris edition of the NY Herald Tribune and the London papers and CNN before we caught up on what was known. Carol's fifteen year old nephew Eric was the first of us who could pronounce Al Qaida. My daughter-in-law Laura's sister worked on Capitol Hill in Washington, and Laura knew that a plane had attacked a site in Washington. She didn't know where, and she couldn't reach her sister. She wanted to go home immediately, but the planes were all grounded. Because the planes were grounded, Carol's niece Alyssa and her husband who were to fly out of Logan Airport in Boston to join us for the second week in the villa were unable to make the trip. Logan was shut down tight because one of the hijacked planes had departed from Logan.

There was a country house next to our villa that was being renovated by a crew of Palestinians, and we used to run into them at the tabac store in Panzano near the bus stop. A day or two after the attacks, we heard them in the tabac store laughing and celebrating the attacks until the owner of the store kicked them out. One night when we got back to the villa after taking the bus into Florence for the day, I found that the side of my rental car had been crushed. Since it could only have happened that day, I concluded that the Palestinian crew working next door had deliberately run into my car with their payloader because they knew we were Americans. They were of course nowhere to be found, and I had no evidence. I had chosen all risk insurance for the rented car so I let Hertz pay for the damage repairs.

In town, worried locals asked us if America would start a war. The local church had a sign on the door reading "Pray for Peace."

By the time the airports in America opened up and the planes started flying again, we were nearing the end of our lease. Gray, Laura and Brayden flew back immediately, but the rest of us stayed and caught our booked flights just a few days later. The rest of our stay in Tuscany was colored by all the questions raised by the attack and the loss of life that was now being reported in great detail. There were no words then, and there are none now. It was a great tragedy that ended American innocence about the depth and quality of Sunni Muslim fundamentalist terrorism. Within a week or two, President George W. Bush ordered the carpet bombing of known Al Qaida locations in Afghanistan. Those locations were deep in sparsely populated mountainous locations and had little effect. Not long after that, despite there being no demonstrable connection between the Sunni terrorist group Al Qaida and the Shi'ite regime in Iraq, the Bush administration initiated a gratuitous and ill-conceived war against Iraq and invaded it. The adverse consequences of that war and its destabilizing effects in the Middle East are still being felt today as I write this.

Back in San Francisco, Carol resumed her headhunting work, and I commuted to Oakland by car from San Francisco as I had done from San Anselmo, albeit via a shorter, more direct route across the Bay Bridge. However, a sea change was evolving in the nature of America's major trade lane.

Continuously since the mid-1980s, the transpacific trade had been fundamentally changing. Through the early 1980s, APL's ships were full in both directions, indicating that America's foreign trade was balanced, both in terms of value and volume. Those were the halcyon days of abundant union jobs paying living wages and a robust manufacturing sector of our economy. In the mid-eighties, however, danger signs were already beginning to appear and liner shipping was a reliable leading indicator of the developing problem.

During the decade of the 1970s, the Japanese *kieritsu*—vertically integrated corporate conglomerates—working in conjunction with the Japanese government (together, "Japan, Inc.")—set the centerpiece of Japan's industrial policy, namely, to promote the two major Japanese industries of automobile and consumer electronics manufacturing through exports. In the space of that single decade, Japanese dumping practices, destroyed the *entire* American consumer electronics industry and took a substantial share of the American market for automobiles. In doing so, America's trade balance with Japan shifted to a $100 billion per year deficit. APL's ships continued to be full in both directions for another four or five years, but the average value of goods being exported from America began to slide as high value exports like electronics and car parts shifted to lower value raw materials. In the late 1980s, our ships were beginning to reflect the growing trade imbalance by westbound sailings that were not fully loaded. The volume and value of American exports continued to decline and the volume and value of imports from Asia, preponderantly from China, increased. Ships sailed westbound with less and less containerized cargo, and returned "down to her marks" full. Something was going on. Class warfare was beginning in America. American consumers had become estranged from American workers.

As Japan made great inroads introducing electronic goods and automobiles manufactured in Japan into the American market, American manufacturers of those products were finding it hard to compete with their lower-cost foreign competitors. American manufacturers appealed to the American government for help in resisting foreign dumping practices by Japan and countering the growing trade imbalance with China. The manufacturers, however, received little support from successive administrations, both Republican and Democratic. Manufacturers correctly came to understand that consumerism trumped industrial policy politically every time.

Confirming that bias, bumper stickers that said "Buy American" were ignored, even laughed at, by consumers. Motorola, GE, Philco, Sylvania, Emerson, RCA, Westinghouse, Admiral, Magnavox, National Cash Register and many other electronics firms withered and closed their plants. Detroit lost market share through dumping and the management technique of "Quality" ironically taught to them by an American business consultant named Deming and universally adopted by Japan, Inc.'s *kieritsu*. The antitrust policies set up in post-war Japan were ignored when the American administration ended.

American manufacturers saw what was happening and understood that help was not coming from the country of their domicile—the country that these same companies and their workers saved through their extraordinary efforts during World War II. American business is nothing if not nimble, so it reacted the only way it could. Manufacturers closed their rust belt manufacturing facilities and abandoned their workers and the communities that had supported them. In doing so, they escaped costly land use and environmental regulations, dissolved their operations, sold their assets, and moved their manufacturing offshore.

American-owned manufacturing firms are now perfectly happy being joint venturers with citizens of China, employers of much lower paid Chinese workers, and non-contributors to the planet's environmental best practices. They are able to profit as Chinese entities exporting to America, something they had been unable to do in their home country.

All of this was progressively measured on APL's ships over the course of three decades as cargo volumes and values shifted 180 degrees. By the turn of the twenty first century, little of value was exported from America because little of value was made in America. America's major moving export commodities were wastepaper, scrap metals, bulk chemicals, bulk agricultural commodities, and softwood lumber—all low valued commodities and all in relatively small quantities. At APL, we disparagingly referred to these cargoes as "rocks and trees." APL's big, increasingly empty ships in the westbound direction carried this meagre menu of cargo outbound to Asia at very low rates. In contrast, those containerships increasingly sailed full from Chinese ports to America groaning with high value cargoes of every description.

In theory, high value commodities would bear a high freight rate, thus making the voyages potentially profitable. In practice, the transpacific shipping companies of the world were so dependent on eastbound traffic to America that they engaged in cutthroat pricing in order to acquire market share. So, Chinese exports to America that should be the fully priced head haul was often priced below cost like the backhaul, thus guaranteeing financial failure.

In the end, despite the victories we had laboriously racked up through unfair trade practices litigation over the years, APL did not make enough money to satisfy the arbitrageurs Hellman and Friedman that controlled the APL Board of Directors, and, in 1997, APL was sold to Neptune Orient Lines, an entity of the Government of Singapore. Under the new ownership, the first casualty within my purview was the end of all proceedings before the FMC and efforts with MarAd and the State Department to eliminate discriminatory restrictions against American shipping companies doing business in China.

The new owners were ethnic Han Chinese and were heavily dependent on China for many things in Singapore, a city which, by its very location, was within the sphere of China's influence. For only one example out of many, if displeased, the PRC could withhold access and landing rights allowing Singapore Airlines to serve Chinese cities.

Anti-discrimination litigation having been a large part of my legal portfolio, and NOL having its own Legal Department for corporate affairs in Singapore, I became surplus. It was a bitter pill for me because I had spent my apex years at the company fighting for a level playing field for the company in China and other Asian countries so that APL could compete with their national flag carriers, only to see APL itself outsourced to Asia. We as a company had lost the fight to survive as a viable American company, and I personally became a casualty.

APL was the first of the three remaining American flag liner carriers in the trade in 1997 to be sold foreign. The other two, Crowley Maritime and Sea-Land Service, were also sold foreign two years later. By 1999, Crowley was sold to Hamburg Sud, a German line, and Sea-Land was sold to Maersk, a Danish line. America, the greatest maritime trading country in the world, was thus left with no merchant fleet of its own to carry its liner foreign commerce.

I was old enough (58) to take retirement, and so I did. Dick Tavrow had already been forced out earlier. The only other maritime lawyer at APL was demoted and assigned to handle legal matters that only required North American legal expertise. I set up my own legal office at 101 California Street in San Francisco (a motor scooter ride from my home on Telegraph Hill.) Through the good offices of its distinguished partner Robert Basseches, I also became "of counsel" for (associated with) the prestigious Washington DC law firm, Shea and Gardner, which had long been APL's outside counsel in Washington. In that capacity I continued to handle APL's legal work referred to me by a severely understaffed legal department.

Two years later, the bean counters in Singapore figured out that they were paying me as outside counsel twice what I had earned as in-house counsel since I charged market-based legal fees as outside counsel. They then ordered that I was to be given no more referred work, as they had "lost face." APL, still overwhelmed with legal work, then referred the work that I had been doing to a Washington law firm which had a much higher overhead and charged much higher rates than I had billed. NOL ended up paying that firm's lawyers *four times* what I had been paid as inside counsel to do their legal work. As I watched that self-defeating drama play out, and as a first hand witness to the willfulness and incompetence of NOL's management, I came to the conclusion that APL's best days were over, and the company would fare no better in the future than NOL's sub-par, minor carrier status that preceded the acquisition of APL had been.

That indeed turned out to be the case. A few years later, to underwrite its money-losing operations, NOL first sold off the multimodal division that I had helped Don Orris establish to a company that Don Orris, also a casualty of APL politics, had independently set up. On the heels of that sale, NOL also sold APL Logistics, our China-based logistics company established after Sea-Land's counsel and I had won the right for our companies to do business in China in litigation before the Federal Maritime Commission and via the resulting bilateral maritime treaty between the U.S. and China. The sale price was a billion dollars. But the money-losing operations continued and the Singapore government forced NOL to ultimately sell the assets of the NOL-APL fleet to CMA-CGM, a closely held, French-based line with a murky pedigree but with access to lots of unidentified capital provided by "Turkish investors."

On the ships of CMA-CGM I have encountered all over the world in my cruising travels, from Singapore to Santarem, Brazil, from Freemantle, Australia to Valparaiso, Chile, and from to Mumbai, India to Rotterdam, I continue to see APL containers still in use in the CMA-CGM fleet.

Just before separating from APL, Carol and I took the most visceral and exciting vacation of our many memorable trips during those years. For our 15th anniversary in October, 1998, we decided to splurge on a trip to sub-Saharan Africa to see the wildlife. Carol arranged for a custom excursion with a South African guide first to Kruger National Park in South Africa, thence to Victoria Falls in Zimbabwe, thence to Pretoria via Botswana on the Blue Train, and lastly to Cape Town and the wine country. That trip subsequently commenced with a too-long trip by a Lufthansa red eye flight from San Francisco to Munich followed by another red eye flight from Munich to Johannesburg plus a connecting flight to Nelspruit, a gateway to Kruger, over two calendar days. We managed it, however, and were met by our guide at the airport in Nelspruit. From there we were driven to our camp at Honey Guide in Mpumalanga province, home of Kruger National Park.

Honey Guide was in the Manyeletti Game Reserve, a section of Kruger Park. Kruger is a Massachusetts-sized reserve on the northeastern border of South Africa, opposite Mozambique. Manyeletti was that part of the Kruger that was reserved during apartheid for the native African population, so the Honey Guide camp was a Hemingway-esque tent camp, much less luxurious than the renowned private game reserves adjacent to Kruger such as Londolozi, Mala Mala, Singita, etc. We thought we should experience both, so we booked Honey Guide as our first stop and Londolozi, a famous leopard viewing reserve, second.

In an interesting bit of public-private cooperation, a number of large privately owned estates border the Kruger Park and have entered into an arrangement with the Park to remove the fence between the Park and their properties. Instead, the private estates erected a fence on the outer boundary of their properties. This had the effect of greatly expanding the area in which the Park's wildlife could range, expanding in turn the animal populations protected in the Park and at the same time give the private game reserve proprietors free access to the Park for their visitors. Win-win.

On the drive through Manyeletti to Honey Guide, we saw elephant, Cape buffalo, wildebeest (gnu), zebra, kudu, waterbuck and impala in close proximity to the road. "Not in Kansas anymore, Toto," I said to Carol transfixed at her car window. We arrived at the Honey Guide camp in the late afternoon of sleep-deprived day two, and very much looking forward to "a bit of lie down." Instead, we were invited to saddle up for the evening game drive. Numb with fatigue, we did. We just had time to drop our gear and change into bush wear before assembling with the other six guests for a Land Rover trek into the bush. The other guests were all Europeans and our guide, Etienne, was a white South African. The complement was completed by a black South African tracker carrying a high caliber rifle. The tracker's name has regrettably been lost. His job was to ride on the hood of the Land Rover in a chair welded onto the hood above the grille to spot animals and their tracks and to protect us. Etienne also had a rifle.

Whatever fatigue we felt vanished at the first nocturnal visit to a water hole. Etienne just drove up to it and parked while we watched through night vision glasses. A beautiful lioness sat regally on one side while on the other, two bull rhino were locked in combat over the contested turf of the water hole. They jousted for a full half hour, heads lowered, parrying each other's horn, until they simply broke it off and walked away leaving us bug-eyed. After the lioness left, waterbuck appeared and hurried down to the water for a wary drink before they too disappeared again into the bush. In a trance, we drove back to camp with just enough energy to enjoy dinner with the others at the long table outside in the warm, dry-season air before turning in. We were escorted to our tent by an armed staff member with the admonition not to leave the tent after dark. A male lion was roaring in the distance proclaiming his turf, and we required no further explanation.

The "tent" was a large, heavy-gauge canvas tent that housed our two cots, two camp chairs, a space for luggage and hanging clothes, and a separate bathroom space with lavatory, toilet and shower stall, all primitive, but clean. The only thing separating us from the lions and hyenas and assorted carnivores in the neighborhood was the thickness of the canvas. But the canvas smelled of oil and so, we were told, the animals did not regard tents or the people in them as food. We fell into our cots that first night and, with the unusual white noise of a lion roaring in the distance, instantly fell asleep.

At 6 am, one of the staff actually played reveille on a bugle by way of a collective alarm clock for the camp. By 6:30, we were assembled at the Land Rover with a filled coffee mug ready for the morning drive on an empty stomach. The morning drive ran from 6:30 to 9:30 with a break for tea and pastry in the bush. Breakfast proper was at 9:45 at the long table. After that, nap/free time, followed by a guided excursion mid-day while the animals rested. Evening game drives were from 5 to 9:30 followed by dinner at the long table. The food was superior camp food—tasty, exotic and plentiful. The warthog and impala stews, loin of kudu, and curried guinea fowl were excellent.

In San Francisco, sunrises and sunsets are orange. In Africa, in the dry season at least, they are red. The sun rises hot and sets late as a ver-million ball through the thorny acacia, overwhelming the brownish-grey landscape. Red sun time is an active time for the animals. Every newly arrived visitor dedicates himself to sighting 'the big five," that is, lion, leopard, elephant, rhino and Cape buffalo. Sightings of these animals must be memorialized in photographs before the visitor can relax. How-ever, the best part of the bush experience came from then on as we spotted the endless variety of exotic animals and birds that somehow live together in the bush. Predators like lions, cheetahs, leopards, hyenas, and wild dogs, and herbivores like elephants, giraffes, rhinos, hippos, and in-numerable varieties of antelope ranging from the majestic sable to the end of the food chain, the impala, replay their eternal dance of death every day. Birds ranging from the dominant martial eagle with a nine foot wingspan to the lovely, speckled guinea fowl abound.

The highlight of the day two morning drive was the lion pride. As our Land Rover approached a dry wash off track, we saw a lioness with a bloody face and two cubs about 75 meters away. She moved toward the wash and we followed until we saw a male lion resting on the other side of the wash. What we did _not_ see, was a second male lion on our side of the wash concealed by dry grass. We first saw him when he charged di-rectly at our vehicle from our right front, his eyes fixed on the tracker sitting on the hood. The tracker made no move and the lion's crouching, snarling run stopped about 20 meters from the Land Rover. It was a "display" charge, as the tracker surely knew, since he never raised his gun from his lap. Then the first male lion charged us out of the wash, roaring and snarling until he too stopped short as Etienne put the Rover in re-verse and eased it backward. When the lions turned, Etienne backed away from them but edged closer to the wash until we could see into it.

I had come equipped with a motor rapid advance camera feature and rigged it for just such an action shot, but my "flight or fight" adrenaline surge at being charged by lions twice in short succession frustrated my intentions. At no time did I have the presence of mind to photograph the charging lions.

What we did see down in the wash was a dead hippo. This was a long way from any fresh water source, so it had travelled several miles in its nocturnal forage to reach this location. Lions do not take hippos; they are too dangerous for lions to hunt and their hide is too thick for the lions to claw or bite them. Our guide and tracker conferred and they opined that the hippo had probably been killed by another male hippo enforcing his territory. The lions seemed to be feeding through a neck wound in the dead hippo which gave the lions an entry into the hippo's flesh. In any event, the pride had enough meat to last it for days. Lions are opportunistic killers, and so they will kill an easy target even if they are not hungry. Fortunately for us, a Land Rover doesn't smell like food to them, and so they merely monitored our presence from a distance.

After breakfast at the long table, the talk was a breathless review of who saw what and how bloody the faces of the lions were and the like. After breakfast, we set out on what was supposed to be a routine bush walk. We were eight visitors, the (unarmed) tracker and Etienne with a rifle. The animals mostly rested during midday, we were assured, so it was *relatively* safe for us to be out in the bush on foot. It was mostly a flora-inspecting, bird spotting nature walk, with a surprisingly interesting focus on scat. The "spoor" or scat of the different animals is readily identifiable to local cognoscenti, and carnivore scat is markedly different from that of the herbivores. We were deep into a lecture on the eight stomachs of a giraffe that produces a spherical cluster of identical balls of scat when someone noticed four bull elephants quite close in a thick patch of bush. They had noticed us first, of course, and were facing us with ears out and slightly shuffling their feet indicating low anxiety. Their heads were above the low bush, but we were blind looking into it. Our guide unslung his rifle and silently indicated by hand motion that we should move slowly to our right flank away from them. We had not gone thirty yards in that direction before we surprised three Cape buffalo in our path. The Cape buffalo is the most dangerous of the big five because they will charge without provocation and never for display. Sandwiched in between the bull elephants and the buffalo, I realized that, for the second time in a matter of hours, we were not in control of the situation. The buffalo stared at us with their crazy looking eyes and, possibly intimidated by the presence of the elephant bulls behind us, simply turned and walked off toward the water hole while we made our retreat. We all had a more realistic view of the elemental nature of life in the African savannah after that, and a certain amount of risk was inherent in it.

We had many exciting wildlife encounters at Honey Guide that I will only summarize. At the end of the day, a cheetah leisurely passed within 10 meters of us and climbed a termite mound without once looking at us as it scanned the grassland beyond us as if to make a menu choice for the evening. Each day we revisited the hippo carcass, which got riper with each passing day. The lion pride was always there, but they seemed to grow more relaxed with our presence. At one point, the alpha male woke up from his meat induced stupor and roared a few times to let other lions in the neighborhood know this was his turf. The roars were so loud they shook our insides.

Elephant are magnificent animals both intelligent and social, and we watched them a lot. They are herbivores, but they are kings of the bush, running any lions off from the water holes when they arrive. They are very destructive, however, and too many of them can destroy the landscape. That is because they eat trees. Literally. It is a strange and painful sight to gaze out across the landscape on a perfectly still day and see the tallest, greenest, prettiest tree in sight begin to shake violently and then flop over at the hands, well, trunk of an elephant. The elephant will chew the bark off the tender branches of the tree and its roots and then move on to another tree. That's why the herds have to be culled from time to time. A herd that is too big can completely denude a landscape. Culling is done by killing complete herds—females, babies and all. That is because any elephant that survives a culling will remember the danger represented by humans and thereafter be dangerous. Culling is a terrible, tragic practice that everyone involved hates, but there doesn't seem to be any way to avoid it.

We grew very fond of giraffe as well. They are among the oddest of unique animals. Watching them eat small tender leaves from among the thorns of an acacia tree is hilarious. I have seen a mule eating thistles with extraordinarily dexterous lips, but they have nothing on giraffe. Adult giraffe don't really have much to fear from lions since they are too tall for lions to reach their backs and their powerful leg kicks can kill. Giraffe are vulnerable when they are young and when they are in the act of drinking which requires them to splay their great legs out and lower themselves to the water, a position from which they cannot react quickly.

We got very lucky one day and came across two juvenile lions batting a ball around in the dirt. They eventually tired of the game and walked off, at which time the ball unfolded itself and became a pangolin. Pangolin are scaly anteaters and are rare and endangered because the tribal witch doctors kill them for their ornamental scales. Poachers also take them for the Asian market which supports all manner of poaching. When moving on all fours, they look like a tiny stegosaurus as they slowly lumber along on their front knuckles. They then surprise you by standing on their rear legs and quickly walk or run away. Upright, they look like a tiny T Rex.

Poachers can be shot on sight, but many a Mozambique poacher will sneak across the border to Kruger and score rhino horn, elephant tusks, pangolin scales, etc., that can sell for ten thousand dollars. To them, poaching is worth the risk.

Our last night was action packed. We lucked out at sundown by finding a leopard on our track and followed it for at least an hour. When it would disappear into an impenetrable wash where we could not follow, the tracker would somehow divine where it was likely to go and direct Etienne to drive where he indicated. Uncannily, five or six times we picked up the leopard again and continued to follow it until we ran out of time. We were a long way from camp at that point, and Etienne was speeding along the tracks to get us back for dinner when we came careening around a corner into a herd of female elephants and their young on the track. We slammed on the brakes with our lights shining on the matriarch who had placed herself between us and the juveniles. Big mistake. Elephants don't like lights in their eyes at night and the females are very protective of their young. She charged us from fifty meters or so, and Etienne threw the Land Rover in reverse, fishtailed backward up the track a couple of hundred meters, and turned off the lights. Then we sat there in the pitch dark listening to animals all around us in the bush and getting more and more fearful about what sort of animals they were, entirely reliant on the fact (?) that a Land Rover does not smell like food to any of them.

Finally, Etienne switched on the lights and saw that the herd was still in front of us but had moved off the track. I also saw a pair of hyenas watching us from our flank. Etienne threw the Land Rover in gear, and we went speeding past the herd as the matriarch wheeled and came after us a little too late. I didn't need a translation of her trumpeting as we raced away. Her benediction was pretty clear to all of us. That night, we had a lot to talk about at the long table. One of the guides said that two weeks before at the Sabi Sand reserve, an elephant had flipped over a Land Rover and spilled its passengers into a pride of lions they had been observing. The startled lions reportedly ran off.

After breakfast the next morning, we reluctantly said goodbye to Honey Guide as Tim Ray, our tour guide, collected us for the drive to Londolozi. Londolozi is over-the-top luxurious. We had a stand-alone casita overlooking the bush below our deck, where we dined in our bathrobes beside floor-standing candelabras as we were served haute cuisine by uniformed staff. Inside, the king bed was enveloped in a gauzy white mosquito net. (I don't remember a mosquito problem at either Honey Guide or Londolozi, but it was the dry season and malaria kills.) On the game drives the next two days, we saw all the big five again, but focused on the leopard. Males were noticeably more muscular and the females presented a lovelier aspect, but both are strong enough to climb a tall tree with an impala in its mouth. They are pretty much spotted only at dusk unless you are lucky enough to see one in a tree during the day draped over a high limb with its kill, which I did once. The leopard's spotted coat looks brilliantly "loud" and conspicuous out in the open, but once the animal is in the grass, it virtually disappears.

We were astonished by the level of luxury dispensed by the resort. The experience, however, did not even come close to that we enjoyed at Honey Guide. True, our lives were never placed in danger once at Londolozi and our accommodations were flawless. But the eye-popping adventures we had at Honey Guide were just not to be duplicated.

Tim Ray picked us up from Londolozi and drove us over two days to the airport in Jo'berg via a long climb up the northern escarpment of the scenic Drakensberg Mountains facing Swaziland. He surprised us with an overnight stay in a Scottish hunting lodge up in the clouds. It was a safe place to overnight. Tim, a former Rhodesian army officer who fought on the losing side in the Jomo Kenyatta-led war of independence for Rhodesia, always carried a gun in his car when ferrying guests. Safety, it seemed, was always a concern.

From Jo'berg, our flight took us to Victoria Falls, Zimbabwe, formerly Southern Rhodesia, where we checked into the old Victoria Falls Hotel with its storied Livingstone Dining Room (as in "Doctor Livingstone, I presume") within view of the mist of the falls. We had two days of walking to the falls through the "frontier" (guard house) at the Zimbabwe/Zambia border through a phalanx of obnoxious, food-thieving monkeys, to watch the bungee jumpers fling themselves off what was then the tallest bungee jump in the world from the bridge down into the Zambezi River gorge. I considered doing it myself until I saw the raging, boulder-strewn torrent of the river a mere twenty meters underneath the end of the rope as jumpers bungeed upside down over and over hanging by their boots until they stopped and were hauled up again. Not.Going.To.Happen, I said to myself and to Carol, who judged me to be mentally defective for even entertaining the idea.

We took a boat ride in the Zambezi below the falls and came within five meters of the biggest croc I've ever seen slumbering on the shore—probably fifteen feet long. Even more concerning was a big pod of hippos in the river that became quite agitated as our boat—a flat bottomed skiff really—approached them for a photo op. We opted for the telephoto lenses.

One entire day was spent with a trip into Chobe National Park in Botswana. Vic Falls is near the four corners of Zimbabwe, Zambia, Namibia and Botswana. The Zambezi River separates Zimbabwe from Zambia and the Chobe River separates Botswana from Namibia. Got it? (Look on a map.) The Chobe has a large delta into the Zambezi that is rich with wildlife. Big herds of elephant and Cape buffalo traipse back and forth through pods of hippo with countless birds everywhere, all wary of the big crocodiles that thrive on the delta. Each riverbank is a separate country but there were few barriers to freely travel from one to another.

Victoria Falls proved to be an unusual blend of old European civilization in juxtaposition with amazing concentrations of wildlife. One taxi driver complained about having to take us all the way through the grounds at night to the front door of the hotel because he'd heard there was an elephant on the grounds. He expected us to walk it?? After our aliquot time in Victoria Falls, we were transferred three blocks to the boarding station for the Blue Train. We had booked passage on one of the world's great trains that harkened back to the days of Southern Rhodesia and the Empire. The Blue Train ran from Vic Falls to Pretoria and beyond, all the way to Cape Town. We had booked the leg from the falls to Pretoria. We had just enough vacation time left to fly to Cape Town and drive out to the Wine Country before returning home.

Our room on the train, for it was a room, consisted of a set of upholstered benches facing each other with a mahogany writing table in between beside a large window. There was a separate, private bathroom with *marble bath tub*. Meals with South African wines were included as were all drinks in the clubby, paneled bar. By merely pushing a button on the wall in our room, a steward would appear with champagne for two.

The train stopped for four hours on a stretch of track in the bush; it didn't pull off onto a siding to stop; it just stopped on the main line for four hours. During those four hours, we were invited to disembark for a game drive that had been arranged for us in the Hwange National Park. Hwange is a big Park with abundant animals in lush and beautiful landscapes, but the piece of it where we stopped exposed us to elephants in quantities approaching those that denude the landscape. There was little vegetation in sight for other grazing animals to eat, and without a population of grazers, there were no predators in sight. Just elephants by the hundreds, and they looked thin. No one mentioned the word cull, but it was on everyone's mind. So, for four hours we saw elephant, but nothing else, and then got back on the Blue Train.

The last car on the train was an observation car with big windows all around for viewing the passing countryside as we travelled at low speeds on the narrow gauge track. Every time I worked myself into a frame of mind in which I could savor the luxury of the experience we were living, the train would roll through a town and I would find myself eye to eye with South African natives beside the track with expressionless faces but taking it all in. Every city and town of size had a modern center where the white population lived prosperously and a satellite, "shadow" city adjacent to it where the natives lived in subsistence-level shanties that might or might not have electricity. Each pair of communities were locked together like twin stars in a shared economic destiny as the white enterprises provided jobs and the natives provided labor for the white enterprises. Whites were never really safe outside their compounds, and blacks never stopped resenting the whites, but, like aboriginal people everywhere, refused to assimilate.

In Cape Town, we taxied to a white commercial district for dinner at a popular restaurant in daylight. After dinner, after dark, we were advised to call a cab and wait inside the restaurant until it came. When we rented a car and drove to the Stellenbosch wine region, we learned to take short stops when pulling over along the road for photos or a view, because natives would materialize and approach demanding money. The racial divide, magnified by the chasm writ large between European culture and native culture, delivered an unsettling, even disturbing experience everywhere we went in South Africa outside of the bush itself. This situation seemed to be South Africa specific. Maybe its history with apartheid was the explanation. Neighboring Botswana is renowned for its good government and gracious people, and Zimbabwe's people are handsome, artistic and polite, notwithstanding Robert Mugabe's long misrule.

The whole experience provided by our trip was unforgettable and educational, but the bush experience was, uniquely, pure joy.

CHAPTER 14

LIFE AFTER ADMIRALTY LAW

My law practice from a solitary office at 101 California Street paid me a good living for two years (1997-1999,) but it wasn't very satisfying. The American "blue water" (foreign trade) Merchant Navy was now gone, and most of the U.S. flag executive maritime legal work I used to do no longer existed. I was too old (60) to start over in some other legal field and had little interest in opening a solo general practice doing wills, divorces and DWI cases. I had a retirement income from APL and was comfortable. So, at the beginning of "Y2K," as the techies called the turn of the century, I made an inventory of all the things I had always wanted to do but didn't have time to do because of work.

I loved to travel. I was interested in wine. I had taken up woodworking and enjoyed making the odd piece of furniture and turning bowls out of blocks of exotic burl. Creative writing had always been an interest of mine. I did a great deal of writing in my legal career, but that was legal writing. I always had an itch for creative writing. However, I deferred all of those interests in favor of an opportunity that must be viewed through the Coke-bottle lenses of the dot-com bubble in order to understand.

By way of background, Carol had suffered from chronic neck pain over the years. Reading a book, in particular, was a challenge for her and a constant source of pain. Being a tinkerer and amateur woodworker, I fashioned a hands-free book holder in my shop that would roll on wheels for positioning beside a sofa or chair or bed, telescope up and down, slide horizontally along an arm, and support a bookrest that would rotate to any angle within 180 degrees from face up to face down (for reading in a reclining position.) I could use existing mechanisms (non-patentable "prior art") to do all that, but I needed a unique device to grasp a book and hold it at any angle while allowing the pages to be turned normally.

So, I had to create custom parts to accomplish the latter, but with extensive tinkering, it came together very well. I tried it out. Carol tried it out. I took promotional pictures of her petting the cat in her lap while reading, sipping a cup of tea while reading, swirling a glass of port while reading—all hands free! Aha! I said. Everyone from disabled people to everyday readers who tire of holding a book up or reading it in an ergonomically bad, head-down position will want one of these. And, it doesn't exist in the marketplace!

It took me the better part of two years to perfect the device, write and submit a patent request for my "BookValet," register the trademark, obtain my patent, register my Internet domain name and design a web page. All that accomplished, I had a legal monopoly on the device and there were no other hands-free book holders on the market. I set up an office at the foot of Telegraph Hill, contracted locally for the manufacture and packaging of my invention. My Internet website would reach comfort-seeking book readers all over the planet! In the interstices of my product development work schedule, I attended bookseller trade shows with my prototype to get real time feedback on the appeal of the device from random book consumers walking past. It was all encouraging.

I read up on startups and the need to hire marketing consultants to determine the market, optimal pricing, and advertising budgets. I priced injection molding of plastic parts for mass production. All of this was going to cost tens of thousands of dollars. I decided to wing it instead, and learn as I went along. After all, I didn't have to support myself with this product, and I had plenty of time on my hands. It was very liberating to afford that approach, and I could have a good time walking through all of it.

I found a cabinet shop in San Francisco with the latest laser cutting tools to manufacture my initial inventory of two hundred BookValets out of cherry wood. I sourced various manufacturers or suppliers of parts that I would assemble to make the patented book holding device. I bought packaging materials for shipping and activated my website. I advertised on ergonomic equipment and book sites and placed Book Valets in two brick and mortar stores dealing with ergonomic equipment. They began to sell, but only at a trickle. I learned that I could not sell many at a price that would cover my costs (about $350,) so I dropped my prices to the level at which they began to sell (about $250). I also learned that while everyone liked the idea of a hands free book holder, since it was basically an item of furniture, few people wanted to have one sitting in their living room at home. It often failed to fit a customer's décor.

I also learned that people with certain disabilities, commonly arthritis, *had to have it* in order to continue reading at all. These were my customers. I ended up selling all my inventory and receiving a fistful of letters thanking me profusely for the device and saying how it had changed the lives of the purchasers. I also learned that I could not make money selling BookValets at prices that consumers would pay if I manufactured them in America. The costs were too high. Given my work history, I found the prospect of outsourcing manufacture of the BookValet overseas to be personally embarrassing.

I got as far as identifying prospective manufacturers in Asia, sending them drawings, and getting a bid on manufacturing them in Malaysia at a price that was well below the retail price level I had identified to be profitable. But I couldn't make myself pull the trigger. I was very disheartened at the prospect of offshoring the manufacture of them. And, I found that I didn't enjoy the way I spent my days. I may have been Chief Executive, Chief Financial, Chief Legal, Chief IT and Chief Marketing Officer all rolled into one, but I was also Chief Warehouseman, Order Taker and Shipping and Receiving Officer. It was mundane, uninteresting work and the market was not a mass market item after all. I would be trapped in an enterprise that, while rewarding in one sense—it was a needed product that made some people's lives better, it was dull. So, I didn't do it. I walked away and closed the business. I did so frustrated by the feeling that I had established a market for a new and useful product of my own creation, but that I had not developed it sufficiently to make it a successful, self-sustaining enterprise. I was unwilling to do what had to be done to make it work, namely offshore the manufacture of it, and spend my time doing the supply chain work required for a niche market item. I did learn a good deal about the burgeoning world of e-commerce however, and that made me a savvier consumer, for what that was worth.

So, what was the next item on my wannado list? By closing the BookValet business, I ended the last reason why we should live in pricy San Francisco. We were land rich, cash poor and we were looking for a retirement scenario. So, Carol and I formulated a plan to retire to the wine country, her other favorite place to live and our go-to place for R & R. But where? We shopped for vineyards in Healdsburg, in Sonoma, in the Napa Valley and even in Mendocino and the Santa Ynez Valley over the coastal hills from Santa Barbara. We found nothing in the gentleman's vineyard category that we could afford and/or appealed to us.

We rented out our Telegraph Hill home to a very young tech millionaire with more money than sense. He had a young wife and baby, but spent his days trying to travel to all of the countries in the world within a certain period of time and set the Guinness Book of Records for doing so. !? So, we moved into a rented country house in the Napa Valley to see whether we liked the wine country lifestyle before making the plunge.

The home we rented was on a hilltop just out of Saint Helena on Spring Mountain Road. It belonged to an elderly widow from an old valley family—in fact, she told us that her grandmother's petticoat was used to make the Bear Flag in the 1846 Bear Flag rebellion in Sonoma that overthrew the Government of Mexico's claim to Alta California. The undermanned military garrison of General Mariano Vallejo in Sonoma apparently surrendered without much opposition. The Bear Flag Republic existed as a sovereign nation in Sonoma for twenty five days in 1846 before General Freemont of the United States Army raised the flag of the United States over the Presidio of San Francisco, and the Bear Flag, or rather the California Republic, was subsumed into the United States as its territory during the then ongoing Mexican American War. But I digress.

We settled into the Saint Helena lifestyle gradually, began to make friends, and toured the many wineries of the valley. Carol's dearest friend, Michele Monson, had married a prominent San Francisco attorney named Paul Haerle, and Paul introduced us to David and Margo Slaby, with whom we became fast friends and, through them, joined the bocce team called "Botched Up" in the Saint Helena Bocce League. We were hooked and within six months decided to make Saint Helena our home.

We sold the Telegraph Hill home and bought a couple of 1031 Exchange properties (named for a section of the Internal Revenue Code allowing for tax deferral on certain capital gains invested in replacement real estate). One property was a junior suite in the Ala Moana Hotel in Honolulu, which gave us a getaway spot in Oahu whenever we needed to exchange fog for tropical sunshine. The other was a small, sixties ranch house on an acre of valley floor land on White Lane just south of Saint Helena. It had a big swimming pool, a bonus room (office) attached to the well house by the pool, a big walnut tree, and lots of good bottom land for a gentleman's vineyard. The latter would prove to be an important option. We decided to remain in the spacious rental house on Spring Mountain and rent the White Lane House out while formulating a plan to develop the White Lane property into our dream home.

Carol decided to reinvent herself again, a facility for which she had real talent. She had already successfully morphed from owner of a sales seminar consulting firm to a head hunter in the biotech field. But logistically, the latter was not something easily managed from the wine country. She had observed that there wasn't much to do in the Napa Valley beyond wine tasting and fine dining. She thought that the women who visited the Valley when their husbands attended the many corporate conferences held in the local resorts needed alternatives. And even the hundreds of thousands of vacationers that come for the food and wine needed something else to do. Being of Italian extraction and a good cook, and having been delighted with the number of high end, artisanal olive oil producers she'd discovered in the Valley, she had an idea. She would form personal relationships with prominent, visitor friendly, estates that produce olive oil, and jolly the owners to let her, and her alone, visit their estates leading small, personalized tours. The olive oil estates would receive a guaranteed amount of olive oil sales from the visit. The retail price for the sale of their olive oil would be double the wholesale price they were receiving from their distributor, so it was an attractive arrangement for the estate owners as well. If the grower also made wine, wine tasting and sales would become part of the visit as well.

Carol would be paid a tour fee by her guests, and her guests would receive artisanal olive oil, a tasting experience, and a wine tasting, if included. It worked. Before long, Carol had access to beautiful estates such as Villa Mille Rose in Oakville, Poplar Hill above Saint Helena on Spring Mountain, and Round Pond in Rutherford, among others. She had a website called Great Olive Tours, and rave reviews began to be posted by her customers. People who knew nothing about the technical aspects of olive oil production or how to use olive oil in cooking and baking were delighted. She was teaching her guests that olive oil was a fundamental part of the Mediterranean life style, and good olive oil was, like good wine, to be coveted. Her tours quickly became ranked No. 1 in Trip Advisor's Things to Do in Saint Helena list.

We had our new life. We decided to terminate our rental and move into the White Lane house. We intended to renovate that house, plant grapes and make wine, but it would be easier and cheaper if we lived there while doing so. I was still going through my wannado list, and Carol was a newly minted good will ambassador to the other industry in the Valley–olive oil. We travelled; we played bocce; we made new friends; and we had fun. In hindsight, Khalil Gibran's poem proved apt once again. "Such prophesies of joy awaken the toad who sleeps away the past under your hearthstone, light forsaken…"

CHAPTER 15

CAROL'S JOURNEY

In the spring of 2001, my mother died of a stroke at age ninety six in her assisted living apartment in Sonoma. While we were moving her things, Carol remarked over the course of several days that she felt unusually tired. Then night sweats set in. She went to her internist in San Francisco, who ordered a blood test. Alarmed by her high white cell count, her doctor then ordered an abdominal CAT scan. A large tumor about the size and shape of a paperback book appeared. It was biopsied. She was diagnosed with non-Hodgkin's lymphoma. The good news was that it was in a single location and, of the nineteen different forms that NHL can take, hers was one of the types that could be cured with chemotherapy.

Like everyone who gets a cancer diagnosis, terrified, we fell into the maw of cancer information gathering, oncology visits and endless tests and procedures. I might just observe that the three weeks between receiving her diagnosis and her first treatments were the worst of my life. The hand-off between internists who diagnose cancer and oncologists who treat it is about as raggedy-ass as anything I've seen. We were advised that she should be treated by a reputable specialist in lymphoma at a teaching hospital. We had UC San Francisco and Stanford medical centers in our area, and I began the search for a doctor. As Carol grew progressively weaker as the tumor sapped her energy, and I spent all day, every day, trying to get one of the doctors to see her. But all of them worked behind a massive screening apparatus. "The doctor only sees new patients on Tuesday. I'm sorry, the doctor is out of the office at a conference next Tuesday. I'm sorry, the following Tuesday he/she is fully booked."

And on and on. All of them. Mind you, she was very sick, with cancer, and needed to start treatment. We finally got her internist to recommend someone in private practice who I reached by phone, and he was responsive. "She needs to start treatment now," he said. He got it. He arranged for her to check into St. Francis Hospital for her first of six chemo treatments called R-CHOP, an acronym for four nasty, poisonous chemicals that kill cells plus one that attaches to the cells that need to be killed and acts as a magnet for the poisons. The day before the first chemo treatment, Carol was so weak she had to crawl up the stairs to our bedroom on all fours.

The day after her first chemo session, however, she woke up and said, "Hey, I feel great. Let's drive up to Healdsburg and have lunch!" I couldn't believe it! The chemo had killed "a few billion" cells, it seemed, including the diseased ones that wouldn't die on their own and were sapping all of her energy. Unfortunately, the acute fatigue, hair loss, and endless procedures involved with chemo-therapy followed. That is how it began. If, gentle reader, you do not wish to read a description of Carol's experience with cancer, please skip to the end of this chapter. However, I do include that remarkable story because it was so medically novel.

The course of treatment filled our lives over six and half years and included the following stages:

1. In the initial course of six chemotherapy sessions, Carol would be infused with the R-CHOP chemicals, get sick, recover, and get reinfused three weeks later. When she recovered from all six treatments, she had no detectable cancer. Her hair grew back. She had apparently beaten her strain of non-Hodgkin's lymphoma. Our lives returned to normal for nearly two years. She resumed her olive touring business and we traveled to Australia and Europe. We were ultimately successful in getting an appointment with the head of the lymphoma practice at UCSF, Dr. Lawrence Kaplan, and Carol switched to his care.

2. In a routine follow up appointment at UCSF two years later, a blood test revealed that she had a *new* blood cancer–leukemia. The chemotherapy she had undergone for lymphoma, we were told, causes other cancers about four percent of the time. The

blood cells now being manufactured by her bone marrow stem cells were abnormal. They would not function properly to sustain her life, and this time the disease was not curable. Her only option was a bone marrow stem cell transplant in which her stem cells would be substantially killed by more chemotherapy, she would get an infusion of new stem cells, either her own ("autologous") harvested before the end of the chemo sessions, or from a third party donor ("allogeneic.") The main risks in autologous transplants are: the risk of infection during the long period (a few weeks) in which the patient is without an immune system due to the extreme chemotherapy, and the risk of reintroduction of diseased cancer cells hidden in the stem cells collected before chemo. The risks of allogeneic transplants are the same risk of infection and also the risk of *rejection of your own body* by the transplanted stem cells of another person that make up the new immune system. That is, the white blood cells of the donor ("graft") would attack the patient ("host"), hence, graft vs. host disease. Both procedures involved a less than fifty/fifty success rate. Carol's oncologists were recommending allogeneic transplant. Carol was too sick to even pay attention, let alone weigh a complex set of options. That was, by default, my job.

Here I ran into a dirty little secret in the American health care system. Each cancer center's protocols, treatments and outcomes data are considered proprietary. The doctors do research for various therapies, patent the effective ones as their intellectual property, and then develop new businesses in manufacturing and selling the new drugs or selling their patents. Hospitals and medical center protocols that are protected by intellectual property laws prosper from the high fees charged to the patients that are tributary to those hospitals. So, there is *no national data base* that tells a patient what the outcomes have been from various therapies. A national data base would be much more accurate than a parochial one, but capitalism prevents it. A patient will get prognosis information from her doctor that is only as reliable as the volume and time span of the doctor/hospital's history of practice. This is one of the strongest arguments for national health care in my opinion.

I asked for and got the meager studies UCSF had done, and then *went on the Internet and did research myself!* I discovered a very large stem cell transplant study within the National Health Care System of Great Britain over five years. It indicated that, for a female of Carol's age, the chances of long term survival with her blood disease were the same with both types of stem cell transplant. I pointed that out to her doctors and also confirmed my reading with the oncologists at the Fred Hutchinson Cancer Center in Seattle, one of the nations' top transplant centers with whom I had been in touch. All agreed that it was an even chance, but the autologous transplant was much safer because, if successful, there would be no graft vs. host disease (rejection) to contend with for the rest of her life. So Carol agreed with me that she should have an autologous transplant at UCSF.

She did. It involved harvesting her stem cells in an easy procedure, then massive chemotherapy taking her close to death, then infusing her own previously harvested stem cells back into her body and waiting the two weeks or so for her stem cells to set up in her bone marrow and begin manufacturing white and red blood cells that would provide her with an immune system. It was successful! She did not get an infection during the period she had no immune system, and she recovered. We resumed our lives again and she was in remission. However, the Sword of Damocles was always hanging over our heads: would the cancer return if cancer cells had been hiding in her stem cells when they had been collected?

3. We resumed our lives again, this time for about a year before another routine blood test revealed, again astonishingly, an *entirely new* blood cancer—something called MDS. It was neither lymphoma nor leukemia and it was not clear whether it came from something in her stem cell collection or whether it morphed from her blood system anew perhaps triggered by all the chemo. She was medically famous at this point. None of the oncology doctors had ever seen this progression of three, seemingly independent blood cancers. The MDS would kill her if left to run its course. This time, there was no other choice. We had tried

the low risk choice of autologous stem cell transplant. Now she had to do the allogeneic transplant. Since the chief risks involved were both infection before, and then rejection after the transplant, the quest was for a donor who was as perfectly matched genetically as possible. The closer the match, the less chance of powerful rejection. We decided to go to The Fred Hutchinson Center in Seattle for this transplant. Its founder won the Nobel Prize for Medicine for his pioneering transplant procedure, and the Center had since grown exponentially along with the disease. We signed up for the program on a visit to Seattle and then rented a condo on "Pill Hill" above the downtown area. Fred Hutchinson was an easy downhill two mile drive to its campus on Lake Union. Meanwhile, the search was on for a donor.

Generous people volunteer to donate their stem cells, and when they do, the details of their blood type and genetic make-up go into a data base that can be searched. Very highly trained scientists do the searching. We had been in Seattle for several weeks, but no luck on a match. I tried not to think of all the cancer patients who lacked the time and resources to do what we were doing.

Fred Hutchinson had developed a brand new cutting edge program that involved the transplant of fetal cord blood stem cells. Their researchers had found that the afterbirth umbilical cords and placentas of babies were a source of fetal stem cells and that the white blood cells produced by fetal stem cells were less aggressive and more adaptive than adult cells. This markedly reduced the risk of rejection, but there was no history for this procedure. It sounded good in theory and their program was growing and building on its recent successes. Carol liked the idea so she chose to do a fetal cord blood transplant rather than risk a poor match and elevated odds of rejection. At the eleventh hour, however, the oncologists had a Eureka! moment when they found an "excellent" match. I was not competent to question the degree of "excellence" at the time, nor did it occur to me to inquire into it. With the benefit of hindsight, I will always wonder whether Carol's team had an interest in settling for a less than perfect match rather than lose her case to a competing program.

Anyway, at the last minute, we switched back to the original program which fast-tracked the procedure. The donor's stem cells were harvested somewhere in the country (a male in his thirties was all we could be told) and shipped by courier to Seattle. Carol got some last minute chemo to eliminate as much of her diseased blood cells as possible. Carol's bestie Michele was visiting her on the day of the transplant, but the donor's cells were delayed getting from the airport. Michele had to leave at about 9 pm to fly back to San Francisco when visiting hours closed. I was alone with her at midnight when her nurse walked in and plopped a plastic bag onto the counter and began to check Carol's vitals.

"Is that it?" I asked.

"That's it," she said. "Just in time, too. These things have an expiration date and time."

So, she hooked the bag to Carol's IV pole and plugged it into her drip line and released the clip. That was it. That was what all the excitement was about, but Carol was asleep, Michele had gone, and the nurse went back to her desk. A life or death moment, unmarked by anything or anyone except the nurse and me in my bedside chair.

4. Carol recovered and her new bone marrow stem cells grew a new immune system. The question was whether her graft vs. host disease would turn out to be "chronic" (mild and manageable) or "acute" (bad news.) She was on a heavy dose of anti-inflammatory Prednisone as a check on rejection, and she was discharged back to our condo. She continued to be monitored. About thirty days after the transplant, she developed a red rash all over her body at the condo. I immediately ran her down to Fred Hutchinson, and her team confirmed our worst fears. It was rejection, which coming on that quickly, meant that she had acute graft vs. host disease. Her new T-cells were attacking her skin (skin is an organ). The team upped her Prednisone and the rash went away. But we knew rejection was going to be the problem from then on.

Anyway, her medical treatments were over, and she was discharged from Fred Hutchinson. We packed up our things in the Seattle condo and drove back to Napa over a couple of days and resumed our life. Carol became a patient of UCSF again and they would monitor her progress. She resumed her olive oil tours and tastings again, although I had to accompany her and take over from time to time when she felt unwell. She began to slowly waste away on the high doses of Prednisone, but she could not reduce the dosages without suffering severe inflammation of her skin and other organs. She became dependent on red blood cell infusions every two weeks or so because her blood could no longer manufacture sufficient red blood cells.

Notwithstanding these problems, she was determined to meet her donor. A year following the transplant, with the consent of both parties, Fred Hutchinson would disclose the names and contact info of the donor and recipient. Carol asked and her donor, "Juan" agreed. We found out he was a 38 year old refinery engineer in Metairie, Louisiana, married with two children. Carol and Juan agreed to meet, and we decided to pay him a visit, to which he readily consented. We put together a trip driving the Florida Keys and then stopping off in New Orleans on the way back. We flew to Miami and enjoyed the drive out to Key West, and then made our way to New Orleans. The visit with Juan and his family was life-affirming. His family was curious, of course, and they all turned out, grandparents, siblings, kids. Carol was thrilled. Juan and his wife took us on an insider's tour of New Orleans, and we all went out to dinner at a fun restaurant in the Garden District where one lucky couple got to dine at a table set up in the back of a pick-up truck. The whole experience was emotional, happy, and satisfying for both Juan's family and for us. It had been perfect.

Another special trip we got to take after Carol's transplant was to Annecy, France to celebrate David Slaby's 60th birthday with the bocce team. The trip came off in a picture perfect manner, like the Alps themselves which loomed over us for a week. Midway through the stay in Annecy, we needed to have Carol's blood counts taken and a red blood cell infusion, if needed. To shorten up the story, we went to the local hospital, made our way to the oncology & hematology department, and saw an oncologist who directed the necessary lab work. We visited the oncologist the next day to get the results. Carol did not need a red blood infusion. The two oncology visits and the lab work cost me the princely sum of 13 Euro. ($20) The French National Health care system is funded by the value added tax, a substantial amount of which is paid by tourists. France returns the favor by giving them access to their health care system. Viola! Health care was so easy and cost-effective! That is when I became a proponent of national health care for the United States.

The final six months of Carol's life were all about the cancer. She got progressively thinner as the Predisone thinned her bones and wasted her muscles. Any reduction in Predizone resulted in stomach ulcers. She suffered spontaneous bone fractures from osteoporosis. I conducted her olive tours and tastings that were booked, but we stopped taking new bookings and then closed the business. That broke her heart.

In San Francisco, Carol always hosted Christmas Eve dinner for Gray and Erin and their families. That torch passed to my daughter Erin over time, and we would spend Christmas Eve at Erin's house for dinner, and watch the grandkids open presents. On Christmas Eve, 2010, she was too weak to make the trip but invited the Fish family up to join us for diner at Tra Vigne restaurant in Saint Helena. As it turned out, we dined without her. She hadn't the strength.

A week later on New Year's Eve, Carol died. The autopsy revealed total body sepsis (infection) from neutropenia (suppressed immune system). She died, cancer-free, from the cure and her new immune system's rejection of her own body. She didn't die at home or in the company of loved ones. She spiked a fever and had to go to the ER in Napa and then to UCSF. She died in the Intensive Care Unit at UCSF hospital as the oncologists fought an infection and the ICU doctors administered life support.

I was pretty much broken at that point. My mind was not working properly. I was at home and had to be called by the ICU doctor to come and authorize taking her off life support. It was 10 o'clock at night New Year's Eve, and I was doing carpentry in our bathroom thinking I had to get it remodeled *in time for her return home!* That's how far I was from being functional. I got in the car and drove into the City that night, knowing that my duty was to authorize pulling Carol's life support. She spared me that trauma. I arrived at the hospital twenty minutes after she died.

CHAPTER 16

PICKING UP THE PIECES

The next two months I was in a slow-motion fog: family and friends were notified, death certificates were provided to banks and brokerage houses, Social Security and Medicare were notified, Carol's personal property was handed out according to her written wishes. No probate was opened as our bank accounts, brokerage accounts and real estate title were held in joint tenancy/community property. I arranged (with the crucial assistance of Carol's nephew Mike and his wife Jennifer) a memorial service in late January. Carol's family came out for it, many of Carol's friends came, my kids and niece Susan from New York came out for it. Even Carol's stem cell donor, Juan, came from New Orleans for it. We had a wonderfully intimate service at the Presbyterian Church in Saint Helena that fittingly had a large stain glass window of an olive tree in the sanctuary.

The service began with a slide show of our life together and as many of her earlier life pictures as I could find. The sound track was Andrea Bocelli singing "Time to Say Goodbye" among other songs. When I prepared it with the technical help of a mortuary staffer, I thought it was lovely, but when actually shown and played at the service, it was brutally sad. Carol's friend Rachael Casey from Poplar Hill spoke and made Carol one last cappuccino, her favorite. My granddaughter Brayden, all of thirteen years old, spoke of her "Nina" with astonishing poise and eloquence, and I introduced Carol's donor Juan to the audience. After the service we exited to the dulcet tones of Izzie singing "Somewhere over the Rainbow."

Emotionally drained, we adjourned to the Napa Reserve for a reception. The Napa Reserve is owned by Bill Harlan and located on the elegant Meadowood grounds. Mike and Jen got Cindy Pawlcyn (owner/chef at Mustards and their boss) to ask Harlan for the favor of letting us hire the Reserve for the day, to which he graciously agreed. If Napa can have a January thaw, we had it that day. It was a warm, summerlike day, the French doors at the Reserve were all open, heavy hors d'oerves (the ones that Carol liked, thoughtfully ordered by Jen) were served on the deck overlooking goats grazing in the hillside vineyard next to us. We were served Harlan's Napa Valley Reserve cabernet sauvignon. I wish Carol could have been there. It was her kind of event.

After the service and everyone goes home, that's when the loss sets in. After six and a half years of holding it together, I could let go, grieve and turn inward, guilt free. Days on end of thousand-yard staring into the landscape began the healing process.

The conventional wisdom was not to undertake any serious transactions for the first year after losing one's spouse. I said, "Screw that." I needed something to do. So, after a few months, I began to plan the demolition of my house and rebuilding a new one in its place. I had, during the time Carol and I lived there, drawn and redrawn my idea of the ideal floor plan for the new house, maximizing the features of the lot, the views, and the seasonal changes in the sun's position. I had tried to interest Carol in that exercise, but she'd refused to think about it or even look at my drawings. I never knew whether she thought it too painful to engage in a project that she likely wouldn't ever get to see, or whether it was just "chemo brain," a very real condition of impaired mental function and personality change brought on by the boatloads of chemo she endured. Whatever the cause, planning for the new house was exclusively mine. I think that helped a bit when I eventually moved into the new house, as I found it largely free of sad associations of my time with Carol when I did.

In any event, I reached out to a contractor we had been talking to when Carol first got sick, and I showed him my floor plan. He gave me a horseback cost estimate based on the square footage of the plan view. That convinced me that the job penciled out. I hired an architect the contractor liked to work with, and he designed the house around my floor plan, adding an inspired "Meadowood arch" over the front porch as a design touch that made the house fit its location. My contractor priced out the drawings and specifications of the architect, and I signed the construction contract.

I rented the guest house annexed to David and Margo's Rutherford winery in Rutherford. My furniture went into storage. I bunked in Rutherford at night and worked out of my poolside office on the property by day all during the nine months it took to build the new house. I think subconsciously I had the Telegraph Hill house in mind as I was doing the floor plan, because the new Saint Helena house had the same rooms with approximately the same dimensions. Thus, when the house was finished and with the occupancy permit in hand a year after the start of construction, I called the moving and storage company and had them deliver and place all of the same furniture into the same rooms arranged in the same way. With new sheer, gauzy, Restoration Hardware-style drapes over the big windows and French doors in the great room and plantation shutters in the bedrooms (also a feature of the Telegraph Hill house), it felt familiar and comfortable, yet without any melancholy attached to it. By the second anniversary of Carol's death, I was a whole and functioning man again, and being on the job site and participating in the construction planning and execution every day was the vehicle for my rehabilitation.

PHOTOS

William Augustus Ainsworth

Inez Ainsworth (Muse)

Harry Lee Vincent

Grace Vincent (Plue-Conover)

William Earl Ainsworth

Carmen Sylvia Ainsworth (Vincent)

William Earl Ainsworth, Jr.

Lt. William E. Ainsworth, Jr. USN

Author at 18 months in Holland MI

Author in Mallorca age 19

Author Senior at Kansas U

Author USMC

Author Age 25 San Francisco

Author with wife Judy, children Gray and Erin

Judy Ainsworth (Harman)

Daughter Erin

Son Gray

Carol Ainsworth (Ingellis)

Author with wife Carol

Son Gray and Wife Laura

Daughter in Law Laura Ainsworth

Granddaughter Brayden Rose Ainsworth

Daughter Erin and husband Eric Fish

Granddaughter Lauren Elizabeth Fish

Granddaughter Julia Gail Fish

Grandson Ainsworth Dylan Fish with Father Eric

Author and Niece Susan Nicole Ainsworth

Author Maritime Lawyer Age 40

Author A Man in Full

Author as docent on SS Jeremiah O'Brien

Author off Vancouver Island

Author with Johanna van Egmond

Johanna van Egmond

CHAPTER 17

BECOMING A WRITER

I am obliged to retrace my steps a fair bit now. In the interest of a coherent telling of this story, I have been narrating life episodes without interruption. In the actual living of life, however, there were things, sometimes momentous things, going on concurrently. Not long after we moved into the Spring Mountain Road rental house and before Carol got her cancer diagnosis, I had dusted off my "wannado" list and ticked the line item for writing a novel.

I had done massive amount of legal writing during my thirty years of practicing law, but that is not good training for writing fiction—except maybe for the stamina part. In order to write a novel, writing stamina is a necessary qualification, and I had acquired that in my legal practice. It isn't easy to write a novel for many reasons, but one of them is that you have to sit there, day after day, week after week, month after month, inside your head, writing. You write until it's finished, not just until you tire of writing, which always comes first. And something about that effort triggers major urges toward procrastination, especially when writing fiction. Fiction writing involves reaching deep into wherever your feelings reside, dragging them up, and exhibiting them to the world. Not for sissies! Nevertheless, while writing stamina was a major hurdle, I was confident about accomplishing that discipline. The emotional part, however, was missing from my experience with legal writing. I had to prove myself in that category as well.

My experience at APL in striving, through trade barrier litigation, to put my company on "a level playing field" with its competitors in their home country but ultimately losing the war (my industry, my company, and my job) was a bitter one. My industry was only one of the many that had been outsourced as the result of America's reckless open markets policy. Throughout the decades that the steady, systematic dismantling of America's manufacturing industry was occurring, economists (who, like lawyers, have paying clients) were opining that things were just fine. America was like a balance sheet, they said, and for every dollar lost to industrial workers, consumers gained as much in consumer savings. The two values balanced out. Enquiry over. But economists do not weigh things qualitatively. For example, economists can't weigh the adverse effects of class warfare where affluent consumers with jobs and incomes benefit from globalization while industrial workers are being driven out of the middle class and into poverty. However, as a writer and an artist, I could empathize with the victims, so I understood that the balance sheet mindset of bean counters was the wrong way to be looking at the problem.

Thus, I did not have far to look for the subject matter of my first novel. In fact, I felt like I *had to write* that story. If I didn't memorialize the injustice and suffering being inflicted on the industrial workers of the country, then no one would. Incredibly, globalization had already been inexorably unraveling the fabric of a big sector of American life for twenty five years *and no one was talking about it.* So, I wrote my first book, *The Chasm*, on that subject. It is a meditation on the class warfare being waged against millions of American families and their communities as a consequence of the vast trade deficits America runs year after year. It focuses on the early beginnings of that period in which the *laissez faire* school of trade policy began to go south in our trade with Japan.

The first section of the book is based upon a characterization of a *Yakusa* chieftain. Implausibly, I had been personally involved with the events recounted in the book and knew them to be substantially accurate. I have had readers tell me that this part of the book is far-fetched. But, as the saying goes, you can't make this stuff up! This backstory to the novel also explained the later spread of this trade disease to America's bilateral trade with China and the exponential increase of economic harm to America as a result.

I don't know what I expected would happen; I wrote the book because I had to write it, not because I had a plan to monetize it. So, guess what? No publisher wanted to publish it and no agent wanted to represent it. I sent query letters to more than forty agents, some of which complimented me on my query letter, but all said "not for us," that is, the ones who responded at all. So, I gave up and self-published the book. It had no advertising. No book-reviewing journals would review a self-published book. Publisher's Clearing House would not review self-published books, and libraries will not order books not reviewed by Publisher Clearing House. Catch-22. I did little to advertise and promote the book myself because I was preoccupied with my wife's cancer at the time, and, I must honestly admit, I have very little taste for promoting my own work. The book was on the Internet via my website and I had used artful metadata search terms so that people searching for books on globalization would get a hit for my book. I figured it had to stand on its own merits and be discovered or not, be liked or not, influence others or not. The book's chances for commercial success were vanishingly small. It was ignored. However, events overtook this issue in a major way. I had the satisfaction of having been right about the class warfare assessment, although I took no satisfaction from the battle that war produced in the 2016 Presidential election ten years later.

I am a big fan of irony, and find it very ironic that the forces that caused a majority of swing state voters to vote for presidential candidate Donald Trump based on his promise to restore their manufacturing jobs were key to his election victory in 2016. None of the political pundit class saw it coming. Like my book, *The Chasm*, the ongoing social destruction from globalization had been discounted utterly.

As I write this four years later, globalization is a hot issue, but the right messenger has yet to come along to deliver the message. Trump, being a deeply flawed, basically incompetent person, let alone trade negotiator, has failed to make good on his promises, not because it they can't be achieved, but because he doesn't know how. He insisted on personally managing something as multifaceted and complex as the Sino-US trade. He should have worked with Congress to legislate a new, clearly articulated policy mandating equilibrium and reciprocity as America's foreign trade standard. Import controls should have been phased in over, say, a ten year transition period, thus incrementally applying the trade tools of import licenses, commodity quotas, and tariffs until the objective of equilibrium in the value of trade goods and services imported and exported was achieved. That approach would have convinced our trading partners, primarily China and Japan, that we were serious and that it was bipartisan policy. American manufacturers would have confidence that if they returned their manufacturing operations to America, they would be able to prosper. In that way, all the players would have time to orderly plan and adjust to the new reality according to a congressionally mandated schedule that would not involve sudden economic shocks.

Instead, Trump ignored Congress, slapped tariffs on imports from China and elsewhere, and provoked retaliatory sanctions against American exports. America enacted no protectionist laws that would convince an American company to relocate its manufacturing to America shores. In the absence of such protectionist measures, an American manufacturer would continue to compete in its home market with the structurally cheaper products made by its overseas competitors, thus forcing them to offshore all over again. The way Trump went about it was unforgivably stupid and doomed to fail, as it did. As I write this, our trade deficit with China is bigger than ever.

My personal frustration continued unabated. No agent was willing to represent a book that warns prospectively of all this on the grounds that they saw no market for books on these phenomena, even as these phenomena played out with devastating effect. A huge market for it existed. I am happy to stipulate that my book was the work of a novice fiction writer and could have been written better and in a manner more appealing to readers. The ensemble-style method of telling a story is hard on the reader. However, that is an invitation for an agent and an editor to do his/her job, critique and develop a book submitted on such a timely topic, and then market it.

The Chasm was published in 2006. I had to cancel my meet-the-author appearance at the Saint Helena bookstore because Carol and I were on our way to Seattle for her second transplant, but it sold enough copies among my friends and bocce mates in Saint Helena to win a place on the "best sellers" shelf for that bookstore. I'm pretty sure that didn't happen anyplace else.

About the time we returned from Seattle and Carol was in remission, I began to get interested in oil and gas production via offshore drilling under extreme conditions in places like the North Sea and Gulf of Mexico and the continental shelf of Brazil. (I did co-major in geology.) The cost of gasoline had been unusually volatile and regular had spiked to $3.65 per gallon while we were in Seattle. Oil companies routinely explained price hikes in terms of higher cost of production and rotating refinery outages. I started reading some of the on-line literature as well as newspaper and magazine articles on the topic. The subject of "fracking" came up more and more often as a possible breakthrough in oil and gas production, but little clear information was available in the popular press. So, in my considerable spare time, I just hacked around the various sources on line and picked up bits and pieces on the market forces at work. I was puzzled by the extreme measures being taken to drill new oil wells. It was very, very costly and difficult. Why had it come to that, I wondered?

Then the Deepwater Horizon blowout happened in the Gulf of Mexico. The news cycle was full of coverage about how deep the ocean floor was at the site (a mile) and how much further below the continental shelf BP had drilled to get oil (another mile). TV reporters were explaining how wells can leak or explode under those conditions and nothing could really be done about it if the blowout preventer were to fail, the preventer being a wellhead valve that is supposed to shut off automatically if the flow pressure gets too high. How can it possibly be profitable to produce oil and gas that way at the market prices we pay? Why would the oil companies' insurers underwrite such risks?

My inquiry led me to the theory of peak oil. Oil and gas are natural resources that took millions of years to form as the remains of marine life accumulated in deep seabed and had been subjected to extreme heat and pressure from the weight of overlaying sediments. There is a finite amount of oil on the planet. No new oil and gas is being formed to replace what we extract other than the glacially slow geological method by which it accumulated in the first place.

The planet's population increased steadily as food supplies expanded, spurred by increased agricultural productivity from breakthroughs in fertilizers. These innovations currently enable our monoculture practices and high agricultural productivity. The global demand for oil and gas expands along with population growth, and more and more hydrocarbons must be used to support the growing population. Renewable energy sources help augment our growing demand for energy, but do not come close to meeting demand. Moreover, even solar and wind generation of electricity can occur only hand in hand with supplemental uses of methane because a power plant has to have a rapidly scalable alternative to the sun and wind during times when the sun doesn't shine and the wind doesn't blow. Hydroelectric power generation is highly desirable, but global warming is lowering the water levels of fresh water reservoirs. Lake Mead, for example, has dropped enough to expose the intake tunnel for the water that powers the dam's generators. Thus, conventional hydroelectric power cannot be increased. Instead, it is decreasing. Geothermal steam is only a tiny contributor. All of the other sources of energy, e.g., biomass, corn as a source of ethanol, nuclear power (declining as plants become obsolete and, for environmental reasons, few new ones are built,) and whiz-bang batteries are also useful augmenters of fossil fuels, but are not nearly enough to meet the planet's demand for energy.

These phenomena were leading us toward the crisis of "peak oil," that is, the point when our ability to generate energy from fossil fuels peaks, followed by terminal decline. When the demand for energy exceeds that which can be produced, an economic crisis follows. The greater the gap between energy supply and demand, the greater the economic crisis. Such a crisis triggers an inexorable progression from recession to depression to collapse.

This looming crisis had developed without any noticeable concern on the part of the public or the markets, not because it was happening in secret–it wasn't–but because few people follow the arcane, cyclical and complex subject of energy and because the oil and gas companies were not sounding the alarm.

It was in this environment that a man named Aubrey McClendon and a handful of others, including former Vice President Dick Cheney, then CEO of Haliburton, were working under the radar on a process called hydraulic fracking as we started the new twenty-first century. During the nineteenth and twentieth centuries, oil was extracted from porous rocks like sandstone and limestones and sandy shales into which oil, buoyed by groundwater, had seeped via slow leaks from oil shales below. The oil rose on the surface of groundwater as it bled with glacial slowness from the source rock of all oil and gas – a non-permeable rock known as shale deposited in former seabeds over millions of years. In those seabeds were the remains of all marine life that ever lived. When this carboniferous waste was subjected to extreme pressures and extreme heat from the weight of all of the rock deposits above them, it formed hydrocarbons we know as oil and methane. These forces slowly squeezed oil and gas out of the source shales over millennia which then migrated upward via groundwater until blocked by geological traps for them where non-permeable rocks like limestone formed an arch or "anticline" cap or where hard rock strata intersected at angles along fault lines.

In the nineteenth and twentieth centuries, oil and gas producers would, through geophysical means, locate subsurface rock structures above oil shales that were likely to hold oil in permeable rock. They would then drill down into to those structures. If they hit oil-bearing rock, and if the rock was permeable, then the extreme pressure of the deep rock would force the oil to flow into the hole and up to the surface for our use. At first, the strikes produced gushers, but then drillers learned to cap those oil wells with a valve that regulated the extraction rate according to their ability to store oil and transport it in pipelines. That production methodology is known as conventional drilling, and has served us well. However, by the end of the twentieth century, pretty much all of the conventional oil reserves on the planet had been discovered and were in various stages of depletion. Discovery of new conventional oil had long been declining. The planet was looking peak oil in the eye as oil companies were forced to undertake more and more extreme drilling to find new oil.

Meanwhile, Aubrey McClendon and his cohort were frantically seeking new technologies that would allow them to extract oil and gas from the source rock itself—the oil shales. These are vast deposits of rock consisting of very fine grains of earth that had fallen on the ancient sea as dust or flowed into it from continental rivers carrying sediments into the sea. These fine materials mixed with the remains of marine life in the sea formed the oil shales in deep water, and over hundreds of millions of years grew hundreds or even thousands of feet thick as they were continuously overlain with other rocks.

Shale, as I said, is impermeable. If you drill into it, the oil it contains doesn't flow into the drill hole. Hydraulic fracking solves that problem. It is a multifaceted method involving pumping water into the shale at high pressures, fracturing the rock in a relatively small area around the drill hole and then forcing special, often toxic chemicals mixed with sand into the cracks and fissures created by the fracturing of the rock. That process enables the trapped oil and gas to migrate to the hole throughout the fracture zone. Because only a relatively small area of the oil shale is able to be fracked for any one well, many oil wells close together are needed to extract all the oil in the shale deposit.

Fracked oil and gas wells leak methane because the concrete used to seal the well does not achieve a perfect seal between the drill pipe and the rock and because concrete cracks. For these reasons, fracked wells spew methane into the subsurface groundwater and directly into the atmosphere. Methane is a greenhouse gas that is thirty times more effective at trapping heat from the sun underneath it than carbon dioxide. There have been widely publicized instances where residential homes above the fracked wells have been contaminated by leaked methane. People living on properties with water wells have been shown on film turning on their garden hoses and striking a match to produce a blowtorch coming out of the hose.

The core developers and innovators of fracking methods, of course, knew all this. When Dick Cheney was George W. Bush's Vice President, he convened a skunk works in the basement of the White House to sort through these problems. Cheney and the White House steadfastly refused to identify the personnel involved or even what they were working on. However, it was during that time that the Republican-controlled Congress inserted a short line item amendment in a voluminous appropriations bill that exempted fracking activities from the Clean Air Act, The Clean Water Act and the laws requiring polluters to clean up the soils and waterways they pollute. Then fracking took off. Hundreds of thousands of wells were fracked during the first decade of the twenty-first century and into the second. Widespread water and air pollution resulted, but the public had no remedies to stop it or force changes in the fracking process. Democratic administrations sometimes banned fracking on Federal land.

Unbeknown to the public, however, peak oil had finally arrived around 2010 for conventional oil and gas production. Maximum production from conventional wells had plateaued and a few years after that had started trending down. Demand had continued to increase with population growth and in the developing world like China, India and the Africa. The crisis predicted by peak oil theory had, however, been averted by the advent of fracking, problematical as it was.

Fracked oil became so plentiful that America stopped importing its marginal oil needs and instead began to export it. Fracking basically saved America's, and the world's, bacon. It came with high environmental costs, however. As I write this, a study has revealed that one half of all of the increase in greenhouse gasses from all sources *on the planet* during the last decade has been caused by fracking in the United States and Canada. Vast areas of surface land in the United States that overlie the oil shales being fracked are denuded by hundreds of thousands of oil and gas wells and their waste collection ponds and machinery. But fracked oil is also finite. Fracked wells deplete faster than conventional wells and global oil production is now forecast to peak around 2040 and earlier in some countries, according to the official reports of The Organization of Petroleum Exporting Countries.

As I became aware of these phenomena, I began to write my second novel, *In Extremis*. It is a meditation on how, exactly, America and the world might slide into collapse as peak oil is reached and a severe shortage of fossil fuels develops. After all, peak oil had already occurred with conventional oil and gas production. Fracking and other extreme or unconventional drilling had intervened to save us in the second decade of the twenty first century as I write this, but that is only a temporary reprieve. And more to the point, after shale oil, *there isn't any more*. We are presently engaged in depleting the source rock.

So, barring a miraculous discovery of one or more replacement sources of energy, which I fervently hope for, our government should be promoting the conservation of the oil and gas we have, along with initiating a high priority scientific search for one or more non-or lesser polluting energy sources to replace fossil fuels. As I write this, there is a large and organized environmental movement to take us off of fossil fuels to mitigate global warming. As the late T. Boone Pickens, a famous Texas wildcatter and founder of Marathon Oil Company, stated in my presence at a Commonwealth Club meeting in San Francisco a few years ago, "We *are* going off of fossil fuels in the foreseeable future." He said that forcefully to emphasize that fossil fuels are finite and we are rapidly exhausting them. The implication of his remarks, however, was that if we did so involuntarily, it would be catastrophic. We don't have enough energy to support the 7.3 billion people on the planet now.

The only non-catastrophic way to go off fossil fuels that would not bring a mass sapiens die-off and global economic collapse is to invent, develop and scale up an alternative source of energy not presently known. Bill Gates has also been quoted as saying that "an energy miracle" is needed. For more on this subject and Bill Gates' important ongoing contributions, see my essay "On Fossil Fuels" in Chapter 30.

A dystopian collapse following peak oil is, then, the back story for my novel *In Extremis*. Again, it is a book I felt I had to write because no one else seemed to be writing it. Whether the book should have been a novel as opposed to non-fiction is debatable. The only book I could write is a novel. And so I did. As a self-published book, it met with the same fate as *The Chasm* met. It languished in obscurity outside of my circle of family and friends.

As I write, we are living at a time of racial conflict and great economic inequality caused by globalization and automation. The chaos unleashed by the presidency of Donald Trump, together with the Wuhan Covid-19 virus pandemic and recession it produced, is upon us. Oil and gas continue to be plentiful and relatively cheap due to the abundance of fracked oil and gas and decreased economic activity during the pandemic.

Energy companies are incentivized to extract oil and gas as fast as they can be sold, even though they are being depleted rapidly. Consumers of fossil fuels are not incentivized to conserve the planet's reserves other than to mitigate global climate change, a more gradual process. So, the exhaustion of our dominant energy source continues to be a sleeping issue overwhelmed by more immediate crises in our daily lives. However, we are still on a speeding train rushing toward peak oil that is getting closer. I pray, as the saying goes, that I am wrong. Also, that Bill Gates will somehow save us.

CHAPTER 18

WINEMAKING

Just as Carol's cancer period overlapped the commencement of my writing career as described above, yet another activity was also going on simultaneously – my winemaking enterprise. Around 2003, David Slaby, fellow lawyer, bocce mate and winemaker and his wife Margo began to include Carol and I in their annual communal winemaking festivities. These events were basically two: harvesting and bottling, each finished with a large and festive dinner at the long table in their backyard attended by their many friends who may or may not have helped with the hard work of a cellar rat in making the wine.

At harvest time, we joined with other friends of the Slabys picking the grapes and, immediately after picking, crushing the grapes of that vintage. The Slaby vineyard was a two acre parcel in the storied "Rutherford dust" appellation – prime Nava Valley cabernet sauvignon country. They sold their wine commercially under the brand name "Slaughterhouse Cellars," so named because their winery outbuilding had been a slaughterhouse a century earlier.

Picking involves getting a small scythe in one hand and putting a thick leather glove on the other and squatting or bending down to the fruit zone on the vines about three feet off the ground. Stoop labor. Hard work. You cut the stems that hold the bunches of grapes to the vine and toss the bunches in a plastic box or "lug" as you move down a row of vines, taking care not to include leaves or other "MOG" (material other than grapes.) When the lug is full, you carry it (about 45 pounds) to the picking "bin" (heavy plastic box about 4' x 4' x 2') placed where it can be picked up by a forklift somewhere near one end of the row. You do that until all grapes in the vineyard are picked and in the bins.

The bins are sized to hold about 1000 pounds of grapes which equates to approximately one 60 gallon barrel of wine. Then the bins are placed next to the crusher/destemmer machine at the winery and the bunches of grapes are shoveled into a hopper at the top of the crusher/destemmer which sits astride an empty bin. An augur at the bottom of the hopper moves the bunches of grapes along to a chute and down into a rotating, paddle arrangement in a steel tube perforated with holes big enough for grapes to fall through. That process breaks the berries from the stems and drops the crushed berries into the bin while sweeping the stems out the end of the crushing tube. The grape juice and crushed grape skins and seeds collect in the crushing bin and make up the grape "must." When you had crushed the requisite amount of grape bunches to make the requisite amount of must, you added a precisely measured amount of a sulphur compound (preservative and killer of wild yeast and bacteria,) winemaker's yeast (choosing which one depends on the style of wine you want,) and nutrients to stimulate the yeast bacteria to "eat" the sugar compounds in the grape juice. That converts the sugars into ethanol, heat and $CO2$. Thus, inoculation of must with yeast commences alcoholic fermentation which, with the requisite amount of nutrients, will ferment all of the sugar into alcohol. Then it is wine.

If you are making a white wine from golden yellow grapes, you must press the juice off of the must immediately after crushing and move the juice to a fermenter. If you are making red wine, you leave the juice on the blue/black skins and seeds in the must, so that the water soluble phenols and aromatic compounds leach from the skins out into the juice as it ferments. Those compounds make red wine red and a good deal more complex than white wine.

After the grapes are crushed and the must is fermented, the wine is usually placed in an oak barrel to mature. Whether the oak barrel is new or previously used, what kind of oak to use, and how much "toast" or char from firing is desired on the interior wood surface, are all elements of the art of the winemaker. Periodically thereafter, every few months, the wine is "racked," that is, pumped off of the "lees" (dead yeast and goo) that falls to the bottom of the barrel and is discarded. The wine becomes progressively clearer and more sediment free with each racking. At some point in the aging and maturing process, the winemaker decides to bottle the wine. When to do so is more winemaker art.

The Slabys left their wine in new French oak barrels for about twenty months. When it was time to bottle, we were invited back over to siphon the wine from the barrel into bottles, whereupon the bottles were corked and a foil cap was spun onto the top before being labeled and put into cases. Another banquet followed bottling, and once again, it would be a joyous affair.

I took an introduction to oenology course at Napa Valley College, a summary course designed to familiarize the student with vineyard practices and winemaking processes. I followed that up with another course in the chemistry of winemaking. Those two courses, coupled with my hands-on experience working with David and Margo, made me confident that I could make wine myself. We were also fortunate to have Enology Testing Services, one of the premier wine laboratories in the world, in Saint Helena. Local winemakers could thus test their wines at all stages to see if their developing wines were chemically within parameters and microbially healthy.

Beginning in 2005, I would decide what kind of wine I wanted to make each year. It was always going to be a variety of red wine because those were my preferred wines. My objective was not to sell wine, but to serve it to friends and family (and drink myself.) In the process, I would learn all about each variety of red wine that I had cultivated a taste for, which was just about all of them.

Once I decided what variety of red wine I wanted to make, I would hunt through the classifieds and postings at various wine bulletin boards until I found a quantity of the desired variety for sale and grown in a good location for those grapes. If the seller would sell to home winemakers—some large growers will only deal in large lots to wineries for tax reasons—I would contract to buy them. Then, as the grapes ripened, I would walk the vineyard and test the sugar levels in them with my field refractometer. When ripe enough (but not too ripe!–more art) I would pick them with friends or hired help and haul them off to my garage to be crushed and destemmed. Alcoholic fermentation would follow.

I designed my label by searching through free clip art on the internet until I found a very moody image of a clipper ship sailing into a fog bank. Then I downloaded the image into my labels folder. I branded myself

Admiralty Cellars because I was an admiralty lawyer and because the maritime influence on the weather is what makes the Napa Valley an especially good winemaking venue. I reused the same design every year, changing only the name of the grape, the calendar year, and adding a maritime term to brand each vintage, for example, the "Silver Oar" cabernet sauvignon, or the "Zephros" pinot noir. Over twelve years, I made three Cab vintages, one pinot noir, one petite sirah, one grenache, one sangiovese, one syrah, and two zinfandels. In 2011, I couldn't make wine as my new house was under construction. One year I bought some bulk Petaluma Gap chardonnay and then clarified and oaked it myself for my house chardonnay.

Immediately after moving into the White Lane house in 2012, I hired a vineyard manager and planted 366 vines of cab, merlot and cabernet franc. My first vintage of fully fruited vines was in 2016, when I harvested well over a half ton (1000 pounds = one barrel = 24 cases = 288 bottles of wine.) My 2017 vintage yielded over a ton of grapes and twice as much wine. The yield would double again with two more years of growth and pruning. A few years of that and I would have enough wine to see me out.

However, contemporaneously with the writing and winemaking sagas, I still had another item on my "wannado" list.

CHAPTER 19

TRAVEL—ON MY OWN

When Judy and I were first married, we had little disposable income for travel. Travel for us was a skiing vacation at Lake Tahoe with the kids. I had, of course, travelled throughout Europe during my junior year abroad and had stops of various lengths in Hawaii, South Korea, Hong Kong, Taiwan, the Philippines, and many months in Japan in the Marine Corps. In Japan, most of my time was spent in Okinawa, but my battalion held a military exercise in the Mt. Fuji area, and I took leave to visit Nikko, Hong Kong (where I bought a Rolex submariner watch in 1963 for $85 which I am still wearing as I write this in 2021) and to attend some Olympic games in Tokyo in 1964. I had a taste for travel, but had scant funds to indulge it.

When Carol and I were married in 1983, we had many more opportunities to travel. We took several two and three week trips to Italy and France on vacation, and toured the Piemonte wine region and the Lake District north of Milan, the Amalfi Coast, the Cinque Terre, Emilia Romagna, Sicily, Tuscany and my father-in-law's homeland in Puglia. We went to Prague and Paris in 1994 and, from Paris, we drove along the Seine to Normandy a month after the 50th anniversary celebrations of the Normandy landing in June, 1944. I didn't know it at the time, but the *Jeremiah O'Brien* had also made the trip back to Normandy for the occasion. In fact, out of the approximately 6,400 ships of all sizes that had participated in the invasion, the *O'Brien* was the *only* ship that had been a part of the invasion to make it back for the 50th anniversary.

Erin and I caught a ride on an APL break-bulk ship from San Francisco to Seattle along with my car, and the two of us drove back past Mt. St. Helens and down the Oregon and Northern California coasts seeing all the sights.

I took a once-in-a-lifetime trip with Gray for his college graduation on a two-week, absolutely stupendous, oar boat trip 212 miles through the Grand Canyon on the Colorado River. Carol and I took other once-in-a-lifetime trips to sub-Saharan Africa for game viewing as described earlier, to Australia's Great Barrier Reef, wine regions of Barossa and McLaren Vale, Kangaroo Island, and The Great Ocean Road drive; and, for my 60th birthday, a cruise to the Society Islands of Tahiti, Moorea, Bora Bora, Raiatea and Huahine.

After Carol died, world travel moved to the top of my wannado list. I deferred travel during construction of my new house because the house required my presence, but as the sweep second hand of my Rolex submariner passed 5 pm on the day I moved into the new house, I began to plan some travel—Paul Theroux-type travel, as in "go far, go alone, ask questions." Not vacations, but travel.

Someone had tipped me to a website called Vacations To Go that had an active travel agency and specialized in booking unsold cruise line cabins at the last minute. As a single, retired person, I was in a position to book on short notice when the deals came along. I began to follow their "90 day ticker," that is, their list of discounted fares for cruises departing in less than 90 days. Good, ocean view cabins could be had for bargain prices for a remarkable variety of cruise locations and durations.

I spotted one that intrigued me because of its itinerary and price. It was an eleven day repositioning cruise on a Royal Caribbean ship departing June, 2012 from Puerto Rico for Lisbon via Saint Martin in the Caribbean and the Canary Islands, none of which I had ever visited. Moreover, the single supplement (they typically charge an extra fee for single travelers as their cabin prices are based on two persons per cabin) was waived so my total cost for an ocean view cabin was $650. That is, $59 per day for transportation to Lisbon with all meals and entertainment. I used United Airlines' frequent flyer miles for a discounted flight to San Juan, Puerto Rico and spent a couple of days in San Juan seeing the sights before boarding the ship. It was June and the South Atlantic was placid so I spent six days quite pleasantly writing in my journal and gazing at the flat blue water. I also wrote the short story "Lisbon" (see *PLACE, Eight Stories*) between Saint Martin in the Dutch Antilles and the island of Tenerife, Santa Cruz in the Canary Islands before landing in Lisbon.

In Tenerife, I learned that Cristopher Columbus discovered the New World by means of a very simple navigational strategy. He sailed south from the Mediterranean along the coast of Africa to the tropics, then turned west. It was known that India was in the tropics. He knew from the Portuguese navigators that the earth was round, but he didn't have a realistic view of how big the globe was. The Portuguese did because they were the most skilled navigators, but Columbus didn't. So, he sailed from Spain to Tenerife, a tropical outpost off the coast from the Sahara Desert, filled up with fresh water and provisions, and then sailed west. He landed in Hispanola, next door to what is now Puerto Rico, and a long way from India and the spices that Europe needed after being cut off from the Arab trading routes by the Arab caliphs that had tired of the Crusades.

I had a lovely time exploring Lisbon and learning about the Age of Discovery and the golden Age of Portugal. I hired a guide to take me around the Douro Valley wine country and one of the places he took me to had twin flag poles, one flying the Italian flag and one the American flag. I remarked on that and my driver said that the owners were Vincent and Kay Bouchard. He was Italian and she was American. The tumblers in my head then fell into place. This was the Quinta do Tedo winery belonging to neighbors Carol and I had on Spring Mountain Road in Saint Helena. In fact, we had brokered the renting of their house and grounds as the site for Mike and Jen's wedding. Vincent was travelling and Kay had gone into Oporto, so I missed them both, but wrote them a note. What are the odds?

The old city of Oporto is on a prominent hill that falls off into the Douro River channel that cuts the old city off from its industrial section containing all the port wineries. J K Rowling sat for hours in Oporto coffee shops a decade earlier after her divorce writing some young adult books about a "muggle" named Harry Potter and some wizard friends. The fabled port houses, however, are down off the river where barges deliver grapes and wine from upriver vineyards to the warehouses where they age their delicious elixirs.

I flew to Madrid to revisit the city I had not seen since my motorcycle trip through Spain in 1960, some fifty two years earlier. I was astonished to find in the Prado Museum, a second identical painting of

The Mona Lisa painted "in Leonardo's studio" just after the original. You could walk right up to it and touch it–no security of any kind and no crowds. The haunting "dark" paintings of Goya were still there.

After tapas in the Plaza Central at midnight and a night's rest, I caught the flight to Paris and connecting flight home to conclude my first solo travel since college. I wanted more, but grape harvest was approaching and there was pinot noir wine to be made.

During harvest, I began to look for another cruise. I was able to put one together after the pinot was safely in the barrel for an October departure by one of Norwegian Lines' ships from Venice for a twelve day Mediterranean cruise. So, for the princely sum of $1,100 (including a small single supplement this time) and a round trip plane ticket, I returned to Venice for the third time to board my ship. Piazza San Marco was awash with increasingly common flood waters and wooden plank sidewalks had been erected for pedestrians to walk on above the foot-deep water. I winced when I saw the ancient mosaics that covered the great expanse of the floors of Saint Mark's cathedral still exposed to the muddy water. Venice was sinking and the oceans were rising.

Usually, a cruise ship sails from the industrial harbor of a city, but in Venice, the cruise ship terminal is shoe-horned in on one of the islands that make up the city. Whether you are on the ship looking at the City or in the City looking at the ship, it is an incongruous sight both to see and to be on a colossal cruise ship sailing in the small, confined canals of Venice otherwise populated with gondolas and *vaporetti.*

From Venice, we sailed to Santorini and Mykonos in Greece; to Kusadasi (Ephesus) and Istanbul in Turkey; to Naples, Rome and Florence in Italy; and finished in Marseilles in France. I had basically a lovely and nostalgic day-long visit at each port. To those who distain cruising on the grounds that they prefer to spend several days getting to know a place intimately, I would say that granted, more time in a city provides a greater learning experience in that city, however, that means fewer places visited. And, given the choice, would you turn down spending a day in each of these destinations? As opposed to not seeing them at all? And, no schlepping in and out! And at "90 day ticker" prices! This trip made me want to return to Greece. My university education did not include much about classical Greece apart from the odd epic poem in a literature class. I knew nothing at all about Greek history, philosophy and governance. I wanted to make an effort to fill those gaps.

My next trip the following year (2013) was not an organized cruise. I determined to allot two and a half weeks to island hopping in Greece on my own—the only way I could craft my own itinerary. So, after a decent interval at home taking care of business, I flew SFO-Chicago-Munich-Athens, a long way that took a long time. I arrived, zombie tired, in Athens on a hot summer day to find that the busses and taxis were on strike. How was I to get to my hotel in downtown Athens with a brain pickled by fatigue? A train from the airport got me within four blocks of my hotel, but from there it was shanks' mare. The hotel I'd booked was not fancy but adequate and well located near The Acropolis, the Acropolis Museum, the Agora (older temples than the Acropolis,) and Ermou Street for shops and restaurants. After a nap, I walked the Agora and the shopping and café districts, saving the Acropolis for the next day.

The climb up to the Acropolis and the Parthenon was work. High humidity, no breeze, a hot midday sun, and a large crowd made for a miserable climb up the narrow trail and innumerable steps to the hilltop on which the Parthenon sits. It is the antiquity of the place, as well as its view that makes it special. The Parthenon dominates the hilltop known as the Acropolis, accessed through the elaborate gateway to it at the top of all of the stairs. Siting demurely next to the Parthenon is the delicate Temple of Athena. On the flank of the hill, the trail passes the Theater of Dionysus, where Greek mythology was fleshed out in great, nuanced detail through Greek plays held there over the centuries.

The Parthenon was undergoing a major renovation when I was there. Its complete upper circumference was being restored by adding replica marble blocks to fill the gaps in the continuous lintel that sat atop the columns on all four sides. This stabilized the column arrangement as a solid rectangle. The top of the building originally had marvelous sculpted marble panels attached to the lintel. The panels depicted count-less scenes from Greek mythology.

Hadrian led the Roman army that conquered Greece circa 131 BCE, but he so revered Greek theater and mythology that Hadrian's Gate, his triumphal arch, became a line of demarcation between ancient Athens and the Roman-occupied city to protect the former from being sacked or disfigured. Regrettably, subsequent Christian occupiers did not feel the same sensibilities. The Christians climbed up to the top of the Parthenon and smashed the marble panels that circled the lintel of the Parthenon with hammers and threw the panel remains to the ground below, shattering them. They did so because the panels depicted pagan beliefs and that offended the monotheistic zealotry of the early Christians. [That history reminded me of the Afghan Taliban recently firing artillery into ancient sculptures carved into stone because they considered them blasphemous.] The Acropolis museum contains all the pieces that have been found and has arranged them, with major gaps, in the continuous relief that would have ornamented the original lintel.

From Athens I took a day trip to Delphi (Del-fee) to visit the former center of the earth. Greek mythology holds that the god of gods, Zeus, sent two eagles to the opposite ends of the earth and had them fly back in a straight line until they met. The fable says they met on the flank of Mount Parnassus. Elaborate structures were built there, such as the Temple of Apollo to commemorate Apollo's defeat of the dragon that guarded the site, He did so by disguising himself as a dolphin ("delphi" in Greek) which allowed Apollo to get close enough to the dragon to slay it. Omphalos, a large, egg-shaped stone was crafted and placed in Delphi to mark the precise location of the center of the earth, aka, the earth's navel. A circus was built at Delphi for chariot racing, an amphitheater for dramas, and most importantly, a Treasury building to safeguard the wealth that was brought to Delphi by pilgrims asking for the favorable benedictions of the Oracle of Delphi. The story of the Oracle is a remarkable one, and it would be hard to overstate the significance of her function during the several centuries BCE when she held court at the center of the earth.

The Oracle was always a middle aged woman selected from the community. She didn't have to be nobility, just be able to play the role expected of her. Once chosen, she was called Pythia and had to leave her family and devote herself to her duties. Those duties consisted of sitting on a tripod over a hole in the floor of the Temple of Apollo whenever foreign pilgrims came to Delphi to consult with her. The pilgrim would stand before her and ask for his fortune to be told concerning any matter of state or quest for discovery or territory. It was recorded, many times and over many centuries, that she would invariably answer in what seemed to be gibberish, but there was always a priest in the next room to "interpret" the oracle. The interpretations of the priest were artful and usually susceptible of being interpreted in alternative ways, no doubt to foster a reputation of infallibility.

The Greeks today tell a story, in the nature of a joke, that Phillip of Macedon had a spirited horse that no one could ride. Pythia told him that whoever could ride the horse could rule the world. Only Phillip's son Alexander succeeded in riding the horse when he realized that the horse was merely afraid of its shadow. Alexander, who came to be known as the Great, then consulted Pythia whether his planned expedition to conquer the known world would be successful. Furious with her answer in gibberish and before the priest could interpret it, Alexander grabbed Pythia by her hair and dragged her off her stool. Pythia exclaimed in clear Greek, "You are unstoppable!" Alexander then, it is said, dropped her, saying "I have my answer!" and left to conquer the known world.

It has long been a mystery whether the Oracle was just a con job by the then clergy bent on earning vast sums of tribute paid to the Oracle and put into the Treasury. However, many give credence to the Oracle legend because history is replete with references to a woman operating as Pythia who was in fact consulted by Greeks, Carthaginians, Persians, Macedonians, etc., *for hundreds of years* and reported on many times by the chroniclers of the day as authentic and accurate in her predictions. With that much exposure, surely a flim-flam operation would have been detected and the Oracle relegated to disrepute. Perhaps the following postscript is instructive:

Carol's niece Christine married a young man named Bjorn de Boer. Bjorn's father, Jele, was a Dutch-born geology professor at Wesleyan University in Massachusetts. Jele and a team of his colleagues set out to determine whether there was a possible geology-based explanation for why and how the legend of the Oracle at Delphi could have continued for so long and been so convincing. For Jele, the prevailing explanation that it was all a con job didn't square with the record. So, he and his team proceeded to Delphi one summer and began to map the geological features of the site. What they found was that two separate fault lines intersected beneath the ruins of the Temple of Apollo in which Pythia presided. Moreover, there were traces of two gasses associated with fossil fuels and vulcanism, one of which is called ethylene, present in the vicinity of the fault lines. Concentrated ethylene is sometimes used as an anesthetic, in addition to other industrial purposes. Thus, Jele's team concluded it was *possible* that, if the Oracle's tripod had been strategically located over a hole in the temple's floor, as reported in the ancient texts, above a fault seam or intersection of seams, any escaping ethylene gas *could have been* present in concentrations high enough to produce altered consciousness. Thus, Pythia's actual state of being drugged or "high" on ethylene would have been authentic and thereby convincing for the many, many close observers of many Pythias over hundreds of years.

After Delphi, I took a bus to Corinth on the isthmus between Athens and Sparta (the Peloponnese.) Apart from being an interesting ancient Greek and subsequently Roman city, now in ruins, Corinth also represented an historically important community of Christians following the death of Jesus the Nazarene. This community was visited by the Apostle Paul twice and his later letters to the Corinthians reinforcing his earlier preachings there are set out in the New Testament of the Bible twice. My visit to Corinth planted a seed in my head that eventually took the form of one of the eight short stories making up my book of short stories called PLACE. The story is called "Corinthians." It explains the remarkable, but little known, legal "proceeding" that identified and validated the theology known as Christianity, and the cast of characters is not to be believed.

Back in Athens after the Corinth visit, I made my way from Athens to the port of Piraeus, and thence, by ferry to Santorini. As the ferry sailed out of Piraeus, I leaned over the rail at the stern of the boat admiring the view. As we passed through the channel between various ships at anchor in the harbor, an apparition appeared off the stern, portside. The shape of the hull and its rigging was unmistakable. It was a Liberty ship! At that time, I was a volunteer docent on the Liberty ship *SS Jeremiah O'Brien* in San Francisco, one of only two operating Liberty ships in existence. (This was yet another concurrent activity I undertook after Carol died.) I had no knowledge of one in Piraeus. Once I returned back home, I researched it and learned that the Liberty ship *SS Arthur Huddell,* which was also in the battle of Normandy with the *O'Brien,* had been specially rigged to lay pipe across the English channel to supply oil to the forces operating in Normandy. After WW II, it was employed laying pipelines under the ocean commercially until officially retired and scheduled to be sunk as a fish habitat. It was rescued from that fate through the good offices of some Greek American officials and gifted to Greece, where it was restored by Greek philanthropists as a museum and renamed the *SS Hellas Liberty.*

Santorini, aka the island of Thira, consists of the remains of a large volcano torn apart by an explosive eruption that devastated the Minoan civilization in nearby Crete circa 1400 BCE. It is visually striking and the villages that sit atop the caldera's peaks are a photographer's dream. Blinding white houses with startlingly blue tile roofs that somehow match the color of both the sky and the sea cling impossibly to the highest rim of the caldera. Donkeys formerly transported visitors from the beach to the rim above the sea, but busses do the job today via a hair-raising, hairpin-turning road only slightly less arduous. I rented a motor scooter and tooted around the small island, visiting a couple of wineries on the slope of the volcano. They have wildly different vineyard practices than ours because of Thira's *terroir* and prevailing winds, but I discovered a very nice white wine that has made a reputation for itself internationally. It's a cultivar called *assyrtico* and closely resembles *sauvignon blanc.*

From Santorini, I ferried to Crete, landing in Heraklion, its major city. After touring the ancient Minoan city of Knossos, home to the athletic sport of vaulting over bulls, I rented a car and traveled west to the seaside resort town of Rethymno and its ancient Moorish fort and Italian harbor ringed with restaurants.

In the opposite direction from Heraklion the next day, I travelled east to the resort area of Agios Nikolaos and its nearby Venetian salt mine and protective fort. Back in the day of the city states, when there was no refrigeration, the demand for salt, like the demand for spices, was high to preserve meat and fish, mask the odors of decaying food to be eaten anyway, and to add flavor to bland food. Prices were very high for salt and spices. The Venetians found it very profitable to sail to the slave market on the island of Delos just off Mykonos, buy a passel of slaves, and force them to work in the salt mines. It was so profitable, they needed a fort to defend the mines.

Ah, and "Zorba the Greek" was filmed in Crete as well in black and white, exhibiting perfectly Crete's iconic black and white pebble passageways and plazas.

From Crete, I ferried to Rhodes which I found to have a fascinating history that I had never heard of. It was a Christian city state. Correction: it was *the* Christian city state. The Crusaders had managed to successfully occupy Palestine and its capital Jerusalem only briefly before they were expelled by Islamic forces in 1291. The Knights of St John, Hospitaller, the name under which they organized themselves, were originally dedicated to health care for the sick, Crusaders and otherwise, in Jerusalem. From Jerusalem, the Knights relocated to Rhodes, and the crusaders operated from Rhodes between 1312 and 1522 as a sovereign city state and headquarters for European crusaders challenging the Muslim occupation of the Christian holy land. However, Suleiman II (successor to Suleiman the Magnificent) ultimately had a belly full of Christian "pirate" ships harassing Muslim shipping and raiding Muslim lands. So, in 1522, he landed 100,000 troops in Rhodes and laid siege to the Crusader palaces of "tongues" (Crusader units were organized into "palaces" or large collective residences having inhabitants that spoke the same language – e.g., English, German, Italian, Spanish, French, etc.) Overwhelmed, the Crusaders quickly surrendered, and Suleiman banished them from Rhodes forever. From Rhodes, the Knights moved their headquarters to Malta where they have resided continuously ever since. The group's full name is The Knights of Saint John, Hospitaller, of Jerusalem, of Rhodes and of Malta. They are not the Knights Templar, another Catholic organization of zealots that operated as a secret society but no longer exists.

My plan was to ferry from Rhodes to neighboring Patmos and check out the cave site where John of Patmos is thought to have written the Bible's Book of Revelation setting out his imaginings of Armageddon. However, I found out "you can't get there from here." I naively thought you could get from any island to any other island nearby via some interconnecting ferry. Not so. Several different ferry lines have carved up the interisland traffic according to routes and schedules satisfactory, or profitable, to them. No one goes from Rhodes to Patmos. You have to go all the way back to Athens and then return to Patmos, likely by air. That didn't work for me as it was to be my last stop and I didn't have time to do a roundtrip to Athens. So, I'll likely never get the full story of the Book of Revelation, but the Roman Emperor Constantine and his bishops decided at the end of the fourth century to include the, um, meditations (hallucinations?) of John of Patmos on the "end times" in the anthology that they prepared and that we call The Bible.

So, it was back to Athens for an extra day to watch the anti-World Bank, anti-EU demonstrations then occurring on a daily basis in Syntagma Square across the street from the Parliament Building. The next morning, I began the relay race consisting of four long flight legs back to San Francisco.

It was a great trip. I, of course, only scratched the surface of Classical Greek history, but it was a deep dive into it for a short period of two and a half weeks that gave me a comfortable awareness of the place and its people. "Z! He lives!"

CHAPTER 20

MORE WRITING

Pretty much throughout the period following my post-retirement, writing had made an appearance on my wannado list, and, along with my two novels, I began to experiment with short stories. I would start something and then put it away, only to dust it off later and try again to give it some coherence. I wrote three rhyming children's books of the sort that I enjoyed reading to my grandkids when they were little. However, those were picture book projects, and I didn't have a killer illustrator to joint venture with. Also, that is a very competitive field, and I wasn't serious about it. So, the children's book efforts disappeared into the ether. But the short stories began to accumulate.

Thunder River Man had its genesis in the oar rafting trip that Gray and I took through the Grand Canyon, but I didn't write it until much later. As I mention in the foreword to my third book, *PLACES: Eight Stories*, I was paying homage in my way to Tony Hillerman, one of my favorite mystery writers who had just passed away.

I wrote *Lisbon*, on the Royal Caribbean Line cruise ship sailing from San Juan, Puerto Rico to Lisbon. It was my first cruise after Carol died and cancer and end-of-life matters were very much on my mind at the time.

I wrote *The Futile Crescent* sometime during America's long, gratuitous and ill-advised interference in the Sunni-Shi'a running civil wars in the Middle East. Beginning with Saddam Hussein's invasion of Kuwait, Bush 41's (George Herbert Walker Bush, the 41st President of the United States and former Vice President to Ronald Reagan, aka "Bush 41") successfully commenced Operation Desert Storm to restore Kuwaiti independence and protect Saudi Arabia from invasion by Iraq. Ten years later, however, Bush 43 (George Walker Bush, the 43rd President, former Governor of Texas, son of Bush 41, aka "Bush 43") invaded Afghanistan following Osama Bin

Laden's Al Qaida-engineered attack on New York's twin World Trade towers. Afghanistan's Taliban regime was then hosting Al Qaida and Bin Laden in the remote mountainous terrain of Afghanistan.

Bush 43 inexplicably invaded Iraq after the invasion of Afghanistan tapered off following its success. He did so on the mistaken grounds that Iraq's dictator, Saddam Hussein, had some prominent role in the 9/11 attacks in New York. As I write this, we still have token deployments of troops in both Afghanistan and Iraq as our two political parties alternate in trying to decide whether America's interests lie with anti-terrorist warfare against the Sunni extremists that attacked New York, or an anti-insurgency policy which targets either Sunni or Shiite extremists who lead armed rebellion against an American-installed regime in each country. Hence, the heavy irony in the short story "The Futile Crescent," a title cynically coined from the region's historical title "the fertile crescent," so-called because of the agriculturally productive valleys of the Tigris and Euphrates rivers.

Girlfriends was a meditation on a man's need for female companionship, not only for the affectionate intimacy needed to be happy, but also on a man's perhaps unconscious inclination to substitute his solitary tendencies for participation in a more sustaining social system organized by women around family and societal communities. That was written during my bachelorhood after Carol died.

Un Elephant was at once a salute to family and a snarky sendoff of the NFL and it's pompous pretensions of centricity to American life while comprehensively self-dealing as a greedy money making machine.

The Nazca Lines was inspired by a visit to the Paracas Coast of Peru on a Holland American Lines ship. The terrain and weather in that bleak but richly ancient place combine to make a visitor wonder if he could ever understand the forces that have come to bear at that singular place.

Corinthians, as already mentioned came to life following a visit to Corinth on my island-hopping trip to Greece. The story of how the Apostle Paul basically invented the modern theology of Christianity that served as a cloak of self-preservation while spreading the teachings of the Jewish Jesus the Nazarene. Paul also won a legal case that not only allowed him to continue to preach about the teachings of Jesus in Roman territory, but legitimized the new Christian theology for posterity, enabling it to continue until it went mainstream with the Emperor Constantine's conversion. Cap those events in Corinth off with a cast of characters about as improbable as one can imagine (the Roman Senator Seneca and his brother and the Emperor Nero himself) and it makes for the best story you never heard of. And the site where it happened, the Isthmus of Corinth, slumbers in a relatively obscurity with no conspicuous marking of the site whatever. Astonishing.

Just within the last two years, I organized these stories in a collection and gave them the serious, pre-publication editing that they deserved. I did not offer them to any agent or take any steps to seek traditional publication. My objective was not to seek fame and fortune, having learned from my experience with the two novels that the odds of getting a book deal from a traditional publishing house that will market it successfully are vanishingly small. Fortunately, I don't have to make a living from my writing. I write because I am compelled to. There are things that I am afraid will go unwritten if I don't write them. Yes, I'm aware that my writing and self-publishing these books is, in effect, practically the same as my not writing them. It's like the old joke that one's odds of winning the lottery are about the same whether you buy a ticket or not. Yet people buy lottery tickets by the millions without a backward glance. And so I self-published *PLACE; Eight Stories* with relish, knowing that family and friends and a handful of others will read them and hear my voice between the lines.

The business of self-publishing has advanced since I began writing. The first self-publishing companies were small business enterprises that sold editing and marketing services, as well as organizing the relatively simple tasks of formatting an e-document, getting a Library of Congress number, an ISBN number, and designing a cover. For these services, the author paid these publish-on-demand facilitators fees in the neighborhood of $1,000 and up, depending on the amount of support desired. As I write, the big printing company, Ingram, has segued into the burgeoning self-publication business by offering its highly automated sales software and distribution logistics for a small fee – in my case $49. It is up to me to find consultants to design a cover, format the interior text, and convert it to pdf format. (It costs less than half what I paid the full service facilitator-publishers of my novels.) Then, I upload the files to Ingram and they insert the electronic file into their inventory of e-book providers and print book providers alike. The book is thus available to anyone, anywhere, on-line or in bookstores, who wants to read or buy the book. A buyer orders a copy, one book is printed, and it is mailed to the bookstore or individual that ordered it. Hence, "publishing on demand." The inordinate delays in traditional publishing are avoided. Agent's commissions are avoided. Royalties are higher and under the author's control. There is no additional editing phase involved by the publisher which sometimes improves the book, or sometimes improves its marketability by dumbing it down. How many ways can I say it? The author's experience is much, much better with self-publishing, assuming you don't have to make a living at it.

The trade-off is a biggie, or course. You kiss off any chance of fame and fortune by not having a publishing house marketing your book. However, even with a traditional publishing house representing the book, after all the delay and unwelcome editing, if the book doesn't generate any buzz in the first couple of weeks, the publisher quits promoting it and it's up to you to market it – the same position you are in if you had self-published. Actually you are left in a slightly worse position, because if you do successfully generate sales with your own marketing, speaking at book clubs, etc., your royalties will be less.

Of course, if you are reading this history, I must have written it. This book is the product of my idle time during the Covid-19 pandemic of 2020, so pandemics are good for something. When my daughter-in-law Laura suggested that I write my memoir, I was not enthusiastic about the project. I was busy polishing the manuscript for PLACE at the time and it seemed like an uninteresting project. Over time, however, I warmed to the idea. I realized that if I were to find an autobiography/memoir written by my grandparent or great grandparent or beyond, I would love to read it. I would be fascinated to learn of the experiences and ruminations of my ancestors in light of his/her unique history. That is what is motivating me now.

Unlike my earlier novels, I am not compelled to write about something I feel to be momentous. Rather, I just feel a kinship with perhaps unborn progeny and would like to share these thoughts and recollections with them as educational trail markers, or if nothing else, entertainment. In return, I presume to ask that you "pay it forward." If you enjoy reading this at some time in the future, I ask that you consider writing your own history to pass along to your descendants and add to the daisy chain of family remembrance.

CHAPTER 21

DOWN TO THE SEA IN SHIPS

I am backtracking again now, chronologically. After my house was finished in 2012, my life settled into a new routine when I wasn't travelling. I planted and tended my 366 vine vineyard and, while waiting the four years until my first crop, I resumed making wine from grapes I purchased elsewhere. I was finishing my novel *In Extremis* and getting it ready for publication by my then publisher.

I volunteered every Friday as a docent on the Liberty ship *SS Jeremiah O'Brien* berthed at Pier 45 in San Francisco's Fisherman's Wharf, and served as a member of the safety and crowd control crew on the ship when it sailed around the Bay on public cruises. Built in 1943 in South Portland, Maine, the *O'Brien* was one of two thousand, seven hundred and ten Liberty ships built on an emergency basis at the beginning of the wars with Japan and Germany. It carried troops and supplies to Omaha Beach in the June, 1944 Normandy invasion. It was the only ship that participated in the Normandy invasion that returned to Normandy for the 50th anniversary in June, 1994. Carol and I visited Normandy and Omaha Beach a month later on our Prague-Paris trip.

[Note: I had a policy of volunteering for some public service ever since joining the San Anselmo Planning Commission in 1980, and that practice had been interrupted during Carol's illness. So, when invited to join the crew of the O'Brien by Captain Mark Schaffer in 2012, with whom I had worked at Matson, I joined up. I continue to explain the workings of the engine room to visitors and walk the decks of the old ship as a docent as I write this.]

My appetite for cruising having been whetted by the Puerto Rico-Lisbon and Mediterranean cruises as well as the Greek island-hopping trip, I determined to do more of it. Not having a wife with a fondness for travelling in style to consider, I wanted to do it comfortably, but inexpensively. So, I doubled down on following the Vacations-To-Go "90 day ticker" deals, looking for longer, more exotic cruises. I soon saw one for a Holland America Line ship sailing from Valparaiso, Chile up the west coast of South America, through the Panama Canal and the Caribbean to Fort Lauderdale over 19 days. I had never been to South America and had never transited the Panama Canal. An ocean view room was cheap, and I could get to Santiago, Chile via United Airlines using my "Frequent Flyer" credits. I jumped on it, and some three weeks after booking, I was winging my way to Santiago.

After a day in Santiago, which boasted of having the tallest building in South America in addition to snow-covered Andes peaks looming in the distance, I caught a shuttle van from the hotel in Santiago to the port of Valparaiso ninety miles away.

My day in Santiago and a morning and midday walk around Valparaiso, home to famed Chilean Nobel Prize winning poet Pablo Neruda, made a strong impression. I had read a collection of short stories on the plane about Neruda and the dark history of the military regime of the 1970s and 80s that overthrew the democratic regime of Salvador de Al-lende. The scale by which that regime arrested and "disappeared" young reformist protesters was beyond shocking, and the experience had deeply scarred the Chilean psyche. Chile is known as "the land of wine and po-etry" and its recent history had been particularly, incongruously awful.

On my first day of cruising on the *MV Zaandam*, I was moved to write the following poem:

The rain and snowmelt steal molecules
     from the pockets of the cordillera,
      inorganic except for bits of *los desaparecidos*,
   in whose pulses of the riverbeds carry them down
    to the crescent harbor,
Staining the *Rapa Nui* current and finally settling
    to form the bar
    across the harbor's mouth
    over which voyagers

from everywhere pass.
Los desaparecidos crossed the bar in this tormented land
    of wine and poetry
    to the moans Tennyson dreaded,
And met their maker, the unknown, face-to-face,
    like those on the other side of the cordillera,
    without ever having the chance to vote "No,"
    leaving an underscored Nietzsche moral.
Asi habla Zarathustra:
    "Beware the man in whom
    the urge to punish
    is strong."

Some background explanation is needed to understand the poem. "Cordillera" is the Spanish word for mountain range, referring to the Andes. "Rapa Nui current" is the ocean current that comes from the area around Easter Island, merges with the Humboldt Current from the Antarctic and sweeps up the west coast of South America toward the equator. "*Desaparecidos* crossed the bar" refers to "the disappeared ones" killed by the regime, and the phrase from Tennyson's famous poem "Crossing the Bar" which uses the mariner's metaphor for death, viz., sailing out of a harbor and over the dangerous sand bars that are found at river's mouth where many a widow mourned the loss of a sailor. The phrase "like those on the other side of the cordillera" refers to the "disappeared" victims in Argentina across the Andes where a concurrent purge of leftists by a military regime also took place. The reference to voting "No" refers to the remarkable blunder by Chile's anti-communist dictator Augusto Pinochet who was so deluded in thinking that he had the support of the Chilean people to purge Chile of leftists (murdering the young) that he put his regime up for a referendum vote. The vote was overwhelmingly against him and Pinochet resigned to be replaced, again, by democracy. The last quotation is from Nietzsche's "Thus Spake Zarathustra" warning about tyrants.

The day before I wrote the poem, however, a much happier encounter took place. After boarding the ship and unpacking, I consulted the daily schedule published by the ship and saw that there was a gathering scheduled in one of the bars for "singles and solos." Hello, I thought.

Just the ticket to start this cruise. Let's see who else is traveling far and going alone to ask questions. I walked into the bar slightly late and was confronted with about fifteen women arranged around a large curved sofa against the wall with a couple of tables in front of it. Two other men were on bar stools facing the tables and sofa. There was one chair empty at one of the tables, and I sat down in it next to a petite blonde lady in a pink dress who smiled at me, which smile I returned.

After introductions all around, I fell into a long conversation with the lady in pink whose name was Johanna and who hailed from Sydney, Australia. Her accent, however, was not Australian, but rather Dutch. She, like me, had recently lost her spouse to blood cancer, and she had been attracted to the same cruise for the same reason I had. She had, however, boarded the *Zaandam* at the beginning of the cruise in Buenos Aires and sailed around the Patagonian tip of South America and up to Valparaiso. Far from the notoriously violent passage she'd expected around the horn, however, the ship had cruised though placid, icy waters in the Strait of Magellan, an inland waterway between the Atlantic and the Pacific.

I learned that her late husband had been the son of a Dutch missionary in Indonesia and had been "interned" in a Japanese camp from age five to nine when Imperial Japan, desperate for oil, invaded the Dutch East Indies (now Java) for its abundant oil reserves. That experience haunted him the rest of his life. After an hour or so of conversation, we all adjourned to prepare for dinner. She had introduced herself as "Joka" Vanderwallen. When pressed about her first name which I found unusual, she explained that Joke (*yo*-ka) was a common Dutch nickname for Johanna. In Anglo-speaking countries, however, that spelling invited too many lame, well, jokes. So, it became Joka.

It was definitely interest at first sight. My memory of the initial meetings Joka and I had on the ship is a little imprecise, but the encounters were of the expected sort–running into each other in the common areas and cafeteria. In the ship's theater (showroom, not movie) when I spotted her sitting alone, I asked to join her. Then she reciprocated. Then we agreed to meet for shows. Then she introduced me to friends she had met from Australia. Then we joined her friends for dinners and shows as a couple. We would take shore excursions together when our sightseeing interests coincided, and met for promenades around the deck while at sea. Sailing north from "Valpo," we visited a Chilean fishing port called Coquimbo, and Peruvian ports at Paracas (the Nazca Lines), General San Martin near Pisco (from which "pisco sour" cocktails come.) Offshore, the Peruvian version of the Galapagos at the Chincha islands were a rookery for millions of birds and a major source of guano. Then to Trujillo for its pre-Columbian ruins; and the Ecuadorian port of Manta for a visit to a coffee plantation before two days in Lima via the port of Callao.

Lima is the capital of Peru and a very old and important city. The conquistadores headquartered in Cartagena, Columbia on the Caribbean side and in Lima on the Pacific side. The Catholic Cathedral in Lima is prominent with a large monastery containing an ancient library and collection. The library made an appearance in my short story *The Nazca Lines*. The conspicuous presence of police scattered around the city center revealed the political tensions between leftist elements (remnants of the insurgent group "Shining Path") and corruption-tainted conservative governments. One of the most popular sights in Lima was the Museum of the Inquisition exhibiting a diverse array of instruments of torture, reflecting badly on the occupying Spanish regime.

The Panama Canal was memorable from beginning to end. The entrance on the Pacific side was, in a head-snapping surprise, actually east of the Caribbean side. On the Pacific side lay Panama City, a smallish, Spanish-architecture-dominated old city containing traditional houses and the administration buildings of the Panama Canal, and, grafted on to it more recently, a huge city of gleaming, high-rise offices and residences. What, you may ask, is the latter doing in the middle of a jungle? A jungle where the Pan American highway ends because no vehicular traffic may transit the wild impassable mountains between tropical Columbia and Panama? Yet, sailing past it is like sailing past Fort Lauderdale and Miami. Did I mention that it is huge?

The answer to these questions has to do with the offshore world of international business, both legitimate and dodgy. Shipping plays an outsized role in the operations of Panama City. There is a little book called *Ninety Percent of Everything* written by an Englishwoman named Rose George. It's about the global merchant marine and how vast it is and how transnational it is. The title of George's book is based on the truism that ninety percent of everything we have and buy and see and use has had a prior move by ship. Giant containerships each carrying thousands of forty foot ocean containers crisscross the globe every day. The ships themselves are a legal cypher, as are the owners, operators, crews, agents, financiers, attorneys, etc. that enable them.

Ships are legal persons, like corporations, and must be registered somewhere in order to call at the maritime ports around the world, but the place of registration is usually determined by the tax-friendly policies of tiny nations who seek the registration fees of ship owners. Panama is one of the leading "flag of convenience" registrars for ships and their corporate owners, operators and agents. So, all of these entities may have a home office in Panama or at least a local representative, usually a lawyer. Ship owners and operators belong to international conventions on safety and navigation which require a contact person and mode of communications in the home port, so technical staff are required. Ships, once registered, must be chartered and financed and crewed, all of which require specialized personnel. Cargo and the ships that carry it have to be insured–billions and billions of dollars of value—requiring more people. Anonymity is a commonly sought aspect of international shipping. Oftentimes, one ship is owned by one corporation, making for tens of thousands of corporate owners and operators globally. One ship can be registered in Panama, owned by a trust for the benefit of many German doctors, but chartered to a maritime services company with headquarters in Switzerland. The captain may be Ukrainian, and the other officers may be Korean, while the crew may be from Goa or the Philippines or China. The hull may be insured by a syndicate headquartered in London, Tokyo or New York. So, if the ship spills oil or collides with another vessel or a dock or bridge in the territorial waters of California or France or Korea or Dubai, who does an interested person, entity or government call? They start with a designated agent in Panama who may or may not answer the phone. If not, from whom do they seek financial responsibility? If the ship is on the high seas, who can take possession of it or arrest the officers aboard it? If it is abandoned as a wreck, who is the insured entity and will it perform the cleanup?

Each such incident is a labyrinthine exercise requiring layers of experts and functionaries. And that is for the more or less legal activities involved in international commerce. Then there is drug cartel activity and that of corrupt governments and self-dealing officials. All require banks and lawyers and government contacts and lots and lots of experts. And so you have the vastness of Panama City in the middle of a jungle at the end of a road to nowhere. It is, however, astride the Panama Canal.

Our cruise ship, the *MV Zaandam*, is registered in Bermuda and owned by a proud and reputable shipping company, Holland America Line headquartered in Seattle. HAL, in turn, is owned by a well-known holding company called Carnival headquartered in Miami. We arrived at the Pacific side of the Canal and dropped anchor to await our turn to transit the canal according to a pre-arranged schedule with the Canal Authority that assessed a fee of hundreds of thousands of dollars for the privilege. There was a colorful Frank Gehry-designed biodiversity museum facing the bay that celebrated the relatively recent geological formation of the Isthmus.

Hundreds of other ships were swinging on their anchors. Some were tramps awaiting receipt of funds from their operators to pay the transit fee. Some were idle awaiting employment. If a containership operating in the Pacific had relatively few containers of cargo destined for the other side, they would elect to save the expense of transiting the Canal and instead off-load those containers at the container terminal on the Pacific side. The Panama Railroad would then load them onto a regular rail shuttle across the isthmus to another marine terminal on the Caribbean side, where they would be picked up by another scheduled ship operating in the Atlantic or Caribbean and beyond. The technology used by the Panamanian Railroad was the same stack train technology pioneered by APL in the transpacific multimodal trade. The Chief Executive Officer of the railroad when I passed through the canal was a former APL executive.

In a what-are-the-odds moment, as our ship entered the Pacific locks, there were three containerships in the locks ahead of us. All three were APL ships! This was after the company had been sold to Neptune Orient Lines of Singapore (the acquisition that cause my departure from the company), but NOL had kept the APL mark on their ships and containers because it was better known, more valuable and a more respected brand than their own. It no longer stood for American President Lines, however, as no such entity operated the ships.

Going through the Panama Canal is one of the greatest maritime experiences one can have. The Canal Authority had just finished construction of a second set of locks at each end of the canal to double the canal's transit capacity and to accommodate the giant containerships and passenger ships then being built which were too big to fit the original locks. So, at the time of my transit aboard the *Zaandam*, the Panama Canal consisted of two sets of three locks in parallel at each end. In the morning, for a prescribed number of hours, ships will enter the canal from both the Pacific and Caribbean sides. The number admitted was determined by the transit time for the first ships to navigate the three locks and then transit Gatun Lake in the center of the isthmus. After that, no new ships could enter. The ships already having entered and transited the entry locks and Lake Gatun would then exit through the Gaillard Cut and Pacific Locks or the Gatun Locks on the Caribbean side before dark.

Each time a ship passes through one lock, the water in that lock, drained from Lake Gatun, is released into the ocean. Multiply the amount of water held in each lock times two sets of three locks at each end times the number of ships passing though in both directions and the result equals the amount of water lost from Gatun Lake each day. Gatun Lake thus has to receive each day a large volume of water to replenish the water lost by operation of the locks. The Chagres River provides that water as it drains the mountain runoff in the tropical rainforest found between the canal and Columbia to the south. This situation is unique to the Panama Canal. The Suez Canal, Kiel Canal, etc., have waters at both ends that are of the same elevation, thus locks are unnecessary.

The Gaillard Cut (named when the French started the project, aka the "Culebra Cut" after the Americans took over the project) between the Pacific side and Gatun Lake was the source of much agony and expense in the building of the canal. It consisted of alternating strata of hard and soft rock standing vertically and running longitudinally along the Isthmus from Columbia in the south to Costa Rica in the north. What the original builders did, first the French under the command of Gustave Eiffel who had successfully engineered the Suez Canal and built his eponymous Tower in Paris, and later by an American consortium after the French enterprise was defeated by yellow fever and bankruptcy, was to simply cut through the vertical bands of rock to create a channel from the Pacific Ocean to Gatun Lake. The vertical strata of hard rock cut through could be left standing almost vertically and remain stable. However, the strata of soft rock in between the hard rock strata was very soft indeed, and in the climate of constant tropical rainfall, it would become supersaturated, liquefy, and slough off into the canal blocking it.

It took the builders many years and many re-excavations of the cut to find the angle of repose for the soft rock, thus stabilizing it. So, passing through the Culebra Cut today, one passes through sheer hard rock cliffs facing the Canal alternating with gradually sloping hillsides rising up from the Canal and riddled with pipes that constantly drain water out of the mud banks in between the cliffs. An accident of geology, combined with omnipresent yellow fever (not known until well into the American custodianship of the project to be carried by mosquitos) made for a disastrous construction effort that bankrupted the French team and nearly did the same for the American team.

To neutralize the outsized influence of the American Government over the Canal as a vital asset in the global infrastructure for maritime commerce, especially the fleet of the People's Republic of China, China solely financed the construction of the second set of locks as part of its Belt and Road system. As chief lender for those improvements, the long term access of its big containerships, bulkers and warships to the Canal was assured.

The day we arrived at the Pacific side and the *Zaandam* anchored while waiting our turn to enter the Canal the next day, I was able to take a bus excursion to the Gamboa National Park at the mouth of the Chagres River. From the vantage point of a treetops viewing tower on a cliff above the Canal, we were able to see sloths and tropical birds in the treetops and an Amerindian village in the jungle along the Chagres River not visible from the big ships like ours that passed by into Gatun Lake from the Culebra Cut. It was hot and very humid. I was learning to move more slowly in the tropical climate. This was only my second experience this trip with exertion in that climate, the first having been the excursion to the coffee plantation in Ecuador. Prior to that, we had been sailing along the Humboldt Current off Chile and Peru in cool, dry weather. At Ecuador, however, the ocean current changes to the Equatorial current which, when it pulses with warm currents, brings El Nino weather to much of the world. Either way, the equatorial current hits the Americas and fans out into a tropical backwash up and down the coast that make for slow moving by perspiring itinerant *sapiens* and a perfect environment for mosquitos.

Joka and I stood on the balcony deck six flights above the main deck and just under the bridge as we watched the *Zaandam* maneuver through each lock. After the ship sailed under the Pan-American or Inter-American Highway Bridge, we studied the Gaillard/Culebra Cut, peered at the tropical flowering trees and marveled at the myriad inlets and coves and cascades of water along the shoreline of Gatun Lake, leaving our viewpoint only long enough to grab some lunch. Then, at the eastern edge of the lake, we entered directly into the Gatun locks and stepped down into the Caribbean Sea, *west* of where we entered the Canal, passing by the containership terminal in Colon and the Caribbean terminal of the Panama Railroad.

[Note: The Pan-American Highway is a network of roads running from Prudhoe Bay in Alaska to Ushuaia, Argentina in Tierra del Fuego, severed in only one place, namely, the Darien Gap in the mountainous rainforests of Panama. The gap is 103 kilometers and the only way to get from one terminus of the highway to the other is by ocean.]

Our first stop in the Caribbean was a tender call at a cluster of tiny islands called the **San Blas Islands**. We anchored off of one of them and took one of the ship's tenders (life boats) to a very small pier. Every square inch of the flat island, perhaps having two meters of elevation at its highest point, was occupied by some path or structure. If not a shop or a house or schoolroom, it would be a pen for animals. We saw a pig pen erected on driftwood above the water. The water was full of flotsam and jetsam, and we never learned where they got their fresh water supply. I suspect, by collecting rain or barge from the mainland. It was obvious that the subsistence of these people came from fishing (their fishing boats were all around) and from visits from cruise ships like ours. Along the narrow streets, women sold panels of Indian motif cloth they had woven, suitable for sewing onto a white T shirt for decoration. If you wanted to take a picture of one of the natives, it was "one dolla." I have a great picture of an ancient, tiny, colorfully dressed woman smoking a pipe with a monkey on her shoulder. One dolla!

These islands are out of the hurricane belt which allows them to survive. One hurricane hit would sweep them clean. Rising oceans due to global warming, however, will finish them. Next stop, **Cartagena, Columbia**.

Cartagena, named after a city in Spain from which most of the crew of the discovering vessel came, dates from 1533. It was strategically situated between the mouths of two rivers, giving the city a defensible position and access to the interior of the northern coast of South America. Spain was able to find gold in Columbia, taking it from the natives. Peruvian gold and silver stolen from the Incas also passed through the port on its way back to Spain. Spain contracted at various times with European colonizing countries in Africa (Portugal, Holland, England, France, and the city state of Genoa) to bring slaves into Cartagena as a source of plantation labor and labor to build the large fort that defended the city from the multitude of pirates attracted by the traffic of gold and silver there.

The Spanish Inquisition established a formal office there and built a palace from which to officiate that can be visited today. The Palace exhibits the sort of instruments of torture the new American democracy banned in its constitution forbidding unreasonable searches and seizures and self-incrimination and guaranteeing the rights of habeas corpus, due process, trials by jury and the like. The Spanish Inquisition was formally ended only when the country of Colombia gained its independence in the early 1800s through the efforts of Simon Bolivar.

Over time, Cartagena yielded its prominence as the center of Spanish colonial activity in the Caribbean to Cuba and Hispaniola. Today, it is an attractive, artistically rendered small waterfront city visited by cruise ships. Passengers can walk the picturesque streets, visit the museums, dine, drink, and climb through the old hilltop fort. It is relatively safe from the violence spawned by the cocaine drug cartels that tend to operate out of Medellin and Cali. Colombia's largest and busiest city is its inland capital, Bogota.

Our penultimate stop on the cruise was at Holland America Line's private Caribbean island called Half Moon Key. It has a long, drop-dead gorgeous white sand crescent beach, cerulean waters, and a watering hole masquerading as an old shipwreck. HAL's development has been tastefully minimal, and the island retains its low key, natural beauty. Joka and I found a small gazebo on the beach with two chairs in the sand under it and promptly appropriated it as the shaded place we could go after periodic swims in the limpid water. That was a nice day.

After another day at sea, we disembarked at Fort Lauderdale. This was crunch time for Joka and me as to whether we were to have a lasting relationship or just concede that the obstacles to seeing each other from our homes half a world apart were too great. However, Joka threw down the gauntlet by saying, "I'm good at challenges," leaving unsaid the implicit question, "Are you?" Not to be outdone, I answered confidently, if recklessly, "No worries. The world is shrinking. Technology is our friend. Let's go for another cruise." With no more of a plan than that, she flew off to New York for a visit with her American daughter-in-law's mother, and I flew home after a ride around the Everglades in an air boat looking at 'gators. [As I write, the iconic airboats are being phased out in the Everglades because of noise pollution and environmental effects.]

As Joka and I corresponded by email thereafter, our plan took shape. After a couple of months at home, she would fly to Napa and spend some time with me. However, I could sense from her carefully worded descriptions of her sons' reaction to that idea that Jan Willem and Adriaan were not altogether comfortable with that. Their father had only died two years earlier, and, reasonably enough, the whole thing was a bit shocking to them. So, as an interim move, we thought it would be fitting if I were to come visit her in Sydney first and sort of present my credentials. If I did so, met everyone personally and got to know them, then her boys (actually, men in their fifties) and their wives might be more comfortable with the idea of mom having an American "boyfriend." Besides, I had liked Sydney a lot when Carol and I were there and was happy to go back. So, I did, and everything went perfectly. I met her family and many of her friends, and it was all very jolly. We firmed up the plan for her to come to Napa, which she did some weeks later. She stayed with me two months, met my family and friends, and we planned my return to Sydney two months after Joka returned home. So, learning as we went along, we had established a two months on, two months on, off, alternating visits, perpetual summer routine. We decided to take a 40-day

Holland America Line cruise from Singapore to Rotterdam being offered at a big discount on the 90 day ticker. We would fly to Singapore together from Sydney to board the ship. At the end of the cruise in Rotterdam, we would visit Joka's sister Helen and brother-in-law Herman in Sassenheim. Her brother Jan and sister-in-law Sylvia from Basel, Switzerland would join us there if possible. While in Holland, we would throw in a trip to Berlin on our own.

The entire trip would be an around-the-world journey for me with a killer itinerary—the trip of a lifetime to exotic places with faraway sounding names. It was a bit of a leap into the dark for both of us to embark on a long voyage in which we would share the same cabin with only having been in each other's company for a few weeks, but we pretty much ignored all those concerns and confidently executed the plan.

As planned, two months after Joka returned to Sydney, I packed up and followed her, taking the fifteen hour direct flight to Sydney and joined her at her home in Avalon Beach, one of the Northern Beaches north of Sydney. While there, we took a quick trip to Tasmania for a week-long walkabout in the north and south of the island and along the east coast. Bushfires were raging all along the western side, so that was not to be part of the trip. We had an interesting and sobering exposure to Port Arthur and its former convict prison, a walk on a 21 mile, blindingly white, beach with sand so fine it squeaked when you walked on it, climbed a saddle between two low mountains to view pristine Wineglass Bay, saw Tasmanian devils, platypuses, echidna (egg-laying, spiny anteater mammals), sea dragons (fancy sea horses), and 'roos galore. We ate scallops from Hobart to Launceston. And that, mind you, was just a warm-up for the big trip.

I should mention that the time spent in Joka's 'hood was anything but empty. The "Northern Beaches" sit on a long, narrow peninsula that juts out into Broken Bay. The headland of that peninsula is called Barrenjoey Head, and it's equipped with an iconic lighthouse. Below it, two broad crescent beaches fan out away from each other forming a sandy spit leading to, on the ocean side, the exclusive community of Palm Beach, and on the bay side, the towns and marinas of Pittwater Bay. Heading south from Palm Beach on the ocean is a string of hilly beach communities with killer views and their own crescent beaches—Whale

Beach, Avalon Beach, Bilgola Beach, Newport Beach, etc., stretching away to the south until you get to Manley at the north head of Sydney Harbor. Each of these towns is a desirable place to live and has its share of celebrities, professionals, and other affluent types.

Joka lives on a beach level street that runs about half a mile from the ocean surf to the calm shoreline of Pittwater, an inlet formed by Barren-joey Head on one side and the Ka-ringgai-Chase National Park bushlands on the other. Pittwater is part of Broken Bay which, with its subsidiary inlets and coves, make up the mouth of the Hawkesbury River where it runs into the Pacific Ocean.

The next town south from Avalon Beach is Bilgola Beach. Neither Bilgola Beach, Whale Beach nor Palm Beach have a shopping District, but Avalon does, so the four villages together form a loosely cohesive economic community at the end of a twisting, cliff-hanging, two lane road from Newport Beach. Each town has its own ocean pool—a large concrete-sided, salt water swimming pool built into the ocean at the town beach and washed by the high tides with fresh sea water. Each town also has a Surf Lifesaving Club that trains young people to safeguard its swimmers and surfers from the hazards of the ocean ranging from sharks to Pacific Man-O-War jellyfish to rip tides. Bilgola Beach has a particu-larly accommodating setting of being hidden from the road, a lovely crescent beach between two imposing rock heads, an adequate parking lot, and a well-equipped café kiosk that serves gourmet coffee, pastries, breakfasts and light lunches. Around the kiosk, there are both sheltered and open air tables and chairs. It is this "place" that serves as the setting in my short story "Billy's."

Australians swim. To the man—or woman—they swim. Either in the ocean or in the ocean pool or both, but swim they will. Their kids ("nippers") learn to swim and surf early and continuously. At Bilgola Beach, there is a rolling group of very agreeable people, mostly retirees or self-employed types whose only common denominator is that they live in one of the villages and come to swim and have coffee at Bilgola Beach every morning. Over time, they have become acquainted with one another, bonded, and established a daily routine consisting of a morning swim followed by socializing over coffee. Joka is a charter member of the group and so, when she brought me along the first morning after I morning after I arrived and vouched for me, I too, became a member of the group. In-stantly, I had fifteen or twenty Australian friends. The group lacks a formal name, but it is commonly referred to within the group as "Billy's" or the Table of Wisdom where no subject is too complex or arcane that it cannot be held up, fleshed out and closely considered.

The women tend to prefer sitting among their own kind and the men do likewise, ostensibly to discuss "secret men's business," a wry and affectionate nod to aboriginal male custom. Barring doctor's appoint-ments, foreign travel, and family demands, members of the group show up religiously every morning to socialize. The characters in my short story "Billy's" are composite characters who have snippets of the features of people both in and out of the Billy's group. The story uses Aussie humor to tell an Aussie story and the group itself plays a starring role in exemplifying the concept of "mates."

So, time spent with Joka in her environs was not only not dead time between cruises, it was a thoroughly enjoyable experience that I looked forward to as much as another travel adventure. I am a lucky man. Joka and I have turned a huge geographical challenge to our relationship into something uniquely nourishing. We had our time in the Northern Beaches, and we had our walkabout in "Tazzie." Time for our departure for Singapore and the next cruise.

CHAPTER 22

SINGAPORE TO ROTTERDAM

Our flight to Singapore was during daylight, and I had a window seat. The flight path was diagonally from southeast Australia to the northwest coast facing the Indonesian islands. It was a cloudless day, and I had an unobstructed look straight down at the Australian terrain from the Great Dividing Range in the east, over the vast outback, and across the more tropical north. Unlike flying coast-to-coast in the States, a trans-continental flight across Australia provides views of ... nothing. No sign of human habitation that is. No roads, no buildings, no farms or fields, not even a track across vast expanses of reddish yellow sand and red rock. There is a single paved highway that runs north and south between Adelaide and Darwin midway across the country. Apart from that ... nothing until you get to the north coast. Aboriginal people make their homes in all that space, but leave few marks. It is a moonscape.

In Singapore, we checked into a hotel along the Clarke Quay waterway and spent two good days exploring Singapore in beastly hot weather. We took a tour boat ride through the downtown area to see the famous architecture of the city and walked Clarke Quay at night lit up like Broadway and 42nd Street. As an extra dividend, we had lunch with a sorority sister of Erin's from Colorado whom I hadn't seen since my last dad's weekend in Boulder twenty years earlier. She and her husband lived there because he was an ex-air force pilot turned military contractor liaison with the American air bases in Asia that used his employer's weaponry.

We had Singapore Slings at the Raffles Hotel (well, I did, Joka rarely drinks), and drinks on the roof bar of the spectacular Marina Bay Sands Hotel overlooking the also spectacular Gardens of the Bay, the harbor, the city, and the Strait of Malacca with countless ships at anchor and aweigh. Singapore is a remarkable and prosperous colony of Han Chinese expatriates that were expelled by the Malays when the Malay war ended and Independence from Britain came to Malaysia. APL (now CMA-CGM) had a gigantic containership terminal there which acted as a hub for its intra-Asia traffic.

On board the *MV Rotterdam*, we settled quickly into our now-standard routine on Holland America Line (HAL) ships. All of the older HAL ships had the same general configuration of public spaces, restaurants and other facilities. Some cruise veterans might prefer varying decor and amenities of different lines from cruise to cruise, but we don't. We like HAL's layout and have come to rely on it. You would be amazed at how often you can be going aft on the port side when you want go forward on the starboard side if you don't know the ship.

Anyway, comfortably settled into our ocean view cabin, we "set sail" for our first port of call on this long voyage, **Port Kelang**, the port of **Kuala Lumpur**. Malaysia is a bifurcated country with a piece on the mainland south of Thailand and another piece on the north side of the island of Borneo. It is territory liberated from Britain after the Malay war of independence that ended in 1957. I will not go into a lot of historical detail about the places we visit on this cruise beyond a few snippets that seem fundamentally important. One such snippet is that the federation of states that formed Malaysia after Independence included Singapore, but Singapore was involuntarily expelled from the country not long after its creation, mainly due to racial and religious differences. The Malay are ethnic Indian Hindus, whereas Singaporeans are overwhelmingly Han Chinese and religiously diverse, but mostly Buddhists.

Our one day excursion in Kuala Lumpur consisted of a highlights tour of the Independence Plaza, the Royal Palace seen from the front gate (yes, there is a king, and the public doesn't get inside the royal grounds) and the unique Petronas Towers. The Petronas Towers are two side-by-side skyscrapers that are mirror images of each other and are connected by a "sky bridge" at the 42nd floor. In an interesting bit of foreign policy accommodation, one tower was built by Japan's Mitsubishi and the other by Korea's Samsung. They were the tallest buildings in the world when built in 1998. The sky bridge is a safety feature that allows the upper floors of one building to be evacuated into the other in an emergency. That feature was put to use on September 11th, 2001 when the twin towers in New York were destroyed. I hadn't been aware of it at the time, but the "twin towers" in Kuala Lumpur were also evacuated on 9/11 as a precaution in the uncertain hours after the attack in New York. The buildings housed the state owned oil and gas company. ("Petro?" Get it?)

One image from Kuala Lumpur will forever stick in my mind, namely, is that of the street lights in the city. They each consisted of a tall pole with an arm arcing over the street and, at the end of the arm, a giant red metallic hibiscus flower with a stamen-like light protruding from its center. That was a fanciful treatment of the national flower by the utility company.

From Kuala Lumpur, the *Rotterdam* completed its northward transit of the Strait of Malacca. (Sharp-eyed readers of my novel *In Extremis* will remember that this strait is the setting for the opening scenes of the book involving the hijacking of an oil tanker from the Persian Gulf bound for China. Those scenes were written several years before this voyage, and this was the first time I'd laid eyes on the real Strait.) Where the Indonesian island of Sumatra ends at the point of Aceh, our ship turned west into the Indian Ocean amid continuing fair weather and smooth seas. Our next stop: **Columbo, Sri Lanka**.

After achieving its independence from Britain, Sri Lanka, formerly Ceylon, fell into a bitter civil war between the Majority Singhalese Buddhists and the Tamil "Tiger" Hindu minority which had migrated from South India. The war had ended with a Singhalese government victory a mere seven years before we arrived. Tensions were palpable, but the island was peaceful. Every sign is printed in three languages, viz., Singhalese, Hindi and English.

Ceylon tea has been world famous for centuries, and we took a scenic and interesting excursion to a tea and rubber plantation high in the mountains out of Colombo. Tea is made from a leaf from the tea plant, cultivated and shaped into a chest-high bush. Workers, usually women, move through the fields of tea plants picking new growth tea leaves and placing them in cloth bags slung over their shoulders. These gatherings are then walked up to the "factory" building where they are sorted, dried and packaged. The drying process involves exposure to hot air from a furnace. Picture working in a hot, humid, tropical climate, in an airless indoor room by a furnace, as the sorting workers did. It was uncomfortable for us just to walk through the room on the tour. For the workers, all of whom seem to be reed-thin, it must have been extremely harsh. Outside, however, working in the tea fields in a lush, green open space seemed pleasant. Perhaps the field workers and the factory workers rotate duties to make it all bearable.

In the forest surrounding the tea fields, there were rubber trees hard at work making lactose milk. The trees bore diagonal cut marks on six plus year old trees, and at the end of the cut, a small bamboo or metal trough and cup would be attached to the tree. The liquid latex rose in the tree from the roots, seeped into the cut, and ran down the cut into the trough and into the cup. The cups were periodically emptied into carrying cans and then, once delivered to the "factory," the latex was pressed and rolled into sheets for drying and handling. Interestingly, the rubber trees come from Amazonia where Portuguese colonists originally prospered hugely by supplying the world with rubber. But the enterprising and ethically challenged British distained paying Portugal for their rubber, and so, like the cacao plant and other Amazonian plants, they sometimes bought but mostly stole seeds and grafts of the plants from Amazonia and transferred them to British colonies that had similar climates. Viola! The Portuguese were cut out of the supply chain. More money for the British. At any rate, Ceylon was not a major source of rubber like, say, Malaysia, but it could be profitably grown as a collateral crop on forested land not suitable for tea cultivation. You sure get a sense of the old British Empire wandering around this part of the world. Next stop: the Jewel in the Crown of the British Empire.

Mumbai (formerly Bombay) has 26 million people. That's a lot of people in one city, even if a city's infrastructure were modern and well equipped. That is most certainly not the case in Mumbai. We were two days in Mumbai, and that involved excursions to the central market—a vast covered space selling everything—and numerous neighborhood markets, where people sell more specialized items from storefronts, from cloths spread out on the sidewalks and from stalls that lined the streets. The bamboo stalls were often two stories, that is, a false ceiling would be erected over the selling space with room enough above for a person to lie down to sleep. Canvas sheets covered the whole to keep (most of) the rain, soot and dust out. One alley we happened into had nothing but burlap bags of dried red peppers running for two blocks—billions of them.

The waterfront was centered on two structures. The first was a great triumphal arch on the central quay facing the fishing harbor. The Victoria Arch was built for a planned visit by Queen Victoria, but she never made the trip. It has always been a popular venue for wedding pictures, and we saw couples queued up for their turn at the site. The second structure, the Taj Mahal Hotel, is set back from the Victoria Arch on the street that faces the harbor. The "Taj" is the most prestigious hotel in Mumbai and was the site of the shocking assault by a group of Lashika-e-Taiba Pakistani terrorists who entered the hotel and began to murder people at random in 2008. Indian government commandos gained control of the hotel after three days of fighting, but 157 people were killed. Holders of foreign passports were singled out by the terrorists and shot to death. It was a major blow to one of India's symbols of power and success, but one from which the city recovered with dispatch. A visitor to the hotel lobby will find a somber waterfall on one side of the lobby with a marble wall inscribed with the names of the victims.

There is a broad esplanade along a crescent beach that fans out from the Victoria Arch for several kilometers. The beach has a low-gradient and provides a deep beach facing the silted-up harbor along the wall of the esplanade. However, residents avoid the beach and the water because it is heavily polluted. It was painful to watch a few small unsupervised children, obviously from low caste families, idling in the filthy water.

In the interior center of the city, our van pulled up and parked on a viaduct, disrupting traffic behind us. Traffic is generally heavy, slow moving, uncontrolled, and characterized by the constant, deafening, honking of horns. Looking down and out from the viaduct, we could see a large area, perhaps a square kilometer, carved up into a rabbit warren of concrete wash basins. It was the city's laundry. Individuals holding themselves out to do laundry collect the garments of their customers and take them to the laundry. Somehow, they get one of the washing pens and wash the garments there. Then, they are hung in the air on lines above the pens until dry. Then, they would be folded and ironed somewhere else as necessary before being returned to their customers. Garment manufacturers in Mumbai used the laundry to stone wash jeans before sale, as fashion dictated. Thus, great swaths of jeans could be seen hanging out to dry. It was one of the most logistically elaborate but primitive systems I've ever seen. It looked like pure chaos.

On the drive back from the laundry we passed the billionaire Tata family home. It was an unadorned block building about six stories high on a busy street. The Tatas control a vast industrial empire in India, including the recently acquired English auto brands of Jaguar and Land Rover. Headquarters are in Mumbai. The Tatas are of the monotheistic Zoroastrian religion being descendants of the community of Zoroastrians that were forced out of Persia (now Iran) and settled in India where they are called *Parsi*. They were expelled from Persia by the Muslin Caliphs who took Persia circa 650 CE.

The highlight of the Mumbai port call for me was visiting Mohandas Gandhi's house. A spacious house by Mumbai standards with a brick exterior, it stood on a leafy residential street of substantial but not opulent homes. Inside, the layout was very western with a central hallway and common rooms running off the hall and a stairway leading to second story bedrooms. Gandhi's room was as spare as one would expect—a thin mattress on the floor, a spinning wheel for making threads for his clothes, a small chest and a wooden chair. In the hallway, there were several photos of Gandhi taken at various historic events with all manner of chiefs of state, but one of them seemed completely out of place. It was a black and white picture of Gandhi and his wife sitting with Charlie Chaplin in which Gandhi and his wife were laughing uproariously.

We were in a somber mood for the *Rotterdam* ceremony of "sailaway" from the Port of Mumbai. Seeing that much humanity crushed together in such stressful circumstances was beyond my experience, but I had nothing but admiration for the Indian souls who live there with dignity, coping somehow, and remaining steadfastly opposed to a more authoritarian, less democratic society. Next, a two day respite at sea while crossing the Arabian Sea to Oman.

Salalah is Oman's second city. The major city, Muscat, is in the north near the Persian Gulf. Salalah faced the Arabian Sea in the more remote south near the border with Yemen (formerly Aden) and just up the coast from the mouth of the Red Sea and the dangerous waters around Somalia and the horn of Africa. A small city of low–rise, white-washed buildings, Salalah nevertheless had a walled royal palace where the king (Sultan) sometimes spent time. When I was there, then Sultan Quaboos, had not been seen in public for several years. It was rumored that he had cancer. That was confirmed when he died in 2020. The same family has produced the governing sultan for over two hundred years.

Oman sits with its back to "The Empty Quarter," a vast expanse of sand that fills eastern Saudi Arabia. In the arid to semi-arid hills of Oman, however, the miniature frankincense tree grows. Frankincense continues to be a cash crop in the area, and markets selling it are common. The tree's branches extruded a pitch-like sap that congeals on the outside of the bark like amber on pine trees. There are varying degrees of purity and higher prices prevail for greater purity. In biblical times, when food spoiled quickly in a hot climate and sewage pooled in open ditches, frankincense, like the more subtle and precious myrrh, was literally worth its weight in gold. A crystal of frankincense could be tossed on the coals of a brazier in a Bedouin tent, and the pungent fragrance emitted would mask all other odors for hours. Outside Salalah, there are ruins of a man-made harbor and port facilities that were used for millennia to export frankincense to the rest of the known world. For Christian believers, the three wise men, believed to have been Zoro-astrians from the Eastern part of the Arabian Peninsula, likely would have obtained their frankincense from Oman and sailed up the Red Sea to the Gulf of Aqaba, thence to the mouth of the Jordan River and on to Bethlehem to bestow it upon the Christ child. I doubt that they would have ridden camels over three thousand kilometers of Empty Quarter.

We did a bit of touring in the city, devoid of vegetation, and visited a "typical" Arab home with its varied living spaces, kitchen tools, food storage jars, and sleeping quarters. We strolled through a souk (bazaar) where cashmere Pashmina scarves could be had for a pittance. We also drove along the coastline and saw unique geological rock formations and long expanses of sandy beaches completely empty of people. We supposed the burkas discouraged swimming for women, but for some reason, not even men or children were in the pristine, calm water. We stopped for lunch at a resort hotel complex operated by one of the European chains, but apart from the western-style café, saw no one around the beachside rooms or on the short-iron golf range under the palm trees.

It felt very remote. Nevertheless, the Sultanate of Oman had its own oil reserves and the revenue earned by the state oil company provided for the general welfare in the country, delivering health care, roads and other infrastructure. The Sultan was western educated and was reputed to be devoted to his subjects' welfare. Right next door in Yemen, the Shiite Houthi rebels supported by Iran were fighting a civil war against the Sunni regime in power, a proxy for Saudi Arabia, at a then cost of over a hundred thousand civilian lives.

When we sailed from Salalah, we picked up a U.S. Navy warship which shadowed our movements down the coast of Yemen and around the point that marks the opening of the Red Sea. Islands belonging to Djibouti and Somalia could be seen in the distance off the port side. This was a prime hijacking lane. Although the *Rotterdam* could make over 20 knots of speed at sea, the ship likely would not have undertaken the route without the military escort. We were very glad to have the U.S. Navy along. For slower tankers and containerships, a naval escort was a necessity.

Once into the Red Sea, we steamed toward Suez without being able to sight the coast of Sudan on the port side or Saudi Arabia on the starboard. I don't remember seeing a single ship passing in the opposite direction. All of the ship traffic that passes through the Suez Canal also passes through the Red Sea, and as narrow-looking the Red Sea looks on a map—remember, Moses was supposed to have parted its waters so the Israelites could escape from Egypt—it is big enough for most of those ships to routinely pass out of sight of each other.

When we reached the Sinai Peninsula, we veered north into the narrower Gulf of Aqaba. Along the way we could clearly see new Saudi Arabian developments on the starboard side and the mountains of the Sinai on the port side tapering down to Sharm El Sheikh on the southern point of the Sinai. The City of **Aqaba** appeared in just a few hours, with the Israeli city of Eilat across the Jordan River from Aqaba.

Jordan is a remarkable place. It is of course part of the historic holy land. As you travel north up the Jordan River, you encounter first the Dead Sea and then, over the border into Israel, the Sea of Galilee. Jordan is a kingdom boasting a total of 1.3 million native Bedouins. Bedouins are nomadic people who cultivate livestock and migrate among seasonal pastures in open public lands. [Note that the Bedouin system of land ownership is more like the former Aboriginal system in Australia than the system of private ownership in the West, that is, land is publically owned and commonly used in sustaining ways.] In addition to the natives, there were more than 2 million Palestinian refugees, most of whom had been generously granted Jordanian citizenship. 370,000 of them lived in camps. So, Jordan lives with the ongoing stresses of the Israeli-Palestinian conflict. Israel is just across the Jordan River for Jordan's entire eastern border of four hundred kilometers, but there are only three border crossings. One of them is between Aqaba and Eilat and is used by Jordanian workers who travel to Eilat for day labor.

The City of Aqaba was made famous in Western circles during World War I. An eccentric British officer, T. E. Lawrence was part of the British military contingent stalled in Egypt in their fight against entrenched Turkish troops in Jordan and Saudi Arabia, the Ottoman Empire having improvidently allied themselves with Germany. Turkey had installed large artillery in Aqaba facing the sea and successfully repelled British efforts to take the city. Lawrence befriended and ultimately marshalled a host of Bedouin tribesmen resentful of the Turks to join him in a torturous crossing of the Jordanian deserts to attack Aqaba by horseback from the rear. The defending Turks were utterly surprised and quickly dispatched by the pistols and cutlasses of the Lawrence-led force. Lawrence and his Bedouin allies also staged raids deeper into the desert to the east and blew up the Ottoman railroad tracks to Messina and Mecca in Saudi Arabia, cutting off Ottoman supplies to those cities. The remarkable efforts of Lawrence "of Arabia" spelled the defeat of Turkey in World War I and the end of the Ottoman Empire.

As I write, Aqaba is a hospitable entry point for cruise ships and their passengers wanting to see the amazing ancient city of Petra and the wild desert landscapes of Wadi Rum, where Lawrence marshalled his Arab corps for the attack on Aqaba. Joka and I were fortunate enough to visit both during our two day port call at Aqaba.

Petra is a two thousand year old community with stunning architectural buildings carved out of the sandstone in a remote canyon. It was "lost" (to outsiders) after the Crusades for hundreds of years, until "rediscovered" in 1812 by a young Swiss explorer from Basel. Access to the ancient city is possible by means of a crack in the deep sandstone surrounds of the place through which a kilometer-long pathway runs. Following that path to the end where it suddenly opens to reveal the vast Siq, or "Treasury" structure has to be one of the most stunning views in the ancient world.

Wadi Rum is reached by road over highlands used by Bedouins to graze their sheep and goats that run down to a wild desert-scape perpetually scoured by desert winds. In the center of it all, a large rock formation towers over the various canyons and expanses of sand and red rock. It is called the Seven Towers of Wisdom, which T. E. Lawrence took as the title for his book about his experiences there. Our Land Rover tour encountered an encampment of Bedouins there, doing I know not what. The only livestock they had were camels and there was no vegetation anywhere. Perhaps they were there as a tourist enterprise because we were allowed to enter their large tent filled with rugs to recline on and a few handicrafts. The only time I have smelled the fragrance of myrrh was in that tent. Myrrh is plant-sourced like frankincense and has the appearance of loose steel wool. Unlike the more pungent frankincense, however, when myrrh was dropped onto the brazier in the tent, it produced a lovely, sweet aroma reminiscent of jasmine or orange blossoms.

Evidently, King Hussein ("Abdullah II"—41st degree direct descendant of Mohammed) was grooming his son, the crown prince, to succeed him because a poster of the two of them together appeared everywhere. His wife, Queen Noor, was an American girl who graduated from Princeton before marrying Hussein.

Jordan was one of the top two or three highlights of our whole trip. But, our time there was up. Next, the Suez Canal.

A quick sail past the Sinai Peninsula and Sharm El Sheikh again and a starboard turn put us into the Red Sea entrance to the **Suez Canal** built by the same Gustave Eiffel who came to grief later in Panama. But this canal was much easier. There were no major rock cuts involved, no muddy banks to liquefy in tropical rains—only sand to be dredged. We sailed past numerous Egyptian communities on the port side, but there were few signs of life on the Sinai side to our starboard. The entrance to the canal was undistinguished in appearance. There were no locks in the Suez Canal as the waters of the Mediterranean and the Red Sea are fortuitously the same level. So, twin waterways have been dredged on the Red Sea side with great piles of sand spoils standing beside the canal. Retaining walls line much of the shoreline to keep the sand from sloughing off into the channel, but dredging is part of the ongoing maintenance of the canal. Car ferries crisscross the canal in close quarters between ship passings in a kind of hair-raising, but obviously well-practiced, ballet. As we passed one large Egyptian city, a frontal road ran all along the canal, and a military vehicle with a mounted machine gun patrolled the road. A passing ship would make an easy target for an RPG (rocket propelled grenade) from a terrorist along that shoreline.

The setting of the canal throughout its length was pretty ordinary. After several hours and without any visual transition or landmarks, we found ourselves out into the Mediterranean Sea at Port Said, with the Nile Delta receding astern on the port side and the Gaza strip fading into the marine haze to starboard. Next: two days at sea, then through the squeaky narrow Strait of Messina between Sicily and the toe of the boot of Italy and up to Naples for some pizza.

I'd spent a day in **Naples** on my Med Cruise two years earlier, and Carol and I visited Pompeii from Positano on the Amalfi Coast when we stayed there on one of our European trips. So, with Joka being a like-minded veteran of Naples, we decided to take in the world famous architectural museum and then just walk. The museum was very interesting, but not subject matter to be covered in this chronicle, so I omit any further mention of it.

It happened to be Easter Sunday, and all of Naples was out in the streets making for a very colorful and lively scene. Joka spotted a couple of guys sitting on a seawall playing their mandolins. Since she played the mandolin a bit and had one at home, she chatted them up. They played a few tunes for us and others who stopped to listen in the shadow of a big statue of Garibaldi. Just down the esplanade was the home of Giuseppe Lampedusa who wrote *The Leopard.* The Neapolitan atmospherics were as thick as a double espresso as we strolled back to the ship for sailaway.

After an overnight sail from Naples, we found ourselves berthed in **Civitavecchia**, the port of **Rome**. We opted for an off-the-grid excursion up the coast to a town called Tarquinia, known to be a hotbed of Etruscan antiquities. A number of Etruscan tombs had been excavated relatively recently (1970s) and the art and artifacts were on display at a former cardinal's residence. Best small museum ever! They had some killer things there, and it was all in a fine villa where you could walk up close to and see everything they had. And no crowd. We even had lunch at a farmhouse nearby that catered to visitors. Who said you can't get off the beaten path on a cruise?

From Rome, another overnight sail brought us to the port of **Ajaccio** in **Corsica**. Now, Corsica is different. It is technically in France because, in an obscure transaction between monarchs a couple of centuries ago, Italy sold it to France. However, France has never supported the place (Corsicans believe,) the residents resent it, and culturally the place is more aligned with, say, Sardinia than with Provence. A popular T-shirt in Ajaccio depicted the grisly severed head of a Moor, neck dripping blood, celebrating the expulsion of North African Berber tribes centuries earlier. The roads in Corsica are terrible because the whole island is extremely mountainous, so getting around from town to town is best done by boat. Ajaccio has the distinction of being the first site in Free France that Charles de Gaulle was able to set foot on after the Allies liberated it in 1943. It is a very pleasant and attractive place to experience.

Spanish Morocco is a tiny island of Spanish territory on the Mediterranean coast of North Africa, surrounded by Morocco and facing Gibraltar across the neck of the Mediterranean. We stopped there for an afternoon on our way from Corsica to Cadiz on the Atlantic side of Gibraltar. The town there is called **Ceuta**, and I visited Ceuta in 1959 when I crossed over from Gibraltar on my way to Tangiers during my trip abroad in college. It is a beach town that Spaniards use for vacations, and it has a fine old fort facing the sea and The Rock of Gibraltar in the distance. Beyond that, I found little to write about.

The next morning, we were docked in **Cadiz,** Spain. Cadiz is next door to **Jerez**, which is the home of Spanish sherry, In fact, Jerez is the Spanish word for sherry wine. So, being a winemaker and all, I had to do a tour of the big sherry house in town, *Tio Pepe*. It was a good industrial tour with lots of sampling and a visit to a special cellar where all the barrels were stained black and all manner of celebrities have auto-graphed barrels of sherry in white chalk. It was fun to spot all the personalities from Lana Turner to Omar Sharif to Picasso to Chelsea Clinton who graced the barrels with their signatures.

On the outskirts of Jerez, there is a facility that breeds and trains Andalusian horses. One of the curiosities of this breed was that they are born black or dark brown as colts, but as they mature they turn snow white. These horses are trained to perform precision dance and other movements individually and in groups in equestrian shows. While Joka took a different excursion, I toured the stables and attended an equestrian horse show after the Tio Pepe visit. It made me want a white horse on which to promenade through Napa of an afternoon.

We could see the end of this cruise now. Our next stop was **A Co-runa** on the northwest tip of Spain, followed by Southampton to disembark some passengers and finally to Rotterdam where the cruise ended. A Coruna was an arty and prosperous port city with the dressiest waterfront I've ever seen. The whole kilometer-long half circle of the wa-terfront consisted of multistory buildings with glass front sunrooms from top to bottom. It was like looking at a city of crystal. However, the tourist draw is not to the city of A Coruna, artistically rendered as it may be, but rather the nearby smaller, leafier town of **Santiago de Compostela** and its renowned cathedral. The Apostle James is credited with bringing Christianity to Iberia. Later, he was beheaded in Jerusalem at the order of King Herod of Judea, a client king of the Romans, for his outspoken criticism of Herod and Rome. His remains were then removed to Santi-ago de Compostela in Galicia where James had been highly regarded. His remains are thought to be in the church's reliquary. The very elabo-rate cathedral dates back to the end of the first millennium and is rich in iconography and relics. It is one of only three cathedrals built on the actual tomb of one of the Apostles, the other being St. Peter in Rome and St. Tomas in Chennai, India. The appeal of James' story for Chris-tian worshippers was enhanced by a good deal of popular mythology about his tomb which I will leave to the reader's research, if desired. The original route taken by James to the town of Santiago de Compostela became a popular pilgrimage trail, and thousands of people hike the Way of St. James every year.

The city is now a university town with the University of Santiago de Compostela as the best university in Galicia and one of the best in Spain. The city's de facto population is made up of students and pilgrims in equal measure. It is a very nice place to spend two or three days if one finds oneself in the vicinity of Galicia just above the top of Portugal.

Sailing away from A Coruna on a clear evening is a celebration of the setting sun ablaze in all the glass windows of the west-facing residences along the esplanade. Probably the roughest weather we had the entire trip was the northward passage across the Bay of Biscay and along the coast of France on the way to the English Channel. All through the Strait of Malacca, the Indian Ocean, the Arabian Sea, the Red Sea and the Mediterranean, the seas had been calm. Now, in the throes of the confused seas caused by the North Atlantic Drift current, an offshoot of the Gulf Stream running into the European Continent at the Bay of Biscay, the waters are perpetually choppy with a strong swell running. Thus, on our way up to the English Channel, it was "one hand for you and one hand for the ship" as walking around involved holding on to something stationary. Inside the Channel, the seas flattened out, and we had tailwinds into the shallow waters of the Solent and the port of Southampton. It was in these waters that thousands of the ships marshalled for the Normandy Invasion on June 6th, 1944, including the *SS Jeremiah O'Brien* , groaning with troops and materiel and departing on the evening of June 5, 1944 for their date with destiny.

Passengers disembarking in Southampton were off in short order, and the ship was soon making way again on its last leg of the voyage in grey seas and under gray skies all the way to Holland. At the berth in the City of Rotterdam the next morning, we (reluctantly) walked down the automated, telescoping gangway onto Dutch soil. Outside, we were met by Joka's sister Helen and her husband Herman who thoughtfully picked us up and drove us to their home in Sassenheim, allowed us to stash our luggage, except for a carryon bag each, and then drove us to Amsterdam's Schiphol Airport. (The distances were not great.) There we hopped a shuttle flight to Berlin for a look-see at that fabled city. Neither of us had ever been there before.

What impressions did Berlin make on me? Tons. I'd been looking at street scenes of Berlin in movies my whole life, mostly in the context of World War II and the Cold War. Names like Check Point Charlie,

Alexanderplatz, the Brandenburg Gate, and Unter den Linden Street re-
verberated in my head. Contrasting images from both sides of The Wall
were familiar to me but only through Hollywood and newsreel lenses.
Berlin had all those things plus an inescapable melancholy that hangs in
the air like fog. One is never very far from a monument to The Holocaust
or other tyranny. Even the architecture gets into the spirit with keystones
on bridges featuring dolorous faces of men long forgotten.

The vast institutions of oppression represented by the Topography
of Terror Exhibit at the site of the Gestapo Headquarters, the undulating
tombs of the Holocaust Memorial, and the imposing Russian Embassy
are front and center. The Topography of Terror Exhibit teaches, for
those who don't know it, that no one suffered more as the result of the
Third Reich than Berliners. The ones who objected to the brutish acts of
the Nazis in the early days and those who resisted them once Hitler was
Chancellor were persecuted and systematically murdered. The survivors
were subjected to Allied bombing to the point of utter destruction. And
after the war ended, the ones trapped east of The Wall found themselves
occupied by the Russians who were as brutish and ruthless as the Nazis.
From 1933 to 1945, Berliners lived under the heel of Hitler's boot and
from 1945 through 1989, those in East Berlin lived under the heel of the
Russian boot for another 44 years!

Nevertheless, Berlin had a progressive face as well. Formerly drab
neighborhoods like Potsdamerplatz were spiffed up with new and pros-
perous-looking office buildings with flash mob theater and chorus
groups performing outside. Crowds of Berliners gathered around the
Brandenburg Gate on weekends and evenings just to socialize. An abundance of gourmet restaurants for the affluent and funky nightclubs for
the City's youth and artistic communities flourished as well.

I was enthralled by the place. I enjoyed looking at everything. The
monument to war dead was heartbreaking. It was in the Cecilienhof Palace
in Potsdam that Truman, Churchill, and Stalin carved Alsace-Lorraine
and the Sudenland out of Germany after VE Day. The Big Three also
decided on their course of action to end the war in the Pacific, namely
prosecuting Japan's unconditional surrender. The end of the Pacific War
was to be accelerated by Russia entering that war along with, though not
disclosed by Truman at the time, America's use of both of the two atomic
bombs it had laboriously manufactured. It was endlessly fascinating.

A stroll down Karl Marx Strasse to Alexanderplatz reminded us again of the ideological currents in Berlin's history. The Reichstag and its showplace dome is popular with tourists, and the new Chancellery Building impresses from across the green space from the Reichstag as the Chancellor's office was recently moved from Bonn back to Berlin, its original home. Humboldt University reminds all who pass that it is one of the great universities in the world. In Berlin, the visitor is guaranteed a surfeit of sensations to take away from this remarkable, historic, and still evolving city.

The flight back to Amsterdam was quick, and, after being picked up by the ever-obliging Herman, we settled into our stay at Helen and Herman's home for a few days. After that visit, I was to fly back to San Francisco on the last leg of my round-the-world sojourn, and Joka was to fly back to Sydney. But first, some fun in Holland.

Gouda was picturesque, even in the rain, and The Hague was busy and visually splendid. In The Hague's main square, one can dine, as we did, on a fair day at outside tables next to Parliamentarians talking shop. The International Peace Building's imposing presence had been entirely funded by Scottish-American Andrew Carnegie and continues to house the International Court of Justice and other important international dispute resolution forums.

One cannot go to Holland without being immersed in the care and functioning of dikes, polders, canals, and other hydrological infrastructure. Before there was an Industrial Revolution, the Dutch used the power of windmills to pump water out of ponds ("polders") created by building earthen levees across the open mouth of an inlet to the sea. Land could be reclaimed from the sea that way. Much of Holland was created by the dike, polder, and pump reclamation methodology. Herman took us to see a remarkable post-Industrial Revolution machine that revolutionized the reclamation process. It consisted of a giant, one-piston steam engine operating six arms with buckets at the ends. Situated at the edge of a large polder, it could lower the large buckets at the ends of the arms into the water, fill them, and then lift them simultaneously to empty the polder water into a canal that ran to the sea. This single steam engine reportedly replaced one hundred windmills and removed all of the water in the polder in the space of a year, thus reclaiming thousands of hectares of land. When aerated to remove the salt, the soil became productive pasture land. The physical stature of Dutch people jumped from small to tall and sturdy with the relatively sudden infusion of milk and cheese in their diet from the exponentially growing dairy industry that nourished the Dutch people in the process.

That single, one-piston pump operating on puny fifty PSI pressure from its twin boilers, is the story of the Industrial Revolution in microcosm. It enabled the exponential growth of productivity and of population. The thoroughly industrialized society that followed the introduction of fossil fuels produced a blizzard of building and manufacturing. It created and sustained urban centers everywhere.

Joka and I vowed to return to Holland and spend much more time travelling around this beautiful and fascinating country. But for now, we had come to the end of a long and remarkable journey. Time to go home and resume our respective lives among our families and friends, make routine doctors' appointments, get medication prescriptions refilled and generally take care of business. During our apart time, with the considerable assistance of information technology and its social apps like WhatsApp, we could plan our next trip.

CHAPTER 23

LEADING TWO LIVES
(AND GETTING AWAY WITH IT)

Reentry into my Napa Valley life was only slightly disorienting. It was delightful to see my children and grandchildren again. They led busy lives and likely wouldn't have even known I was gone but for the steady drip of emails I sent them with arresting photos from exotic places attached. I checked in with my bocce mates in Saint Helena and reentered our much anticipated summer bocce league play. I resumed my docent duties aboard the *Jeremiah O'Brien* on Fridays. And, I resumed writing short stories. My impressions of Sydney's Northern Beaches along with some from Berlin and Holland made it into the short story "Billy's."

After a couple of months tending the home fires, Joka joined me at me at home in Saint Helena. She bought a pretty, Delft-blue bicycle that she named Beatrix after the Queen of Holland, and, when I would spend too much time writing or tending the vineyard, she would take off on Beatrix and ride the private road through the vineyards down to the end of White Lane and Nancy and Paul Pelosi's wine country house. (Nancy was Speaker of the House of Representatives and third in succession to the Presidency at the time.)

I decided that Joka needed more exposure to the good old US of A, so we took an excursion to Santa Fe. Americans tend to look to Northern Europe regarding early American history. The Norse had a small presence here first in the extreme northeast. Then the Dutch East Indies Company had a major presence throughout the northeast, especially the Virginia, New York and Massachusetts colonies. They established prosperous plantations around what was New Amsterdam from the early 1600s until the English muscled them and some tentative French colonies out. Peter Stuyvesant surrendered New Amsterdam to the British Navy in 1664, and the British commander promptly renamed the city after the Duke of York.

Spanish expeditions pushing up from Mexico into the Southwest in search of gold had earlier settled Santa Fe beginning about 1610, and the Presidio there had already burned down once before the Pilgrims landed at Plymouth Rock. Santa Fe offers a unique slice of Americana and has always been one of my favorite places. So, off Joka and I went. We checked into a small inn in a residential neighborhood within walking distance of the Plaza and started walking. Out Canyon Road were the art galleries. Downtown there were more art galleries and many jewelry stores featuring turquoise mined locally and set in Pueblo Indian motifs. The historic hotels and churches and government buildings were satellites around the main square where everyone gathered for a paseo in the evening and to listen to live music.

Santa Fe art is an entire genre to itself, with Georgia O'Keefe as its lodestar. It has the outdoor landscapes of New Mexico, the architecture of the pueblos, and the spiritual designs of the Pueblo and other Native American cultures that inhabit the area. And Santa Fe *style* is an art form that escaped from the pueblos, mountains and dry washes of Northern New Mexico into the art communities of cities throughout the world. Eager to do my part, I made a "spirit bear" out of a block of manzanita burl and inlaid a silver "heartline" with a coral arrowhead after one of my visits to Santa Fe. I gave it to Joka for Christmas in 2019, and it resides in Avalon Beach, New South Wales.

The Delgado Street Bridge in Santa Fe was the drop point for a Los Alamos-based scientist named Klaus Fuchs when he passed America's nuclear secrets to Russian spies during the Cold War. There's nothing to see there now except a small bridge over the small, leafy *arroyo* and river and a walking path. An out of town day trip to Los Alamos and its museums and monuments made for a great excursion. I was so taken with it in an earlier visit that I made Los Alamos the sanctuary place to "scatter and adapt" after the collapse in my novel *In Extremis*. A drive to the biggest Catholic pilgrimage site in America at Chimayo is a must. In a church chapel there, pilgrims can scrape dirt from a small pit in the floor believed to be holy and curative for the lame and halt. This holy place made it into my short story *Lisbon*.

The last day, we drove the high road to Taos through Milagro, the setting of Robert Redford's film, "Milagro Beanfield War." In Taos, we found more art and more galleries, but also more funk. The Taos Pueblo is the highlight of a visit to Taos. It is authentic and the Pueblo Indians have been living there for centuries while battling the white man's government for control over their lives, including for jurisdiction over a nearby lake that is the source of their water and figures prominently into their spiritual stories.

Surfeited with Santa Fe style and southwest cuisine, we made the drive back to Albuquerque airport and caught our flight home. Joka loved it and soaked up all the novel culture. Mission accomplished.

After two months, Joka went back home, and our now customary two month hiatus apart followed. Then in the fall, I hopped a direct United Airlines "Dreamliner" flight (fifteen hours going, fourteen coming back) to Sydney in time for the holidays, Down Under-style. Joka's oldest son Jan Willem married his college sweetheart from Cornell, an American physician, Devora Lieberman. There is no Thanksgiving holiday in Australia; however, Devora made a Thanksgiving dinner at their newly finished showplace home in Avalon Beach and spread a little of the giving thanks idea around.

Joka and I spent the Christmas and New Year holidays in Avalon Beach, which of course was high summer. Christmas carols were sung, not by the fire or within the sound of sleigh bells, but on the beach with food trucks assembled to provide fish and chips, ice cream, and the like. It was a disorienting experience for me, but full of good will and that's rather the point. Australian merchandizers were just as eager to sell their wares as American ones, so Christmas sales were thoroughly hyped there as well.

Mostly, when we were in residence at Joka's Avalon Beach home, we followed her routine. It was fixed—as in invariable. That is not a complaint. For me, her daily routine was as close to perfection as it possibly could be—certainly better than any I have ever managed to put together at home. It consisted of sleeping until we woke up, showering and dressing, having a light "brekkie" of toast and fruit, and then driving four kilometers to Bilgola Beach. At the beach, there were options. Did I mention that Australians are swimmers? Once can swim in the ocean or in the salt water ocean pool. One can walk the length of the beach at the surf line to the headlands that separate Bilgola beach from Avalon Beach and return, about a kilometer. Or one can take a challenging walk up a series of timber stairs and follow a trail over the headland between Bilgola Beach and Newport Beach, taking in a spectacular view along the way of the surf rolling onto the beaches and crashing into the headlands, of breaching whales and rolling pods of dolphins, and of ship and small boat traffic offshore in the Pacific Ocean. Joka mostly swam, and I mostly walked.

After our daily exercise routine, we would meet at the café kiosk and there rendezvous with Joka's friends. This group had no organizing principle other than the members come to Bilgola Beach every morning to swim, have coffee or "brekkie" and socialize. To do that, one had to be retired or self-employed, and so they tended to be in the 60-85 age range. This group created a monkey's knot of friendship that was beyond my experience. Every "member" of it drew daily sustenance from their morning meetings at one or more large picnic tables outside the kiosk that would be co-opted for the occasion. At the Table of Wisdom, they thoroughly hashed out the daily news, travel plans, family goings on, cultural opportunities and the like. They followed American politics more closely than most Americans do.

For a more soulful meditation on the group dynamics of the group, larded with composite characters, histories and concerns, please refer to my short story "*Billy's*. In any event, this social experience, set in a drop-dead gorgeous crescent beach and cove, was a daily routine for Joka and me. Not too shabby. And given this routine, there was little stimulus to pick up and go somewhere else. So, when we did venture out into the greater world, it was usually in the late morning or afternoon for a run into Sydney on the B Line bus, or by bus connecting with the Manley Ferry into Sydney, or by car for a museum visit or a concert at the Opera House or the sculpture walk between Bondi and Tamarama Beaches. I can happily spend my two months stays with Joka engaged in nothing more than the aforesaid routine. Nonetheless, we both had long legs and looked forward to our next trip.

CHAPTER 24

OUR VIKING EXPERIENCE

After my next two month home break, Joka joined me in Saint Helena and we gathered momentum for a couple of weeks before setting out for our next adventure. We'd booked two back-to-back cruises, the first a Baltic Cruise around Scandinavia and Saint Petersburg, and the second a North Sea Cruise to Norway, Iceland and Britain aboard the *M/V Zeiderdam*. We flew to **Copenhagen** together two days early for a couple of days of sightseeing in Copenhagen before embarking. Joka's sister Helen and husband Herman drove to Copenhagen from Holland to join us as a nice surprise. We stayed at a converted multi-storied warehouse called Admiralty House on the quay near The Queen's sailing yacht and across the channel from the glass and concrete opera house gifted to the city by A P Moller Maersk, a shipbuilding and operating conglomerate.

The world headquarters of Maersk Lines, one of APL's chief competitors and the largest shipping company in the world was also just down the quay from our hotel, as was the iconic statue of the Little Mermaid on its base about ten yards out into the channel. We prowled the picturesque small boat harbor called Nyhavn, and took a boat tour around the central part of the city and the outer port featuring an array of wind machines providing alternative energy to the city.

Copenhagen sits on a cluster of islands which form the point of the Jutland Peninsula facing Sweden. That point narrows the waterway between and separates the North Sea to the West and the Baltic Sea to the East. Denmark sits astride the top half of the Peninsula with the German border below it. Denmark would be very small country indeed, but for the fact that it controls the vast, ice-sheet-covered island of Greenland three thousand kilometers away. A bridge spans the narrows between Copenhagen and the Swedish city of Malmo, through which narrows pass the ships trading among the Baltic ports of Eastern Germany, Poland, Estonia, Latvia, Lithuania, Russia, Finland and Sweden on the one hand and the outside world on the other.

At the time I write this, there is a plethora of crime novels and cable television crime stories that feature Swedish or Danish detectives solving crimes that are set in Malmo and Copenhagen and involve much crossing of the bridge in the gray gloom and marine haze that typically shrouds Jutland and the Baltic, e.g., Wallander, Beck, The Bridge, Ragnarok, Game of Thrones, and others. However, Joka and I had good weather and witnessed no murders in Copenhagen. I much preferred those crime series to American cop shows because there were no guns or car crashes in them!

We embarked on schedule via a different Holland America Line keel, this time the *M/V Zeiderdam*. Our ports of call were, in addition to Copenhagen, Tallinn, Estonia; Helsinki, Finland; Saint Petersburg, Russia; Stockholm, Sweden; and Kiel, Germany. **Tallinn** had a unique museum focused on the victimization of the Roma during the Holocaust. **Helsinki** is a fine walking city, and **Kiel** is of interest to history buffs as the manufacturing center for German shipping, including its submarines in WW II, and for the Kiel Canal.

Saint Petersburg is a west-facing city that has been profoundly influenced by its intercourse with the West. It was laid out by Peter the Great to evoke the canals and style of the Dutch city of Amsterdam, a city the czar greatly admired. As the capital of Russia for over two hundred years and the only Russian port on the Baltic, it was a beneficiary of the old Hanseatic League of countries that acted as a sort of maritime co-prosperity sphere in Northern Europe. That exposure guaranteed the city and Russia a place at the Northern European table within the Baltic and among the North Sea countries of Norway, France and Great Britain outside the Baltic.

Its original name was Saint Petersburg or Petrograd, but after the Communist Revolution, it was changed to Leningrad, and Moscow was designated the capitol. When the USSR collapsed from within over seventy years later in 1991, the citizens of the city renamed it Saint Petersburg. The core of the city is characterized by glorious buildings that reflect pre-

Revolutionary Russia. The Hermitage, Peterhof Palace, Catherine's Palace, St. Isaacs Cathedral, the Church of the Spilled Blood (a more elaborate but less famous onion-dome-ornamented church than St. Basil's on Red Square in Moscow,) the Admiralty Building, and a host of palaces that belonged to the aristocracy under the czars arrayed along the canals built to evoke Amsterdam's urban design. We toured the Hermitage collection of French impressionist paintings and the famous collection of Faberge eggs that two tsars made a tradition of giving to their tsarinas at Easter. And, we got to stretch our legs at the Admiralty Building and its surrounding neighborhood of canals, and again at the Church of the Spilled Blood and the palaces of former nobility that populated that district.

The outer regions of the city, however, consisted of Soviet-style hirise concrete apartment blocks on a huge scale—monolithic, bleak, and soulless.

We took a train to **Moscow** from Saint Petersburg, a four hour (one-way) journey of 650 kilometers. The train was crowded and the terminals at both ends were crowded. Food service on the trains was amateurish and served by young women dispensing soft drinks. They seemed dour and uncomfortable among foreigners.

The thing that struck me about the train ride to Moscow was what I saw out the window. Or rather what I didn't see. The forests were very pretty because, like most of Scandinavia, the dominant tree was the birch. So the forests consisted of countless white-barked trees with a bright green canopy, and they occupied more land than the interspersed meadowlands. An occasional grouping of dachas near the railroad tracks could be seen.

What was not to be seen, however, were any signs that the land was being cultivated. Land, of course, was owned by the state. If no government impetus to develop a parcel of land existed, it was not developed. Thus, for a Westerner to see hundreds of miles of uninterrupted swaths of fertile land standing idle is shocking, while across Russia's border with Estonia, Latvia and Belarus, the meadowlands and plains are laid out in geometric patterns of cultivated farms as we in the West would expect. I suppose the birch forests were used for lumber, but they were not thick trees and they were hardwood, so their usefulness would be limited. The dachas appeared to be grouped on small plots along the railroad right of way and situated on tiny plots gifted to citizens by the tsar and the Soviet government to be used for recreation and, importantly, gardening to help feed the citizenry. So, it is very common for a Russian citizen to have a tiny dacha on the outskirts of whatever city in which he/she lives and works.

In any event, the absence of any incentive to work fertile land was the on-going cause of this disuse of land in Russia. Private ownership would inject that incentive into its owner that would produce an entirely different social and economic result. Taking the long view, however, as non-socialist countries exhaust their land and destroy wildlife habitat elsewhere around the world, perhaps the "wilding" of the land inherent in Russia's socialist regime may pay dividends yet.

In Moscow, we had poor weather, cool and rainy. From the train station, we were bussed straight to Red Square and the Kremlin. The Kremlin is a fortress inside the urban center of Moscow, and for centuries it had stood as the symbol of power for its rulers, first the Tsars and then the Communist Government. There were no prisons or barracks of any kind in the Kremlin; it was instead a showplace of iconic buildings, dominated by a large, Romanesque administration building from which the head of state, Vladimir Putin, governed. Flanking the administration building were a large, modern auditorium called The Congress, the former palace of the head of the Russian Orthodox Church (that quasi-governmental position was eliminated by the Communist regime,) four, count 'em, four big Christian Orthodox churches, and the smallish former palace of the Tsars. The entire compound was surrounded by high red brick walls and towers with a few gates to provide controlled entry to the Kremlin. Outside the walls and facing Red Square, was the perpetually guarded tomb of Vladimir Ilyich Ulyanov, better known by his alias, Lenin.

After de-Stalinization in 1956, all monuments and markers of, or making reference to, Josef Stalin had been eliminated. The other giant of the Communist Revolution, Lev Davidovich Bronstein, aka, Leon Trotsky, was also entirely missing from the pantheon of Russian monuments. Trotsky was an ideologue who favored a more democratic council of proletariat over the strongman role of leader of the Communist Party and so fell afoul of Stalin as Stalin consolidated power after the revolution. Trotsky lived in exile in Mexico for several years, taking Frida Kahlo as a mistress among other achievements, before he was assassinated in Mexico by Stalin's agents.

Visitors were being freely admitted to the **Kremlin** for tours via one of the gates which was set up to handle long queues of tourists for ticket sales at multiple booths. We got in one of the lines and stood in the rain as we inched up to the admission point. Our guide arranged for the tickets for our group, and, as we went through security, Joka volunteered that she had a knife in her pack, and pulled out a small paring knife she used to slice apples for snacking purposes. Pandemonium! The line came to a halt as the alarmed guards considered what to do. Joka offered to surrender it to the guard facing her, but he threw his arms up as though the knife were radioactive and said he didn't want to touch it. Joka was told she would have to get out of line and go into a nearby building which had lockers. She could stow it in a locker for the duration of the tour. Joka was adamant that she wasn't going to go through the admissions line again, and the tour didn't have time to wait for her anyway. People in the line behind us began to shout and gesture at the delay. One of the guards finally took the knife and pushed it down into a crack in the mortar between the stone floor and the stone wall of the building until it disappeared. Security breach solved.

We were admitted for a tour of the outside of the buildings. The Kremlin is spacious and attractive and festooned with rows and rows of cannon captured from the retreating French army during Napoleon's ill-fated attempt to take Moscow.

From the Kremlin, we had a bus tour of the rest of the city's highlights. The University of Moscow is big and imposing. I spotted an Uber car at the main entrance. The financial district looks like any major city's financial center. Rows of modern skyscrapers house the headquarters of the oligarchies controlling the energy, metals, technology, banking, telecom, and transport industries. A number of the large venue buildings built for the 1980 Moscow Summer Olympics are also architectural contributions to the landscape. It will be recalled that sixty six nations, led by the United States under President Jimmy Carter, boycotted the Olympics that year in protest of the Soviet Union's entry into the insurgent war in Afghanistan against the mujahedeen. Subsequent events made that American gesture an ironic one indeed.

After a full day of touring in Moscow and another four hour train ride back to the ship in St. Petersburg, we were tired puppies by the time we crawled into our berth after midnight. It had been a fascinating day, though.

After sailaway from St. Petersburg at night and an overnight cruise to **Stockholm**, we decided to get an overview of the Swedish capitol by means of the "hop-on-hop-off" bus that looped around the city's landmarks. The first stop was the amazing *Vasa* museum. It seems Swedish king Adolphus was at war with his rival in Poland and needed some serious fighting ships. So he contracted with a Dutch shipyard to build two magnificent 64-gun ships out of oak. The first to launch was the *Vasa* in 1648 with its guns on the third and fourth deck and very top heavy. Before launch, the captain had been concerned about its stability and arranged a test in which thirty men together ran from side to side on deck. He terminated the test after three roundtrips for fear the ship would capsize. However, the king insisted on sailing the ship because he was anxious to send it against Poland. On its maiden voyage, the ship sailed out into the harbor at Stockholm with all of the gun doors open for display. A squall hit immediately thereafter, and the ship heeled over in the wind until the open gun doors took on water flooding its lower and upper decks. It quickly sank twenty five minutes into its maiden voyage.

The hull languished in the cold waters of the harbor for 313 years until it was raised in 1961. Fortunately, the harbor waters were thoroughly polluted for centuries, thus killing the microorganisms that would normally eat a wooden hull sitting in mud. It was in surprisingly good shape when raised. The extent of the ornamentation on the high stern section is remarkable, and much of it is still there. Nevertheless, seventeen years of careful conservation involving saturation of the wood with polyethylene glycol and drying it over and over was required before the ship could be displayed erect and intact. The city build an entire museum building around the reconstructed ship, and it has three levels of catwalks for visitors to inspect every aspect of the exterior of it from the keel to the crow's nest. The only maritime museum that equals or exceeds the *Vasa* museum in my opinion is the *Titanic* museum in Belfast. More about that coming up.

The second ship of the *Vasa* class followed, but the design and construction was modified by adding a mere one meter to the width of the hull. The second ship was thus made stable and went on to serve the king for many years.

After the *Vasa* museum we got back on the hop-on-hop-off bus, but Joka began to feel unwell, courtesy of a bug she would have picked up in Saint Petersburg or more likely, the train to/from Moscow. So she returned to the ship, and I wandered Stockholm. The Tivoli amusement park was prominent. I was also serenaded from the door of every souvenir store I passed with the dulcet tones of ABBA's "Dancing Queen," "The Winner Takes It All," "Mamma Mia," "Take a Chance On Me," "SOS," "Fernando," and on and on.

My final stop was almost as good as the first stop at the *Vasa,* namely, the Nobel Museum. Alfred Nobel was a nineteenth century inventor, industrialist and philanthropist. He was a prodigious inventor with hundreds of patents, the most famous of which was dynamite, and he made a large fortune making and selling munitions for all of Europe. When his brother died in Southern France, the French newspapers mistaken published an obituary on him in which they referred to him as the "merchant of death." Appalled at the legacy he was leaving, he decided to leave most of his fortune in trust for prizes rewarding worthwhile human progress. He endowed an annual prize for each of the fields of chemistry, physics, literature and medicine to be awarded by the Royal Swedish Academy of Sciences. A fifth prize was to be awarded for Peace by the Norwegian Parliament in Oslo. Why Nobel chose to go out of the country for that is unclear. This year, the year that I write this history, will mark the one hundredth awarding of the Peace Prize. My vote would be for Greta Thunberg, a saintly, Joan of Arc-like maid who has spoken truth to heads of state all over the world and shamed them for deliberately taking the world headlong into environmental disaster.

Across a waterway from the old town section housing the Nobel Museum is the Stockholm City Hall. It is a large and imposing building that serves as the site for the formal granting of the Nobel Prizes to the winners for their contributions to chemistry, physics, literature and medicine. The Peace Prize, as mentioned, is awarded in Oslo.

My time in Stockholm was remarkably full and fascinating for being just a cruise ship stop. After Stockholm, we headed for Warnemude, Germany, a port from which a day trip can be arranged to Berlin (with difficulty, given the distance to Berlin.) However, Joka and I had just spent time in Berlin. Also, Joka was recovering from the flu, and I was coming down with it. So, we did not go ashore there or in Copenhagen again (rainy, still sick and quarantined by the Captain.)

After sailaway from Copenhagen the second time, we were bound for two Norwegian cities, **Alesund** and **Bergen**. Both are picturesque and highly enjoyable stops, but descriptions of them and our (once again healthy) impressions would likely not make interesting reading for future readers. The uniqueness of Norway itself, however, is worth some print. For centuries it languished as a country supporting itself from fishing, shipping, lumber and mining. Of course, its Viking population had an outsized role in the early exploration and settlement of the entire North Atlantic.

Norway faces west, and that has always determined its prospects. Although located in high northern latitudes, unlike the Baltic Sea countries, Norway faces the relatively habitable waters of the Gulf Stream. So, Norsemen Eric the Red, Leif Ericsson (Eric's son, get it?) sailed west to Iceland, to the British Isles, to Greenland, and to Canada and what would become New England.

They also inhabited the north coast of France aptly named Normandy after that territory was settled by a Viking named Rollo. So, after an early and rich history as a fierce, curious and dominating people, they settled into a civilized role more in line with its limited assets. Fast forward, in 1969, Norway struck oil on its continental shelf. Since mineral rights are owned by the sovereign under Norse law, an enlightened government has managed the enormous wealth generated by its petrochemical industries to provide for the general welfare of its citizens, including national health care and old age pensions, among others. However, as I write this, Norway's oil fields are in an advanced state of depletion, although gas reserves are still high. The government is turning toward privatizing industries like technology that require access to financial markets. Still, it remains on a very solid financial standing and the standard of living for its citizens is very high. On to the remarkable island of Iceland.

Iceland is unique in all the world for its landscape. It is the only land form on the mid-Atlantic Rift, and it formed astride the rift over a geological hot spot. It too is located in the outer reaches of the Gulf Stream, and so its climate is more temperate than one might expect that far north.

A north-south seam may be found right down the middle of Iceland from which the North American Tectonic Plate is emerging from the bowels of the Earth's mantle west of that line and is "flowing" (breaking and bending and floating) off toward the west. Immediately adjacent to that emergence the Eurasian Tectonic Plate is emerging and "flowing" toward the east. In the center of the island along the rift line, there is a remarkable place where a waterfall drops off of cliffs on the American Plate and forms a steam that flows along the rift for a kilometer or so and then crosses over onto the Eurasian Plate to form a broad lake. This site is called **Thingvellir,** and it was the site of what was perhaps the world's first democracy. Norse tribes that occupied the island at the end of the first millennium used to meet annually at Thingvellir and settle disputes, make laws and coordinate tribal activities. The entire body of then Icelandic law would be read aloud at "Law Rock" before each annual session and then revised as needed by majority vote among the tribal chieftains at each annual meeting. Sometime around 980 CE, the King of Norway converted to Christianity and issued an ultimatum to the Icelandic tribes. Either they converted or else. Legend has it that the chief of the principal tribe threw his statue of the primary pagan god into the Gullfoss waterfall from Langjokull glacier as evidence of his compliance with the Norse King's orders.

The government of Iceland, like that of Norway, has been clever about the use of its earth resources, in particular, geothermal energy. We visited one power plant near **Reykjavik** that consisted of a series of wells drilled into a geothermal reservoir underground to capture the steam to power generators for electricity. These wells also extracted hot water to route through a system of pipes circulating throughout the city to heat dwellings and offices. The cooled water and condensed steam was then returned to the underground reservoir to replenish the water there and to reheat. Energy, then, is abundant and cheap and non-polluting and *perpetual.* In fact, Iceland successfully attracted Alcoa Aluminum Corporation to build a plant there to which its bauxite ore from the Caribbean mines is shipped. Alcoa uses free or cheap energy in Iceland to smelt aluminum from the ore before shipping it out again to world markets.

Active volcanism is constantly occurring over the Icelandic hot spot resulting in the reformation of the island. Since the volcanic eruptions are usually, but not always, of the plastic flow type rather than explosive, they have over time occurred under glaciers and resulted in flatter mounds under the ice rather than the peaked volcanic cones we are used to. Hot springs, waterfalls from glacial runoff, fumaroles, thermal pools and lava flows abound.

We also stopped at the ports of **Akureyri** and **Isfajordur** for separate sights of fiords, glaciers and volcanic fields. We took an excursion to the second largest glacier which involved a walk down into the ice via a tunnel. Unlike many glaciers around the world that are melting, that glacier was actually growing. We could see the line of volcanic ash down in the ice that had been deposited by an explosive eruption about ten years earlier. It was interesting to walk around inside a glacier and look *up* through a crevasse. There is a great deal of liquid water inside a glacier.

We were scheduled to make a final tender stop (no wharf available for the ship, land visits by life boat only) at a spot with the catchy name of **Djupivogur** to see Iceland's biggest glacier, but the visibility was so bad the tenders couldn't find the boat landing. So, the captain made a command decision, and we were off to Scotland with an extra day to play with.

The Orkney Islands appeared as misty shapes along the way past John O'Groats House and into the Firth of **Dornoch** in the extreme northeast of Scotland. We docked at **Invergorton** across from Inverness, and Joka and I took separate excursions ashore, she being a teetotaler and me being partial to a wee dram of Eastern Highlands single malt scotch (for medicinal purposes only, heh, heh.) The village of Dornoch was full of surprises. First, it had a golf course that is on the PGA tour along with St. Andrews. Second, it was the ancestral land of Andrew Carnegie, and he maintained a vacation home in the area. Lastly, it had the storybook church where Madonna married Guy Ritchie. Outside of town, there is a well-known distillery that makes Glenmorangie, a shining example of the aforementioned Scotch whisky. I learned (between wee drams) that the chief difference between Eastern Highlands scotch and Western Highlands and Islay scotch, apart from the tongue-twisting Gaelic names of the latter, is that the Eastern Highlands scotch does not use peat in its distilling process. Thus, the notes of smoke that may be found on the nose of, say, a Laphroaig or Johnnie Walker scotch are absent from, say, a Glenmorangie scotch.

Another surprise in the Firth of Dornoch: obsolete offshore drilling platforms from the North Sea oil patch are parked there. Lined up like a row of corn, they are. I suppose it isn't that easy to dispose of them once they have reached their useful life, but they add nothing to the seascape of the Loch while they await expressions of interest from ship breakers and salvors.

After **Invergorton**, the *Zeiderdam* steamed around the easternmost point of Scotland and down to the Firth of Forth (Translation: Fiord formed by the River Forth) and **Edinburgh**. Our cruise formally ended in Copenhagen, but we had arranged to disembark in the penultimate port of Edinburgh so that I might fulfill a bucket list goal of mine. More about that later. The point is, the ship was berthed at a dodgy pier that was underwater at high tide and sloppy wet at low tide when we disembarked. We dragged our luggage the length of the pier over the wet, pebbly surface to the head of the pier and hailed a cab. A mere half hour later, we were checking in to the Royal Scots Club, a reciprocal affiliate with the Marines Memorial Association Club in San Francisco of which I am a member. We looked forward to a couple of days of sightseeing in Edinburgh before driving down to Manchester, England and a small village on the Bolton-Bury Road named—wait for it—Ainsworth. But first, the ancient city of the descendants of the Vikings and Picts who first combined to defeat the Romans, then divided into clans, and then involuntarily united again, however uneasily, under the English crown.

Edinburgh Castle, always flying the cross of St. Andrews looms over the city of Macbeth, William Wallace, Bonnie Prince Charles, Mary Queen of Scotts, Sir Walter Scott, Thomas Hobbes, Adam Smith, and many more. It was nearby in Culloden that the clans led by Bonnie Prince Charles were finally defeated by the English in 1746, and, continuously since then, the British crown has rested on Catholic Scotland and Edinburgh Castle. Down the Royal Mile is Holyrood Castle, one of the Queen's (Elizabeth II, as I write) properties, but it is used only for ceremonial purposes as the Windsors prefer the more commodious Balmoral Castle when in Scotland.

I decided that I would like to spend more time in Scotland in future just wandering aimlessly around in a rental car and letting myself age a bit on the lees of the local single malt elixirs in between rounds on the golf links. Joka would sign up for the trip as well, but more for the fresh air and hikes over the moor and through the heather.

Hertz was kind enough to rent us a car, so we signed ourselves out of the Royal Scots Club and into a midsize sedan for the drive to Manchester. On the way, we passed within sight of Loch Ness, the Falls of Clyde, and the village of Lockerbie where Pan Am Flight 103 fell out of the sky, for you numerologists, at 1:03 pm on a December Day in 1988 after a bomb planted by a Libyan terrorist at Heathrow in London exploded. If the crossing from Scotland into England was marked by a sign, I missed it, and about 160 kilometers south of that border we found ourselves in the outskirts of Manchester. A turn to the east took us to the small city of Bolton where our lodgings were located. After checking in, we set off again on the five or six kilometer drive from Bolton to **Ainsworth** on the Bolton-Bury Road.

For a full recount of my genealogical pursuits in the area, please refer to the Genealogical Appendix to this volume. In general, however, I was there to learn what events in English history produced migrations of Ainsworth-surnamed people from Lancashire to the New World locations of America, Canada and Australia, as well as to Ireland. I learned during this visit and subsequent research that these events included The English Civil War, religious persecution of Calvinist believers at the hands of the Anglican Church, periods of extreme poverty, and the Industrial Revolution in and around Manchester, the textile center of England. I learned that I was a descendant of either (1) a Norman knight surnamed d'Euins to whom the Cocky Moor area of Lancashire was given after the Battle of Hastings (1066) and after whom the village was named, or (2) someone whose surname was taken from the place of his domicile after the naming convention of the time (e.g., Leonardo da Vinci, Thomas of Ainsworth, etc.) My ancestor likely migrated to the American Piedmont well before the American Civil War either due to pressures following the English Civil War (Ainsworths were on the losing Royalist side when Cromwell prevailed and perhaps had to flee to the New World) or simply sought a better life than that offered by a feudal agrarian economy in a place with bad weather. My dad's family came from Ainsworths who emigrated to South Carolina and the cotton belt in the mid-1700s. From there they migrated throughout the cotton belt of the Carolinas, Alabama, Mississippi, Louisiana and Texas, with my immediate ancestors settling in Rankin County, Mississippi.

Armed with information obtained in Ainsworth from the Vicar of the Presbyterian church, the caretaker of the Methodist Church, the official church records of births, deaths, and incarcerations in the Bury Poor House, as well as the good offices of a man named Phillip Parker whose family owned the property on which Ainsworth Manor had stood and which land boasted artifacts left by the Romans, I was able to do a good deal of research on line to put this picture together. I got substantially what I came for, i.e., an idea why people with the surname of Ainsworth immigrated from the village of that name to the new world, seeming in pulses, over a considerable period of time.

Joka and I then moved on by means of a short flight across the Irish Sea to **Belfast** in Northern Ireland. There, we checked into a small hotel in the city center. Our first official act was to take a hop-on, hop-off bus ride through Belfast, which revealed the several neighborhoods occupied by warring factions of Catholics and Ulster Protestants during the period called "The Troubles." The open civil war between Catholics seeking unification with the Catholic Republic of Ireland to the south, and the Protestant majority which sought to preserve their association with the Protestant government of Great Britain, had just been settled, however fragilely, by a power sharing arrangement called "The Good Friday Accord" engineered by the Clinton Administration some seven years earlier. The history of assassinations and retaliation assassinations had embittered the two segments of the population against each other in ways too lasting to fade over a mere seven years, so revenge killings still took place at the time we were there, but on a scale that could be considered crime and not civil war. Whole neighborhoods were still walled off and closed to intercity travel at night by massive gates. But the peace has held and the City shows signs of civic pride and self-promotion to the commercial world.

In our tour of the City Hall, an imposing structure, I walked up the grand staircase and passed a young woman coming down. She wished me a pleasant good day as she passed, and I responded in kind. An attendant at the top of the stairs then informed me that she was Lord Mayor of Belfast.

We had two full days in Belfast; one to be spent at the Titanic Museum where, as the museum's name suggests, the *SS Titanic* was built by the British White Star Line. The other day involved a bus tour to the geological site known as The Devil's Causeway on the extreme northern coast of Ireland. We did the second tour first and we were fortunate to have what passes for a fine day in Northern Ireland in which to do it. It didn't rain, the wind was only moderately strong, and it was cool, but not cold.

The site itself was remarkable. It consisted of an area in which lava flows consisting of basalt rock had fractured over time into hexagonal columns, something basalt does naturally because of its crystalline structure. But these columns had weathered unevenly along the coastline as some areas were inundated by the storm surf more than others. The result is a striking visual of hexagonal columns perhaps twelve inches wide of uneven heights undulating along the shoreline for hundreds of meters. It was easy to walk up and down the steps provided by the columns and made for a great photo op. My favorite part of the geological story behind the Devil's Causeway is the fact that sixty six million years ago, the lava eruption that created the basalt deposit took place over the hot spot that is now Iceland. In other words, the volcanic eruptions took place where Iceland is now, but then those rocks moved the distance from where Iceland is now on the Great Atlantic Rift to where Ireland is now on the Eurasian tectonic plate. That journey took sixty six million years as the Eurasian plate continuously forms along the Rift zone and migrates to the east. Having just come from Iceland, that factoid resonated.

Back in Belfast the following day, it rained hard and made the hop-on, hop-off bus trip to the Titanic museum miserable, but the museum itself was spectacular. It is a new museum—perhaps five years old as I write—built on the site of the ship way in which the great ship was built. In the gift shop, there were T-shirts for sale reading "She was fine when she left here." The ship launched successfully, and sailed to Southampton and other English Channel ports to embark on its maiden voyage to New York. But, Murphy's Laws being alive and well, the ship's captain was attempting to set a speed record across the North Atlantic regardless of the *known presence of icebergs* along the route. Also, the ship sailed from Southampton *while fighting a fire in its coal bunkers* that weakened the structure of the hull in the area where the iceberg eventually struck. The rest is history. Its sister ship, the *SS Olympic*, also built in Belfast, had a long and distinguished economic life.

The museum consists of a scale mockup of the Titanic which can be toured by means of a unique gondola ride that lifts and twists the viewer from the keel to the bridge and throughout the ship showing different phases of construction from to riveting to pipefitting to outfitting. *Titanic* was an amazing work of construction a hundred years ago, and the museum does a terrific job of making the project visual and comprehensible to a visitor.

The next morning, we took the train from Belfast to our final stop in **Dublin**, Republic of Ireland. Dublin was pure, relaxed sightseeing for us. We took a bus excursion to neighboring highlands to see heather and peat bogs and the Guinness family estate used to film episodes of "The Vikings," "Game of Thrones," "Star Wars" and other notable movies. We also found the headwaters of the River Liffey that bifurcates Dublin. In town, we prowled the famous Temple Bar. This is a neighborhood built up on a sandbar in the River Liffey, although in the Temple Bar neighborhood, just to make it confusing, there is a pub called The Tem-ple Bar. We toured the prestigious Trinity University and visited its incredible library. Founded by Elizabeth I in 1592, it served to develop a Protestant educated class in Ireland. Admission to Catholics was re-stricted until 1892 when the university was opened to them. The Pope's response to that reform was to forbid Catholics from attending the uni-versity *until 1970* . Thus, in a predominantly Catholic land, a university education at its most prestigious university could not be had by Catholics for nearly *four hundred years*. This history is only one example of the centuries-old, baked-in animosity between the British Anglicans and Irish Catholics that dates back to Henry VIII and his single minded quest for an heir, and acts as a prism through which English-Irish affairs must be viewed when approaching "The Troubles" in Northern Ireland. Also, before that, relations between Great Britain and the German-sympathizing Republic of Ireland in World Wars I and II were warlike. It is one of the most persistent and intractable conflicts between populations in Western history.

With that, our revelatory exploration of the Baltic, the North Sea, Iceland, and the British Isles came to an end. We flew back to San Francisco together for another week or so in Saint Helena before Joka returned home. Another long and spectacular trip!

CHAPTER 25

ADDICTED

Joka and I were now in an alternative universe where we lived at polar opposite sides of the earth from each other yet easily went back and forth to our respective domiciles, together and apart, travelling to whichever parts of the globe struck our fancy. That was, of course, beyond reason, but I loved it. I identified with Australia a lot, and Joka was pleasantly surprised by how much she enjoyed the States. It seems her family members had experienced only New York and Columbus, Ohio, where her oldest brother settled after the war. Neither place appealed to them. Not that there is anything wrong with Columbus, Ohio, home of astronaut and Senator John Glenn and "the Golden Bear," Jack Nicklaus. However, compared to Holland and Switzerland, it came up as unremarkable.

By now, Joka had toured the California coast south as far as Los Angeles, lived with me in the San Francisco Bay Area experiencing the Mediterranean weather and lifestyle in the Napa Valley. She had explored Fort Lauderdale and Key West, Florida and the high desert beauty of Santa Fe/Taos/Los Alamos, New Mexico. She looked forward to a talked-about future riverboat trip down the Mississippi through the Antebellum South from Memphis to New Orleans. So, life was good, airfares were cheap, and technology had fostered our relationship via free facetiming apps that kept us in daily contact even when apart. Who knew the world really could be our oyster?

We held the view that our "duty" at our age was primarily that of taking care of ourselves and not making demands of our children who had busy lives to lead. Our presence was not particularly needed by either of our families, except for holidays and special events, and we were fortunate to both have enough means to travel. So, as long as our health held up, we were free to follow this peripatetic lifestyle that we happened

261

onto by sheer, dumb luck. After two months at home in Napa "taking care of business" and catching up with family and friends, I flew back to Sydney for my by-now customary two month stay, featuring daily, not-to-be-missed, visits to Bilgola Beach, among other interests.

There was the annual Sydney-Hobart single-hulled "Maxi" yacht race. On race day, the sleek boats sprinted from Sydney Harbor past South Head, and, with a right turn at the marker buoy into the Southern Ocean, they were gone. They faced a wild two-day crossing of the Tasman Sea fighting typical "Roaring Forties" seas all the way to Launceston, Tasmania.

We, on the other hand, sailed the placid waters of Pittwater Bay with friends, ferried up the Hawkesbury River for lunch at a waterside resort with Devora's father visiting from New York, and again for a 50th Anniversary celebration with Joka's long-time friends, Richard and Willy Barton back from their Cook Islands home. We took in the annual "Sculptures-By-The-Bay" art event that follows a path along the coast from Bondi Beach to Tamarama ("Glamarama" to its neighbors) Beach.

The time passed too quickly, but, when the two months was up, I packed up again and went home for the holidays. All four grandchildren were on hand, two of whom were back from college (Brayden from Chapman and Lauren from Syracuse.) Julia, a high school senior and Ainsworth, a freshman in high school were still at home. Thanksgiving and Christmas were hosted by my daughter Erin and son-in-law Eric at their stately Kentfield digs, formerly one of the family homes of William Kent himself, a wealthy, three-time Congressman, conservationist and philanthropist who donated Muir Woods to the State of California.

I should clarify that Joka and I had visa restrictions that determined how long each of us could visit the other's country. Neither of us could remain in the other's country for more than 90 consecutive days, although we were free to return multiple times during the one year period of the visa. Visas could be renewed annually and indefinitely, so we were able to go back and forth indefinitely, as long as we didn't exceed 90 days in any one stay. As mentioned, we had a goal of perpetual summer, that is, we tried to be in Sydney during the winter months in California and in Napa during the winter months in Sydney. We couldn't always adhere to that program because of the way that holidays or other obligations fell and because of the scheduling and itineraries of the cruises we took. But mostly, it worked.

Henceforth in this chronicle, I won't keep to a strict chronology of our back and forth travels to spare the reader a head-snapping exercise in trying to keep track of the multiple legs of our schedule but will simply summarize those goings-on of interest. From here on, I will focus more particularly on the cruises Joka and I took.

When Joka next visited me, we drove to **Mendocino** for a bit of New England in California. The county of Mendocino is a heavily forested, sparsely populated area of coastal mountains, with a lovely and wild seascape on the ocean and a tidy vineyard landscape inland in the Anderson Valley. Interspersed in numerous clearings in Mendocino's forests, illegal marijuana growing patches appeared in clearings, but out of sight of the roads. The economic prominence of marijuana was measured only by the mysterious bulge in currency in the regions' banks that could not be explained by the logging, tourist and winemaking industries. These hidden growing sites were no-go places for law enforcement and forest hikers alike as they were defended by armed drug entrepreneurs. De facto toleration of the "weed" industry was largely explained by the fact that there existed a great deal of popular demand for the product among the residents of Northern California.

After the Mendocino excursion, in June, 2018, we booked a "90 day ticker" deal on Holland America Line for an **Alaska** cruise aboard our old friend from the South America cruise on which we met, the *MV Zaandam*. It was a 14 day round trip cruise out of Seattle up past British Columbia and via the inside passage to Ketchikan, Juneau, and Glacier Bay to Anchorage and to Denali, Kodiak, Homer, the Hubbard Glacier and back down the ocean side to Sitka and into the Strait of Juan De Fuca to Victoria, B.C. The cruise ended back in Seattle, but we arranged to disembark in Victoria so we could spend some time there.

Holland America Line had conducted Alaska cruises longer than the other lines that now crowd southeast Alaska waters. Also, its ships were smaller than most others in the trade. Its longevity and ship size meant that a HAL passenger could get into three ports that were not on the itinerary of most cruise liners, namely, Glacier Bay at a native people's village, at Homer on the Kenai Peninsula, and at Kodiak Island.

Our first port, **Ketchikan,** stood out as a colorful mining town in the rainforest worthy of a day's walkabout among the charming shops located in the former brothels of the town. If the weather was not terrible, a float plane excursion into the misty fiords could also be easily arranged. We did the former, but not the latter because it was raining and the ceiling was too low. We did take a gondola up a local mountain for a walk in the rainforest and to measure our wingspans (arms from fingertip to fingertip) and compared them to those of the much bigger wingspan of the bald eagles that looked menacingly at us from their cages at the exhibit.

Our second port up the Inside Passage, **Juneau,** was an amazing stop for two reasons. First, a float plane ride took us over five, count 'em, five glaciers that grind their way to the sea from the coastal mountain range. The sight of those glaciers was merely the first of many glacier encounters we were to have, but it was an exciting introduction into the glaciology of southeast Alaska. The second major attraction in Juneau, apart from the state capitol across the street from it, was the Red Dog Saloon. This place was an old fashioned bar with a pair of swinging front doors and to hell with the weather. Its style was Northwest honkey-tonk with moose and bear heads on the wall and sawdust on the floor. Live country and western music was dispensed at the hands of the singer/guitar picker *du jure,* and it was a hoot. It was Joka's first experience with real country and western music, ambiance and clientele, and she had the time of her life. And the beer was excellent. We stayed right up to the bitter end before the ship pulled up the gangway to sail away. Fortunately, the ship was berthed right across the wharf from the saloon, a circumstance that saved many travelers over the years who needed to stagger onto the ship at the last minute. Joka filmed me in a cringe-worthy video singing along to John Denver's "Take Me Home, Country Road…" Yee-haw!

The next stop was **Icy Straight Point, Glacier Bay,** an outlet to the ocean from the Inland Passage north of Juneau. Specifically, we were visiting a community of Tlingit Native Peoples residing in a village called Hoonah on the island of Chichagof. Though the name doesn't exactly trip off the tongue, Chichagof is the fifth largest island in the United States, and Hoonah, its "first class" town, boasts 788 souls, per the 2018 census. Jobs there were mostly government jobs, but they did have an industrial pier for supply ships, and it was big enough to berth the *Zaandam.*

Those of us who chose to go ashore were there to get a look at the native village and to take a bear walk. The town consisted of an uninteresting collection of homes and government buildings arranged in no subdivision plan that I could discern. I doubted that Euclidian zoning laws had made it that far into the bush. The bear walk was the main draw, as the island has a large population of Alaskan Brown bears—a larger, fish-eating coastal cousin of the Grizzly. The Tlingit people live together with the bears, that is, there are no bear barriers in the village of Hoonah. The natives learn the ways of the bears and their diet, and it seems the Tlingit are not a part of it. I was told by our guide that he was unaware of any fatalities in his community involving bears during his lifetime. You do, however, have to be cluey enough not to get between a female and her cubs. Bears are omnivores, but there were plenty of fish, berries and other edible plants, including a broad leaf plant called "bear cabbage," available for them to eat. They also scavenged the carcasses of moose, caribou, deer, and other mammals as they found them.

We hiked a trail into the bush with two Tlingit guides, one of them carrying a high caliber "kill anything" gun for protection, looking for bears in the wild. We hiked through interesting flora, some dwarf varieties due to highly leached, shallow soils in some meadow areas, and along streams. We frequently encountered fresh bear scat and pawprints among the bear cabbage and stopped at viewing platforms built by the natives to look for them. We saw no bears on our walk. However, when we got back to where the van was parked, took our seats, and the van turned onto the gravel road back to Hoonah, there were three bears on the road, a female and two juveniles. They were apparently accustomed to seeing vehicular traffic and seemed relaxed, but as we crawled toward them for a better look and photo op, they disappeared into the forest. It was well worth the stop just to be able to glimpse how they lived in that wild and remote place in the summer season.

The environmental stresses faced by us urbanized and well-supplied sapiens from the south were nowhere to be seen. True, the face of the local glacier had retreated a mile or so over the last fifty years, but the glacier was still seventy five miles long, the water was pure, and the eagles and whales and bears and salmon and caribou were present in countless numbers. The environment did not register as unhealthy to my untutored eye. Next stop, Anchorage and Denali.

I don't remember how many float planes there were in **Anchorage**, but it was more than any other place in America and possibly on earth. We had booked an excursion on one of them for a flight to see Mount McKinley, aka Denali, up close and personal. It was contingent, though, on decent weather, and the day dawned ominously dark and raining. Just as I was trying to locate someone in the ship's office to cancel, the clouds broke and the sun came out. So, off we went by taxi to the harbor and found the right float plane berth among hundreds of them. At the appointed time, we took off in a six-seat Canadian-built de Havilland aircraft. The distance from Anchorage to **Denali National Park** is about seventy five miles, and the route follows tundra, streams of glacial runoff, and forests of conifers being killed off in alarming numbers by a bark beetle due to warming in the Arctic. About 20 minutes after take-off, we were at the base of Denali itself. The mountain loomed above us as a brilliant white peak among the Alaska Range. I say it loomed above us because, although we were in an airplane, the de Havilland could only climb to 10,000 feet of elevation, and the mountain rose to 20,000 feet. It was HUGE.

Joka neglected to tell me beforehand, but she was terrified of heights and was unable to look out the window and down into the vast glacier that circled off the mountain or at any of the hanging canyons filled with untouched ice and snow. So, it was white knuckles time for her the whole way, but I took a lot of pictures for her to look at back on the ground. Also, I knew from an email from my daughter Erin that a neighbor of hers whom I had met, a former Navy Seal, was on the mountain that day trying to summit it with a climbing team. Looking into those ice fields and razor sharp ridgelines surrounding the peak on all sides, I couldn't imagine attempting that feat, but people do and he was. I telepathically sent him my very best wishes as we circumnavigated Denali, America's biggest mountain.

The pilot unnerved us once when he asked us through the headsets we were wearing to let him know if we saw any other airplanes flying near us as we banked into and maneuvered within the various mid-mountain faces of the peak. There was no air traffic control in the Denali National Park.

The airplane's window on the front passenger side wouldn't close the final half inch, and it grew seriously cold in the cockpit after a half hour or so, it being roughly thirty degrees below zero Fahrenheit outside at our elevation. So, eventually the pilot dropped down to several hundred feet above the glacier and wound down the mountain with the glacier. The view of Denali and two neighboring peaks of nearly the same height, ninety percent brilliant white in the sunshine and ten percent black volcanic rock, with the entire Alaskan Range trailing off to the north is a sight I will never forget. Most visitors to the park do not get to see Denali at all because it is normally covered by clouds. We had been unreasonably lucky weather-wise and were able to inspect every square meter of the mountain—from a safe distance in the plane circumnavigating the mountain.

On the lower part of one flank of the mountain, the pilot landed on an Alpine Lake so we could stretch our legs and warm up. The water surface was so smooth and the reflection of the sky so clear and blue that the pilot remarked that he could not judge the distance between his pontoons and the water as we landed. I tried to estimate it myself as we came in for the landing and couldn't do it. We finally just hit the water with our pontoons, taxied, and the prop wash pulled us to the beach. There was a lot of brown bear scat on the beach and in the surrounding berry bushes, so we had to stay alert, but it was a beautiful and lonely spot, and the sun was warming. Then we took off again and flew back to Anchorage calling out to each other all the moose sightings along the way. What a day!

The city of Anchorage is not a tourist destination. It is a normal, small-sized city in appearance, with streets lined with office buildings, banks, and stores. I had been there briefly once on APL business when we built the container shipping terminal at Unalaska in the Aleutians, but had little memory of it. In any event, downtown Anchorage was not on our itinerary, so it was back to the ship for our customary champagne sailaway.

After Anchorage, we called at the ports of **Homer** on the Kenai Peninsula and the island of **Kodiak**, each featuring wildlife excursions to see whales (humpbacks, greys, orcas and minke), eagles, sea otters, puffin birds and penguins. In Homer, there was also another famous saloon called The Salty Dawg to be sampled and enjoyed. This enduring saloon had a tradition wherein patrons sign and pin a dollar bill on the wall or ceiling so that if a thirsty wayfarer without means were to show up, the funds would be there to pay for his drink. Evidently, not many indigent drinkers show up because there are thousands of dollars pinned on the log cabin's ceiling and woodwork.

After Kodiak, we sailed over to the **Hubbard Glacier** on the mainland. The Hubbard is THE Alaskan cruise destination because of the sheer size of the glacier. It is 76 miles long and near the lower end is joined by the Valerie Glacier, forming a seven mile wide face of ice that pushes into Disenchantment Bay. The ice face is 75-100 feet high and the below-water depth of it is multiples of that. Cruise ships anchor just off the face of the glacier from which vantage point passengers are treated to regular, sometimes spectacular calving events that would swamp a small boat. In addition, the sounds emitted from the millions of fractures in the shifting glacial ice are hugely entertaining, ranging from screeching noises to assorted pops and snaps through thunderous booms that sound like artillery fire. One is happy to stand at the ship's rail for hours and listen to the glacier's symphony of percussion while sipping a cup of hot chocolate or split pea soup thoughtfully provided by the stewards. Navigating room is limited, however, and eventually we were obliged to yield our position to another, newly arrived ship and move on.

From The Hubbard, we sailed to **Sitka**, a pretty little port just north of Vancouver Island and facing the Gulf of Alaska. Because of its relatively southern latitude, it had the feel of a more temperate climate. We were amazed to see the size and abundance of lush azaleas in bloom all over town in mid-summer, much later than in Napa. The architecture of Sitka reflects a Russian influence from the eighteenth and nineteenth centuries when Russian whalers and fur traders ranged as far south as Fort Ross in Sonoma County, California.

The colonial advance of the Russian czars in North America was eventually blocked by the string of twenty one missions, with military garrisons at Monterrey, San Francisco and Sonoma. These had been built by a Spanish quasi-military expedition, the initial nine of which were built by Father Junipero Serra, starting in San Diego in 1769 and extending to, not coincidentally, Sonoma in Alta California opposite the Russian Fort Ross in 1823. After many years of the static face-off in Sonoma, the Russians finally abandoned Fort Ross and, with the purchase of Alaska by Lincoln's Secretary of State, William Seward, for seven million dollars in 1867, withdrew back to Russia entirely. The town of Sitka predates that Alaska purchase and so many of its old buildings look Russian, notably the St. Michael Archangel church with its onion domes.

From Sitka, it was a short leg down the west coast of **Vancouver Island** and east into the **Strait of Juan de Fuca** to the picturesque town of **Victoria, British Columbia** where we disembarked and moved into a hotel downtown. Had I done my due diligence, I would have booked us into the Union Club, a dressy private club and hotel having reciprocal privileges with the Marines Memorial Association Hotel in San Francisco. The Union Club was perfectly located across the street from the landmark Empress Hotel near the water, but the latter had been fully booked when I made the arrangements on short notice before the trip. So, we settled for an ordinary, three star hotel a half block away. Still, we thoroughly enjoyed walking the streets of Victoria, visiting its museums and restaurants, and of course touring the mini-miracle of the Bouchart Gardens. United Airlines had a direct flight from Victoria to San Francisco, and, on departure day, we were back in Napa in a matter of hours.

A couple of weeks later, Joka's time in the States was up, and she returned to Sydney. I took the occasion of our two months separation to work on editing the short stories I had written thus far and drafted a new one that would eventually become *Billy's*.

CHAPTER 26

HOME AWAY FROM HOME

On my next trip to Oz (Australians informally call their country Aus, or Oz), I immediately rejoined the Bilgola Beach morning coffee and avocado toast society as Joka and I resumed our very comfortable routine. I had joined the Avalon Beach Returned Service League ("RSL") a private club with historical connections to veterans but now a venue for eating, drinking, and gambling. Upstairs there were slot machines, horse race betting windows and card tables. Downstairs, there was a bar and restaurant and events like trivia clubs and private gatherings were hosted there. Jan Willem and Adriaan served as my two sponsors, and I was in. I could now play the ponies and lunch at "my club."

Misfortune began to have its way with our group as a natural consequence of aging. Joka's longtime friends Agnes (Dutch-born like Joka) and her husband Andre (Indonesian-born merchant marine captain) were dealing with Andre's advancing motor neuron disease (Steven Hawking's disease.) Longtime friend Richard Barton had a severe stroke at his home in the Cook Islands, and he and his wife Willy moved back to Avalon Beach to receive care. Longtime Bilgola Beach morning swim group member John Stone's Parkinson's Disease progressed to the point where he had to move into a care home, and a founding member of the Bilgola Beach coffee and swim club, Ross MacPherson, was descending into dementia, a great worry to his wife Rae. Ross was content to sit smiling at the table long after he lost the ability to follow a conversation. Joka and I were thus reminded of the relentless passage of time and our precarious place along the life span continuum. Nevertheless, we vowed that, as long as we were going to be here, we might as well be here. We decided to take up a long standing invitation from some friends who lived out in the country to come visit.

We drove west into "the Riverina" of New South Wales to visit a couple we had met on the South American cruise. Len and Annette had been a part of Joka's and my meeting and getting to know each other experience, and we decided to go to their home in Leeton, NSW. It is about a 600 kilometer drive from Sydney to Leeton, and we did some sightseeing along the way. I won't go into all the New South Wales towns we passed through, but two of them merit comment. After climbing into the Great Dividing Range through the Blue Mountains, the road comes out into rolling pasturelands and a town named **Cowra**. Cowra was known for having one of Australia's enemy alien internment camps during World War II. At the outbreak of the war, any Italian, German or Japanese personnel, military or civilian, unlucky enough (or, it could be argued, lucky enough) to be in Australia were instantly enemy aliens. Crews of merchant ships or airlines, students and academics, visiting businessmen and the like were stranded and had to be confined as prisoners of war.

Cowra housed both Italian and Japanese prisoners of war, each in a separate part of the camp. The Italians were a peaceable cohort and were generally happy to wait out the war in Australia as farm workers. They were not confined by day, and they assimilated with the farm families to which they were assigned, often forming life-long friendships with their host families that survived the war.

The Japanese prisoners, however, were a different lot. As the war in the Pacific progressed, surviving crews of Japanese ships sunk in Australian waters and airmen who crash landed during the air attack on Darwin were imprisoned there. Culturally ingrained in each Japanese internee was the conviction that it was a disgrace to be captured alive. They lied when initially giving their names and personal information so that there would be no reports given by the Australian government to Japanese diplomats that could get back to their families as to their whereabouts. Captivity would disgrace their families. They were militant prisoners and were considered dangerous potential escapees, even though an escaped prisoner in the countryside around Cowra had nowhere to go, nowhere to hide, and no way to return to a Japanese military unit.

Nevertheless, they plotted and executed an escape in August, 1944 when over 1100 prisoners broke out, killing nine Australian guards but suffering hundreds of dead and wounded among their own as they were machine gunned by their guards during the escape or killed as they resisted being recaptured over succeeding days. The purpose of the breakout was simply to die trying, thus regaining the perverted (my opinion) sense of honor they thought they had lost by being captured alive. It will be remembered that throughout the Southeast Asia theater of war, the Japanese Imperial Army engaged in gratuitous acts of beating, starvation, beheading, bayonetting, shooting, withholding of medical care, and generally wholesale murder of captured British, American, Canadian, Australian, Philippine, Chinese and other allied troops.

They did it in Nanking, in Corregidor and Bataan, in Singapore, along the Thai Burma Railroad, at Sandakan, and many other places because of their mindset that any soldier allowing himself to be taken alive merited being either summarily killed or worked to death. It was what we Westerners can only consider a defect in their humanity (again, my opinion) that compelled them to commit such atrocities on such a large scale and without remorse. After the American atomic bombs were dropped on Hiroshima and Nagasaki, the members of the governing war council didn't even convene a meeting to discuss surrender because they were no more concerned about their own citizens' lives than they had been during the firebombing of Tokyo that had killed even more Japanese than the A-bombs. It took the subsequent Russian declaration of war against Japan as the Allies had agreed at the Potsdam Conference to produce the Japanese unconditional surrender. Apparently, Japanese leadership simply chose to be occupied by Americans and not Russians.

At any rate, the Cowra breakout was notorious for exhibiting this Japanese character trait since there was no object to it other than be killed and to kill Australians in the exercise. Should that character trait be forgiven today on the grounds that it was the misguided indoctrination of the Japanese military culture at the time? Or that the benevolent American occupation and rebuilding of Japan administered by MacArthur cleansed any such instincts? It would be comforting to think so and many blithely assume so, if they think about it all as they buy Japanese cars and electronics from the same Japanese corporations that supplied the Japanese Imperial Army its war materiel. However, this writer is not convinced.

At the Cowra museum as I write, baseball caps are purchased by Japanese pilgrims to Cowra that have "The Great Escape" written in Japanese characters above the bill. The major political party in Japan operates a shrine that honors the perpetrators of atrocities throughout the war and the war dead equally on the grounds that all died honorably in the service of their divine Emperor. Japanese schools today teach students nothing of those atrocities and instead characterize the Japanese military operations in Asia in WW II as resisting Western colonialism. They do not acknowledge the Rape of Nanking. They do not admit or apologize for using Korean women as "comfort women" on a mass scale. They do not repent. To their credit, however, they have never sought to reinstate their prior culture in disregard of the MacArthur era constitution imposed on them that forbids Japanese military engagement.

At Cowra, there is an expansive "Peace Garden" that was built by a famous Japanese landscape architect and funded by a Japanese industrialist. Is it a left-handed admission of Japanese atrocities during the war? An affirmation of basic human civility? Or is it a face-saving way to mollify the sensibilities of its Australian customers to promote the business of Japanese *keiritsu*? It will be generations that follow my own that will judge. For my own view, I borrow from Fredrick Douglass:

…there are no bygones in the world, and the past is not dead and cannot die. The evil as well as the good men do lives after them … The duty of keeping in memory the great deeds of the past and of transmitting the same from generation to generation is implied in the … moral constitution of man."

[Note: At the time of this writing, men are gradually being sensitized by shifting legal norms and the judgement of history to yield more power to the opposite gender in many areas of human behavior. That should be no less true with it comes to assigning blame for wars and the atrocities that were committed by men. Let the record reflect that the atrocities committed by the Japanese male gender implying a character defect during World War II may not be fairly imputed to the female gender living at that time, just as it must be noted that it was not women who fired on Fort Sumter, nor Sunni women who today kill Shi'a. There is much to be learned in that regard by sapiens going forward.]

From Cowra, we proceeded on to **Leeton** and Len's and Annette's home. Len had a pharmacy in Leeton for forty or fifty years and Annette was a homemaker. Len took me to a Rotary meeting as his guest. Both of them engage in charitable works, particularly foster parenting and hosting exchange students as a regular part of their lives. They are the salt of the earth.

Leeton is in the middle of the Riverina, a vast and productive agricultural zone in New South Wales. The Darling River, the Murrumbidgee River and the Murray River all run west from the Great Dividing Range and converge there forming a vast irrigation zone that produces all manner of crops. Think San Joachim Valley in California—Big Ag, hugely productive. Len arranged for us to visit a large "station" outside of Leeton which was owned by a friend of his. This fellow kept track of his holdings by means of a small two passenger aircraft called an "ultralight." He took me up in it to see the property. His land extended far into the distance in all directions; wheat and barley fields, rice paddies, walnut and almond orchards, vineyards, fields of canola (an oil producing grain), etc. Some crops were in multiple plots that had been staggered in planting so that, say, barley could be harvested periodically throughout the year for the beer industry. We buzzed the 'roos off the wheat and the ducks off the rice.

Back on the ground at the station, I struck up a conversation with a very tall, good looking young man wearing a ten gallon hat. He was American visiting from the Modesto area as an ambassador from his family's agribusiness there. He was in Oz to study water conservation methods as well as animal husbandry and farm labor management. We would call it networking. In any event, he knew one of my shipmates on the *Jeremiah O'Brien*. Small world indeed!

Nor did the coincidences end there. We also visited a winery near Leeton called Lillipilly, which is the name of a native tree in Oz. I shamelessly played the winemaker card ("I'm a winemaker from the Napa Valley …") and he pulled out all the stops. We tasted as many of his wines as I could take, and the owner gave me lots of bottles of his wine to enjoy with Len and Annette. In the course of our conversation, he explained that a few years prior he had received a call one day from a wine broker in the Napa Valley who supplied cruise ships and airlines with the wines

274

they served the public. The caller said he had just tasted a Lillypilly late harvest wine that he thought was excellent and thought the Aussie wine-maker should submit a sample to KLM Airlines which was looking for a dessert wine for their first class service. My new Aussie friend and Lilly-pilly owner did, and KLM bought it. Then Quantas ordered it also as the word got out. This development instantly made the Lillypilly winery a financial success and it grew from there. The winemaker didn't know, however, how this broker came to taste his wine in far off Napa. I told him that my late wife's nephew in Napa, Mike Ingellis, worked for a large wine distributor, and I would ask him if he had provided the tasting with the broker for the airlines. I later did query Mike about that, and he confirmed that his distributor did indeed carry the Lillypilly brand and that he was familiar with their late harvest wine and thought it very good. Mike didn't recall doing a tasting of the Lillipilly wine with the broker but thought it might have been his predecessor in the job who had done so. That act had dramatically changed Lillipilly's fortunes seven thousand miles away. Crazy.

After saying our goodbyes to Len and Annette, we set off for a small town called **Lockhart** they had recommended we visit. There was a small museum there, they said, that was well worth the trip. Lockhart's down-town sported a two-block-long commercial strip with early twentieth century Victorian architecture and lots of filigree wrought iron orna-menting the balcony levels on the storefronts that marched down the street. The covered verandahs kept the hot sun off of shoppers. It wasn't hard to find the museum, and we were fortunate to find it open, as its hours depended on the personal schedule of the caretaker. The museum exhibited antique farm implements and the work of a single artist named Doris Golder, a recently deceased woman whose husband ran a large sheep station out of Lockhart. She was an artist, but didn't have access to a reliable supply of art materials where she was, so she created a new art form using material she did have available—wool.

She gathered samples of wool in every gradation of color from snow white to black from their shearing shed and then combed them so there was no foreign matter in the wool. She then painstakingly pulled out little bits of the varicolored wool and placed them on a board until, using only gradations of color, she created portraits of famous Australians

(John Newcomb-tennis player, Paul Hogan-Crocodile Dundee actor) and landscapes of Hereford cattle and stands of eucalyptus trees. The astonishing thing about her work was how precise it was. The detail of the eyes or teeth of a subject in a portrait, for example, were sharply delineated, and the hair or eyebrows in a portrait or the hide and fur on animals, for example, were perfectly lifelike.

Apparently no other artist in the world worked with the medium of raw wool, so the art market struggled to put values on her pieces. Some found their way into art museums, but much of her work remains on display in her own private museum in Lockhart, NSW on the road to nowhere. Wacky, but extremely cool.

On the way home, we passed through The Rock, a town situated at the base of a big rock sticking above the surrounding plain. The Rock is about seventy five kilometers from the micro-metropolis of Wagga Wagga (not to be confused with Walla Walla, Washington, although there is also a Walla Walla in New South Wales.) We spent the night in the wine country town of Yass, named after a tributary of the Murrumbidgee River.

It was my second experience in the semi-arid "bush country" of Australia. That is not quite the same thing as the "outback," a desert landscape in the center of the country. Carol and I had stayed on a sheep station in bush country near The Grampians National Park in Victoria during our earlier trip. The overwhelming majority of Australians live within 100 kilometers of the coast, so trips into the country, let alone the outback, are relatively rare. In fact, there is only one transcontinental passenger train from east-west and no cargo trains. The only major city in Western Australia is Perth, a mining center, and the closest big city to Perth is Singapore. So, goods move trans-continentally mostly by ship or plane, although the "road trains" of trucks with articulated trailers hundreds of feet long do pound through the outback on the one paved highway and the red dirt roads on more local routes. There is also one south-north passenger train and one paved highway that runs between Adelaide in the southern wine country and Darwin in the tropical north.

Alice Springs and Uluru lie in the center of the country but not much else does in the way of urban development built by "whitefellas." The aboriginal people, in all of their multi-tribal variety, do inhabit the outback, as well as the more hospitable lands around coastal areas which brings them in contract with whites. The two types of people in Australia do not mesh well.

The white colonizer assumption is that the aboriginals must assimilate, that is, adopt white European customs, language, legal systems, economic systems, educational systems, mores and norms. It has taken white Australians—the ones who think about it at all (many never or rarely lay eyes on an aboriginal or Torres Islands Strait ("ABTIS") person)—this long to realize that assimilation is not going to happen. The aboriginal people are militantly proud, different in just about every way it's possible to be different and are convinced that they are being occupied by barbarians. They are perfectly adapted to the land on which they have lived for upwards of *50,000 years*. The Europeans do not sit easily on the land and over time, tend to ruin it (and the air, and the water, and the fisheries, etc.).

Also, the concept of land is wildly different between the two peoples. The ABTIS people don't recognize the concept of private ownership of land. They consider land that the people walk on is land they are all responsible for safeguarding for others in the future. What an idea! Anyway, it is beyond the scope of this chronicle to meditate on the Australian ABTIS people "problem," but let it be recorded that the "problem" is alive and well.

[Query: since Australia is the only place on earth that has a continuous record of *sapiens* activity for over 50,000 years (vs. 5,000 years in, say, Asia Minor, Africa or Europe, which would be just about the outside limit of European peoples' data bank,) wouldn't you think that *sapiens* everywhere would consider it a priceless resource of information about the nature of, and therefore prospects for, *sapiens* going forward? Do they/we? Of course not! By the way, the primary DNA of aboriginal people in Australia is that of the Denisovan people, a separate branch of *sapiens* from either Neanderthals or *homo sapiens.* Denosivans are believed to have migrated down from Siberia through China and the Indonesian islands.]

Back home in the Northern Beaches, Joka and I planned our next trip. It promised to be a doozy. HAL had a 55 day cruise on the *MV Veendam* that sailed from Fort Lauderdale, ranged down through the Caribbean to the Antilles and Devil's Island, down the east coast of Brazil to Rio de Janeiro for Carnival, back up and into the Amazon River 900 miles, and then back through the Caribbean for more island stops. Yikes! After I go home for my two months' taking-care-of-business homestay, Joka is joining me and we will make the journey to Fort Lauderdale in time for a February departure.

CHAPTER 27

BRAZIL

Joka arrived in Napa in late January, 2019. Being in the northern hemisphere in January violated our perpetual summer program, but we were headed back to the southern hemisphere on our cruise. We flew to **Fort Lauderdale** the day before embarkation day and checked in to our pre-and post-cruise hotel, the Pier Sixty-Six Resort and Marina we remembered from the South America cruise on which we met. A stroll around the marina revealed a goodly number of mega-yachts owned by Saudi princes, Russian oligarchs, and a sleek, racy-looking one belonging to Steven Spielberg. But, we did not allow the green-eyed monster Envy to consume us and shrugged such ostentation off. We had our own, even bigger ship that we could call home for the next two months of exploration—The *MV Veendam*.

The next morning, we slept in, had a big brunch at the hotel, and lounged around the palm-studded garden and pool complex until it was time to taxi to shipside. Embarkation was, by now, a familiar routine—dump the luggage on the pier, go through immigration, check in with HAL's reception, answer a general health questionnaire, ride the elevator up to Lido Deck for a light snack, then find our ocean view cabin where, by then, our luggage would have magically appeared. Then it was unpack (surprisingly, there was more than enough closet and drawer and bathroom space for our stuff), and then back to the upper decks for sailaway into, quite literally, the sunset. Then dinner, then the floorshow in the theater, then piano bar with the lounge singer *du jure*, then to bed with a light rolling of the ship to lull us to sleep. In the morning, Key West.

Key West was more pure Americana for Joka. I like the place too. We visited the Harry S. Truman "Summer White House" on the old Naval Base dating back to 1890. Harry and Bess had enjoyed staying in an apartment probably built for the commanding admiral at some point. It had been used as a vacation spot for, in addition to Truman, Presidents Taft, Eisenhower, Kennedy, Carter, and Clinton. Being from Missouri, Truman found the tropical vibe there relaxing. Unlike Ike, Harry Truman was not a golfer, so he just did a bit of deep sea fishing and caught up on his reading. One of the most significant pieces of official business Truman accomplished at his Key West quarters was to issue an executive order banning racial discrimination by government contractors of the Department of Defense. This was the first official Federal Government act targeting segregation and employment discrimination since the WW II emergency executive orders, and before the Supreme Court decision in *Brown vs. Board of Education* (1955) struck down the noxious "separate but equal" doctrine of *Plessy vs. Ferguson.*

The historic district in Key West is not a large area, so it was an easy walk to Ernest Hemingway's House, complete with the latest generation of his six-toed cats. Then, the "Duval Crawl" down Duval Street past Jimmy Buffet's Margaritaville, to Sloppy Joe's, where Hemmingway maintained a booth as a sort of combination office and drinking spot. Then to Mallory Square, the Customs House and the Federal Courthouse, where a good deal of the admiralty law (my legal specialty) on salvage was written over the years. A large number of shipwrecks had occurred over time in the Florida Keys, either by reason of the hazards of navigation presented by the surrounding coral reefs or by reason of thieves who moved lanterns to the wrong locations causing ship strandings so that their cargoes could be stolen. As a consequence, a large body of maritime law was created courtesy of the Federal courthouse in the Keys.

I renewed the quest previously undertaken the last time I was in Key West with Carol to search for the best key lime pie available. Lunch at Margaritaville, however, was my only opportunity this trip. I gave their pie three and a half stars out of five. The *Veendam*'s dining room, however, offered key lime pie from time to time, which I always sampled for purely academic purposes.

Our last walkabout stop in Key West was the Conch Republic Marker, southernmost location of the continental United States and some 90 miles from Havana. Key West boasts that it was a sovereign republic at one time according to a story that goes like this: In 1982, the

Florida Highway Patrol set up a roadblock on the main causeway road at the direction of the Federal Government. All vehicles were searched for drugs making their way from the Keys to the rest of the States. Since that severed all traffic and commerce with the mainland at great inconvenience to the residents of Key West, the Mayor claimed that the road closure was in the nature of a frontier or border established by the U.S. Government and an involuntary expulsion of Key West from the United States. He then declared Key West as having succeeded from the U.S. as a sovereign nation and named himself as Prime Minister. There are numerous anecdotes that arose from these circumstances, including one incident in which the hostilities became kinetic when the native "Conchs" (as the locals were called) hurled pieces of crusty bread and shot water cannons at a battalion of U.S. Army personnel who happened to be in the area on a training mission. Shortly thereafter, the highway check point was removed, and Key West rejoined the Union.

Three sea days out of Key West, we found ourselves in the **Dutch Antilles**. The first island was **Curacao**, the largest of the islands having Willemstad as its capital. West of Curacao is **Aruba**, capital Oranjestad, within sight of Venezuela and its offshore drilling rigs. East of Curacao is **Bonaire**, the smallest of the three and the least developed. Centuries earlier, the islands traded ownership between Britain and the Netherlands, depending on the alternating successes of each in their European wars. In the Caribbean, the fortunes of each island depended on the fortunes of their European sovereign.

Most of the action in the Antilles took place in the 1600s. A young Peter Stuyvesant went to Curacao for the Dutch East Indies Company and presided over its colonial plantations there and in the neighboring islands. The Spanish, however, attacked and took the Dutch settlement on Saint Martin, a more distant island. As part of Pope Alexander's allocation of colonial space in the Americas between Spain and Portugal (Brazil went to Portugal, Venezuela and the West Indies to Spain) Saint Martin was fair game for Spain. Peter Stuyvesant led a Dutch expedition to take it back. In the ensuing unsuccessful naval battle for Saint Martin, a Spanish cannonball took off Stuyvesant's lower leg.

During a long and painful recovery in Holland, he acquired a wooden leg with a handsome silver collar. It was when he was so equipped that he was appointed to be the last (as it turned out) Governor

General of Niew Amsterdam on North America's northeast coast. Britain and its navy finally got the best of the Dutch East India Company and the Dutch ceded Niew Amsterdam to Britain. The British officer in charge promptly bifurcated Niew Amsterdam into New York and New Jersey. But it was "Peg Leg Pete" as he was popularly called, who led the Dutch presence in the New World during those formative years. [For our family ancestral connections to the early Dutch in Niew Amsterdam, please see the Genealogical Appendix.]

But that was then and this is now. Our time in the Antilles was spent touring each island by van, stopping at the scenic beaches, walking the streets of Willemstad and Oranjestad, finding agreeable lunch spots, taking boat tours of mangroves with their teeming marine life incubation, and watching flocks of flamingos eating the pink shrimp that give the big birds their color. In the case of Bonaire, a huge salt mine had been operating for centuries. The Dutch and British had punctuated their hos-tilities with periods of economic cooperation where warranted. One of those cooperative periods was in the late seventeenth and eighteenth cen-tury when the Dutch ships would procure African slaves for British plantations and salt mines in the Caribbean after anti-slavery reformists made it difficult for British slavers to operate. It was highly profitable for both sides. The slave "houses" (6'x 8' concrete block houses) are still vis-ible on the beach near the salt mine in Bonaire.

While we were in Bonaire, the Maduro regime was trying to expel U.S. diplomats from Venezuela, but the American legation refused to honor the demand because it officially recognized only the government of President Juan Guaido. As I write, the contested government of Nicholas Maduro is still unresolved and hyperinflation is destabilizing the country. Oh, and I marked my seventy ninth birthday on Bonaire.

From the Dutch Antilles, The *Veendam* sailed to **Trinidad** and then to **Tobago.** These two islands comprised the Independent Republic of Trinidad and Tobago. They received their independence from Britain in 1962, the capitol is Port of Spain in Trinidad, and the culture is creole. Port of Spain is a city of nearly a million people, and they are well dressed, polite and relatively well-off thanks to the country's oil reserves. Trinidad is also just offshore from Venezuela, is much larger than Tobago and has a prominent wildlife reserve populated with exotic tropical birds like the brilliant scarlet ibis which I was delighted to spot in the mangroves. Tobago is smaller, prettier and has lovely beaches making it the favored tourist destination.

From Tobago, we went to **Barbados**. I sometimes struggle to keep Bermuda, Bahamas and Barbados straight, but Bermuda is a lone seamount in the Atlantic Ocean off the coast of North Carolina. It is an elegant British colony and has, in its capital of Hamilton, a world class reinsurance industry and is a popular tax haven for incorporating companies. It also serves as a flag of convenience for global shipping. Its currency is the American dollar. The Commonwealth of Bahamas consists of an archipelago of islands off the east coast of Florida and is an independent government of which Nassau is the capital. The Bahama Islands are a popular tourist destination for Americans.

Barbados, however, is a small island in the southeasternmost Caribbean next to the French "Departments" of Martinique and Guadalupe. It is an independent nation that is part of the British Commonwealth and has gorgeous white and pink sand beaches. Its business, apart from flying fish, is tourism and cruise ships. We had a contact there as Joka's son Jan Willem went to Cornell with a fellow from Barbados, and Willem suggested that we give him a call and meet up, which we did. Francis Gonsalves was his name and he took us to his upscale but casual beach club, the Royal Yacht Club, for a coffee and then to the local fish market so that Francis could lay in some seafood supplies for his two restaurants. It was there that we watched with amazement while a skilled fisherman was filleting a small flying fish, a local delicacy, with a machete. I would not have thought it possible to do such fine work with such a big knife, but the fillets came out perfectly every time with none of the flesh wasted. We said our goodbyes to Francis, and Joka took a kayaking excursion to some sea caves while I toured the Foursquare and Mt. Gay rum distilleries. Yo ho ho!

From Barbados, the captain pointed the bow of the *Veendam* toward **Devil's Island**, a French penal colony just offshore from mainland French Guiana. It was made famous for our generation by the movie "Papillion" starring Steve McQueen and Dustin Hoffman. It had been made infamous much earlier in a French political scandal known as the Dreyfus Affair, a shameful instance of anti-Semitism in which Dreyfus, a Jewish captain in the French Army was falsely accused of betraying

French Alsace and Mosel then being annexed by Germany. In a bewildering confluence of military and political pettifoggery and anti-Semitic misconduct, Dreyfus was convicted and sent to Devil's Island where he was singled out for abusive treatment for years. Influential people marshalled to his side, and he was eventually retried and his sentence commuted, allowing him to return to the Army and fight for France throughout WW I.

In the case of the Frenchman simply called "Papillion," before the penal colony was closed in the 1950s, Devil's Island was made famous again by an inmate named Henri Charriere. He was known for the tattoo of a butterfly (Fr. papillion) he wore and for his propensity for escape. Charriere was a safecracker who had been framed for murder by his mob-ster boss after Henri kept some of the diamonds he stole on a job for his boss. He was sent to Devil's Island. For his constant attempts to escape and other breaches of discipline, he survived one two-year stretch in sol-itary confinement and one five-year period in solitary before ultimately escaping successfully and permanently.

There is no wharf to berth a cruise ship on Devil's Island, and so visitors from cruise ships must "tender" in to the small prison dock in life boats called tenders. Joka and I did just that in punishing heat and humidity, and we hiked up to the top of the island where the prisoners' cells were. The place is mostly in ruins now and infested with monkeys as the jungle reclaims the place, but we could get a clear picture of how miserable prisoners would have been. There would have been no relief from the backbreaking work of crushing rock with sledges, or from the heat, tiny cells, poor rations, malaria, and sadistic treatment by camp officers and guards. The facility itself, even apart from the miscarriage of justices that sent people there, does not reflect favorably upon the French Republic at the turn of the twentieth century.

Back on the ship, we took cold showers and cleaned up for sailaway to the Brazilian port of Belem, our first experience in Amazonia. But on the way, we became enamored with a charming, elderly French couple named Victor and Nellie.

They grew up in the country near Limoges in France. As small children, they lived under the Vichy regime during WW II, and that part of France was spared heavy occupation by the Germans. Nevertheless, the

Vichy government collaborated with the Germans extensively. Nellie's father was entrepreneurial by nature, and he decided their community needed more bread to survive the war. So, he set out to grow wheat where wheat had never been grown. Disregarding the ridicule of his fellow farmers in the area, he planted his farm in wheat, and it turned out to be very productive. Nellie's mother used some of the wheat to bake bread for sale which was locally acclaimed to be excellent. They prospered from their bread income. Largely out of contact with German troops and officials, they hid a Jewish couple in one of their outbuildings that had a double wall. The couple worked on the farm by day and slept in the hidden space by night. All of their neighbors were aware of this, but none of them reported it to the authorities as the Vichy officials were held in contempt. Toward the end of the war, Nellie's parents raised a pig, which was illegal since all pigs had to be surrendered to the Vichy and the Germans to feed the German army. The officials heard reports of the pig and searched for it, but it was kept hidden on their and surrounding neighbors' farms. During the winter of starvation in 1944-45, they slaughtered the pig and shared the pork with the other co-conspiring farms and the hidden Jewish couple, allowing all of them nourishment.

Nellie married Victor, who aspired to be a brewmeister, and they immigrated to Canada to work for a brewery in the 1950s. In later life, they retired and moved to Austin Texas, to be near their children. In the small world department, Nellie said she and Victor had recently been on a cruise where they ran into a couple from their village near Limoges who remembered the wonderful bread that Nellie's mother made during the war. Nellie and Victor, a sunny and impish man with a strong French accent, were very popular dinner companions, and we were delighted whenever we ended up at the same table with them.

Belem called itself the city that rubber built. It was located just below the mouth of the Amazon River on a vast marshy bay fed by Amazonian waters. A city of two and a half million people of Portuguese, Amerindian and African slave origins, it dates back to the 1500s. In the nineteenth and twentieth centuries, it was the booming gateway to the Amazon for the rubber trade. Now, the handsome buildings built by the Portuguese rubber barons look a bit down in the mouth, but the aura of decay is counterbalanced by all of the activity that still goes on there. The fishing fleet was large and the open air market adjacent to the wharf area vast, fascinating and fun. We saw countless items of produce that we could not identify, and some that looked vaguely familiar like durian and acai and brown husks containing Brazil nuts. There was one counter where a woman displayed maybe seventy five used plastic drinking bottles filled with varicolored liquids that she was selling as having medicinal benefits. Any ailment known to man had a cure in one of her bottles, including, she said as she zeroed in on my inquiring countenance, one for erectile dysfunction. Apparently there are no pure food and drug standards whatever in effect in Brazil.

We watched a storm cell approaching from the jungle across the bay and a tropical downpour opened up just as we arrived at the covered market. By the time, we had canvassed the market completely, the storm had passed leaving the poorly drained streets overflowing.

Visually, the town was disconcerting. High rises for the affluent lined a sandy beach with shanties shoe-horned into the interstices between them. Iron bars covered every first story window, concertina wire sat atop every wall, and armed police were everywhere, usually in groups for self-protection. But there was also an elegant, 150 year old opera house built for the rubber barons that was in use for a rehearsal when we passed through on a tour. We also toured a gems and minerals museum that displayed specimens mined from all over Amazonia, including solitary quartz crystals as big as a wheelbarrow.

The tour bus guide spoke openly about the corruption of the government and police and the fact that everything was skewed for the benefit of the rich classes behind their walled compounds. However, he also said that the markets were full in plentiful variety and that "nobody goes hungry." And, apart from a bit of electricity, houses (shanties) do not require heating and don't receive cooling, so little energy is required on a consumer level. Brazil is an oil producing state and the export revenues earned by the government from that source are available for running the country, at least that margin not siphoned off by corrupt officials.

After a day's sailing due east from Belem along and then rounding the shoulder of Brazil, we arrived at the "Venice of Brazil," **Recife.** If Belem is the city that rubber built, Recife is the city that sugar built. It was the port most tributary to the sugar cane fields in northeastern Brazil in the seventeenth, eighteenth and nineteen centuries. I have mentioned before how the politics and wars of Europe determined the fortunes of the Caribbean colonies of European participants. One of the more interesting and unanticipated outcomes had to do with the Iberian Jews. When Spain and Portugal purged their respective populations of the Sephardic Jews that migrated to those countries via North Africa over the second millennium, they fled to Amsterdam, a place known for its religious tolerance. Calvinist Christians from England, including some Ainsworths (see Genealogical Appendix), made similar pilgrimages to Amsterdam to escape harassment by the Anglican Church. In the case of the English Calvinists, frustrated by the Dutch system of guilds that monopolized the trades and therefore relegated immigrants to menial work, they emigrated again, this time to Virginia and Massachusetts.

In the case of the Sephardic Jews, however, many relocated from Iberia to the Portuguese territory of Brazil. However, they did not go to the territories that were controlled by the Portuguese, their oppressors in Iberia to begin with. They went instead to the city of Recife which was Dutch territory in the seventeenth century by virtue of successful aggression by the Dutch West Indies Company. Pope Alexander had allocated territories in the Americas as between Portugal and Spain, however, the Pope's *terra nullius* decree was not binding on the non-Catholic British and the Dutch, who continued to raid and harass Portuguese territories in Brazil. The Dutch took control of the sugar that flowed through the port of Recife.

Iberian Jews flowed to Recife from Holland to seek their fortunes, which, being a clever and industrious people, they found. Jewish families in the sixteen hundreds did well there, some becoming rich and powerful families from the sugar trade. The first Jewish synagogue in the New World was built in Recife and still stands there today. It is believed that the first Jewish immigrant to Niew Amsterdam, now New York and New Jersey, arrived from Recife.

Recife sits on a long broad beach with a shallow gradient so that the waves range from small far out in the water to tiny at the shoreline. As in Belem, high rise buildings line the beach front housing for the affluent but with scattered shanties among them. On the outskirts of town, there is a UN World Heritage Site. It is a hilly village called Olinda that was built by sugar-wealthy folks back in the day, with lovely Mediterranean–style villas in a wooded setting. We enjoyed our stroll through Olinda which, with Carnival less than a week off, was filled with early dancing and celebration.

Again, clumps of police were always visible to keep a lid on things and protect the tourists. The markets groaned with fruit as Recife was also a busy port for mangoes, bananas, and pineapples headed for Europe. The signs of upcoming *Carnivale* were everywhere. Spontaneous groups of samba drummers and dancers sprang up like flash mobs, despite the heat and humidity. It is amazing how much zest and enthusiasm springs up in anticipatory rejection of the inhibitions of Lent.

Our next stop was a short one in a small city named **Macieo** just south of Recife. Joka and I took no excursions there and simply took a bus to the city center and walked around. We stopped at an open air market and at the cathedral, the interior of which, though open to the air was magically and delightfully cool as opposed to the hot humid air outside. We lacked the stamina for that level of heat and humidity, so we caught the next bus back to the ship. The only welcoming presence at the port for our arrival had been a brass band wearing military camo uniforms sitting in the shade of a bridge overpass playing pop music. They too gave it up as they were not there when we returned.

A short transit overnight brought the *Veendam* to the pretty city of **Salvador de Bahia** on the point of a peninsula with a cooling trade wind. At sea level, a shelf of land along the shoreline contained the public market and some high rise office buildings. However, the rest of the city sat high on a bluff above the waterfront. In a piece of engineering knowhow borrowed from the Chiado district in Lisbon, there was a large public elevator that, for a modest fee, took people in at the waterfront level and deposited them a couple of hundred feet above on the edge of the bluff where the old town was situated.

Further down the waterfront, there were two steep cogwheel trams that transported people up the same hill. Clearly, the fashionable part of Salvador is on top in the Old Town. Mediterranean-style plazas filled with people were arrayed along the bluff. One of them had a cathedral with more gold leaf that I've ever seen. Since it was a cathedral of the

Franciscan order, the word schizophrenia comes to mind. When I mentioned to a tour guide later that St. Francisco would not approve of such ostentation, she explained that the sugar barons insisted on it and to a large extent, paid for it, in order to exhibit their status.

As with the other cities previously visited, there were pods of police stationed always within sight of each other, leaving no areas of town in a blind spot. The ship's cruise director exhorted us before every port call in Brazil not to wear any bling or expensive watches and not to carry cash or credit cards in wallets or purses. We were never accosted or threatened in Brazil (I like to think it was my Clint Eastwood-like, "go ahead, make my day" game face that cleared our way,) but many others were victims. One elderly lady strolling in town with her walker was pushed to the ground by a well-dressed young man in a business suit who then took her laptop. Despite our political conditioning as Americans to dislike the omnipresence of military/police in a country's civil spaces, Joka and I were grateful for all the protection they offered in Brazil's cities. We tourists, who would otherwise be prime targets for the criminality that exists in a country with the social and economic disparity that Brazil has, were certainly beneficiaries of the high police presence.

The Afro-Cubano-Amerindian samba beat was louder in Salvador de Bahia that it had been earlier. We were four days away from Mardi Gras in Rio, and the celebrations were beginning to take over. Gorgeous decorations were everywhere, and samba dancers and musicians and elaborately costumed ladies were on the sidewalks making music or advertising something. For the first time, we were beginning to grasp the "soul" of Brazil, and it was infectious.

A short overnight transit from Salvador de Bahia brought us next to **Ilheus,** a small city and port at the mouth of the Rio Cachoeira. It is the home of a locally famous writer named Jorge Amado. In addition to touring the museum home of Amado, we took an excursion to a cacao "plantation" (farm) where we learned all about chocolate. Cacao originated in Central America, but the Portuguese cultivated it in Amazonia and it became a major cash crop for them. Britain resented paying Portugal so much money for chocolate so agents of Britain stole (Brazil's view) some of the seed pods from Brazil and commenced growing cacao in Britain's colonies in Africa. These African sources over time have become the world's principal sources of chocolate.

The cacao tree is smallish and grows in the lower canopy of the rain forest along with rubber, Brazil nut, banana, mango, papaya and other trees. The cacao tree produces seed pods, which are papaya-sized, ribbed and elongate. Inside the soft shell, a layer of white, slimy pith protects the cluster of seeds in the center. Seeds are the size of large bean and, when ripe and "fermented" (heated for five days in the sun) can be cracked open and the interior paste can be separated into cocoa powder and cocoa butter. Cocoa powder can be mixed with milk and sugar and reblended with cocoa butter to make chocolate with varying degrees of concentration. Delish!

The plantation we visited clearly involved child labor in the harvesting of cacao pods and Brazil nut pods (which are very tough—like a coconut.) Children chopped them open in their unprotected hands with a machete. But, this was a family farm and children always work on a family farm, even in America. I had no way of knowing to what extent children were used in the commercial processing of cocoa.

Just below the entrance to Rio de Janeiro harbor is the small resort town of **Buzios,** our next stop. Buzios has a number of claims to fame. First, it is locally famous as a seaside getaway for citizens of Rio for whom Copacabana and Ipanema beaches do not provide enough R and R. Second, on the Atlantic side of the promontory occupied by Buzios, a coastline of cliffs and islands has been identified as identical in terms of crystalline structure, fossils and age to a corresponding rocky coastline on the west coast of Angola, in Africa. This unique geology confirms yet again that Gondwana was a geological fact and that the Americas split from Gondwana by the forces of the Mid-Atlantic Rift into separate continents. It will be recalled from the discussion of Iceland in Chapter 24 that, in a similar fashion, Northern Ireland has migrated eastward from the present location of Iceland. Greenland has migrated west as the result of the same tectonic movement away from the Mid-Atlantic Rift. So, the same separation occurred below the Equator to separate the Americas from Africa. The third claim to fame for Buzios is that Brigitte Bardot dated a Brazilian playboy for several years and the two of them spent a lot of time in Buzios. There is a bronze statue of her near the seawall sitting on a piece of luggage and gazing out to sea, waiting. Her well-formed bosom, revealed by a low-cut sleeveless T-shirt, has been highly polished by the hands of her many well-wishers over the years. This is the second town, along with San Tropez, that was put on the map by Brigitte. XO, Brigitte!

Another short overnight cruise a bit further south brought us to a town and island of the same name, **Ihlebella**. This was a pretty little village and getaway playground for the citizens of Sao Paulo. The marina had big yachts, lots of high end restaurants and nice small hotels. There were, I was told, numerous waterfalls in the interior of the island, some swimmable. Ihlebella had the obligatory church and, like every other place in Brazil we have visited, a large, former gaol. These abandoned gaols speak volumes about what life was like in Brazil during its colonial period. The colonial authorities had many slaves to discipline during both the long period of slavery and after emancipation. Today, the gaols invariably serve as ready retail venues for crafts, clothing and costumer jewelry as the former cells are ideal for vendor stalls and shops. Joka went off to check out the shops, and I sat on the seawall under a big acacia tree contemplating the huge (meter long) purple seed pods on it the likes of which I had never seen.

The time for the major attraction had arrived. After departure from Ihlabella and a slow overnight cruise, we sailed into the harbor at **Rio de Janeiro**. The name means January River. The narrow mouth of the harbor was dominated by the famed rock/mountain called Sugarloaf on the left. Across the narrows was the remains of an old fort whose guns defended the harbor. Beyond and spread out along the circular shoreline inside the harbor were the high-rise offices and apartments and the favelas that house the six million people who live there (seven and a half million during Carnival.)

The capitol of the country is Brazilia about 400 miles inland, which, like Washington DC, was located as a political compromise. Rio and San Paulo are the two most important cities for business and industry in Brazil, with Sao Paulo in the lead. Both host all of the traditional manufacturing industries necessary in a big country as well as newer tech-nology businesses. The port of Rio played a bigger role in its early development than it does now. Tourism plays a significant role in Rio's economy as well.

This was actually our second sighting of Rio. As we cruised from Ihlabella to Buzios past Rio two nights before, a sick passenger had to be evacuated in Rio. So, around sunset, the ship nosed its way into Rio's harbor and met the pilot boat that picked up the sick passenger just opposite Sugarloaf. So, we had a nice view of the harbor as the lights were coming on before continuing on to Buzios.

Brazil was "discovered," together with its Amerindian population, in 1500 by the Portuguese explorer Cabral just six years after Vasco de Gama accomplished what Columbus failed to do, namely, found a way to India and its treasure of spices around the cape of Africa. These discoveries gave rise to the epochal name of The Age of Discovery that followed. The spice trade from the Far East alone made Portugal a rich and influential country for two centuries, thanks to its accomplished navigators. Portugal's colony in Brazil developed over time and allowed Portugal to do what it did best, namely, supply much-needed commodities to Europe. Portugal built Brazil into the world's leading supplier of sugar, rubber, coffee, and cacao, and its plantations also provided bananas, mangoes, breadfruit, calabash and other exotic produce. It also had the dubious distinction of being the world's largest importer and user of slaves. Portugal's heavy investment in commodity production and the slavery that enabled it also resulted into it being dragged, reluctantly but inexorably, into the age of human rights as the last country to free its slaves in the 1880s.

After the slaves were freed, they migrated around the country with work opportunities in Brazil's agribusiness and mining industries and its growing service industries. Out of the African population came the tradition of the native "circle dances" from Angola which fused with the Catholic liturgical calendar to produce the festival of Carnival. The word itself, *carni-vale,* means "meat goes away," a descriptive term for the fasting of upcoming Lent. So the days before Lent were celebrated with dance characterized by percussive music and hedonistic abandon; hence, the spectacle of Carnival today. Obviously, similar cultural influences gave rise to Mardi Gras in New Orleans as well. (I wonder whether the holiday of Carnival/Mardi Gras would disappear if the Catholic Church were to cancel Lent?)

Over time, the localized celebrations of Carnival resulted in the development of "samba" schools throughout Brazil and finally in competition among the schools. Carnival in Rio is the Super Bowl of samba competition. During three days in March before Lent, competing samba schools form a parade of marching bands, dancers and floats that are among the most elaborate in the world and form an unbroken line of samba performers through the "Sambadrome" in Rio. The Sambadrome is a three-block-long stadium through which the samba route runs. The performances start at 9 pm and run through 7 am (avoiding the heat of the day) for three consecutive days to accommodate all the best schools— not all of the schools who apply, mind you; only the best ones. And what a spectacle it is.

Our ship arrived on March 3rd, 2019 the first day of the Sambadrome show, and the *Veendam* had procured a block of stadium seats for us to attend. Joka and I spent the first day doing a city excursion that featured a split gondola ride first from street level to the top of a mid-sized intermediate rock/mountain and then another gondola to the top of Sugarloaf for a killer view of the entire city and harbor basin of Rio. On another mountain in the distance stood the statue of Christ the Redeemer, arms outstretched and facing its twin in Lisbon a long way away.

Our tour included a stop at Copacabana Beach for a short exploratory walk along the beach and its trademark black and white wavy sidewalk (which in turn was patterned after the foreshore in Lisbon.) Neither Copacabana nor the more distant Ipanema Beach neighborhoods were considered safe for tourists and so we were not given the time or freedom to individually walk those areas. It is a pity that lawlessness is so rampant in Brazil, but it is. When the poor are not invested in the national economy, whether by exclusion at the hands of the elites or abandonment by the authorities, the result is brutish. After our tour, it was back to the ship for dinner and to get organized for the Sambadrome.

It started to rain just it was time to go to the Sambadrome, and it was not just a passing shower. So, we dressed down in shorts and T shirts, and, remembering the warnings of our minders, left our valuables on the ship. I just took a photo ID (my driver's license,) about $50 worth of rials for snacks, and one credit card in my wallet which was in my front pocket. My Rolex Submariner stayed in the cabin safe.

We were bussed to the Sambadrome and then walked and climbed stairs and walked and climbed some more until we finally exited into Section 109 of the stadium above the "box" seats along the parade path. Our Row Q stadium seating consisted of a level concrete bench—no seats or seat-backs and only a guide-issued plastic pad about 1/2 inch thick to sit on. Each seat was 16" wide and 18" inches deep and had to accommodate the butt of the occupant and also the feet of the person sitting in the next row above and behind it. And so we sat in the rain on the cement with no back support and waited for an hour and a half until the parade began an hour late. Meanwhile, there was a deafening, non-stop rendition of samba music pounding from the loudspeakers that lined the stadium on each side and facing the other side. We were getting it big time from the battery of loudspeakers just across the street and facing us. The whole scene was so festive and crazy that we could only laugh and soak it all up.

The schools of samba that competed had to tell a story. Each school chose its story and revealed it to the judges two months before the competition. During the competition, they were judged by highly trained samba experts on the quality of their costumes, dance, drumming, enthusiasm and the *three or four* floats each school built to act as their mobile stage. Each story involved a King and Queen and they had exactly one hour and twenty minutes in which to tell their story during their transit through the 'drome. The men were elaborately costumed and the women were semi-nude with elaborate headdresses and enormous feather plumes mounted implausibly on G-strings like a peacock tail. The floats were enormous, electrified, automated affairs several stores high with dancing platforms built into them at various levels. There are no words that can adequately express the elaborateness of the costumes, floats, stagecraft and preparations created by these samba schools. One must experience it for oneself, and trust me, the sensory experience is HUGE.

It quit raining a couple of hours into the show, and we sat in wet clothes the rest of the time. It was so warm and humid, though, that it made no difference whether we were wet or dry. We sat on the hard concrete upright, so as not to sit on the feet or press against the legs of the persons behind us, until about two or three in the morning. By then, the accumulated body and eardrum fatigue was too much, and we gave up. We were free to leave at any time and so formed a small group which was then led by a guide down through the stadium and crowd back to where our excursion bus was parked.

When I got back to the ship, I noticed that my wallet was gone. I had removed it from my front pocket a few times while we were in the 'drome to pay for drinks, but I pushed it back into my front pocket each time. Whether it fell out when I got up to leave, or, more likely, it got lifted by a pickpocket in the stands or during the walk back to the bus, I'll never know. But whoever ended up with it made $683 in charges by the time I reported the credit card lost the next day. The charges were reversed, but my driver's license was gone.

I still had my passport and other debit and credit cards in the safe, along with, miraculously, a duplicate driver's license (I'd recently obtained another veteran's license) to use for car rentals and supplemental ID for the rest of the trip. I spent a good part of the next day trying to report my credit card loss with the port's wifi down due to five other ships in port and tourists overwhelming the system. We were groggy and it was hot and humid that day, so we confined our activities to a pleasant walk along the fairly secure waterfront area of municipal buildings and museums. That allowed us to see more parade floats for the next night's Sambadrome performance as they marshalled in the side streets to the Sambadrome not far away. I bought a new wallet for 20 rials (about $4) from a street vendor.

Being in Rio at Carnival is desirable, of course, in order to see all the festivities. It is undesirable, however, in that the other sights of Rio like museums and art galleries are closed or, if outdoors, jammed with crowds populated with muggers and pickpockets, among other bad actors. So, other than our trip up Sugarloaf and along Copacabana Beach, the Sambadrome blowout, and the walk the following day through some of the public spaces in the heat of the southern Equinox, we had limited exposure to the city of Rio. But even that much was enough.

The next two days we spent pleasantly at sea. No matter how hot it is, being at sea is always comfortable with fifteen or twenty knots of wind over the bow. At Rio, the *Veendam* took on two new lecturers, each of whom was hired to deliver a series of lectures during our transit. One was a military expert who recounted the history of WW II in the South Atlantic, including the famous Battle of the River Plate that resulted in the German battleship *Graf Spree* being scuttled in Montevideo to keep its radar out of the hands of the British. The other speaker was a botanist who spoke on the variety of flora and fauna found in the Amazonian rainforest toward which we were now steaming.

But first, we had another stop on the upper shoulder of Brazil in **Fortaleza**. My journal notes on Fortaleza reflected that it was an active port for containerships picking up refrigerated containers carrying mangoes, bananas and other fruit. I saw a CMA-CGM (the company that now owns the former assets of APL) ship with four shipboard whirly cranes loading and unloading with the help of one whirly crane shoreside. There were no proper container gantry cranes to be seen. It looked like a scene from 1968. Can you spell low productivity?

My notes also reflected that we went into town by bus and saw the inevitable gaol-cum-crafts market and a fine cathedral modeled after the cathedral in Cologne. Must have been the sugar barons showing off again. More than that, my notes didn't say, except that I spent two hours in the terminal building using the port authority's free wifi catching up on email.

During the sea days after Fortaleza and before our first port up the Amazon River, I contemplated the comparative experience between South American countries having agrarian economies in the eighteenth and nineteenth centuries with that of the American Cotton Belt during the same period. Both economies were totally dependent upon the leverage provided by slave labor. Unlike Brazil and the others, though, the American South was not Catholic and did not rely on the church's doctrine of *terra nullius* as authority for their cruel economic system. That proved, I concluded, that it is the economic leverage of slave labor that determines its use, whether or not the church supports it. Not that it should let Pope Alexander off the hook for his dreadful papal bull.

On March 13, 2019, Carol's birthday (RIP), the *Veendam* tied up at the berth in **Santarem**, Brazil, some 400 miles up the Amazon River in the supersized state of Para, the same state in which Belem may be found far to the east. Santarem was a prosperous Indian chiefdom before the Europeans arrived and continues today as a busy port for exporting soybeans grown on the expanding farmland being reclaimed by agribusiness in cutting/burning the Amazon forest uplands. Any tofu in salads or on noodles eaten in California probably passed through a silo on the wharf at Santarem. Cargill is the soybean company and it is beloved by the locals for the jobs it creates and the market it provides for the upland soybean farmers. The environmentalist preoccupation with burning and clearing of the rainforest in Europe and America was wholly absent from the Amazonia I visited.

We took a riverboat boat excursion to "Lake" Maica (a piece of Amazon waterway bounded by the floating jungle and having the appearance of a lake) which locals use for recreational purposes. We saw pink dolphins in the "lake" and a sort of drive-in restaurant for boaters was popular there.

The floating jungle is an interesting aspect of Amazonia. There are countless mud banks and sand bars created by the currents and eddies of the Amazon River and its tributaries. There is also a wet season and a dry season. During the dry season, these banks and bars are out of the water a few feet, and in the wet season, they are submerged up to thirty feet. But trees and grass and bushes have acclimatized themselves to this cycle and during the wet season appear to be patches of dry land with trees growing from them and expanses of bush and grasslands under the trees. In reality, the trees are tropical hardwoods rooted underwater and the grasslands, while actually grasses and small broad-leafed plants, are floating rafts on top of the water. So, as we rode in our boats in the channel between the floating forests, they looked for all the world like riverbanks. In fact, though, we could turn our boat perpendicular to the channel and drive right through these floating riverbanks in our boat. Sometimes, there would be some giant Amazonian lily pads in evidence among these floating grass rafts that revealed the true nature of the river "banks."

We saw a sloth high in a tree with a forked crown. The sloth was spread eagled across the forked limbs staring at us while we stared at him. We saw a toucan fly by, the only time I've seen one in flight. Then we went fishing for piranhas. You get a line with a small hook and bait it with fresh meat (not fish—you need blood) and a lead sinker, and you drop the line into still water. With a short wait you will usually get a hit from these gold, red and gray-hued fish with big mouths and very sharp teeth. It was strictly catch and release, but our guides were the only ones who undertook—carefully—to remove them from the hook and throw them back. The fish are throughout the Amazon and people swim in the River and its tributaries without hesitation. I myself waded up to my waist in piranha-infested waters once to cool off. In the absence of blood in the water, these fish will not attack a swimmer.

One vital fact quickly appears when travelling on the Amazon River. Human settlements are never located on the banks of the Amazon itself. Its main channel is filled with brownish red sediments washed down from the Andes in strong currents. Human settlements are always located on the banks of a dark, tea-colored tributary to the main channel a short distance up from the place where the waters merge. These sections of the river are characterized by a visual line down river from where the tributary water comes in, thus delineating the separate currents and called, logically enough, *encontras des aquas*, or the merging of the waters. But the vital fact about these mergers of tributaries into the Amazon itself is that the Amazon's water is acid neutral—its pH is about 6. The tributaries, however, have so much plant material leached into them by filtering through the floating forests that they are highly acidic with a pH of around 4. I have made wines with a pH of 4 and wine is an acidic drink. Water with a pH of 4 is too acidic for mosquito larvae to gestate in; hence, human dwellings on the banks of tributaries to the Amazon are free of the deadly malaria, yellow fever, dengue fever and other mosquito-borne illnesses that can and do decimate human populations in Africa and other tropical locations. So, Santarem with a million inhabitants situated at the merger of two tributaries, the Arapiuns and Tapajos Rivers, just upstream from the Amazon, and Manaus, further upriver with 2.5 million inhabitants near the merger of the Amazon on the aptly named Rio Negro, are spared those mosquito borne illnesses, as are all the little villages up and down the Amazon safely tucked upstream beside the dark waters of some tributary.

Joka and I took an excursion into the city of Santarem away from the port area and were immediately surprised. The city was tidy with no graffiti and no visible police presence. The people were relaxed and friendly. There were no limits on our movements and so we wandered until we found a hotel with free wifi and spent an hour catching up on our email. It would have been interesting to learn why there would be such a difference in the urban vibe in Santarem relative to other Brazilian cities. I noticed that the population is seemed more Amerindian and less Afro-slave. Also, it was a Cargill company town providing solid employment opportunity.

At sailaway, we had an odd and I thought reckless encounter with another Holland America Line ship, the *MV Prinsendam*. The *Prinsendam* arrived headed downriver in the main Amazon channel and then turned into the tributary in which Santarem is situated. It passed us on our berth and headed up the tributary. Then, just as the *Veendam* was beginning to let go its lines and head into the current of the tributary and head down into the Amazon, the *Prinsendam* made a sudden U-turn and then sailed back past us, cutting us off from our exit route. This required the *Veendam* to use its bow thruster to push us back to the berth while the *Prinsendam* cruised past. Throughout this whole exercise, the ships' horns were blasting back and forth at each other in a manner that struck me as angry. A couple of days later, in a Q and A with our captain in the ship's theater, the captain was asked about that incident. He said in a joking manner that this was the *Prinsendam*'s last voyage before retiring and being scrapped, and its captain had been our captain's mentor, so they were just saluting each other and having a bit of fun. Well, that made a good story, but it didn't seem to square with the events at the time as I witnessed them. I'll never know what took place that day, but I am experienced enough as a mariner to know that what I witnessed was not a safe maneuver.

The next morning we found ourselves at the village of **Boca de Valeria**. As the name suggests, this village was located at the mouth of the Valeria River. Too small to have a berth for our ship, we had to tender in to the village in our lifeboats to the "pier" (some wooden planks on the low bank.) Holland America had a deal with the locals that HAL would donate a lot of school supplies for their one room school if the village would accommodate our visits. So, the villagers turned out in their tribal finery with their exotic pets animals to let us take photos of adorable children with baby sloths hanging on their necks, giant catfish, and colorful birds for 1$ per picture. It was the "one dolla" scene all over again. It was hokey and authentic at the same time.

We took a small riverboat ride around the large wetland where the two rivers merged and found the best photo op of a big expanse of giant lily pads we encountered the whole trip. We also had a first rate opportunity to inspect the floating grass rafts and floating forests up close and personal in a small boat.

This village sat at the base of a hill that had some elevation to it. So, this village was at the edge of the Amazon River floodwater basin where it transitioned into the upland agricultural areas that are so much in the news for all the not-so-*sub rosa* clearing and burning activity that goes on to create farmland in Amazonia.

The next day, March 15, 2019—the Ides of March—a hard tropical rain greeted us as we berthed in **Manaus**, nine hundred miles up the Amazon and Amazonia's biggest urban area. We were to be in port for two full days. Our first excursion was to the Botanical Garden, which is operated by the military (?) and features a center for the treatment of the Amazonian manatee. These sea grass-munching animals are grey in color unlike the Florida specimens which are cream colored. Apart from color, they seemed indistinguishable to my untutored eye. The site was populated with rubber trees, cacao trees, Brazil nut trees and many other species, together with ant colonies and symbiotic bee and termite colonies in the trees. The rubber tree seed pod consisted of a hard shell that held four seeds. It was these seeds that the British pilfered back in the day when they set out to create rubber plantations in Malaysia and other tropical realms of the Empire. Today, rubber is not even in the top ten commodities exported from Amazonia.

An adjunct part of the military Botanical garden is the military zoo. (?) There we saw many different species of monkeys (howler, spider, capuchin, marmoset) as well as an assortment of tamarin, tapir, agouti, and jaguars, including the only black panther I've ever laid eyes on. Why the Brazilian Army is involved in the study of Amazonian flora and fauna was a mystery until one of the officers explained that, given that its neighbors are Venezuela, Bolivia, Surinam, etc., a major part of the Brazilian Army's capability is fighting in that environment. They know from their conflicts with natives in the past that a knowledge of the terrain includes the behavior of the animals and the characteristics of the plants of the jungle. Hence, the emphasis was on training that considers the totality of the jungle environment. Okay, that made sense. When I was being interviewed for a covert CIA job after the Marine Corps, I was informed that an early part of an agent's training was jungle training in Panama. Same idea.

The evening of the first day, we attended the Manaus Opera House, a famous baroque-style anomaly in the jungle built by the rubber barons a hundred and fifty years ago. The performance we attended was an interesting concert by the local jazz orchestra playing a number of Afro-Cubano-Brazilian samba-esque rhythm numbers in the loud, discordant, modernist style. Their adaptations of pop pieces like "Tequila" and "The Girl From Ipanema" driven by an unrelenting samba beat were nearly unrecognizable. Not my cup of tea, but a heck of an accomplishment given the setting.

The Opera House itself was Belle Epoch with rows of small, intimate chairs set on the ground level and a surrounding oval section with three vertical tiers of boxes under an ornately decorated ceiling. A vast, tapestry curtain completed the look. Under the seats along the floor, there were perforated ventilation pipes which piped forced air into the audience space. This antique arrangement was preserved and put to good use before modern air conditioning was installed much later. The acoustics were terrific. The Manaus Opera House is a major municipal asset, as well as a curiosity. It really is true that when one goes to Manaus halfway up the Amazon, an urban island in the jungle with no access other than by river, one goes to the opera.

The second day, we took a six hour river boat excursion into the Rio Negro, the tributary that hosts the city of Manaus. Below the city, the 'merging of the waters" takes place and the dark waters of the aptly named Rio Negro are mixed and ultimately consumed by the muddy Amazon. There used to be a bridge over the river running north and south that was part of the solitary road that runs from Venezuela to the interior city of Rhondonia in the southern highlands. Unfortunately, the floods, landslides and jungle encroachment upon the roadway since it was built has rendered it impassable. So, Manaus is an island in Brazil, unmolested by much of the crime, poverty, official corruption and drug infestation of other Brazilian cities. It is clean, graffiti-free and sports, in addition to the Opera House, an ornate Customs House, showplace rubber barons' former homes, and some municipal "palaces." Unemployment is modest—

around 7 percent—and that is believed to be a real number, unlike the phony number concocted by the United States Government with its thumb on the scales. The reason for such a prosperous city is an unlikely one, but one which integrates Manaus squarely into the Global Village.

They make motorcycles and small motors in Manaus. Tons of them. Honda, Yamaha, Suzuki and, yes, Harley Davidson motorcycles are made here. Stihl chain saws are made here, as well as Yamaha and other outboard motors. Probably half of all the outboard motors manufactured in the world are put to use throughout Amazonia, and so it is logical to make them where they are used. In any event, many of the world's motorcycles and small motors have been made here for some time. It is its own version of Motown, and it makes its citizens relatively well-off and contented. A riverboat ride past the entire length of the Manaus riverfront provides ample evidence of its hyperactivity.

Outside the confines of the City, the ecotour commenced. Pink river dolphins rolled in the eddies, toucans, parrots and eagles crisscrossed the river, howler monkeys in the treetops chronicled our progress, and the floating forests provided an infinite variety of insects, insect-eating fish, and raft-adaptable vegetation.

The grass rafts alone are fascinating. They serve as habitat for insects and fish spawn and have a seasonal life cycle like land grasses. They start out as pond scum made up of tiny sprouts and over the growing season, grow into lawn length grass, and then finally shoulder high cane that dies and breaks down in the slowly migrating water.

The piranha get all the press, but the biggest river fish is the pirarucu which can reach twelve feet in length. It possesses large, hard scales which the natives use as fingernail polishing tools because of their rough surface. They are also a popular eating fish. The *Veendam* served filets of it in the dining room one night, and it was excellent. Like other fish in Amazonia, pirarucu are rarely found in the main river channels. They congregate in the floating forests where the insects are.

Venomous and constrictor snakes can be seen coiled on the branches overhanging the river and in the trees, either enjoying the view or waiting for a small animal to float by.

Sailaway from Manaus at 4:00 pm on the second day took place in a nice light with no rainclouds on the horizon. Along the banks of the river where the tributaries came in and mud banks formed, small patches of land appeared above the floating forests. That was a sign of drought as this was the rainy season and the river level should have been up to thirty feet higher. Global warming, they said. As it was, the natives were taking advantage of the presence of dry land to rehabilitate former shanties now out of the floodwaters. The shanties provided shelter from which they could husband their livestock. We passed one small circle of land maybe ten meters in diameter with eight white and brown horses standing tightly together with their hooves just out of the water. I could relate.

The following morning, as we headed back downstream toward the mouth of the Amazon, the *Veendam* anchored off the Amerindian town of **Parintins,** home to a hundred thousand souls. Average temperature year around, I read in the ship's bulletin, was 34 degrees Celsius (93F). Humidity was north of you-don't-want-to-know. I was definitely in a glass-half-empty mindset. I had been fighting an upper respiratory infection for the last three weeks, the excursion staff was urging everyone to stay aware of their surroundings, wear no bling, don't give personal infor-mation to anyone and the like. The only excursion ashore was one to see a dance folklorico show at the "Bombadromo" featuring two competing dance groups acting out the story of a legendary ox. I passed on that. Joka, indefatigable world traveler that she is, did tender in to the town and did some shopping. I stayed on the ship and rested on my, ah, laurel. Sailaway again took place in an artist's light and under a cloudless sky.

Our final stop in the Amazon was at a small resort town near San-tarem called **Alter do Chao.** It is a hilly area with an unusual combination of white sand beaches and recreational waterways. When it is not flooded, that is. When we were there, the beaches were half submerged, so the usual March crowd of Cargill technocrats from Santarem were absent. After ten-dering in to the beach, we walked along the foreshore in oppressive heat and humidity, finishing at the town square featuring a shuttered church and scattered bars and cafes. We joined a surprising number of people sit-ting at the cafes sipping cold drinks and listening to live music from a small band. We found that siting in the shade motionless for a goodly period of time can restore one's physical comfort, notwithstanding the heat and humidity. That phenomenon tends to keep one in such an inert position for as long as possible. On the walk back, it was instant overheating, and I waded into the river up to my waist (with the piranhas) to cool my "core." We then wandered back to the dock and caught a tender to the *Veendam* and its blessed air conditioning.

I entered Amazonia on February 17th and now it was March 19th as we crossed the bar of the Amazon River into the South Atlantic. *Not once* did I see a mosquito. I spent over $400 on a yellow fever inoculation, malaria pills, and super-duper insect repellent based upon the strong recommendations of the county health officials in San Francisco and Holland America Line. Nada. Butkis. Zip. Whisky Tango Foxtrot?

The *Veendam* plowed out of the mouth of the Amazon with the far banks on both sides vanishingly faint. The two headlands must be forty or fifty miles apart. The muddy fresh water of the Amazon's outflow extends tens of miles out to sea. The water was still muddy brown when we picked up the swells of the ocean. Gradually, the water turned brackish green, and then suddenly, deep blue as we crossed the tideline, with long strings of yellowish brown sargassum trailing along in parallel with the wind—escapees from the currents that circumnavigate the wide Sargasso Sea to the northeast.

The Sargasso Sea and its eponymous plant mass is one of the most important factories for sequestering carbon dioxide on the planet, even rivalling the Amazon basin itself. The Sargasso Sea was so named by Portuguese fishermen because of the tiny air bladders that keep the floating seaweed at the surface so that photosynthesis is enabled. These little hollow berries, it is said, take their name from a variety of Portuguese grapes with a similar appearance.

The Sargasso Sea is the only "sea" on the planet which is not bounded by a land mass; it is surrounded entirely by ocean currents which form a vast gyre containing little else besides sargassum. In addition to sequestering carbon dioxide, this mass of sargassum acts as an incubator for all manner of sea life from fish to sea horses to turtles. It is bounded by the Gulf Stream to the West, the North Atlantic Drift above Bermuda to the north, the Canaries current running down the West coast of Europe, and the North Equatorial Current to the south that drags hurricane vortices across the Atlantic from Africa to the Caribbean during hurricane season. In its center gyre, largely out of the major trade lanes of ship traffic, the Sargasso Sea performs its ecological magic largely unseen. Except that is, for ships transiting from north to south through the North Equatorial Current between the coast of Brazil and the Caribbean Sea.

After three blissful days at sea in tropical waters, we dropped anchor at **Castries, San Lucia.** The weather (and climate) had changed. In clear skies, moderate humidity and a temperature, both in the air and the water, of 80 degrees, we delighted in the northeasterly trade winds washing the island. We were pretty close to the intersection of the Prime Meridian and the Equator at the time of the Vernal Equinox. How many people can say that?

San Lucia is an island state about 25 miles south of Martinique and is part of the British Commonwealth. It is a constitutional monarchy with Queen Elizabeth II as its queen, and two houses of parliament, like Australia. It has a viably diverse economy and its people are primarily descendants of slaves. They speak English and a French *patois*, given the proximity of the French "departments" of Martinique and Guadalupe. From a tourist standpoint, it is a beautiful, off-the beaten-track vacation spot with good hotels, good beaches and watersports and nice, quiet atmospherics. This volcanic island has two iconic peaks called Les Pitons.

We hired a car to drive us from the Port of Castries to an interior viewing point for Les Pitons and back through a couple of fishing villages. Loved it. Great photos to be had. We stopped at a banana plantation and learned the various stages of growing and harvesting bananas. I know from my shipping days that one of APL's innovations in container shipping that had a huge influence on the banana trade is that of atmospherically controlled refrigeration. The carrying temperature and levels of gasses present within a reefer container can be set and monitored throughout the ocean voyage and during terminal storage. The mix of gasses inside can also be controlled to slow the rate of ripening to the extent desired.

On the way back from Les Pitons, we passed a spanking new, too-large middle school that seemed out of place. Our driver said it was built by the Peoples Republic of China as part of its Belt and Road Program. They are everywhere!

The PRC uses its trade surplus of dollars from the U.S. to build infrastructure in third world countries financed by loans from China. The good will and coercive effects of the loans means that China has a disproportionate and growing foreign policy influence throughout the world. For example, if the United Nations is voting or a policy position having to do with, say human rights, China can use its influence in all of these debtor nations to stack the votes in support of its position. As I write, the United States is just beginning to realize that it has been out-witted and out-influenced by China, using America's own money, even in America's back yard. So, contemporary readers, think twice before you fill up your car with Walmart purchases, four fifths of which are made in the PRC. The money you spend is being used against you.

Our final port call on this amazing, fifty five day cruise was, fittingly for a Dutch ship, **Saint Martin [Sint Maarten].** It is an outlying island in the Dutch Antillies, and, it will be recalled by the careful reader, the place where "Peg Leg Pete" Stuyvesant lost his lower leg fighting the British before heading off to govern Manhattan. Carol and I had been to St. Martin on one of our trips, and I knew how small it was and how the island was bifurcated into a French and a Dutch side, the latter being much more developed. It was an easy sell for Dutch-centric Joka, and so we never ventured out of Phillipsburg, the main beach town.

First, we participated in a mock America's Cup race. There are two former single-hull America's Cup racing boats in Phillipsburg, the *Stars and Stripes* (American, of course) and the *True North,* a Canadian boat. We and the other participants chose up sides and became the actual crews of the two boats. Then, we sailed out into the harbor and were assigned duty stations and duties, mostly manning the rotatory winches to change to sail positions when coming about. When we were pronounced ready, the starting shot was fired and the two boats commenced to race around the harbor course. Joka and I were on *True North* which got shellacked by *Stars and Stripes*, but the experience was a real hoot.

Back on the beach in Phillipsburg, we stopped at a bar that sported a huge collection of Ohio State football memorabilia. The owner went to school there for a year or two and was a big fan. After a glass or two of suds, it was a ferry back to the ship for our final sailaway of the cruise. When the playlist on the ferry's sound system got around to Neil

Diamond's "Sweet Caroline," all of the seventy five or so passengers on the ferry spontaneously broke out in the chorus at the top of their lungs. One forgets how culturally dominant American music and movies are around the world.

In the ship's theater that night, an American singer and piano player played a repertoire of Jerry Lee Lewis numbers. The place was rocking out. The perfect ending of a perfect day to finish a perfect cruise.

The return flight from Fort Lauderdale to San Francisco and the airporter bus ride to Napa were a weary blur. Joka had only a few days with me in Napa before jetting home to Sydney. I would follow in a couple of months, and we would try something new.

CHAPTER 28

FNQ, FREO

Not much happened that seems publishable during the two months I was at home taking care of business. But it was these breaks at home that allowed us to manage our affairs, our health and our properties, whether or not newsworthy, and enabled our crazy lifestyle. I thus resume this chronicle with the booking of a flight back to Oz. Joka had kept me advised of plans to take her family up to Port Douglas in FNQ (Far North Queensland), the prime jumping off place for the Great Barrier Reef. It was to celebrate, you see, her 80th birthday. Over there, the custom was for the person having a big birthday to host it. It is a thoughtful custom in that it saves the invited guests the expense of having to attend and pay for a celebration not of their choosing. And, because the host is paying, the size and make-up of the group is determined by the closeness of the relationship as determined by the host, thus, tending to insure that the group will be small and close knit.

So, in early September, 2019 I arrived back in Sydney on the United Airlines direct flight from San Francisco in a mere fourteen and a half hours. That does not count the time Uber-ing to the Airporter in Napa, bussing to SFO airport, going through check-in and security, and enduring the cattle calls for Groups 1,2,3,4, and 5 to board the aircraft for an 11 pm departure. Nor does it include the disembarking time it takes for a jumbo jet to dislodge 500 sleepy people wrestling with their carry-on baggage at 8 am two calendar days later (the international dateline was crossed) and walking what seemed like three kilometers through a labyrinth of secure corridors to get to immigration—or rather to the line to immigration for non-citizens. After clearing immigration, it was off to the newly automated customs gates and surrender of forms which must be processed but which never, ever, seem to result in any baggage actually being inspected. Then, outside in the main lobby, I had to locate the correct airport shuttle to the Northern Beaches, and, when located, settle in for the two hour ride to Avalon Beach. It is about a twenty-four-hour exercise. Despite my hundred-mission-crush appearance when delivered to her door, Joka was always glad to see me, give me a cup of tea, and let me take a nap.

As soon as I awoke and began to acclimatize, Joka brought me up to date on the birthday plans. We would join her two sons, their spouses and Adriaan's three children and fly to Port Douglas north of Cairns for a week of sightseeing, beach combing, snorkeling and feasting associated with her birthday on September 28th. Also, before the trip, Joka's brother Jan and wife Sylvia from Basel, Switzerland would arrive for a visit in Avalon Beach and would join us for the week in Port Douglas. Jan and Sylvia subsequently did join us for a few days of play before they flew to Brisbane and then drove leisurely up to Port Douglas.

The plan unfolded smoothly and we in the family cluster all arrived together at the Cairns airport where we rented a van and a car for the seventy kilometer drive to Port Douglas. We had two multi-bedroom apartments at a nice inn with pool just two blocks from the main commercial street in one direction and Four Mile Beach in another. Jan and Sylvia arrived at the same time and they, Joka and I, all octogenarians, shared one two bedroom apartment and the rental sedan while the brothers and their families shared another apartment and the van.

We had seven perfect days sometimes doing things together and sometimes splitting up, taking turns cooking for the assembly, going out for special meals, walking Four Mile Beach and the headland trail, and taking a river excursion up Packer Creek by boat. On the boat ride, the driver pointed out salt water crocodiles among the trees and vegetation on the banks of the creek. Saltwater crocodiles. Hmmmm. I began to connect the dots. There were no barriers between the bush and creek at the edge of town and the town. Also, there was no net or barrier at the mouth of Packer Creek to separate the creek from the ocean at Four Mile Beach where people sunbathe and swim. Even if there had been, the crocodiles could simply walk around it. In other words, there was *nothing* separating us from the crocs, either in town or on the beach. When I asked a local about that, my concerns were dismissed. I was told with a typically Aussie disregard of the life-threatening hazards that abound in their country that the crocs don't want to be around a lot of human activity and anyway we are not on their menu.

Generally speaking, I concede that those are the facts. Generally speaking. But what about the exceptions …? Crocs take humans in Australia all the time. The fact is, the locals just accept a certain amount of risk as inherent in their environment. And that is true. There are a lot of things that can kill you in Australia. There are sharks, box jellyfish, lionfish, blue ringed octopus, nine types of venomous snakes plus pythons, and funnel web and other spiders. And salt water crocodiles. A former Prime Minister, while in office, went into the surf for a swim *and was never heard from again.*

Cassowaries, an ostrich-like, ill-tempered bird, are found in the rainforest and look and act like a velociraptor. The big bird has a large central claw with a nail on it that can rip you from north to south in a lightning stroke. Fortunately, it has a beak and not a mouthful of incisors. We, apparently, were going to venture into the environment of the crocs and sharks and cassowaries and snakes. But, the odds were always going to be with us, so no worries mate!

Natural risks aside, we did the things we wanted to do without hesitation. We took a day's excursion to the outer Barrier Reef for snorkeling. The weather was unsettled that day with tropical showers buffeting the dive boat during the thirty mile trip to the outer reef. Once at the reef, the currents were strong and the surface bumpy, but the subsurface was gorgeous. There was no sign of bleaching at all where we were and sea life was abundant and strikingly colorful, even without camera lights. Giant clams, stars and sea cucumbers, a giant Maori Wrasse, a shark, a scattering of turtles, a great variety of live, spawning corals, and an endless variety of tropical fish filled our underwater vistas. Joka and I and Jan and Silvia stayed reasonably close to the dive boat because of the wind and currents and our limited stamina, but Adriaan and the kids were fearless and ranged far and wide. It was a rewarding day on the reef—like my other day on the Great Barrier Reef twenty years earlier when Carol and I took our dive. It is one of the world's great diving venues.

We took the antique railroad trip from Cairns to Kuranda, a scenic town up into the Great Dividing Range rainforest that runs along the spine of the York Peninsula. We also took the 7.5 kilometer super gondola Skyrail that runs just above the forest canopy as it transitions from temperate eucalyptus forest by the coast to dense rainforest.

We took a walk through the Mossman Gorge area of Daintree National Forest that is reserved for aboriginal tribes in the area. Our mandatory aboriginal guide took us on a forest orientation walk that I can say, without exaggeration, was an attitude, if not life, changing event for each one of us. It began with a "smoke ceremony" by which our guide built a smoky fire out of paperbark eucalyptus peelings and as we walked through the smoke, he called on the spirits of the forest to safeguard us along the way. It sounds hokey as I write about it, but that's the fault of my writing. It was a very authentic experience. He showed us many things, including how to communicate with others in the forest by banging a rock on a huge fig tree root that made a sound like a drum.

At one site beside a small creek, he selected different rocks and ground pieces of them into pigment with which he drew symbols on his arm that identified him as a member of his tribe in the York Peninsula rainforest to any other aboriginal man not of his tribe that he might encounter. Then he took leaves from a tree and wet them with water from the stream and rubbed the leaves until they foamed. Using the foam as soap, he then washed his arm clean.

He told us of the Dreamtime (creation) legends of his people and how those stories meshed with the volcanic geology of the granite gorge in which we were standing. It will be remembered that Aboriginal legends go back over 50,000 years—old enough to encompass past volcanic eruptions. He played the didgeridoo for us, which was astonishing because to play it, one must, and this is the truth, exhale and inhale at the same time to make a constant sound. Try that sometime!

The time we spent in the company of our aboriginal guide was unforgettable. The kids were mesmerized, and Adriaan, very much at home with nature of Australia, was also. Jan and I and Joka and Sylvia were gobsmacked. The experience led me to read a popular Australian book called *Dark Emu* by Bruce Pascoe. It asks the question: Since Aboriginal and Torres Strait Islander people have lived sustainable lives in harmony with nature for 50,000 years plus, and European colonizers have lived there for only one hundred and fifty years, denuding the land and polluting the air and water over that time, wouldn't it be prudent to at least study how the natives managed it and possibly learn from it? The question suggests the answer, of course, but Canberra took no notice. Just as non-native Americans and their government are largely oblivious in their pursuit of what Greta Thunberg has called "The Fairy Tale of Continuous Economic Growth."

The yoke of occupation of their land by European types does not sit easily on the aboriginal and Torres Strait Islander people. As mentioned before, the latter have not assimilated and do not share the values of the European population. They do not accept the notion that they must work in "whitefella" endeavors and earn a salary in order to be able to live in their land. They do not believe in the private ownership of land.

Our guided tour of aboriginal land reserved for the Mossman Gorge tribe was part of an experiment with the state of Queensland in which aboriginals can learn to be comfortable sharing their heritage with "whitefellas" and by which they can earn money with which to support themselves. Our guide, a handsome and dignified man in his late forties, obviously schooled and well-spoken, was superb just being himself, and we felt privileged to be in his company.

The capper of the trip was a group dinner to celebrate Joka's birthday at a local restaurant in Port Douglas. Joka was delighted by the surprise attendance of her favorite nephew from Southern California, Gerard ("Josh") and his brand new fiancée.

The trip to FNQ had to come to an end, and so we were obliged to pack up and leave at the end of the week. But we had the memories. Jan and Silvia continued their travels in Australia by flying to Darwin and then to Broome in Northwestern Australia. There they were to rent a car and drive leisurely down the coast, seeing the sights along the way, to Perth before flying home.

Joka and I had not been back in Avalon Beach more than a week before we got the idea of flying ourselves out to Perth, meeting up with Jan and Sylvia there for a couple of days before thcy left, and then doing a bit of a walkabout in the famed forests of Southwestern Australia. So, with the magic of cellular communications and the Internet, we arranged to book into their hotel in Fremantle (port of Perth, aka "Freo") and then flew out to meet them. They drove in to Freo the evening of the day we arrived.

We spent the next two days separately seeing the sights in Fremantle, a university town, by day and dining together in the evening. Jan and Sylvia took the ferry to Rottnest Island, where a small, unique mammal called a quokka resides in the wild. Joka and I were intent on seeing the maritime museums, including the one housing remains of the Dutch ship *Batavia* shipwrecked in 1629 on a reef by the "Roaring Forties" (referring to the rough seas and stormy weather in the latitudes around forty degrees south that blow from the southern tip of Africa straight into southwestern Australia.) We also toured the big convict-built prison in Freo as well as Victoria Quay in the port.

I set myself on a special mission to view Victoria Quay because of its ties to the Liberty ship *SS Jeremiah O'Brien* in San Francisco on which I performed docent duties. It seems that, after the *O'Brien's* momentous mission to carry supplies to the Normandy beaches during and after the June 6, 1944 landing for Operation Overlord, the *O'Brien* was then dispatched to the war in the Pacific. It made two voyages in that ocean, during the last of which, the Pacific war ended. The A-bombs were dropped on Hiroshima and Nagasaki and Russia declared war on Japan while the *O'Brien* was sailing westbound with cargo bound for Shanghai and Calcutta. The *O'Brien* proceeded to those ports, discharged its cargo, and was then ordered to Subic Bay in the Philippines. There the Armed Guard (a detachment of Navy gunners aboard the armed, merchant Liberty ships) was taken off the *O'Brien,* thus freeing up some of the crew berths. The ship was then ordered to Fremantle, Western Australia, to pick up a parcel of commercial cargo bound for California.

On December 7th, 1945, four years to the day from the attack on Pearl Harbor, the *O'Brien* arrived at Fremantle and berthed at Victoria Quay. There it took on a load of 16,000 bales of merino wool. In the bunk facilities just vacated by the Armed Guard personnel who disembarked at Subic Bay, the *O'Brien* also took on nine Australian war brides of U.S. Navy personnel and three of their children. The *O'Brien* then sailed to San Francisco where it was unloaded by my old employer, Matson Lines. After being unloaded in San Francisco, the *O'Brien* was laid up in the Suisun Bay Naval Reserve Fleet for thirty three years along with other militarily useful ships to have available for national emergencies—a resource the country lacked at the onset of both World Wars I and II.

In 1979, well after the advent of containerization in the merchant marine, the military usefulness of Liberty ships having wasted away, the *O'Brien* was gifted to the National Liberty Ship Memorial as a museum ship. As such, it continues to make news as I write, it having survived the fire that engulfed and destroyed the shed at pier 45 where it was berthed in 2020. That survival was courtesy of San Francisco Fireboats Nos. 1 and 3 who kept the shed fire off of the *O'Brien* and saved it. The *O'Brien* has always been a lucky ship.

Incidentally, while sitting on a bollard at Victoria Quay in Freo contemplating the sweep of history and the role of the *Jeremiah O'Brien* in it, I cast my eyes across the channel to the new container terminal on the other side. There, a CMA-CGM containership was working under the port's big gantry cranes plucking import containers from and stowing outbound containers onto the ship. Scattered around the container yard adjacent to the ship were some APL containers. As mentioned earlier, APL had been sold to the Government of Singapore's Neptune Orient Lines in 1997, and NOL and APL had been resold to CMA-CGM in 2016.

CMA-CGM, headquartered in Marseilles, stands for Compagnie Maritime d'Affreighment and Compagnie General Maritime, two former French national merchant shipping companies acquired by an opaque Swiss-Lebanese named Jacques Saade. Saade reportedly had "Turkish investors" with apparently unlimited funds with which to invest in an asset-heavy, chronically unprofitable industry like liner shipping. (See comments about the murky offshore world in Chapter 20's discussion of Panama City.) I digress again.

Jan and Sylvia ran out their allotted time Down Under and flew back home to Basel, Switzerland from Perth over Dubai. Joka and I pointed our rental car toward the Southern Forests and the Margaret River wine region to have a look-see. Neither of us had ever been to Western Australia. The history of European exploration of Western

Australia dates back to the late sixteenth century with early explorations made by the Portuguese and probably the Chinese. Throughout the seventeenth and eighteenth centuries century it was explored by several ships of the Dutch East Indies Company. As mentioned, the Dutch ship Batavia wrecked on the shoals north of Perth and its artifacts are in a Fremantle museum.

French ships also explored the Southwest Coast at the beginning of the nineteenth century, and one French mariner named Vasse was washed overboard in a storm. He was presumed drowned, but then reports surfaced over the years of his existence ashore in the Margaret River area. The oldest winery in the area (Vasse Felix, 1967) was named after him.

Leeuwin Estate is another big name derived from the geographical feature to the south called Cape Leeuwin where two great oceans, the Indian and the Southern meet. There are several hundred wineries in the Margaret River area now and it is a popular getaway spot for city dwellers from Perth and Fremantle as well as visitors from all over the world. Joka and I found a B & B there for two days of seeing the sights and tippling. Although the locals have a high opinion of their wines, claiming them to be Bordeaux-style, I found them to be unripe and on the astringent side. But, in fairness, big, ripe Napa-style wines are distained there as being too powerful and therefore food unfriendly. So, different spices for different rices.

After Margaret River we were off to explore the giant Karri and Tingle trees near Walpole and Pemberton. The Tingle trees are second only to the slightly taller California Coast Redwoods as the tallest trees in the world and the girth of the oldest Tingle trees is comparable. There is one solitary Tingle giant near Walpole that is the broadest at the base of any tree I've ever seen. We found it early one morning by parking at the designated spot on a dirt road and then hiking to the tree. We were surprised to find a Dutch backpacker already there. He had walked all the way in and was just sitting at the base of the tree communing with nature when we arrived. The Tingle's bark resembles a Western Cedar, but it is a variety of eucalyptus, of which there are hundreds in Australia.

The other tree for which the Southern Forests are famous is the Karri with its smooth pale bark and tall, straight growth patterns. It is also a type of eucalyptus, and it too rivals the California Coastal

Redwood in the tallest sweepstakes, coming in just ahead of or behind the Tingle. The forest management people in WA have thoughtfully built an elevated walkway through the Karri canopy near Walpole. From the top, a visitor sees that the Karri forest extends for miles and miles throughout the low mountainous area. It is a tropical hardwood and makes absolutely gorgeous furniture, but I didn't get the feeling that it is logged extensively—perhaps because the big old groves are protected like the virgin groves of Sequoia in California.

There are three individual Karri trees in the area that are strategically located, each being on high ground. These three trees have been adorned with steel rods that have been drilled into the tree in a stair step, escalating fashion that circles the tree from bottom to top. These trees were intended to be for fire spotters to use by climbing to the tops and, from a platform constructed at the top of each, viewing a large section of the forest for smoke and fire spotting purposes. They are in fact used for that purpose; however, the minute the steel "stairs" were installed on these three trees, the general public also took to them as extreme sport challenges. Australians are not as litigation happy as Americans and the authorities have done nothing to exclude the public from climbing the trees and enjoying the views, despite the inherent danger.

Joka and I climbed up twenty or thirty "steps" just to get a feel for the exercise, but we quickly realized that the entire climb would be highly strenuous and the act of one ascending climber and one descending climber passing one another would be hazardous and tricky. The risk of slipping off of one of the steel rods, which have been thoroughly polished by all the boots that have used them, is somewhat reduced by the envelope of chicken wire that encircles the "stairs" to catch climbers who slip before they fall all the way down the spike stairs. We concluded that this attractive nuisance was not intended for octogenarians, and so we exercised self-restraint after our initial experimentation and just watched some youngsters doing it.

In the forest around Pemberton, there was more of the same. Very impressive forests and small towns spaced out in meadow or waterfront areas among the trees. Civilization had not even begun to burden this landscape. We left it like we found it, and, out of time, drove back to civilization, this time to Perth, a big city about twenty kilometers up the

Swan River from Freo. Perth is a financial center for the mining industry, a substantial part of which may be found in the outback to the north and east of Perth. Big high rise office buildings boast building-top signs for BHP (Broken Hill Proprietary), Rio Tinto, Fortescue, Newcrest and other mining companies. These companies are major players in the global market for iron ore, coal, copper, aluminum, oil and gas, gold, silver and many lesser metals. Their biggest customer is China, and Australia increasingly finds itself conflicted by the economic need to toady up to China as its chief market on the one hand and on the other its political inclination to associate with the political values of America, the UK and the West. So, the Perth economy is closely attuned to the government in Canberra a continent away, while being geographically isolated. The closest big city to Perth is Singapore.

As I write this, China under Premier Xi, is flexing its economic muscles to punish Australia for several public positions the Government has taken against Chinese interests, real or perceived. For instance, Prime Minister Morrison has joined in the call to thoroughly investigate the origins of the Covid 19 corona virus in Wuhan, China, home of a major laboratory studying viruses. For another, Australia has joined America and four other Western countries called The Five Eyes, to monitor China's expansionist moves in the South China Sea. In any event, China has retaliated by imposing punitive tariffs on Australian exports of timber, wine, lobster, barley, red meat, and cotton, but not yet Australia's major export commodity, iron ore, which China needs. The Xi regime picks out countries it thinks will be vulnerable to its market power and moves against it without hesitation, while not behaving in the same way against America and the EU.

I called an old APL colleague, Dan Pendleton, for whom I did legal work when we were setting up APL's multimodal systems. Dan had a career with the railroads, and APL's traffic from Asia to the "BosWash" corridor (urban areas from Boston to Washington, DC) was growing exponentially in the 1980s. Working under Don Orris, the head of rail operations for APL, Dan and I hammered out the terms and conditions of our contracts with the Union Pacific, Denver Rio Grande, Chicago Northwestern and Conrail to give APL's shippers their first through multimodal, door to door, containerized shipping service. When APL was sold to Neptune Orient Lines (Singapore), Dan retired as I had, and he subsequently married an Australian woman and settled in the wine country just outside Perth on the Swan River. So we chatted by phone and caught up a bit on the intervening twenty five years since we last saw each other. He had been involved in two exploratory ventures to bring transcontinental containerized rail service to Australia, but neither one came to fruition. With a population of only 25 million people in the entire country, including aboriginals, the projects just didn't pencil out.

Joka and I wandered Perth's impressive Botanical Garden that contained flora I had never seen before, such as the Bottle Tree that looks like a jug of green fruit juice and the Baobab tree which grows abundantly in Madagascar. The Baobab is also found in Northwestern Australia, proving once again that the earth's land masses had been joined as one "Gondwana" until about 180 million years ago. Australia's north west coast had broken off from Africa's east coast and Asia's south coast 140 million years ago, just as the Americas had separated from Europe and the west coast of Africa.

After the Botanical Garden, we found Perth's downtown area, though bustling and modern, to be marginal tourist fare, so we spent our final day back in the colorful, artsy, university town of Fremantle. Across the Esplanade in Freo is the Little Creatures Brewery and Pub where hours may be profitably spent lunching and quaffing.

I was lucky again and scored a window seat flying back to Sydney. The first twelve hundred kilometers of flight covered the vast Nullarbor Plain, a perfectly flat, brush-covered landscape that runs from the Nullarbor cliffs along the Great Australian Bight to the Great Sandy Desert to the North. An Australian peculiarity is to be found on the Plain in the form of a golf course that is spread out some 1300 kilometers with one or two holes situated at each municipality along the only highway that traverses the Plain from west to east. The separation between municipal areas might be a hundred and fifty kilometers, hence the long, looonng single golf course.

After the Nullarbor Plain, the aircraft's trajectory took us out over the Bight and the Southern Ocean with its Mediterranean blue waters, then crossed back over the coast near Adelaide and its wine country. From there, it tracked the Murray River Basin to the Riverina, over The Great Dividing Range, and down into Botany Bay and the Sydney Airport. This was my second transcontinental flight over Australia in daytime under cloudless skies. One cannot help but be impressed by how big and how empty Australia's center is. On the ground, of course, there are camels and 'roos and wombats and dingos, etc., and hundreds of thousands of aboriginal people who have called it home for pushing *sixty millennia.*

After the allotted two plus months in Oz, I returned to Napa and enjoyed seeing Erin and family for Thanksgiving and Christmas, at which Gray and his family joined us in NorCal. Christmas Eve has been a "thing" with us beginning with the special Christmas Eve dinners that became a tradition when I was married to Carol. Her Christmas Eve dinners were like Babette's Feasts (a French movie about the soul-satisfying joinder of friends and family and good will with terrific food and wine), and we all looked forward to them. After Carol got sick, Erin picked up the baton and continued to host them.

After the holidays, and necessary home maintenance and repair, and doctors' and dentists' appointments behind us, the urge to travel returned to Joka and me. Being winter in California, it was not in keeping with our *modus operandi* for her to come to Cali, so we planned a fourteen day Holland America Line cruise from Sydney to Auckland, New Zealand via Tasmania. The cruise went on beyond Auckland to Fiji, the Cook Islands and Tahiti, Hawaii and ultimately San Diego, but the ship was booked full beyond Auckland. Apparently, lots of people don't mind spending the winter months in the South Pacific, and many were embarking at Auckland. Hence, a few cabins on the Sydney to Auckland leg were available on short notice and discounted. We jumped on it. So, I flew back to Sydney in time to celebrate my 80th birthday with our Bilgola Beach comrades, complete with a birthday cake for "Dinky Di" (genuine, true, authentic Australian) Dave.

CHAPTER 29

NEW ZEALAND

Four days after my birthday, we embarked on the *MV Maasdam* at Circular Quay in Sydney for one of the most beautiful sailaways on the planet. Midmorning on a balmy February (high summer) day, the ship let go its lines in front of the Museum of Modern Art at The Rocks, eased out alongside the Harbour Bridge and the iconic Sydney Opera House, and cruised past Mrs. Macquarie's Chair in Darling Park next to the Opera House, past the Governor General's Mansion on Cremorne Point, past Rushcutter's Bay, Rose Bay, and Watson's Bay to starboard and the headlands at Tauranga to port. We waived at our pals assembled on the headlands to see us off, and glided finally past South Head where the Sydney to Hobart yacht race starts and then out into the Pacific. Magnificent.

After a sea day, we arrived at Hobart, the biggest city in Tasmania. Joka and I returned to Port Arthur on the southeast corner of the island and revisited the remains of its penal colony. Since Port Arthur is described elsewhere in this chronicle, I don't repeat any of that here. One can't go to Hobart, though, without going back to the eccentric Museum of Old and New Art. My faves were: 1) a machine that digests food by reproducing, at various stages, the functions of *all* of our alimentary canal, including flatulence and elimination, and 2) a computer-operated water droplet emitter at the top of a two story, illuminated sandstone face that forms random words in water droplets which then fall to the base and splatter on the rocks before flowing away.

As we sailed from Tasmania, we rounded a point of land that was deposited as a lava flow and had fractured into the classic hexagonal basalt columns like The Devil's Causeway in Northern Ireland. The whole headland was high cliffs of hexagonal columns going for miles but largely invisible from the land side.

The Tasman Sea between Tasmania and New Zealand is a patch of rough water created by the Roaring Forties winds, and our ship was moving around quite a bit during that crossing, despite having its stabilizers out. I stood in front of a floor-to-ceiling mirror in the elevator lobby and took a photo of my reflection with the floor tilting away in one direction as the ship rolls and me leaning away in the opposite direction to stay upright. The camera was oriented in between, and the visual effect was funny and as disorienting as walking around the ship. The next morning we were in Milford Sound.

The southwestern corner of New Zealand's South Island is wild and remote. The Roaring Forties slam into the land mass on the west side making it inclement as well. However, there are a number of fiords along that coast, and they provide beautiful vistas for cruise ships. We sailed first into the quiet beauty of **Milford Sound** surrounded by soaring cliffs dripping with slender cascades of rainwater and snow-capped peaks in the distance. The next entrance to the ocean moving southward along that coast was **Doubtful Sound,** so named by Captain Cook, its discoverer, who declined to sail into it because he was unsure whether he could get his sailing ship back out given the onshore winds. We were not so limited, however, and went in to enjoy the view. Upon exiting the sound, we did what Cook had done, namely, take an inside passage parallel to the coast and coming out into the ocean again at the bottom of South Island.

After a night of slow steaming, *Maasdam* arrived at **Oban on Stewart Island**, a tender port off the tip of South Island. It was a small, picturesque village with a cruise ship oriented economy that provided tours of the island's rainforest, giant ferns, and kiwi (the bird) habitats. The kiwi is a large, flightless bird that is nocturnal, favors dense undergrowth and is rarely seen. And so, we never caught sight of one in the wild. We did glimpse them in natural history museums, and, even there, they could be viewed only in subdued light.

From Stewart Island, we proceeded to the port of **Dunedin** on the South Pacific Coast of South Island. Dunedin is a small Scottish-influenced city and the port, like many in New Zealand, is a softwood timber exporting port. China, India and South Korea are big consumers of softwood logs from New Zealand's sustainable pine forests, and NZ ports commonly have great piles of them awaiting export on bulkers.

Joka and I took a van excursion to a private wildlife center out on a high promontory overlooking the ocean. Next door was a center for the study and rehabilitation of injured Wandering Albatross, the biggest bird in the Pacific and one that has a solitary lifestyle largely spent at sea for months or even years at a time. We, however, boarded a small, six wheeled all-terrain vehicle and took off overland to see the Little Blue Penguins, the smallest of these ocean birds at a penguin sanctuary. The owners had a private beach that served as a nursery to this species of penguin, and by hiking down an enclosed, man-made, wooden chute, being very quiet, and sliding a wooden window in the chute aside, we were able to look directly into the eyes of surprisingly relaxed nesting penguins perhaps eighteen inches away.

At another of the owner's beaches, we rode down to a small cove where National Geographic had filmed a pod of orcas herding, trapping and devouring seals in the bull kelp of the cove. On the day we were there, the seals hadn't a care in the world.

Another overnight cruise on the *Maasdam* brought us to the center of an extinct, partially submerged volcano. It had eroded down to the point that there was a channel into its core that would accommodate a cruise ship. A small town called **Acaroa** sat on the edge of the flooded center of the caldera and provided a picturesque place to stroll, lunch and shop. It also served as the jumping off place for tour busses to Christchurch, some seventy miles away. I elected to go to Christchurch, and Joka chose to idle in Acaroa.

Christchurch had been heavily damaged in a major earthquake in 2011, killing 185 and injuring hundreds more, It did extensive damage to the architecture of the second largest and most European of New Zealand's cities. Eight years later, it is doing what cities do when they are substantially damaged or destroyed by *force majeure*. They rebuild using the style of architecture in fashion at the time of the rebuilding. Hence, Christchurch's buildings were a random mixture of modern glass and steel high-rises and also renovated low-rise grey granite Victorian and Palladian buildings. A number of buildings were in obvious limbo with steel struts propping them up to prevent further collapse, but no work was being done on them as their owners no doubt struggled with the decision as to whether to sell, renovate or tear down and rebuild. Seismic risks are not generally insurable, so a catastrophic earthquake is a big hit to a local economy, despite the stimulus of reconstruction.

Christchurch is a university town and the University of Canterbury campus stands just on the edge of downtown astride a lazy stream that flows through it, providing a park-like atmosphere. Canterbury is the largest and most visible university in Christchurch, and Lincoln University, further away from town, is a 1990 spin off from Canterbury that specializes in land-based fields of study such as agriculture, life sciences and architecture.

Less than a month after I was there, an Australian white supremacist and Islam hater troubled himself to journey to Christchurch, arm himself with semi-automatic weapons for which he had obtained a license in New Zealand, bought illegal high capacity magazines via the Internet to convert his semi-automatic rifles to automatic ones, and murdered 51 people in a terrorist attack on Christchurch mosques. It was the worst mass killing in New Zealand history and the worst by an Australian in Australian history. The perpetrator admitted guilt and received a life sentence for his crimes.

After the obligatory highlights drive through town on the tour bus, we were given free time which I spent walking around the Canterbury University campus and the river park. On the tour bus ride back to the ship in Acaroa over a high, winding and very scenic road, we stopped at a sheep farm and were treated to a demonstration of sheep dog herding—something I had never seen before. The dogs were highly trained and could be directed by shout or whistle, sometimes at distances of hundreds of meters, to turn the sheep in any direction, stop and hold them, or retreat and let them graze. We were also treated to scones with fresh cream as well as a nice cup of tea by the missus in their lovely Victorian farmhouse in its pastoral setting. It felt like Nebraska or Kansas in the 1950s.

Sailaway from Acaroa was back out the channel from the heart of the volcano. If I had seen White's Island by then, I would have been nervous, but more about that later. Overnight, we left South Island, crossed the Cook Channel separating the two islands, and pulled into the North Island harbor at **Wellington**, the capital city of New Zealand. Wellington was a free day for us, that is, no booked excursions. So, we walked through town until we came to the cable car that climbed up the hill to the top of the Botanical Garden. At the top, we found ourselves at the highest part of the park and started following a winding path downward through changing displays of trees and flowers and plants found in various parts of the world. Tropical plants were reserved for greenhouse displays along the way, since the weather in Wellington was much too temperate for them. But, many of the Northern Hemisphere's trees and lesser plants were familiar to this Californian. The Norfolk Pine, however, is native to the lands bordering the Tasman Sea, and in New Zealand, as in Australia, they grow into big trees.

Toward the bottom of the path, past a tea house in the rose garden, was a cemetery. In the park. Apparently, there wasn't a problem incorporating it into the park when the park's designers laid it out. Below the cemetery a few hundred meters, the path ended at the Wellington Civic Center with the Parliament House and "the Beehive," a building that looks like, well, a beehive, and where the executive offices of the national government are to be found. Wellington is an attractive and modern medium-sized city, but I don't recall there being a lot of hits on the things-to-do-in-Wellington meter, so we just spent the day walking and doing lunch.

There was an extinct volcano on the peninsula to the northwest of Wellington that Joka would have liked to see because it is named Mt. Egmond, her maiden name. Just as all Ainsworths have ancestral ties to the village of Ainsworth in Lancashire, all Van Egmonds come from an important family centered around the town of Egmond in North Holland featuring lots of lords and counts and even kings of ancient Friesland. Like me on the Medici side, heh, heh. (See Genealogical Appendix) But, alas, Mt. Egmond was 100 kilometers away, and we had not the time. Besides, Joka's information was that there wasn't much to see apart from a goodly sized conical mountain that dominates the vista like Vesuvius dominates the horizon around Naples. So, we took our leave from Wellington with the tide that evening as the *Maasdam* headed for Napier.

Napier is a popular destination on North Island because the entire town consists of art deco buildings and public art. It wasn't always that way. In 1931, New Zealand's biggest earthquake shook the city for a full two and a half minutes, followed by over 500 aftershocks. The earthquake and the fires that started in the demolished buildings wiped the entire city away. As I have noted before, when a place is wiped out by a catastrophic event, it is rebuilt in the style of the era in which the rebuilding takes place. Viola! The new Napier is entirely 1930s art deco. I enjoyed myself walking all over downtown taking photos of the exteriors of the various stylish buildings and architectural features, while Joka inspected the interiors of the shops they housed.

One sight stopped me in my tracks. I was walking by a small cherry red sport utility vehicle and happened to glance at its logo. It was a familiar brand, but one I had not seen in a long while—MG. Curious, at my next free wifi stop, I searched the brand name and learned that the British MG brand had been sold to the Chinese. The Chinese are making MG branded automobiles now and selling them in the West—or at least in New Zealand. I have not seen or heard of them in the U.S., but I suppose it is just a matter of time before they show up in the States. Or maybe not. Maybe China has been advised in preliminary marketing surveys that the American government and public might not appreciate additional competition in its domestic automobile industry, especially given the advanced state of decimation of the American auto industry caused by Japan's automobiles. Future readers of this chronicle may wish to take note that this was a very early example of Chinese-made consumer cars to be seen in the West.

Napier and its nearby community Hastings, also art deco for the same calamitous reasons, sit in the center of Hawkes Bay, a prominent viticultural area on North Island. The area is a popular destination for locals and visitors alike.

From Napier, the *Maasdam* made the journey to **Tauranga** by way of White Island, a place that will always give ocean cruise passengers pause as a reminder of the dangers that lurk for the unwary and unlucky. Uninhabited White Island sits about thirty miles off North Island's northeast coast all by itself. It is privately owned and is the largest active volcano in New Zealand with the bulk of it sitting on the seabed. It erupted for twenty four consecutive years ending in 2000, and some eight times since—all at times when no one was present. However, on December 9, 2019, just four months before our arrival, that luck ran out.

The active main vent had in the past blown off one side of the caldera, leaving the mouth of the volcano accessible by sea. It was possible to approach in a small boat, beach it on the ash and rock beach, and simply walk to the vent. Helicopters flew tourists out from the mainland and landed on the beach area as well. On December 9th, 47 tourists from a cruise ship tendered in to the beach and walked into the center. A helicopter had landed with its passengers who were also walking to and from the volcano's vent. Suddenly, the volcano "burped." It didn't erupt with lava; there was no discharge other than the one, but that one was explosive. Volcanos erupt explosively when there is a significant amount of ground water that comes in contact with magma. As water turns from its liquid state into its gaseous state, it expands fifteen hundred times (the principle of the steam engine) creating enormous pressure.

If the steam is not allowed to expand because it is contained within a rock formation, say a volcanic plug, then it is only a matter of time. When the sustained pressure reaches an amount that can overcome the weight of overlying material, a sudden and explosive eruption occurs. That happened on December 9th, resulting in an ash and rock explosion that suffocated fourteen people on the rim and broke the rotors on the helicopter making it inoperable. The others made it back to the water's edge with their burns and other injuries and were rescued. In a matter of a few days, the ash cloud dissipated as the volcano went quiet again.

Maasdam approached the island from windward and sailed past the beach some three hundred meters away. I could see the helicopter sitting on the beach covered with ash, its rotor blades broken in half. We cruised downwind until we were catching up with the gas plume blowing off the island, and then *Maasdam* reversed course and sailed back past the island headed upwind. Incongruously, a huge colony of seabirds called gannets nested on the windward side of the island. They fairly turned the surface of the island white on the few points of land that made up their rookery. Apparently the volcanism next door was not a problem for them. The ship made no announcements over its public address system during any of this, perhaps out of respect; it was hallowed ground. Eventually, *Maasdam* glided back out to sea, and we proceeded to our berth in Tauranga.

The port of **Tauranga** is a jumping off place to go to other places. In our case, we were headed to **Rotorua**, a geothermal showplace in an important Maori settlement. We opted not to take a ship-sponsored excursion and instead went in search of a local tour operator. We found one that had an exhaustive itinerary, and it turned out that we were the only ones on it. It was conducted by an older woman who owned the business, and she was a delight. The first stop was the largest geyser in New Zealand, the Puhuto ("Big Splash") geyser which erupted twenty times a day and its plume reached thirty meters into the air. (Old Faithful in Yellowstone can reach over fifty meters.) It was surrounded by thermal pools and fumaroles (bubbling mud pots), all emitting the familiar, disagreeable odor of sulphur gases.

Just adjacent to the geothermal park was the entrance to a Maori ceremonial village at *Whakarewarewa*. At the entrance there is a big sign with a bold print caption that reads:

TE WHAKAREWAREWATANGAOTEOPETAUAAWAH

I had no idea what that was telling us, but, judging from its sheer span of sounds expressed, I assumed that it was big medicine. I don't mean to be flippant about the Maori culture; in fact, I was quite taken with it.

To backtrack a bit, the Maori are Polynesian people and they arrived in New Zealand a mere 800 years ago. Until this trip, I admit being confused about the difference between Australian aboriginal people and the Maori right next door, thinking them somehow related. Not so. The Australian aboriginal people migrated eastward over the islands now known as Indonesia from South Asia as *sapiens* migrated out of Africa. The Maori came westward from Tahiti and the Cook Islands and Hawaii about the time the Franciscans established the alternative Pope in Avignon, that is to say, pretty recently.

The Polynesians were in fact brilliant navigators, despite not having sextants. They knew the seasons and the constellations, the wind and ocean currents, and the birds and sea life in various parts of the South Pacific. They put together very seaworthy ships by lashing two long war canoes hollowed out from tropical hardwood trees and lashed them in parallel with a stout bamboo pole structure above and spanning the war canoes, thus creating an ocean-going catamaran. On the bamboo deck they could carry supplies and erect masts bearing sails to increase their speed and control.

The South Pacific is a vast space, and they explored all of it from New Zealand in the southwest to Easter Island in the southeast to the Hawaiian Islands to the north. The first party arriving in what is now New Zealand saw the elongated land structure consisting of two islands arranged end to end under a band of clouds that hovered over the land mass. They named it the "Land of the Long White Cloud"—in Polynesian, of course.

There are many cultural and language similarities among the various Polynesian Islands, but New Zealand is somewhat more isolated and has had enough time on its own to develop its own unique cultural characteristics not shared with the other South Pacific Islands. For starters, it is a much bigger land mass than any of the other islands, thus giving them room to grow into a larger, more complex population. My visit did not make me an expert in these matters, but certain matters made a very vivid impression on me that I will never forget.

The first was seared into my memory at the "challenge ceremony" in the village at *Whakarewhatewah*. We were advised that this ceremony was to take place at 2 pm and to assemble in front of the large ceremonial gathering house. Our tour guide, who was expert in such matters, positioned me strategically in the center of the walkway and next to her, which signaled to the Maori that I was the nominated participant in the challenge ceremony and that she vouched for me. She then told me that I would be selected and instructed me on how to behave. I should never smile or laugh, and remain still, no matter what happens.

As the Maori players began to form up, a village elder woman came up to me and led me partway up the path to the gathering house to await the ceremony. Soon enough, a Maori warrior with a spear appeared from the gathering house and proceeded to perform an elaborate *haka* (more on that later) involving much shouting, scowling and thrusting of his lance in my direction as he got closer and closer. When he got in front of me, he made a particularly passionate recitation with accompanying shoves of his spear toward my midsection, and then calmly laid the tip of a silver fern on the ground in front of me. The silver fern (a large, common fern with an underside that is silver in color) is the Maori symbol for New Zealand. I came to understand that I was playing the role of a visiting warrior chief being offered a welcome to their land if I should accept their challenge of entering into their custody.

As instructed, I then stooped and picked up the silver fern and held it in my hand, unsmiling, thus indicating my acceptance of the challenge. At that point, the mood changed into all smiles and I (the visiting chief) and Joka (my wife) were escorted into the gathering house along with all of the other hundred or so visitors observing the ceremony. Joka and I were seated on a bench in the front row and we all enjoyed a performance of more *haka* dancing and chanting on the stage. We received no oral or written explanation of any of this. At the appropriate time in the ceremony, I was invited up on the stage and proceeded down a reception line of six Maori warriors. I "kissed" (I don't know of a better word) each warrior by rubbing noses with each of them, taking care not to touch foreheads. After that, it was over, there was much smiling and clapping on backs as we filtered out of the gathering house. I kept the silver fern in my hand for most of the afternoon. It seemed like a travesty to just throw it away.

Okay, so a "*haka*" is a dance form, which involves a chant along with certain gestures, but the performer has some discretion as to what gestures he/she elects to use and at what times. Some of the *haka* are famous and known to all Maori. Some are regional and less well known. There is one that is nationally known and seems to have more significance to more Maori. It is called the *Ka Mate haka*. It begins with "*Ka mate, Ka mate*, (This could be my death) *Ka ora, Ka ora* (this could be my life)…" and goes on to tell the story of the chief of the majority tribe in the southern North Island and the northern South Island as he is being pursued by his enemies, his hiding in a pit to escape, and his finally coming up into the sunlight and receiving protection from the chief ("the hairy man") of an affiliated tribe. Something must be lost in translation because this somewhat awkward tale engenders in the Maori teller of the *haka* the most passion and intensity imaginable, accompanied with fist clenchings, hand quavering, squatting foot stomps, and full-tongue-out fierce faces. In fact, the New Zealand National Rugby Team, the All Blacks, perform one of two *hakas* before each game they play, and "*Ka Mate*" is the most favored. I have seen them perform this haka and by the time they are finished, their faces have a truly intimidating countenance that reflects the passion they feel. Oh, and by the way, despite New Zealand having a smaller population base by far than most of the other national teams they play, the All Blacks rarely lose.

I was moved by my experience to buy Brayden, my oldest grand-daughter, a Maori "greenstone" (jade) breast plate as a college graduation present. It is said to offer protection and strength to the wearer. The plate had an unusual mixture of forest green jade with clouds of white jade in it symbolizing the ancestral Maori "Land of the Long White Cloud."

Also at Rotorea that memorable day, our guide took us to a city park which featured a steaming, malodorous geothermal lake and stream travers-ing an otherwise urban, normal-looking park. And finally, we stopped at a forest of Northern California Coast Redwoods that had been planted sev-enty five years earlier by a philanthropist who had seen the virgin redwoods in California and was moved to plant some in New Zealand. The climate must have been a good match as the trees are now all uniformly healthy, big and lush. One might think he was standing in the Rockefeller Grove of the Humboldt Redwoods in Northern California but for the fact that the un-dergrowth in the Rotorua grove consists exclusively of silver ferns.

Sailaway from Tauranga was a bit wrenching for us. We had reacted powerfully to our experiences at Rotorua and left wanting more. But, it made for the climax of our cruise and, after a day at sea, we found our-selves docked in New Zealand's largest city, Auckland, and our destination.

Auckland was a pretty city situated on a scenic bay with islands scat-tered around to enhance the views. It had a lovely, popular waterfront packed with trendy restaurants and good hotels. However, it sat in an active volcanic field, including one volcano just offshore and facing the city—Rangitoto Island. As a local museum demonstrated dramatically, if/when that volcano erupts explosively again, the city will be swept away by the thermoplastic cloud and tsunami that follows before residents would have time to react. But, perhaps like the residents of San Francisco sitting astride the San Andreas Fault, the good citizens of Auckland man-age to suspend their knowledge of how things might (probably will) go in the long run and bet the farm on how they might enjoy life there in the short run.

There is a space needle in Auckland like that in Seattle, only Auck-land's has a glass floor at the observation deck. Not a good experience if you are afraid of heights.

Auckland marked the end of our cruise, but not the end of our trip. We rented a car there and set out on a limited tour of North Island. About two hours out of Auckland, we entered the **Corundel Peninsula** on the eastern shore. It is a sparsely populated area with a mountainous spine and scattered seaside resort towns on the ocean. The authorities in New Zealand have largely resisted the urge to rename all of the settlements in New Zealand with English names and instead have kept the names of the Maori settlements that predated Captain Cook. So, on the Corundel Peninsula, we stayed one night each in **Whatianga** and **Whatamata**. (The "wh" letters are pronounced "f.") At a seaside restaurant in the latter, live music was provided by an aging rocker playing and singing Eagles classics. He was very good, and you could tell he was a professional. We had an entertaining chat with him and bought a copy of his CD.

From the Corundel Peninsula, we turned inland and headed for **Lake Taupo** in the center of the Island. It is a big freshwater lake (236 square miles) and was formed by the flooding of a huge volcanic caldera. An alert reader will by now have noticed that New Zealand is riddled with volcanoes. In fact, the entire country is formed from successive volcanic eruptions over the eons and they continue today. Anyone considering emigrating from America in frustration over its declining quality of life and governance should bear that in mind.

Lake Taupo had **Huka Falls**, a picturesque continuous cascade that drained the overflow from the Lake. There was a popular boat trip I wish we could have taken around the lake to see geothermal features and some spectacular Maori rock carvings of warrior faces and various animals in the basalt. Regrettably, our schedule did not allow enough time to take that tour.

Instead, we headed off for the glow worm caves in **Waitomo.** I don't know if these organisms exist elsewhere in the world, but it was the first time I experienced them. They are worms that hang down like short spaghetti from the roofs of caves in several locations in New Zealand. They congregate in the pitch black interior of caves that have fresh air exposure and a lot of ground water. They have a phosphorescence that emits not just an eerie glow like the wake of a ship at night, but a very bright spot of light. It seems that insects that fly into the mouth of the cave in search of water and a resting place out of the view of predatory birds, are attracted by the light, and fly toward it only to end up stuck to and eaten by the worms.

For us, it was safer. We climbed into a boat at the mouth of the cave and floated through a series of caves tethered to a line until, when it was pitch black, we rounded a turn and entered a larger chamber with the ceiling covered by thousands of spots of light that glowed blue white. Up close (seen with binoculars) the worms look like a luminous string of pearls hanging vertically. It was astonishing.

From there, we drove back to Auckland for another night in our waterfront hotel and another good dinner before returning to Sydney the next morning.

Not long after our return to Sydney, the Covid pandemic had begun to spread like wildfire around the world. Cases were popping up everywhere. Travelers from China had already been banned by Australia and United States before we set sail for New Zealand, and more travel bans were being openly talked about in those countries and others. I became increasingly concerned that I might be unable to return to the States, and so I reluctantly booked a flight out a week or so earlier than I had planned. A few days after that, I flew home, thus ending not only my most recent stay in Oz, but also the peripatetic ways I had embraced for the last five years. Travel to Australia and the United States did indeed cease shortly after that as the global pandemic spread around the globe.

Joka and I were not just separated. We were "stuffed." The legal barriers to our visits to each other and to travel the world were ironclad and open ended. Thus began the long period of enforced separation for us, but also a period within the United States of enforced mask wearing, social distancing, and inability to gather in restaurants, theaters, churches, stores, or even out of doors venues with more than a few people at a time. I took advantage of the opportunity/enforced idleness to write this chronicle during that period. I therefore finish the book some fifteen months after returning from Australia and New Zealand. In the interim, several vaccines against the Covid virus have been developed around the world, and I have been vaccinated with a vaccine with 94% efficacy. Joka, however, has not yet been vaccinated as Australia failed to pursue a national policy of aggressively acquiring the vaccines and inoculating its citizens. The barriers to travel between the two countries have not be relaxed and we don't know when they will. And that, gentle reader, accounts for the abrupt end of this book not at some logical or climactic point in my story, but simply because the pandemic has interdicted the trajectory of my life. So be it. Another determinative fork in the road.

CHAPTER 30

ESSAYS

Thus ends the chronology that is my story, or at least the first 81 years of it. The balance of this volume consists of short essays on topics which have preoccupied me during my lifetime and on which I have the urge to meditate in my old age. These are thoughts on matters that seem important and that I would like to pass on to posterity—or at least that small part of posterity that will ever see this record.

The Covid 19 Pandemic:

In January, 2020, prior to the departure of our New Zealand cruise, the "Covid 19 corona virus" pandemic had broken out, initially and inaccurately reported by the Chinese Government as originating from a wet market in Wuhan, China. The Wuhan market originated as a seafood market, but as the Asian oceans were increasingly overfished, wild animal meat or "bush meat" was increasingly available in the markets, some species having been imported from distant parts of China. Bats, perhaps, some said, were the source of the virus. Or not. Now, a year plus on, it appears that the virus was circulating in Hubei Province in China the summer before, but its origin was unclear. Roughly thirty percent of the first known infected Chinese had no connection with the wet market. The Chinese Premier, in an extraordinary piece of belligerence and reacting to President Trump's penchant for calling the virus the "China" virus, the "Kung Foo" virus, and other slurs, suggested that the virus originated in an American laboratory in Maryland. Despite this petty deflection by the Chinese Communist Party, the working consensus is that it originated in Hubei Province, including the City of Wuhan, but from an unknown animal source from which it was transmitted to humans, possibly, but there is no evidence of it, via the agency of the official Chinese biomedical lab located in Wuhan.

American scientists visit this lab and coordinate with their Chinese scientist brethren on matters of mutual scientific interest. One theory is that the virus was developed in that laboratory as germ warfare or was derived from bat or other animal populations and inadvertently released into the population. There seems to be no evidence to support this hypothesis. But, the virus came to America, Europe and elsewhere both directly via travelers from Wuhan and indirectly by way of Wuhan travelers to intermediate locations and then transmitted by relay to America, Canada, Europe and ultimately, everywhere.

A reputable Chinese biomedical doctor publically announced the existence and identification of the virus and the threat it represented to the world via social media as he himself was dying from it. The Chinese Government first silenced him for promulgating rumors that portrayed China in an unfavorable light, and then, after wiser heads prevailed in Beijing, the particulars of the disease were publically, but still inaccurately disclosed by Chinese sources together with the false or erroneous conclusion that it was not transmissible from human to human. By February 10, 2020, there were 40,000 diagnosed cases of the corona virus worldwide, and 99% of them were in China. By then, however, it was making its way around the world on daily jumbo jets out of Wuhan.

Australia and America had closed their borders to flights from China in January, but neither had a mechanism for screening out persons from Wuhan but flying in from a third country. Prior to the border closures, Americans had been flying to and from Wuhan, a major industrial center in China. A Boeing wide-body passenger aircraft arrived in Sydney and San Francisco *every day* from Wuhan.

We embarked on the *Veendam* on February 14th, weeks after the Australian border had been closed to Chinese visitors. We assumed that the closure guaranteed that no one coming into Australia from China would be on our ship and that our cruise would therefore be free from virus risks. New Zealand had no cases. We failed to appreciate that the virus could have hitched a ride with someone from Wuhan and triangulating in from a third country or infecting someone who would then visit Australia from another country.

Nevertheless, we were lucky and we enjoyed the entire cruise with no outbreak on the ship. Nor did we see any sign of the virus in New Zealand. However, back in Sydney upon our return in early March, it was huge news. There were by then many cases in Australia in general and New South Wales in particular, and a full blown pandemic was getting started in the States.

As this contagion spread, my granddaughter Lauren was having the time of her life in Sydney as a junior-year-abroad student at the University of New South Wales. She was living the life in the Bondi Beach neighborhood with six other girls from Syracuse University. She and her mates had just returned from an excursion to Thailand, Bali, and Singapore.

By mid-March, however, the Covid virus angst had risen to medium anxiety. I witnessed an escalating series of travel restrictions being rolled out around the world, and I made a command decision to cut short my stay in Avalon Beach by two weeks and return home to avoid the risk of being stranded. My daughter Erin and son-in-law Eric arrived right then on their long-planned trip to visit Lauren in Sydney and to tour Australia. Their itinerary took them first to Tasmania and then to Sydney. By the time they arrived in Sydney, they received word that the University of Colorado had cancelled classes for Lauren's sister Julia, and she was on her way home. Further, grandson Ainsworth's high school classes had been cancelled as well. So, Erin and Eric had to jump on a plane and return home after a mere four days in Australia. I flew out right behind them.

Lauren and her friends, ever the optimists, wanted to stay until the end of their apartment lease in late May. A week after I returned home, however, the UNSW had cancelled all classes, and Lauren was on her way back as well. Shortly after that, travel became impossible as travel visas were cancelled or restricted in domino fashion throughout the world. We were all locked down in our respective countries in an attempt to "flatten the curve" of virus transmission by wearing masks, practicing social distancing, and following hygienic hand washing and sanitizing practices. This was to prevent a spike in cases that would overwhelm the health care system as had happened a century earlier with the "Spanish Influenza."

That was fifteen months ago, as I write this. We have been under various levels of voluntary or involuntary quarantine and social distancing discipline throughout the intervening time. We try not to interact outside our non-infected family and social "bubbles" without wearing a mask and remaining at least six feet apart in public. As the rate of infection would dip, restaurants were allowed to serve inside at reduced capacities. When infections increased, they could serve take-out or patio dining only. Barbershops and beauty shops, theaters, churches and stores were closed. Businesses were limited in the numbers of persons that could be within certain spaces. Unemployment soared. A mortgage and rental holiday was declared in most states, and Congress enacted a per capita payment program to keep households intact. However, these benefits expired over time and Congress became paralyzed by the political gridlock that characterized the Trump Presidency.

The Trump White House and the Republican Party, the latter having been cowed into submission by Trump's capacity for vitriol directed at anyone opposing his views, shamelessly pursued an official policy of doing nothing to control the virus. Trump ridiculed those who wore masks and practiced social distancing while he held in-person fund-raisers and rallies while practicing neither, thus infecting thousands of his fans and killing some of them (e.g., Ben Carson).

Donald Trump was a hotel and resort developer and was losing a lot of money because of the pandemic economic downturn. So, in urging business-as-normal, he was serving his own self-interest at the expense of the lives of Americans he was supposed to serve and protect. And his supporters didn't seem to be able to connect the dots. The mind boggles.

As I write this, Joe Biden has recently been elected as President, and Donald Trump is in disgrace on so many counts that I will leave it to the historians to explain. Trump's disgrace, however, is not recognized by his hard-core supporters in our society, a basket of what Hillary Clinton called "deplorables" comprised of racists/white supremacists in and out of the former Confederate States, religious zealots who treasured Trump's conservative appointments to the Supreme Court (who will presumably protect gun rights and erode abortion rights,) and rural populations that seem to be deeply hostile to city-dwelling "elites" and diversity-tolerant urbanites. There is another and very legitimate cohort of Trump supporters who see him as a champion of industrial labor who tried to right the wrongs done to them in the course of globalization. (More on that subject in the essay that follows.)

The problem is that there were, in the aggregate, 70 million of those Trump supporters that voted, compared to 77 million supporters of the victorious Presidential candidate in 2020, Joseph R. Biden. So, the country is deeply divided as I write this—more so than at any other period in my lifetime. However, you, gentle reader, will have the benefit of knowing what transpires from now on and why, so I will not share any of the speculation that preoccupies us at the time of this writing.

On Globalism:

I can't resist the urge to revisit the backstory of my first novel, *The Chasm*. In the book, I basically forecast that there would be hell to pay for the betrayal of industrial labor by American consumers and American government. Donald Trump has rewritten the ending of my book, but the theme of it remains substantially correct.

Globalism or globalization are terms we used to identify the group of issues arising from the fact that technology has enabled the ready movement of capital around the world, while labor remains largely static within the confines (jurisdiction) of nations. Thus, a factory making appliances can be shut down in Cleveland, funds sufficient to build a new factory in Guangzhou can be wire-transferred to China, workers can be hired in Guangzhou under a contract negotiated quickly, and the resulting products can be manufactured and shipped to the American market by containerships with a two-week transit time. The unit cost of manufacture is more than halved, U.S. land use and other environmental constraints on manufacturing avoided, and worker health care insurance and pension costs avoided.

The formerly well paid union industrial workers were, over time, left impoverished, and their communities were burdened with higher welfare costs but with drastically lowered tax revenues with which to meet them. Note that this was not "creative destruction"— a process of replacing obsolete goods and services with currently needed ones, e.g., ceasing production of rotary dial telephones and replacing them with cellular computer phones. This was replacing modern, needed articles, usually having been innovated in America, with the same products made cheaper in third world countries offshore.

As stated, this process was devastating to industrial labor and to the communities that the displaced workers call home. It was enabled, even driven and accelerated by a Federal open markets policy; that is, allowing foreign manufactured goods to freely enter the stream of American commerce without penalty, duty or tariffs. There are no barriers to foreign entities doing business in the United States. This is an American trade policy that exalts consumer prices and choices over industrial policy. American wages and employment opportunity declined as a result, but consumers benefited. It is class warfare between those wage earners with a secure source of income and industrial laborers whose lack of income impairs their consumption. That pool of disenfranchised industrial labor has been suffering and growing and coalescing into a voting pool of Americans who feel betrayed by their government with its thumb on the scales of consumerism.

Outsourcing American manufacturing needs in this way also damages the national economy by reducing GDP. (The value of manufacturing activity, including retailing the manufactured goods, lost far exceeds the value of marginal retailing activity gained, if any, from selling imports.) Outsourcing also forfeits the industrial base that leads the country out of economic recessions. At the bottom of a recession, a shift in consumer confidence results in increased consumer spending, but if the commodities being newly purchased are made in China and Japan, *those* economies are stimulated in a recovery while the American economy languishes. A current review of all of the recessions that have occurred in America since WW II reveals that recessions have grown consecutively longer beginning in mid-1980s when the offshoring phenomenon began to take off and America's trade deficit ballooned.

This is the phenomenon that prompted me to write my first novel— a muckraker about this class warfare. But, my book was no "Grapes of Wrath" by John Steinbeck or "The Jungle" by Sinclair Lewis or "The Octopus" by Frank Norris. My book received no public attention at all. The millions of industrial laborers that made up what we now call "the Rust Belt" fell into poverty silently, without support from their former champions, the Democratic Party. The labor unions that formerly represented these workers in Washington, dwindled in membership numbers until they too became relatively irrelevant in lobbying power.

The fate of these workers was sealed. They remained an ignored lump of misery and abandonment in the body politic for decades, but they seethed with fury. It was Donald Trump that discovered them. He had no experience in politics and his string of bankruptcies revealed that he cared little for his workers. However, in plotting a Presidential campaign calculated to enhance the Trump brand, and in search of issues upon which to campaign, he commissioned a political consultant to do a poll on what made voters angry. He reasoned that he would fashion a campaign around meeting the wants of whoever is angry to form a political base that would serve as a platform from which to build his brand. His consultants gave him his answer. A huge number of Americans were very angry about America's open markets policy and outsourcing. Disproportionally, these voters were domiciled in the formerly Democratic swing states of Pennsylvania, Ohio, Michigan, and Wisconsin.

So, with absolutely no idea of how to actually do it, Trump promised to bring all those lost living wage jobs that had been outsourced back to America. It was a masterstroke. In addition to the white hot fury of industrial labor, he also pandered to Christian evangelicals, white supremacists, anti-Muslim and anti-immigrant bias, and elitist anti-urbanites. That led him straight into the White House in 2016.

The heavily favored Democratic candidate Hillary Clinton and the Democratic Party were left in the dust, bewildered, as the formerly "blue wall" states of Wisconsin, Michigan, Ohio, and Pennsylvania flipped for Trump. Moreover, the down-ballot wake of the victorious Trump vote gave the majorities in the House of Representatives and The Senate to the GOP now dominated by Trump.

The result has been a catastrophe. We have had four years of Donald Trump's unabated nihilism. He has been a veritable fountainhead of pathological lying, immorality, self-dealing, treasonous alliances with autocrats, notably Vladimir Putin of Russia, unlawful conduct and obstructions of justice, tax cheating, foreign affairs blundering, racism, contempt of Congress, and fostering an attempted insurrection and coup for good measure as he incited a riot on January 6, 2021 to prevent the Congress from receiving the electoral college vote for Joe Biden.

Trump lost his bid for reelection after having been abandoned by the voters of Pennsylvania, Michigan, and Wisconsin for, among many other things, incompetence in failing to accomplish anything he promised them. Only Ohio went for Trump in 2020 of the former "Blue Wall" states. I'm confident that the future reader will have the benefit of a clear, 20-20 picture of the post-Trump years as they unfold. But I would be very surprised if the voters of the Rust Belt—the formerly middle class, union card carrying, industrial workers—continue to be sacrificed to the gods of globalization in silence. It is clear that no political party can win the White House without them. Even celebrity economists like Paul Krugman who have been on record as chronicling globalization "*uber alles*" have admitted their myopic blunder.

On Fossil Fuels:

I also can't resist the urge to revisit, or rather update, the backstory to my novel *In Extremis.* That book meditates upon the fact that sapiens are exhausting perhaps the biggest resource needed for long term survival, fossil fuel energy, without having developed alternative energy sources sufficiently.

There has been a school of thought that the concept of "peak oil" (oil and methane gas are a finite resource, and production of it will peak when demand exceeds depleted supply and then terminally decline) has been discredited. Perhaps that is due to industry observers having been numbed to the idea of oil and gas exhaustion by the cyclical nature of the industry and the temporary market gluts that keep prices down. Doubtless all of the *faux* science injected into the discourse is contributes to the confusion. The tobacco industry and the NFL unleashed concerted lobbying campaigns claiming that the nexus between lung cancer from tobacco and brain damage from football concussions are somehow propositions on which the science is disputed. Well, those propositions are not disputed, and peak oil isn't either.

The evidence that has surfaced since writing *In Extremis* shows that peak oil from the *conventional* extraction of oil and gas *has in fact peaked already*. Peak production reportedly occurred sometime around 2010-

2012, after which it has platcaued and begun to decline slightly. We continue to use fossil fuels in the manner to which we have become accustomed and the supply of it can easily be met by industry *now*. Producers meet the demand spikes of national and global markets by pumping available reserves out of the ground as needed. However, this lulls us into a false sense of security in that our ability to enjoy the energy benefits of hydrocarbons on a day-to-day basis bears no rational relationship to the unconsumed quantity of those resources still in the ground. Oil and gas reserves are finite and our continuing use of them is exhausting them faster than we realize.

In my novel, I posited that peak oil would occur around 2035. That was based upon projections that, by 2035, Saudi Arabia would become a net importer of oil and that the fracked oil boom would peak in the 2020s and deplete faster than conventional oil did. From where will Saudi Arabia import its future oil? And what would prevent Saudi Arabia and all of the other oil and gas producing countries from connecting the dots between dwindling reserves and their own energy needs and adopt conservation policies long before reserves are actually exhausted? The prospect that oil producing countries will stop or reduce exporting oil and gas seems more likely than not; hence global scarcity of oil and gas could arise suddenly absent the discovery of some miraculous new source of energy.

Well, the other shoe has now dropped. OPEC, that is, the Organization of Oil Exporting Countries, has just last year (2020) admitted that peak oil will occur in the global market circa 2040 and in some countries, before that. Unh, ohhh. That is nineteen years from now.

The issue has thus been taken out of the realm of conjecture and placed into the mainstream empirical record. It would be a mistake not to heed what OPEC is saying, namely, existential shortage is just around the corner (one to two decades). OPEC countries have a powerful interest in exporting oil and gas. They pay for the infrastructure and welfare programs for their people with that money. If they are making this admission against their own interest now, they are admitting that they contemplate the need to conserve their own reserves for their own future use. If they decide at some point to reduce or curtail further exports, that would precipitate an energy crisis for oil importing countries by accelerating scarcity earlier than 2040.

Against that looming catastrophic scenario, we have the chaos theory possibility that somehow, someway, a miraculous substitute for fossil fuels will appear in a globally distributable and economic form to save the world's population of 7.5 billion people (at this writing and growing.) The problem is that such a scenario isn't likely. Nuclear fusion technology is talked about, but is not even close to being available. Hydrogen powered engines to generate electricity are being talked about, but again are not forthcoming. Anyway, these alternative sources are not going to fly airplanes, propel ships, and propel railroad cars and trucks and autos, let alone power homes and businesses and industries all over the industrialized world, never mind the undeveloped world. Certainly not within one or two decades.

On a micro level, solar and wind power will provided alternative power solutions. There is an on-going movement among enlightened people on Planet Earth today to minimize/discontinue use of fossil fuels in order to avoid/minimize the adverse effects of global climate change due to greenhouse gas emissions. To the extent that the activism of these people reduce *sapiens'* carbon footprint, so much the better. That will not only slow whatever effects greenhouse gas accumulation has on the Earth's climate, it will conserve fossil fuels, thus buying us more time within which to find and perfect an alternative energy source for the world's needs.

The good news is that sapiens will go off of fossil fuels, if only because we exhaust them. The bad news is that if *sapiens* goes off of fossil fuels involuntarily, that is, because we exhaust them *before finding a replacement energy source*, it will be catastrophic for many (most?) sapiens.

[*Note:* For the roughly five thousand years prior to the advent of the Industrial Revolution around, say, 1800, the earth's population was approximately 500-700 million people. As I write this, some two hundred twenty years later, the earth's population is 7.3 billion. Exponential growth of that kind during the era of fossil fuels will stop because it can't be sustained. The energy shortage that will stop global population growth will cause population decline.

Further Note: If we do appear to be headed into a catastrophic shortage of oil and gas, the earth has a goodly, but also finite, amount of coal. However, coal is dirty and it adversely effects the environment. We have long since lost the infrastructure to use coal for heating and transportation and electricity generation, and it would take a lot of effort to get it back. Moreover, coal mines are not located where power plants are. Railroad train engines to haul hopper cars full of coal to power plants burn oil. So, back to coal fired steam engines? And back to ships with coal fired steam engines? All over the planet? Can that reversal occur quickly enough to mitigate oil and gas energy shortages? And that would only work for a limited period of time until the coal runs out.

Final Note: When I wrote *In Extremis*, I struggled with the idea of writing a non-fiction book about peak oil versus a fiction book in which peak oil is the backstory. For a lot of reasons beyond the scope of this essay, I decided on the novel route. My concern about using the novel form was well grounded. The book has been self-published and has been read by almost no one. It has had no effect whatever. People look around and see a glut of fossil fuel energy year after year. What shortage? However, we are in luck! We will now have a non-fiction presentation of the problem in an empirical form by the one person on this planet in the best position to do it: Bill Gates.

Gates apparently feels guilty about having warned us all five years ago that a pandemic was coming and that we should prepare for it. However, he didn't follow through with a campaign, and no one did anything to prepare. The global coronavirus death toll is two and a half million one year in, and that is an undercount. Now Gates is also warning us about the energy crisis, but he is cleverly doing it in the context of global climate change, a more slowly developing crisis but one we can relate to. *And he is making it a campaign.* With the great fortune of his foundation at his disposal, and his brilliant mind, and his status in the world that gives him access to anyone, anywhere, as well as the world's biggest megaphone, we can hope for a more impactful advocacy for new energy sources. His bestselling book is *How to Prevent a Climate Disaster.* And in case you thought he is not all in on this subject, he has formed an investment venture group called Breakthrough Energy Ventures and has started his own cutting edge energy firm, TerraPower.

As I write this, he is constantly on media making his case for new and cleaner forms of energy. We must quit making steel and cement the way we do, he says. Too much hydrocarbon burning is required and too much CO2 and ozone is created. Well, we ask, how then should we make steel and cement? And fertilizer that supports monoculture in farming that experts estimate support two billion people currently? Answer: We must develop new sources of energy from nuclear fusion or fission, new storage batteries, hydrogen engines, etc. *Solar and wind are not enough.*

We must stop powering our ships and planes and trains the way we do. Well, how do we do that? And so on. But Gates is casting the problem not in terms of peak oil which has proven not to resonate when oil is paradoxically widely available. Instead, he is advocating going off of fossil fuels in the more popular context of global climate change to avoid the fires, floods, droughts, violent storms, and other extremes of weather that threaten us more and more and that are apparent to everyone. And he is not being disingenuous. The two issues of peak oil and climate change are two sides of the same coin. Both issues call for new clean energy sources and we need them quickly to avoid refugee-creating crises from both climate change and energy shortages. I certainly wish Gates well and am personally grateful for his appearance on the scene and taking up this burden. Our lives depend on it.

These unanswered questions await those who come after me. It does appear, however, that, to the extent one of more of these energy miracles are not perfected and implemented in the next twenty years or so, a corresponding die off of *sapiens* will occur. If/when that happens, the aboriginal people of the world will return to the fore. After all, the Australian aboriginal people carry the genes of Neanderthal people and, to a greater extent, the Denisovan people from 60,000 years ago. Their methods are more resistant to extinctions than those of modern *sapiens*.

On Immigration

This is a big subject, and one on which I am not competent to opine other than in generalities. I can only point to yet another conundrum. It is so true as to be a cliché, but America was founded on and grew by immigration. Of course, ice age migrants carrying the genes of the Bering Sea people came to the Americas some 13,000 years ago and, within one or two thousand years of what must have been hunter-gatherer prosperity in the productive land they found and its huge population of animals, settled the entire twin continent land mass.

In the last five centuries, immigrants came from Spain, via Mexico into what is now Santa Fe. Not many decades after that, some religious zealots from England formed the Virginia and Massachusetts colonies. Then came the Dutch East India and British East India Companies' push into the American continent followed closely by the French in Acadia and up the Mississippi River from the Gulf of Mexico. Then came waves of other Europeans.

As America involved itself in foreign wars and foreign trade, it attracted slaves from Africa, Chinese from the Far East, then Philippine people, Japanese, Koreans, Vietnamese, Middle Easterners and waves upon waves of the Hispanic poor from Mexico and Central America. For the most part, at least until recently as I write, immigrants were welcome, even invited first to settle the country and then to work in America's factories during the Industrial Revolution.

People seeking land for farming came from everywhere to stake out their claims based on European concepts of real property and at the expense of the Native Americans and their communal attitudes toward property. Labor was forcibly imported (African-American slaves) to feed the agri-capitalist need to leverage labor for the neo-feudal plantations of the former Confederate states. Irish poor were needed and Chinese poor were recruited to build levees and railroads.

A certain false folklore grew up that came to be inscribed on the base of the Statue of Liberty ("Give me your poor, downtrodden...") I say false because America's immigration laws were always about exclusion. Nevertheless, there was schizophrenia in America's immigration policy and the popular belief persisted that refugees might find a home here, and for good reason. America grew rapidly, and the economic engine of capitalism propelled it. World Wars I and II cemented America as a world power, and then *the* world power, and there was never a time when its economic engine did not need fresh immigrant labor to leverage profits for capitalists.

Fast forward to the present as I write. America is overpopulated. The planet is even more overpopulated. Large swaths of the world's population is unemployed or under employed and dependent upon tax-funded public assistance or charity. Recent automation in the form of computers and robotics have contributed greatly to America's surplus of labor and made it permanent. The advent of artificial intelligence will accelerate and worsen this situation. American labor has come unmoored from GDP. A rising tide does not life all boats anymore. Capitalism has a problem.

People who have technical skills needed by capitalist managers will prosper, and people who own and employ capital and leverage labor and earn a return on their investments will prosper even more. But people who labor for wages will do worse, the lower-skilled margins doing much worse. This is the stuff revolutions are made of. It's just a matter of numbers, the lapse of time and a catalytic event.

Karl Marx and Friedrich Engels were not wrong when they wrote *Das Capital*. They merely catalogued, exhaustively, the abuses of market power of *laissez faire* capitalists in 19ᵗʰ century and early 20ᵗʰ century Europe. Those practices and conditions were uncomfortably close to the contemporaneous situation in America as well whenever the marketplace is deregulated. The conditions described by Marx and Engels resulted in the advent of socialism and in Russia's communist revolution.

In America and in Europe as well after World War I eroded Europe's monarchies, voters demanded reforms. Trade unionism was hard won but established and regulation of capitalist behavior thorough legislation became the norm. In America, the Sherman Antitrust Act was passed by the Congress in 1890, and the myriad "trusts" by which horizontal competitors in various industries bound themselves together to eliminate competition and maximize their market power were outlawed. That was preceded two years earlier by the Interstate Commerce Act which closely regulated the behavior of the railroad barons whose caprice and predation ruined countless businesses and drove farm laborers into poverty. Whole communities were desolated in the course of competition among the railroad barons.

Muckraking novelists helped stimulate further regulatory revolution in the form of the Fair Labor Standards Act, the Child Labor laws, the Pure Food and Drug Act, the Labor Management Relations Act, the Shipping Act of 1916, the Social Security Act and many others. Regulatory agencies were created by those laws and charged with the administration of the legislative objects and policies of their enabling legislation. This regulatory revolution *saved capitalism*. The collective improvement in the prosperity of and the working conditions of ordinary workers that followed in this country defused the political pressure that led to socialism elsewhere. This collectivism has tended to go further to provide welfare states in Europe than in the United States, as capitalism has managed to fiercely defend its interests here marginally better than in Europe.

One of the consequences of that history was that the working classes increasingly prospered over time. Experienced or skilled workers sought and obtained employment that delivered a fair opportunity to achieve what became known as the American Dream. But as that progress unfolded, a perpetual need was created for new laborers who were willing to do the menial labor. Immigrants were *necessary*. Capitalists welcomed them as cheap labor to leverage. Industrial labor mostly resented them. Early English workers resented the Irish when they came and the Germans and Scandinavians when they came. The Irish resented the Italians. All resented first the Chinese and then the Hispanics when they came more recently.

Each wave of immigrants created pressure on the wages and conditions of workers already here, but with strong unions and an ever growing economy, that pressure remained manageable. Capitalism, regulated by government and moderated by collective bargaining with unions, was able to survive politically, even throughout the Great Depression. The eventual stimulus provided by World War II created opportunity for everyone, businesses, farm labor and industrial labor alike.

The fifties, sixties and seventies were prosperous in America. Regulation of capitalism delivered a fair opportunity for all except the racial minorities, and the civil rights movement was slowly eroding the old prejudices—not fast enough and not effectively enough to satisfy those minorities or to deliver equal opportunity, but enough to keep America as a whole functioning at a high level.

In the mid-eighties, the wheels began to come off. Not only was third-world labor, especially Hispanics from Latin America, migrating faster into the American workplace, but American living wage jobs began to be outsourced in greater and greater numbers. By the mid-eighties, the trade deficit was large and growing. The *trade deficit*, by netting out the value of American production exported against that of foreign production imported, *is the measure of the amount of economic harm being done to the economy* by a foreign trade imbalance. A trade surplus is the measure of the benefit of foreign trade. America's non-petroleum trade balance went from beneficial to harmful during the eighties. The amount of the deficit harm continued to grow throughout the nineties and into the first two decades of the twenty-first century as Japanese-made consumer electronics and automobiles and Chinese-made consumer products of all kinds, all made more cheaply overseas than they could be made here, flooded into the country without limitation.

Millions of Americans were laid off from their living wage jobs during this period as the impossible was expected of American industrial labor, namely, to compete with third world wage levels or else. This situation was exacerbated by rising Hispanic immigration into the American workplace, effectively bringing third world wages to America in the industries of agriculture, construction, meat packing and hospitality services. This was all blatantly unfair to American labor, because American laborers, facing a higher standard of living, required higher wages. They could neither compete with the foreign workforces that made the products Americans needed nor the newly arrived third world laborers inside the country who were willing to live in congested, poverty-level labor camps for the opportunity to repatriate their earnings back to their families at home.

The economically disenfranchised American workers affected were driven out of the middle class and into poverty by the consumerist policies of the United States that denied them a living wage. The ones that took jobs that were now available to them earned minimum wages in which they were actually competing with third world immigrant labor. It was impossible for them to even subsist at the wages paid by the jobs that were available, e.g., at Walmart as a warehouseman or a cashier, in the hospitality industry as a food server or dishwasher, or as a farm laborer.

Those displaced workers morphed into an enraged class of voters concentrated in the former industrial states of Wisconsin, Michigan, Ohio, Indiana, Illinois, Pennsylvania, Kentucky and a scattering of New

England States. That population congealed into a lump of misery and abandonment, seething with rage at having been sacrificed unfairly to the great god of big box store consumerism. Then Donald Trump came along, told them that he understood their situation, believed it to be wrong, and promised to restore their jobs by rebalancing America's foreign trade. It got him elected as all those industrial labor states voted for him. He, it turned out, was both incompetent and a fraud and accomplished none of those things. So, the angry industrial labor demographic remains a destabilizing factor in American politics.

The net effect of all this has been that immigration and immigrants have become fruitful ground for political conflict. The fact that it is and always has been a necessary ingredient in the American economy has been lost. Enraged Trump supporters are not interested in judiciously parsing which Hispanic workers are needed and which ones are arguably not. Those voters are not inclined to accept diversity as a desirable social objective and do not want new religiously and culturally alien Muslim and Asian refugees to come here and make things even more diverse (worse.)

The situation is one that calls for Congress, as the repository of legislative power to enact new immigration laws that address these issues by capping immigration at enforceable levels, and providing for work visas for those needed by the agriculture and other industries with low-end jobs that Americans won't take. The President, as the possessor of the bully pulpit, needs to work with the Congress to do just that. However, neither the Congress nor the residents in the White House have been willing or able to do that necessary work, being paralyzed by the money contributed to their campaigns by industry which is perfectly content to preserve the status quo which provides them with very low wages and therefore maximizes capital's ability to leverage labor to increase profits.

As I write this, I don't see any forces at work that are likely to break this logjam. Industrial labor doesn't seem to be a cohesive political force anymore given the withered state of trade unionism following the offshoring of American industry after the 1980s. There is great danger in the status quo, however. Climate change, regional and civil wars abroad, and overpopulation around the world are creating a pool of refugees that will form a tidal wave of illegal immigrants for America and elsewhere. Energy shortages, when they appear, will greatly magnify the problem of refugees.

At this time, there are approximately 26 million permanent refugees around the globe. This is up from 10 million in 2010. Of those 26 million, several million, when polled, have expressed a desire to immigrate to the United States. Since very few of those can be accommodated by legal immigration quotas, the pressure to enter the United State illegally and through asylum-seeking increases. The sheer number of refugees displaced by wars, climate change, extreme poverty and, when it comes, energy shortages, threatens to overwhelm us and the rest of the western world going forward. Given the fact that this problem will worsen, not improve, due to on-going climate change and diminishing resources of all kinds to support the world's existing and forecasted population levels, the need for the President and Congress to confront this situation with forward-looking legislation and regulation is urgent. Yet, the Congress today, while rhetorically bashing immigrants, continues to bask in the campaign contributions of employers who favor no controls, thus continuing to give employers a large and growing de facto third world population inside America to leverage in their pursuit of profits.

On Democracy

Democracy means one man, one vote. Not all men are equal in knowledge or quality of judgement, but the premise is that they are created equal and should have equal privileges and immunities of citizenship. But pure democracy is not workable. To our way of thinking, one man, one vote carries the real, in fact inevitable, risk of tyranny by the majority. Thus, the American Constitution provides for a *constitutional* democracy, by which we mean that there are certain essential human rights that are not subject to elections and officials. They are constant and inviolable. The cultural values of the drafters of a nation's constitution ultimately determine what rights are to be held inviolable. In America, the culture that informed the framers of our Constitution was that of The Enlightenment, as it boiled up out of the Protestant Reformation and the Thirty Years' War in the low countries of the European continent. It came out of Holland via England, the two leading countries that did not subscribe to the doctrines of the Roman Catholic Church.

So, the implied "social compact" between the Federal Government of the United States and the citizens of the United States, provides that the rights enumerated in the Constitution, as amended, namely, such things as the freedom of speech, and of religion, and of the press, and of the right to assemble, and the right of habeas corpus, and the right to form militias and bear arms (this one, uniquely tied to the shift from confederacy to a federal system, has proven to be troublesome), and freedom from unreasonable searches and seizures, and of a criminal trial by a jury of one's peers, and of the equal protection of the laws, and all the other enumerated rights in the Constitution. These things may not be infringed by the President or other officials of the Federal Government's Executive branch, nor may the enacted laws of the Congress infringe upon those rights. The Judicial Branch of the Federal Government declared early on in *Marbury vs. Madison* that it shall be the final arbiter of questions of "constitutionality." That pronouncement by the Supreme Court has been accepted and observed ever since by the Executive and Legislative branches, a defining and miraculous element of our democracy.

All of the powers of government not specifically delegated to the Federal Government under our Constitution are vested in the States that make up the nation. The Constitution's enumeration of civil and criminal rights of its citizens has been construed over the years by the Supreme Court to make those same human rights binding on the governments of the States (and on their counties and municipalities and other subdivisions) as well as the Federal Government.

The American form of constitutional democracy—the world's first—is derived from the unique circumstances of its history. These were mainly two: First, the timing of its creation following The Enlightenment by Dutch and English philosopher-influenced colonists, and second, the reluctant ceding of power by the original Confederate states to the new unifying Federal Government. So, our well known constitutional checks and balances identify us. I trouble you, gentle reader, with this background to lay a foundation for the following:

America has just experienced its closest brush with autocracy in the person of former President Donald J. Trump. It had an earlier brush with autocracy in the person of Huey P. Long, former governor and Senator from Louisiana, but Long operated only on a state level. (He was considered a rival of Franklin D. Roosevelt for the Democratic nomination for President in 1932, but that prospect was mooted with Long's assassination by a local enemy.) By the time you read this, there will have been many histories written on Trump, and his flaws, failures and popular attributes will have been cataloged aplenty. What I want to tell you is that, during this experience, the Executive and Legislative Branches of the Federal Government have been tested and come up short. The Executive Branch was systematically purged of opponents and independent-minded public servants by a corrupt, self-dealing President who replaced them with slavishly loyal, but weak-minded people who cared not a fig for the democratic principles on which the country was founded or the moral code of the Greco-Christian-Hebrew traditions of Americans, viz., honesty, trust, honor, selfless patriotism and sacrifice.

He was twice impeached for his transgressions but twice acquitted by a Republican majority of the Senate along a party line vote. Partisan-ship trumped (pun intended) principle, law, and morality. The Republican majority in the Senate, led by Kentucky Senator Mitch McConnell, proved to be an enabler and protector of Trump throughout Trump's incumbency. Thus, the Legislative Branch was tested as well as the Executive Branch, and it too was found lacking. There was sufficient popular support for this corrupt and autocratic cabal in the Republican-led White House and Senate, bottomed on the appeals of their President and Senators to the ignorance and biases of their constituencies, to enable the aforementioned circus to take place. In that sense, the American pub-lic was tested as well and it too came up lacking.

But the constitutional line of checks and balances held on the thread of a single branch of the government—the judicial branch. In the trial courts, in the appellate courts, and at the Supreme Court, all of Trump's meritless lawsuits, (more than seventy) failed to invalidate the popular and Electoral College votes of states that proved determinative of Joe Biden's election. So, nine justices of the Supreme Court, with nary a soldier or weapon at their disposal, by the sheer weight of truth and the public policies enumerated in the Constitution, delivered the correct re-sult in this crisis. Six of them were Republicans and three of those had been appointed by Donald Trump. By a vote of 9-0, they refused to consider the lawless attempt to overturn the legitimate vitory of Joe Biden in the Electoral College and the popular vote and substitute the votes of the Republican majority state legislatures instead. If five of those nine justices had voted Trump's way, Trump's enthronement as tyrant would have been easier than Adolf Hitler's selection as Chancellor in 1933 Germany. It has been a sobering experience for us, and one that underscores that democracy is a continuing experiment in this country and cannot be taken for granted.

It should also be noted that simple professionalism on the part of state bureaucracies in certain swing states performed with distinction as well. States with Republican administrations like Georgia and Arizona were subjected to strong personal attacks by Trump as he attempted unsuccessfully to get them to "find" more votes for him and other corrupt methods of changing the official vote in their states. They steadfastly refused and defended the integrity of their voting processes that had resulted in a Biden victory in their states.

[Note: The reference to Hitler is not hyperbole. There are apt par-allels up until 1933. What occurred later by way of the scale of secret police tyranny and the Final Solution is *not* parallel, but it was enabled by making Hitler Germany's nationalist autocrat. In a double-twisting irony, a majority of American Jews supported Trump throughout his Presidency despite his racist disregard for civil rights and dog whistles to white supremacy because Trump validated the Zionists in Israel by del-egitimizing all of the Palestinians' claims for land, civil rights, and recognition.]

On Family

It may not have escaped the reader's notice that this history is perfunctory in its references to those who were close to me and whose love or friendship helped shape the events chronicled herein and produced the considerable happiness I have enjoyed during the many and sustain-ing bright intervals of my life. There are three reasons for that. One is that I am loath to say anything that could be interpreted as critical of or defamatory to any person, living or deceased, whether by word or by omission or by degree of emphasis. Another reason is that this is not a memoir. There is no story arc, no dramatic tension, no perfectly times cascade of obstacles overcome and followed by resolution and reflection. This is not that sort of book. I am not writing for contemporary readers interested in learning my personal secrets (not that there is anything wrong with that; it is human nature to want to know the secrets of oth-ers.) I have troubled myself to write this book on the off chance that future generations would like to hear about the life and times of an an-cestor as I myself would have loved to read the autobiography of a distant ancestor. This is period piece. My loves, friendships and personal dealings with those who have affected me are simply not germane to the purposes of this history. Omitting mention of them in no way minimizes those vital, formative and sustaining relationships. The third reason is that including a treatment of family and friends would add at least a hundred pages to the book. You're welcome.

Epilogue

"If I haven't done my share of work, I have at least reached the time by which I ought to have done it." *Mark Twain In Paradise*

As I looked in the bathroom mirror this fine spring morning, with birdsong drifting through the open window, I saw the countenance of an elderly bald man with a full beard of white shaving soap about to be scraped clean.

As the title of this book posits, I asked myself, "So, where are you marching to, Globoman? Whither goest thou for the unexpired balance of your life?" Like the narrator in my short story *The Nazca Lines*, I answered truthfully. "I have no idea." But, as Standing Bear, Chief of the Lakota Ogallala Sioux famously said, "I will just keep going." Hopefully, leaning into the wind. And, if the miraculous Covid coronavirus vaccinations currently being administered on an unbelievable scale here and around the world is any indication, the fair Joka and I may before long be leaning into the wind over the bow of a cruise ship bound for more exotic places.

David Ainsworth Napa, California April, 2021

GENEALOGICAL APPENDIX

Reflections on the Ainsworth Surname

In my later years, I have been increasingly intrigued by the archipelago of information I keep running across involving the fairly uncommon Ainsworth surname. First, the variations—Ainsworth, Hainsworth, Aynesworth, Unsworth. Then, random discoveries of some factoids were provocative: the Ainsworth Psalter (hymnbook) on the Mayflower, the Ainsworth Latin Dictionary, and nineteen Victorian novels by William Harrison Ainsworth, a mentor of Charles Dickens. Also intriguing was the diaspora of Ainsworths in the United States and Canada—many in the South like my ancestors, a steamboat captain in the Mississippi and the Columbia Rivers, Great Plains pioneers with towns named after them like Ainsworth, Iowa and Ainsworth, Nebraska, New Englanders (railroad men), and Canadians (lumbermen.) In current affairs, a Minister of Defense in the U.K., a gaming machine billionaire in Australia, and a pitcher for the San Francisco Giants.

Through the Ainsworth website and forum on Facebook, I learned of the Village of Ainsworth, near Manchester, England, the historic center for the British textile industry during the Industrial Revolution. Since my ancestors come from cotton country in the American Piedmont, I thought there could be a tie-in between the British sourcing of cotton in the American south and textile making in Lancashire, England. I also uncovered an Ainsworth connection to the Protestant Reformation (see following paragraphs.) So, I determined to add a visit to the Village of Ainsworth into my itinerary following a planned Holland America Line cruise of the Baltic and North Sea areas in July, 2017. I wondered if all Ainsworths were related and/or came from this lone, small village on Cockey-Moor on the Bolton-Bury Road in Lancashire, England. And if so, what prompted them to migrate to the New World, seemingly in waves.

My trusty companion on this quest was my lovely girlfriend, Johanna (aka Joka, who is Dutch but resides in Sydney, Australia and whom I met on a Holland America Line cruise in Valparaiso, Chile, as more full related in chapter 21). On a vacation in 2016, the very same Johanna and I found ourselves in Amsterdam following a Holland America Line cruise from Singapore to Rotterdam. Johanna knew Amsterdam well from her many visits there while growing up in nearby Sassenheim (of tulip fame, her father having been a tulip bulb grower and exporter) and subsequent trips back to Holland in later years. While showing me the sights, she took me to a unique Amsterdam neighborhood consisting of an arrange-ment of housing around an oval green on which exists an ancient chapel originally of the Begijnhof Catholics, but in 1578, following the Oran-gist reform government's purging of "Popish idolatry," was turned over to Protestant reform people and became known, as would be made clear to me shortly, as the "English Reform Church" in Amsterdam. The hous-ing was originally for Begijne women who dedicated their lives to doing good works—not as nuns, but as devout single women whose housing and subsistence was provided by the Begijnhof church as part of its charitable mission.

Johanna and I walked the gardens and marveled at the charming arrangement of attractive houses and then visited the modest chapel. There, lightning struck! On the wall of the sanctuary, I was startled to see my surname on a brass memorial plaque! The plaque had been presented to the church by a sister congregation in Chicago in 1909 commemorating the three hundred year anniversary of a significant event in the Protestant movement. The plaque read:

"From Scrooby [Nottinghamshire, England] to Amsterdam Ainsworth, Johnson, Robinson, Brewster, Bradford [families] by a joint consent resolved [in 1607-9] to go into the Low Countries where they heard was freedom of religion for all men and lived at Amsterdam."

Subsequent research revealed that this community of Puritans had been systematically targeted by the Archbishops of York in the Church of England preventing them from freely practicing their religion and other deprivations of liberty. This community of five families made their way in different voyages to Holland and formed a congregation in

Leyden (now Leiden), but, as foreigners, they were unable to join the guilds and work in skilled trades and so lived in poverty. They also saw that their children were growing up to be Dutch, and so they resolved to immigrate again, this time to the New World. This kernel of Protestant Puritans subsequently made up roughly half of the emigres to Massachusetts on the Mayflower in 1622 (the other half being Puritan residents of Eng-land.) There were no Ainsworths on the Mayflower, but the Ainsworth Psalter was aboard as the group's hymn book, authored by one Henry Ainsworth, an activist figure in English religious affairs at the time. William Bradford, author of the language quoted on the plaque in the Begijnhof Church in Amsterdam, was part of the Scrooby/Amsterdam group on the Mayflower and founded the Massachusetts congregation of Puritans. The quoted language on the plaque is from his book, "Of Plymouth Plantation."

So, I had a partial answer to my question why Ainsworths migrated out of England, at least in the early 1600s; they sought relief from oppression by the Church of England against those of Calvinist persuasion. Similar treatment of Protestants by the Spanish Inquisition in Holland (then considered by Spain a colony) culminating in the Thirty Years War provided stimulus for the Protestant Reformation. However, these Ainsworths came from Scrooby in the border area between Nottinghamshire, Yorkshire, and Lincolnshire, well east of Cockey-Moor in Lancashire where the village of Ainsworth can be found. So, while some in the Lancashire community of Ainsworths may have migrated to the Scrooby area, nothing in the Scrooby-Amsterdam migration story confirmed this. On the other hand, the parish village of Ainsworth in Lancashire had been formed hundreds of years earlier, and so a migration of less than 100 miles to the Scrooby area over that time period by some of them seems entirely plausible.

I contacted the Lancashire Archivist's office before setting out on my trip to Ainsworth, but was cautioned that it would be very difficult to find records that would address the question why a person or group emigrated. The public and church records have to do with census information, births, deaths, marriages, criminal records and the like. To find out why any person or group migrated would likely have to be discovered from family records. Alas, my family records on that question are lost in antiquity.

At the end of July, Johanna and I disembarked from the *MV Zuiderdam* in Edinburgh, and on July 30, we drove a rental car south, past the Falls of Clyde, past the melancholy-tinged town of Lockerbie (into which portions of Pan Am Flight 103 crashed after being blown up by a Libyan terrorist in 1988), and into England, arriving at our hotel in Bolton, a Manchester suburb that thrived in the 1800s during the Industrial Revolution. Bolton is separated from its neighboring town of Bury by 10 kilometers or so, and the parish village of Ainsworth lies midway between them on the Bolton-Bury Road.

We only had that afternoon and the next day to explore Ainsworth, so we dropped our bags at our hotel, The Last Drop Inn, and drove to Ainsworth. Our first stop was the Methodist church, which was closed (on Sunday,) and we saw no Ainsworth headstones in its graveyard. Then, we walked across the street to the Presbyterian Church, and, at the fair Johanna's initiative, conversed with someone who referred us to the caretaker of the church, a Mr. Horrocks, whom we found nearby in his garden. He graciously offered to open the church and show us marriage and death listings of Ainsworths and other old records and pointed out some Ainsworth surnames in the headstones of its cemetery. The church, largely idle and without a pastor, is very old, poorly heated and consists only of family boxes partitioned off from each other by waist high wooden panels. Parishioners were obliged to pay rent on their boxes. There were no pews or benches. The last time I saw that interior arrangement was in St. George's Church in Bermuda built by the Jamestown, Virginia settlers (first English settlers in America) while they were shipwrecked in Bermuda in 1612.

It was cold and raining and getting dark so we thanked Mr. Horrocks for his information and adjourned to our digs at The Last Drop Inn in Bolton to warm up, dry out and enjoy some "bangers and mash" washed down by artisanal English ale.

The next day, we visited the First Church of Christ, dating from 1513 as the parish Church of England. Again, through the good offices of the fair Johanna and her interrogation of two ladies placing flowers on their family graves, we were directed to the nearby home of the Vicar, Reverend David Thompson. We knocked on his door and he graciously invited us into his office and answered my questions as best he could. He showed me a book that had been written by his predecessor called "The Story of Cockey Moor, Otherwise Ainsworth" by K. P. Bullock that pro-vides a history of the area. The book is out of print, and I could find no copies for sale on eBay later. Vicar Thompson confirmed what our search of the graveyard indicated, namely, that there are no Ainsworth surnamed people in the graveyard of his church.

Vicar Thompson and Mr. Horrocks, caretaker of the Presbyterian Church, are both long time members of the Ainsworth Historical Society, and they both confirmed what I had seen repeatedly in my on-line research as to the origin of the name Ainsworth. "Worth" was a common Saxon word meaning "enclosure" or, likely, farm. Saxons migrated to Britain in 449 CE, so there was a long period during which one or more Saxons could have established a prominent farm on the hills that became Cockey Moor. To put the pagan Saxon arrival in context, that coincided with the withdrawal of the Romans from the British Isles. The Roman exodus took place about sixty years after the Roman Emperor Constan-tine converted to Christianity at the end of the 4th Century. Thus, for sixty years, the Roman armies were enablers for Holy Roman evangelists for Christianity and monastic enclaves in England.

Earlier, in the 900s, the French king allowed a group of Norsemen under Rollo to settle in the north of France opposite England. They prospered and their progeny hosted Edward the Confessor during his exile from England, thus beginning the Norman involvement in English political affairs. Upon the Norman arrival and defeat of Saxon King Harold's army at Hastings in 1066, various Norman knights traversed England suppressing opposition and confiscating land for their own.

In feudal times, adoption of a family name having manorial rights over a property was an emphatic way of broadcasting that fact. So, "Ains" would likely have been derived from a pioneering person's given name. A number of Saxon names are phonetically close to it, but Phil Parker, a resident of Ainsworth (whom I did not meet while I was there, but with whom I corresponded following an exchange of postings on the Facebook Ainsworth genealogical website) has supplied the most credible answer to that question, Mr. Parker advises that a Norman knight named D'Euins appropriated the land in the vicinity sometime following the Battle of Hastings and what phonetically turned out to be Ains likely began as D'Euins. Most of the actors at the time were illiterate, and so by the time most surnaming conventions evolved, the name became, variously, "Ains", "Hains", "Aynes", "Haynes", "Uns" and the like.

Phil Parker points out that because England and France were at war many times over the millennium in question, those English families with French sounding names dropped the French-sounding parts of their names. (Hence, de Lancaster became Lancaster.) Also, spelling was not taught until recent times, so when later scriveners sought to write English letters to convey the French "Euins", they were choosing among the sounds of the vowels a, i and u.

Surnames, of course, evolved over time and progressed from first or given names to added surnames that differentiated people by their place of residence. Hence, Leonardo da Vinci from the Tuscan town of Vinci near Florence, William of Orange, etc. My late wife Carol's last name was Ingellis which she received from her Puglia-born Italian father. The name is an archaic Italian word for "English." One can reasonably assume that some English sailor or adventurer washed up on the shores of Puglia long ago and started a clan identified by his place of origin.

The following are my conclusions—mostly educated conjecture—as to how we all came to have the Ainsworth surname. English and other European surname conventions branched out from location-based names to also include names based on blood lines or clans (Johnson, Swenson, Peterson) and occupation (Carpenter, Miller, Shoemaker) and other, less common conventions. Hence, as old as the surname Ainsworth is and given the prevalent surnaming convention at the time as being geography-based and manorial rights-based, the location was likely named by merging the Norman "D'Euins" with the Saxon word "worth" meaning farm. Probably, however, it is no longer exclusively a clan-based name in which all Ainsworths are blood relatives, but rather also was used as a surname for any John or James or Levin or William, etc., from the Ainsworth parish vicinity, his place of domicile. The Ainsworth diaspora likely consists of both, but all come from ancestors from a small, ancient Saxon/Norman parish that sits atop Cockey-Moor in Lancashire, England.

Phil Parker also advised that the site of Ainsworth Hall (formerly owned by his family and demolished as a derelict structure in 1966) is thought to date back to a Roman outpost called Coccium. He reports that there have been Roman coins and urns found in the vicinity and that some Roman stones are believed to have been incorporated into the building of Ainsworth Hall by the descendants of D'Euins or their successors. That Ainsworth clan is believed to be identified with the Ainsworth coat of arms depicting three single-bladed battle axes against a red field and the motto *"courage sans peur"* (a French phrase meaning "courage without fear") thus tending to corroborate the Norman origins of this feudal, manorial family and a militaristic outlook. I have a copy of this coat of arms, a gift from an in-law years ago.

It is worth noting that the D'Euins/Ainsworth history roughly parallels that of the more prominent and more thoroughly researched Lancaster family, originally the Norman "de Lancaster" of Lancaster Castle, Lancashire in which museum of heraldry the Ainsworth coat of arms I have is reportedly displayed.

During the English Civil Wars, the Ainsworths descended from the D'Euins family would likely, since their feudal status was given to them by the King, have been allied with the Royalist side. Other Ainsworths, perhaps of unrelated clans but who had taken the surname of Ainsworth because that was their place of domicile, may have sided with the Parliamentarians led by Cromwell as, for example, did most of the town residents of neighboring Bolton. As evidence of the bitterness of that schism, Phil Parker pointed out the infamous incident in which a Royalist army of 12,000 led by Prince Rupert (German mercenary military commander on hire to the crown) massed on the high ground of which Ainsworth village is now a part (musket balls and weapons smelting paraphernalia have been found on the Ainsworth Hall property) and then massacred the citizens of Bolton. During the English Civil Wars, the monarchy was overthrown and later restored.

The fortunes of the Royalists and Parliamentarians reversed twice. As happened with Lancasters, and as related by Phil Parker about the Ainsworths, Royalist Ainsworths were likely first disenfranchised and exiled to Ireland and the New World with the overthrow of the monarchy and then subsequently had their properties restored when the monarchy was restored. The fortunes of any Ainsworths who were Cromwell activists would have seen the reverse, hence providing a stimulus for emigrating by both family lines at different times. Phil Parker related a history in which a family of Ainsworths who had immigrated to America during the first English Civil War, returned after their properties were restored.

Enter the steam engine. Once the science of physics and mechanics merged to create the applied steam engine in the early 1800s, and fueled by abundant coal, the Industrial Revolution was born, and the Manchester Area of England figured prominently in it. The Town of Bolton was a center of textile industry activity, especially in weaving and the dyeing or bleaching end of things. Earlier, a branch of that family in 1396, had married into the De Winkley family of Pleasington, near Blackburn. The De Winkley family seat thence became through marriage the family seat of that Ainsworth clan, namely Pleasington Hall. Pleasington Hall still stands about 12 miles from Ainsworth. It is that branch of the Ainsworths from which the "bleacher" Ainsworths descended. That family figured prominently in the Bolton area textile industry with its textile dyeing and bleaching business and also coal mining at various sites on Cockey Moor to fuel its operations. That branch prospered and acquired another prominent local home, Smithills Hall, which was never renamed and continues to exist as Smithills Hall.

The De Winkley/Ainsworth branch took its own coat of arms—the one appearing in the Facebook website, namely, three silver spades and a motto in Latin, "Spes Meliora" translating as "hopes for better [things or times]" indicating an agricultural and perhaps melancholy outlook.

The textile industry in the Manchester area declined during the American Civil War when the supply of cheap, slave-labor-produced cotton was severed for many years. It took another hit later from competing textile producers elsewhere using Egyptian cotton.

So, what were the causes of various Ainsworth migrations, first to the American colonies, then to the United States and Canada, then to Australia over the course of five hundred years? Much is conjecture, of course, as previously noted, especially relating to the earliest events, but conjecture based upon historical reality. We know from the Scrooby-Amsterdam migration that Puritan persecution by, and flight from, Church of England orthodoxy and its grip on secular power in the late 1500s/early 1600s was a cause of emigration to Holland and the northeastern lands of America. Later, each of the English Civil Wars created a new brace of winners and losers—upheavals that reversed themselves as many as three times over a score of years, e.g., when the Catholic king Charles was first overthrown and then returned to the throne after Cromwell's commonwealth failed following his death; then yet again when William of Orange reversed the religious poles upon his arrival. Each time, if people from Lancashire sided with Catholic Royalists or Parliamentarians or Dutch reform advocates and ended up on the losing side, they would have had an incentive, sometimes lifesaving, to try their fortunes elsewhere.

Interestingly, in our meeting with him, Vicar Thompson downplayed the severity of the effect of these religious changes in the village of Ainsworth during the English Civil Wars, pointing out that the Unitarians and the Episcopalians shared the use of his church at the time by staggering their services. Perhaps the remoteness of the village and a sense of community moderated the effects of those reversals.

If there were any Quaker Ainsworths in the substantial community of Quakers in neighboring Bury, they may have been part of the 23,000 strong Quaker emigration from the English midlands to America from 1675 to 1725 triggered by both oppression in England and reportedly a sense of destiny.

It is well documented that Britain exiled a large number of its convicts to its New World colonies, first to America and then, after the Revolutionary War, to Australia, to provide a labor workforce to further its colonial ambitions in those places. Some of them were doubtless Ainsworths. I was browsing some computerized convict records in Sydney one day with Johanna and found that one William Ainsworth of Manchester had arrived under a sentence of seven years labor in 1877.

Finally, there is the obvious incentive of economic opportunity to consider as a cause of emigration. Doubtless, some Ainsworths migrated simply seeking a fair opportunity to prosper in the Americas and later Australia. Ainsworth clans prospered greatly at times, and during the Industrial Revolution, the De Winkley branch of Pleasington Hall employed many local workers, some of whom were housed in the worker's cottages that still sit astride the Bolton-Bury Road in Ainsworth.

Mr. Horrocks, caretaker of the Presbyterian Church, produced a logbook recording eighty nine instances in which members of that congregation were incarcerated in the Bury Poor House during the second half of the 19th century. Poverty on that level would have been a powerful motivator to emigrate to the Americas or Australia at the time just as it did in the Irish communities during the potato famine.

It befalls those present Ainsworths with a stronger interest in genealogy than I to massage the immigration data of the Americas and elsewhere to see if any census data bulges correspond to any of this host of developments. DNA from multiple living Ainsworths can possibly identify which ones of us are clansmen of the D'Euins and which were simply people who took the name of their place of domicile in Ainsworth as their surname. I don't know from which line I come.

The fair Johanna and I finished off our sojourn into the mysteries of Cockey-Moor with a visit to The Duke William, one of the two pubs in Ainsworth (the other being The White Horse.) It is a comfortable, working man's establishment with good beer and a rolling group of patrons who seemed genuinely glad to see each other.

We caught an early flight to Belfast the next morning and were immediately confronted by another history—that of "The Troubles"—which has unfortunate parallels to the English Civil Wars, namely, that each side of the religiously/politically divided country can be satisfied only when the other is vanquished entirely. (See also, the Israel-Palestine conflict, the centuries old Sunni vs. Shi'a conflict, Crips vs. Bloods, etc., *ad nauseum*).

As to my purpose in going to Ainsworth, I am content that I now know what it means to stand in the firmament of Americans with that surname. By the time a Norman arrow, fired perhaps at random, pierced the eye socket of Harold, the Saxon King during the Battle of Hastings in 1066, the site that would later become known as Ainsworth had already existed for hundreds of years. It took its current name thereafter from a Norman knight, and the fortunes of the village have risen and fallen since then along with political and economic change. Whether from a single Norman clan, or other clans who adopted the surname identifying themselves as being from the place of Ainsworth in Lancashire, all now have progeny throughout the English-speaking New World. Many of them have distinguished themselves, and some of us are just fellow travelers.

Muse Family

My paternal grandmother, Inez Muse, came from a long line of migrants from England named Muse, or occasionally Mewes. I say that with authority, not because I have any information about her history beyond the fact that she married my paternal grandfather, William Augustus Ainsworth, gave birth to my father and his three brothers and one sister and died a tragically early death at twenty nine of pellagra. Rather, a search for the name on line produced a very large number of Muses who immigrated to America from England over approximately the same period of time the Ainsworths did, initially to Colonial Virginia and then dispersing via their offspring throughout the southern states, including Mississippi. I simply don't know any more about my grandmother Inez.

My Dutch Heritage

My maternal grandmother Grace was a Conover from Titusville, Pennsylvania, where the first oil well was drilled. The surname Conover was a renaming of the Dutch surname, Van Kouwenhoven, which evidently proved to be too much a mouthful for the family in English-speaking America. The earliest Van Kouwenhoven, according to Wikipedia, was one Walphert Gerretse Van Kouwenhoven, an original patentee and founder of the New Netherlands colony for the Dutch West India Company circa 1625. He founded the first European settlement on Long Island, New Amersfoort in 1632 and "played an active role" in founding the communities of Manhattan, Brooklyn, Albany and Rensselaer. He managed the farm properties of Kiliaean Van Rensselaer for several years before acquiring his own plantation in what is now Flatbush.

He and his wife had three sons and they, in turn produced many descendants, including the notable U.S. Presidents Theodore Roosevelt and Franklin Delano Roosevelt, two William Harrimans (a diplomat and a railroad baron), actor Michael Douglas, and, of course, yours truly, among many, many others.

One genealogist came up with the following poetic chronicle of the Conover-Van Kouwenhoven (also Couwenhoven) name:

The Old Family Tree
Planted in America 1630 A.D.
Written by J. Taylor Conover b. circa 1834
Tune of Marching Through Georgia

From over the broad ocean the Holland people came,
And planted in New Netherlands the Couwenhoven name,
Since sixteen hundred thirty, this old family tree has stood,
In all its pride and beauty, the bright glory of the wood.

*****

Couwenhoven is old style and Dutch, too, if you please
But as honest and as true as the sunshine or the breeze.
The oak, too, is old fashioned and long has it stood;
In all its life and glory it's the pride of the wood.

Hurrah then for this tree of our forefathers that still stands,
The pride of all our people that have sprung from these bands;
Whose word was e'er their bond, and whose blood was as blue
As the best in the land, the azure Holland hue.

Descended from old Holland stock, New Amsterdam vein,
Of old Manhattans early men with Knickerbocker fame,
Their names are told in story oft of hard and stormy times,
And the lives of their descendants are recorded in these lines.

*****

Vincent

My maternal grandfather, Harry Lee Vincent, was born in the Titusville, Pennsylvania area. I know nothing of his early life there, except that the oil business was born when the first commercial oil well came in there some fifteen years earlier in 1859. Since his wife, Grace Conover, was born in 1875 and was raised in the area and she and Harry Vincent married there, I am assuming that Harry was born about the same time as Grace was.

[Note: Other places in Louisiana, Russia, China and the Caucuses also claim to be the, or among the first oil wells drilled. But the Drake well in Titusville was the one that launched the oil industry as we have come to know it.]

Both Harry and Grace grew up in a boomtown with the oil industry rapidly expanding into the energy space of the American economy replacing whale oil as the preferred home and industrial source of energy. The whaling industry that had powered the Civil War began to decline precipitously, never to return—fortunately for the whales which were being hunted to near extinction.

In any event, Harry acquired the skills required on a drilling rig. Early on, he went to work for the Standard Oil Company as a driller, and just after the turn of the nineteenth century, he was posted with his family to Ploesti, Romania. The Romanian oil fields were shallow and easily worked by the rudimentary drilling technology (timber drill stems!) then existing. My mother was born there. (See discussion in Chapter 1 regarding my mother Carmen Sylvia.)

Harry died relatively young of Hodgkin's disease, possibly due to his continuous exposure to a cocktail of chemicals found around oil fields and drilling rigs.

Toward the end of her life, my grandmother Grace offered me a scrap of paper—a torn piece of an envelope—on which some genealogy tracings appeared. She told me that if I ever wanted to join the Sons of the American Revolution, the group's requirement of being a direct descendant of someone who fought in the Revolutionary Army during the war of America's independence could be satisfied by the intelligence she was giving me. The family tree shown on the paper indicated that her late husband Harry was a direct descendant of one Colonel Salisbury Vincent of the Revolutionary Army, unit unknown.

I have been unable to locate any record of a Salisbury Vincent in the Continental Army or its militias; however, what much later struck me as significant about the scrap of paper my grandmother had given me was the entry that showed who Salisbury Vincent married, namely, one Mace **di Medici** in Baltimore in 1790! Di Medici is not a common name like Smith or Jones, and 1790 was a year after the French Revolution. The Italian Medicis were in France from and after Catherine di Medici's marriage to the French King Henry II in 1537. Catherine was queen consort for twelve years. It is possible that at a time when French aristocrats found it necessary to escape France to save themselves, a marriageable young di Medici woman might have married a reputable American to find refuge. I have not been able to verify any of the information provided by my grandmother Grace Vincent through casual on-line genealogical research. Too bad. I would love to be able to claim Florentine nobility among my ancestors.

Lightning Source UK Ltd.
Milton Keynes UK
UKHW020649230721
387648UK00010B/661